Surviving Well
is the
Best Revenge

Book One

A Novel of Cuba: 1958

by

Patric Ryan

Sarawak Studios Press & M.L. Ryan Publishing

Fiction by Patric Ryan

The Fogo's War Trilogy
Book One
Summer Wars & Winter Schooners
Book Two
Schooners Are Black & U-Boats Are Grey
Book Three
The Final Acts of Fogo's War

The Paris Shooter's Union

The Burning Islands

Surviving Well is the Best Revenge: Cuba

Surviving Well is the Best Revenge: Montreal

Surviving Well is the Best Revenge: Newfoundland

Non-fiction

Closing The Newfoundland Circles

Screenplays

Winter Schooner, Fogo's War & Ellie's Boat

Short Stories
*Rum Runners & River Rats, The Last Fisherman,
The Skipjack Wars
& The Man From Chicago*

Surviving Well is the Best Revenge

A novel of Cuba 1958.

by **Patric Ryan**

Author of *The Fogo's War Trilogy, The Paris Shooter's Union & The Burning Islands*

Sarawak Studios & ML Ryan Publishing
535 9th St. E.
Owen Sound Ontario Canada N4K 1P4

Email: patric@patricryan.com
www.patricryan.com

Cover design: Sophie Ryan

Canadian Cataloguing in Publication Data
Ryan, Patric D.M.

Surviving Well is the Best Revenge: Cuba
ISBN 978-0-9698003-2-3

1. Ryan, Patric D.M., 2. Cuba 1958, 3. Fidel Castro, 4. Cuba and the Cuban Revolution. Drama. Fiction

For John The Poet

A special thanks to Sophie for her cover creativity
and to my patient editors: Sarina and Dorie

&

Jason: who guides me through the mysteries of
electronic publishing

Prologue

The world slumbered between wars, but Cuba was poised on the brink of another defining moment in her tortured history. It began with the arrival of the Spaniards and continued in turmoil and greed and slavery until, after many bloody rebellions, a young exiled lawyer was leading a ragged but disciplined force against Batista's garrisons. For Christian the Cuban Revolution was only rumours and rumbles, like distant thunder out of the Sierra Maestra far to the east.

It was a dangerous time to be in Cuba. Fidel Castro inflamed the people to believe a revolution could finally succeed. Emotions burned. Spilled blood was the badge of commitment. A Canadian could be mistaken for a Yankee Imperialist with sympathies for the corrupt dictator, Fulgencio Batista. Or a Castro mercenary infiltrating Cuba to overthrow El Presidente.

Christian James Joyce fled Montreal's emerging sub-culture of Bohemian socialist rhetoric, always heading south, if obliquely. Running from himself in a haze of drugs and music. He wanted only to hide out in Cuba for awhile, get clean. To be at peace in his villa above the sleepy harbour of Los Espiritos, waiting for Renée.

Surviving Well is the Best Revenge

Part One

Paradise Undone

The Self-Taught Man said: "If I were ever to go on a trip, I think I should make written notes of the slightest traits of my character before leaving, so that when I return I would be able to compare what I was and what I became." *Jean-Paul Sartre. Nausea. 1938.* The Self-Taught Man never ventured beyond a library reading room.

Christian had at least made a start. He escaped to Los Espiritos, a small fishing village on the west coast of Cuba. Now he sits in the ruins of his villa, letting the journal slip to the stones of the terrace. He shuts his eyes, exhausted by the events of the last four weeks. Fulgencio Batista fled Cuba on New Year's Day. Fidel Castro is in Havana, the Revolution sweeping Cuba like a wild fire. In Havana and Santiago they are still celebrating in the streets, even as the trials are beginning, and the killing. The army is in disarray, many are dead and more will die in the reprisals. Los Espiritos is charred rubble and his own villa damaged by a tank shell, but Christian has survived. A light breeze from the Gulf flips pages to the last journal entry...

...A strange and confusing year. I met Maartyn on the supply boat to Bimini and then Renée and Paulo in Nassau. We hung out on Andros Island and argued about Sartre. Paulo went to jail in Nassau for dealing drugs. I came to Cuba to play in a jazz combo in Havana but found Los Espiritos. I didn't know what happened to Renée. I thought I'd lost her too. And here in Los Espiritos I met Miguel, Juanita and Escobar. Rosa and Esa.

The trouble really began one year ago on the lower east side of Chicago, in a cold water flat above a jazz club. The club was called El Cubanna and had 'a painted moon over a cardboard sea', fake palms and nothing to do with Cuba. Chicago was a frozen island in an ocean of snow, whose only hope was the lake. But the lake was frozen too. Jazz clubs are a refuge for itinerant musicians like me. Walk-down owners hire bottom feeders who don't ask questions. The elevated railway, viewed through the frost-etched and fly-specked window of my room, the only link with civilization. I woke up that morning, after the Lenny Bruce concert, wrapped in dirty sheets, freezing. Really strung out. I thought I was dying. It's hard to accept dying when you've lived a thousand days, thinking one day you'll just quit the scene. They told me I would never quit on my own. So, I took my sax, rode the el to the outskirts of Chi Town and started hitch hiking.

Instead of going home to Montreal I headed south to some place warm. At university I had a girlfriend from the Islands, Haiti. She was dark and warm with life. She said to go there but don't take myself with me. I didn't know what she meant, at the time.

Withdrawal on the highways of America was an experience. One time, near Macon, Georgia, I thought the highway was a giant zipper holding the body of America together and the truck was the zipper thing. America was spilling her guts behind me and I couldn't look back. Somehow I made it to Florida and took the supply boat to Bimini. And then I ended up in Cuba, in time for the Revolution.

So here's the story so far. Dedicated to Old Jocinto, eternally playing his fabulous guitar.

Los Espiritos: Cuba, December 16th 1958

Maartyn arrived without warning.

"Chris! Hey, dick head! Y'all in there?" The chill crept up his spine. The iron gate opened, but did not close. Confident strides clicked across the stone walk. The knock, loud and impatient.

"I'll get it, Miguel." Christian opened the heavy door. "Hello, Maartyn."

"Here I am, ol' buddy. In the flesh."

"I didn't expect you, so soon."

"What? Don't want me?"

"No, no. It's just that...you should have let me know."

"Well, we didn't exactly have a number."

"There's no phones."

"So this' our new flop, huh?" Maartyn pushed a beat up Marine Corps duffle bag past Christian, stepping into the cool of the stone house. "Dark in here, man!"

That morning Miguel woke Christian after sunrise, put the glass of salt water on the wooden box, and opened the bedroom shutters facing west. The Gulf of Mexico looked iron grey through the bars of the window.

The aroma of coffee boiling in the pantry pulled Christian out of bed. He dressed in a musty T-shirt and cut offs, rinsed his mouth, spit into the toilet hole, then took a cup of coffee and his saxophone out on the terrace. He played soft music to the rising sun and fading stars, the notes floating easily over the village below. The villagers had been at work for two hours. Some mornings he translated stories about the Revolution in the Havana papers. Miguel brought the newspapers from Juanita's Cantina every few days. He also read the Miami Herald to compare what the Americans were saying about Fidel Castro.

Later he and Miguel walked down to the beach with fishing gear and rowed the old skiff out through the anchored boats to the reef, returning before noon to have lunch of fried fish and corn bread. For the rest of the day he would write, play music or sleep in the afternoon when it was hot.

Maartyn looked about the room as if checking for a way to escape,or a way in. "Real classy little dump," said Maartyn, tossing the duffle bag on a worn sofa. "Where do I sleep?"

The world slumbered between wars, but Cuba was poised on the brink of another defining moment in her tortured history. It began with the arrival of the Spaniards and continued in turmoil, greed and slavery until, after many bloody rebellions, a young exiled lawyer was leading a ragged but disciplined force against Batista's garrisons. For Christian the Cuban Revolution was only rumours and rumbles, like distant thunder out of the Sierra Maestra far to the east.

Miguel, his houseboy, sulked in the stone pantry near the terrace, watching Christian Joyce. His young boss, jazz musician and writer, an artist in cut off jeans and faded Madras shirt with long sleeves to hide the marks, was part Ivy League prepy and part Bohemian smack head. He had good Irish features and careless, straw coloured hair, but the blue eyes were sad or lonely. Miguel also watched the intruder, an American, dressed in black chinos, downtown leather shoes and white T-shirt with the sleeves rolled up over a soft pack of Lucky Strikes. Dark, almost handsome, angular and narrow hipped, with cropped hair and shifting, dangerous eyes. The mole on his left cheek a hot button. 'Señor Maartyn talks like a Yankee thug,' said Miguel later.

Christian opened more shutters for Maartyn. The late sun flooded the room. The villa had a stone fireplace and brown tile floors. Sparsely elegant, furnished with an American couch and long monk's table with benches near the pantry that doubled as the kitchen. The bedroom had an oversized, carved Mediterranean bed. The bathroom with no fixtures, had a hole in the floor. Maartyn looked disgusted. Christian steered him to the terrace. "Miguel, bring rum, please."

They stood apart. Silent. Two friends sharing almost nothing in life, other than being on the run. Miguel made the drinks and judged Maartyn St. Jacques from the shadow of the pantry. "Well, this sure is you, ol' buddy."

"The view's good," Christian offered. Maartyn barely noticed the Gulf and the small islands to the west. Los Colorados Archipelago, standing offshore like a fleet of white ships with green sails. Below, the hot white sand, the clear, turquoise water and the fishing boats at anchor. To the east rose the humping limestone hills with the blue Viñales pines and between the hills, the rich red soil of Pinar del Rio tobacco fields. The best land belonged to Havana cigar makers. Guajiros worked the fields or fished. Little prosperity to be seen other than the Catholic church at the beach level, and to the south, in the pines above the beach, a large white stone villa with a red tile roof, belonged to an eccentric old man, Ernesto Escobar. A white Cuban with a Spanish history. Miguel brought the drinks and left them on the table. Christian handed Maartyn a glass of dark rum with warm, flat cola.

"So, why this place?" Maartyn sipped and pulled a face.

"It's peaceful."

"Dead, y'all mean."

Los Espiritos floated in dusty sunlight, suspended in the dry heat, waiting for nightfall. Eternally dying Royal palms scraped bony fingers over the tin roofs of shacks straggling along the foot of the curving hill, separated by crumbling stone walls and winter-dry shrubs and old wooden fences laced together by drying vines. Women in faded print dresses foraged in the tangled gardens. Shirtless fishermen wandered up from the boats carrying gutted fish. Naked children laughed and played in the clear water. Dogs and babies slept.

He had offered Maartyn the bench by the rough plastered wall in the shade of a wisteria bush, its pods dropping black seeds on the terrace stones and dry leaves. The seeds falling on the leaves sounded like ice rain on the tin roof of the wood shed behind the family apartment in Montreal. Christian sat on the crooked chair in the sun, staring at the last island in the chain. He didn't know the name of the island. Subtropical Cuba was only a temporary refuge, like a lifeboat slowly drifting ashore.

"Real nice, Chris. The little hideaway y'always went on about."

"It's okay. Not much happening."

"Looks like it, man. Nothin'."

It was a dangerous time to be in Cuba. Fidel Castro inflamed the people to believe a revolution could finally succeed. Emotions burned. Spilled blood was the badge of commitment. A Canadian could be mistaken for a Yankee Imperialist with sympathies for the corrupt dictator, Fulgencio Batista. Or a Castro mercenary infiltrating Cuba to overthrow El Presidente.

Christian James Joyce fled Montreal's emerging sub-culture of Bohemian socialist rhetoric, always heading south, if obliquely. Running from himself in a haze of drugs and music. He wanted only to hide out in Cuba for awhile and get clean. To be at peace in his villa above the sleepy harbour of Los Espiritos, waiting for Renée.

"Yeah, real quiet, an' spooky," said Maartyn. "Ya know, man, I thought Los Espiritos was a nightclub in Havana. I looked all over the goddamned place."

"How did you find me?"

"Some Latino chic in a bar gave me directions, so I banged'er good."

"Out of gratitude?"

"Least I could do, man. Can't believe I found this burg."

"We're practically invisible."

"Oh, yeah?..." Maartyn put the small black revolver on the table and pointed it at Christian. A Saturday Night Special, 38 caliber, deadly only at close range. Available on street corners in American cities for twenty-five bucks. The carved walnut handle didn't make it a thing of beauty.

The little revolver always made Christian uncomfortable. He got up and walked to the terrace wall. "Did you have to bring that thing?"

"Y'all need a piece, man. Never know when some Gook's gonna sneak up an' cut yer throat."

Christian watched the sun falling into a voluptuous bank of clouds with an explosion of tropical colours, regretting the intrusion. He was too familiar with Maartyn's attitudes. "Look, there, Maartyn. Have you ever seen such clouds?"

"Sure! So?"

"Incredible aren't they? Amorphous but lyrical."

"So, what makes these so special?"

Christian felt the familiar prickles on the back of his neck. Maartyn never understood allusions. Still, he liked to push the edges. "The angle, see? Los Espiritos is seven degrees further west than Andros Island."

"An' that makes sunsets better?"

"They last longer, dig?"

"What are you talkin' about, man?"

"Closer to the place were the sun goes down."

"You goof!"

"No. The world's flat. Look..." Christian swept his hand across the broad expanse of the Gulf of Mexico. "Flat as anything. The edge's over there, where the sun goes down. Only it doesn't go down, it goes over."

"What?"

"The edge."

Maartyn drained his glass and shrugged. "Call yer boy. If I have to drink this swill."

"Call him yourself."

Maartyn let his empty glass drop beside the gun. "Hey, you, boy!" The sound brought Miguel to the door. "What's this nigga's name?"

Christian knew some of Maartyn's history so wasn't surprised. He used the word for anyone darker than himself. "Miguel Echevería Santamaria Diez. He likes to be called The Archangel."

"The hell I will! Hey, Amigo...drinks! An' put some goddamn ice

6

in it this time!"

"Take it easy. There's no ice."

"No problem. Cold beer?"

"We could go down to Juanita's."

"What a screwed up country! That bus ride from Havana, man! An' then the one from that Peanut Della Riva place! Old women an' chickens. Bawlin' kids."

"You could have walked from Pinar del Rio."

"Never walk."

"Nobody does," said Christian, regretting his own lethargy. They were both silent again, waiting for a new topic to fill the intellectual space. "Well, you look pretty good, for smack head," offered Maartyn.

"So does the surface of the moon, from a distance."

"You off the junk?"

"So far."

"What do for kicks?"

"Rum's cheap. It's enough, if I don't drink too much, or think too much."

"Not enough for this crap," said Maartyn, gesturing at the Miami Herald scattered across the terrace with the Cuban papers.

"What *this*?" asked Christian.

"Goddamned Fido Castrol guy!"

"Fidel. The other end of the island. The Sierra Maestra. Six hundred miles away. Even farther than Andros."

"Feel better already."

"We can just hang out here 'til they sort it out."

"Hope Batista kicks the livin' Jesus outta them Commies!"

"Socialists."

"Same thing."

"Let's not talk politics," said Christian, sitting down on the crumbling terrace wall.

"Bunch'a bearded monkeys. Chewin' sugar cane an' doin' Mary Jane." Maartyn snapped his fingers and laughed.

Christian felt obliged to laugh. He finished his rum, shifted his back to the wall of the villa and slid down, facing the sunset. Eyes closed. "Too bad about the ice."

"Yeah, too bad." Maartyn spat over the wall.

"The price of revolution in warm countries. Always the first to go, even before newspapers and human rights. In Canada there'd still be ice, but we don't have revolutions."

"Canada? You have ice all the time, right?" Miguel approached cautiously and set a fresh glass beside Maartyn's empty glass. Maartyn grabbed the glass in his rough hand. "To all the ice in Canada."

Miguel handed a glass with straight dark rum to Christian. "Gracias, Miguel."

"The rum's all gone, Señor Christ," said Miguel in Spanish. "So's the cola."

"Okay. I'll go down to Juanita's later."

Miguel picked up the empty glasses and faded back into the shadows. Maartyn watched him go. "He walks like a girl on the rag."

"You walk like an ape."

"Screw you!" Maartyn's body tightened and his thin lips drew down slightly. In that pose he looked more Latino than Louisiana Creole. Christian had seen the look. Maartyn being too cool to show emotion. "Miguel doesn't like me."

"You're just a another big mouth Yankee," Christian said, pushing a little further into Maartyn's thin veneer. Knowing there was a boundary, but Christian could get deeper than most.

"Don't call me Yankee! Genuine Louisiana red neck."

"Cubans don't bother with the political geography of their dangerous American neighbours. Too busy with their own problems."

"Americans fill this stupid little island with money."

"Not much reaches Los Espiritos. And your greenbacks aren't going to stop Castro from taking Havana."

"Thought y'all don't want talk politics?"

Christian took a sip of Cuban Dark, rested his head against the stone wall and gazed at the comforting sameness of the Gulf. "Not politics, just a fact of life."

"Then our filthy greenbacks'll buy Batista more'a these." He caressed the gun lovingly and rotated it to point at Christian.

Christian shifted away. "You don't get it do you?"

"What's to get? Communists want take over the world. We gotta stop'em." He moved the gun to point at Christian again.

"Do you mind?" Christian started to get up.

Maartyn picked up the revolver and stuck it into Christian's crotch. "Stick 'nough these up their Commie butts."

"Take it easy. Jesus!" Christian moved out of range. "Maartyn, have you ever had a commitment?" Maartyn looked blank. "A driving passion?"

"Women!" Maartyn spat over the wall. "You?"

"No. But Castro does." He crunched down at a safe distance. "And he has the peasants. Batista only has the military and the corrupt bureaucrats. It's just a matter of time before the Cubans kick Batista out."

"You Commie too?"

"I doubt it. Apolitical." Christian stretched his tanned legs into the slanting sunshine. "First generation Dublin Irish. Catholics, without baggage. Two uncles in the IRA but we never hear from them, except when they want money. Mom and Dad would argue for hours. Mom hates the IRA. Said we're Canadians and don't need a war with Ulster. Let Ireland and England settle it, she said. Canada can take the moral high ground."

"Yeah, an' we have to fight yer battles. Like that last time? Kick Japs off Pacific. Then Korea an' them Chinese Gooks, man!"

"Go ahead, fight the good fight. It's all the same to me."

"Not very patriotic," said Maartyn, feigning disgust.

"Don't need to be. We watch you Americans have gigantic parades on television to celebrate blowing up a hundred thousand Japanese. And don't forget the Spanish War right here in Cuba. You love beating up on small countries."

"An' we won that little war against that guy Hitler!"

"You weren't alone. Germans had already beaten themselves by attacking Russia. And you should do some history on the war in the South Pacific, chum. You weren't exactly alone there either. By the way, the French are getting out of Indochina. Why not take a whack at them?"

"What's *them*, more Gooks?"

"Asians are opposed to European colonialism."

"We already saved yer dumb ass from those Commies."

"Thank you," Christian said dryly.

"Welcome, jerk."

Christian studied his guest. Maartyn tried to be a one dimensional animal but Christian knew that beneath the street thug crust there was an intelligent, if culturally deprived, young man. It was hard to resist trying to enlighten Maartyn about the world. "Maartyn, what's a real communist, in your estimation?"

"Estimation? What's that?"

"Opinion, then."

"Hell, I don't know...Gooks. Chinks. Reds. All same."

"Think Miguel's a Commie?"

"How should I know? He's yer nigga."

"Right," Christian sighed. "He just brings the drinks."

"Without ice."

9

"He's only fourteen but he talks like a post pubescent university student who just discovered ideological socialism somewhere between biology class and girls. I'm not sure if he likes girls...His mother washes my clothes."

"So?"

"Father fishes and works the fields. Tobacco country. Did you know that? Pinar del Rio. Havana cigars, loved by kings, dictators, tycoons and American gangsters."

"So?"

"Youngest sister's got some mental defect."

"So what?"

"Oldest sister's a prostitute to help the family."

"So, what's the point!?"

"They're just simple folks with problems."

"Okay, so Miguel's a poor kid who can't find us any ice?"

"Ask him about Batista's ice."

Maartyn protruded his lips. "Him yer slave, no speaka ma language."

Christian winced. "Houseboy. Batista and his generals have ice. The majors have ice. Even the sergeants have ice."

"Y'all tellin' me that's why the Commies are tryin' to take over?"

"That's about the size of it. The Cubans don't want another corrupt dictator."

"Dictators! Commies! Seems I just landed in another stupid country."

"Running out of options?"

"Yeah, well, there's still Mexico."

Christian pointed west toward the darkening Gulf. A dry breeze had wandered in ruffling the harbour. "Yucatan Peninsula. Two hundred miles."

"Lots'a Mary Jane in Mexico, man. Good beer. Horny women."

"An' more trouble."

"Don't need more trouble," said Maartyn shaking his head. Eyes honest and sad for a moment.

"Amen to that." Both of them lost in thought. They could hear Miguel moving about the house closing shutters.

"Too bad about Paulo," Maartyn said finally.

"I guess," agreed Christian reluctantly. Another topic he didn't want to explore.

"He's a little crazy. But he's got balls," admitted Maartyn.

"You hate him."

"Kill that mother, first chance." Maartyn laughed and squinted into the sunset. "Maybe we should get him out of jail though."

"No. Better he does time," said Christian, relieved that his nemesis was safely tucked away in a cell.

"That Ambassador in Nassau could spring'im."

"Consul."

"What?..."

"French Consul. Ambassadors do Embassies."

"Who gives a shit, man? Some political jerkoff."

"Paulo's a dumb Basque tossed for smuggling a key of grass. That doesn't turn a consul's crank. You have to do something special. Murder. Assassination. The French are big on political crimes. It's their culture."

"You don't dig the French?"

"I grew up in Montreal," Christian said. Maartyn looked blank. "The Colonies? French Canadians?"

"Oh. Y'all still dig Renée then?"

Christian hesitated. "I guess."

"Too skinny."

"Says you." Christian looked at Maartyn for a reaction. Decided Paulo was an easier topic. "Paulo was just plain stupid."

"Stupid jerk asshole!" Maartyn's nostrils flared and his dark eyes flashed like the sunset. "Crazy fucker! Almost pulled it off though."

"Close only counts in horseshoes and hand grenades," Christian said, instantly regretting the reference.

"Yeah! Frags, man. Lob'em over the wall when they come."

"Maartyn, don't even say things. Batista's people are very nervous."

Maartyn waved the gun at Christian, dismissing the notion. "Okay..." He pulled the pin of an imaginary hand grenade, mimed tossing the bomb over the wall. *"Brrrrchaam! Blam!"* Maartyn giggled.

"Don't do that!"

"Okay, I'll just shoot'em up the butt. Silencer! Dig?" Maartyn howled with laughter.

"You're the one who's crazy."

"Yup, me an' Lucille. My best girl."

"Just don't shoot anybody, okay?"

"Commies an' cops everywhere." Maartyn waved the gun at the village.

Christian inhaled deeply. "Maybe you shouldn't have come, Maartyn. It's too peaceful here. Was peaceful."

Maartyn shrugged. "Y'all told me to get out of Nassau.

"I was afraid you'd end up in jail with Paulo."

"Maybe. I had this one fight..."

"Where's Renée?" Christian asked, looking straight at Maartyn. He needed to face the truth.

"Huh. Y'all know Renée, man."

"Did you sleep with her?"

"Kiddin' me?" Eyes flickered, scanning the horizon. "She's too screwed up for this Louisiana boy."

Christian knew he was lying. "At least she refuses to fly with the flock."

"Tight-assed dodo bird. Flew away one day." Maartyn laughed and punched Christian hard on the arm.

"Hey, she's *my* girl, okay?"

"Sure. Pity you."

"What's that supposed to mean?"

"Gone's what I mean."

"Maybe it's better," said Christian. The loneliness increased. He breathed the new land breeze from the hills that smelled of dust and tobacco. Last year's crop fermenting in the drying sheds. The sun glided lower smearing the last of the good heat on his cheeks. He studied the sky above the sun. Pink-tinged, high cirrus. A cold front coming in from the north. "It's probably snowing in Montreal."

"Man!...How'd'ya survive in a country that's frozen all the time?"

"Why do you think I'm here?"

"Well, Chris ol' buddy, it sure as hell ain't the night life."

"A quiet place."

"Deceased, more like."

"Los Espiritos means literally, The Holy Spirits."

"Yeah...like freakin' ghosts."

"Maybe some ghosts too. There's voodoo priests and Santerias mixed in with the Catholics. Very Afro-European."

"Why's it always about weirdo religions?"

"Cuba's a good Catholic country, just confused about origins."

"Even Catholics have to have fun, man."

"Hey, Maartyn, Catholics have more fun than Presbyterians. Jehovah's Witness aren't allowed to have fun. Muslims might have fun but they won't admit it. By the way, never trust anyone who doesn't believe in wine and brandy. Leave it to the Catholics. Monks make brandy. Catholic countries throw the best parties. Take the French for instance..."

"They know how to party all right," agreed Maartyn. "Mardi Gras!"

"The French invented Mardi Gras."

"In New Orleans."

"Exactly. Where jazz was born. Played a club there once. We'd groove all night. Sunrise over Lake Pontchartrain, drinking Gallo on the levee, shootin' up, watching the chemicals coming down from Baton Rouge. Very colourful."

Maartyn, not listening but thinking, took a sip of rum. "My ol' man could party." Maartyn looked over the terrace wall. Low tide. The wide, wet beach glowed pink and orange. Fishing boats scattered on the sand. A gentle clutter. "...Not much of a party down there right now."

"What did Renée say?"

Maartyn's perfect white teeth dazzled. "That you're a lousy lay."

Christian bristled but said gently, "Tell me."

"Okay," he said finally. "Maybe she was goin' to Paris."

"She hates Paris in winter."

"We needed sheckles."

"Were you that broke?"

"Well, yeah, actually. Momma sent a plane."

"Doesn't sound like Renée. She rejected their money."

"A real idealist, like?"

"Everybody could use some."

"Screw idealists! Makes you stupid. Turn yer back on a fortune an' live like a hermit in some way out dump like this."

"Living within my means. There *is* a difference."

"Only the very rich can, dig?"

"I wouldn't know about the *very* rich."

"Renée's loaded. That's why y'all jumped on'er isn't it? The money?"

"I didn't know about the money, at first. Renée walked away from it. Said she was looking for a higher level of consciousness. The Sartre thing? Existentialism?" Maartyn just shrugged. "Here and now. Nothing and nothingness. The ideal of nothing."

Maartyn made a face. "Man, idealists are such simpletons. If Marilyn Monroe was naked at yer feet you'd say, pardon me mam, an' cover her up."

Christian was tiring of the conversation. "Miguel?..." Christian called softly, "What's for dinner?"

Miguel appeared at the pantry door. "The fish we caught this morning, Señor Christ. Some wild onions from the garden. There's corn bread left from breakfast."

"Okay, I guess it's fish." He turned to Maartyn. "Fish?"

"There's a choice?"

"Hunger."

"Tell'im to cook fish hot. Burn it. Lots of pepper," said Maartyn. "Burn it!" he shouted at Miguel. "Black fish on rice, like a nigger in a cotton field. The way we do it in Louisiana."

Christian translated about the heat and the pepper. "...And slice the onions fresh on the side. There's a bottle of wine." When Christian rented the villa he found a case of Campo Vieja Rioja hidden in the stone cellar beneath the pantry. The rest of the bottles were still in hiding.

"Should I really cook the beautiful fish the way the Gringo says?"

"Yes. Blackened fish is very good."

"Cuban cooking's not good enough for the Gringo?"

"Just do the fish."

Miguel shrugged back into the dark pantry. A match flared. Yellow light spilled across the rough stones of the terrace. Then the single gas burner hissed blue. Night sounds started up in the dry acacia beside the wall. Voices floated up from the village. Guitars and melancholy songs. A man and woman talking, loud, then yelling too fast for Christian to follow. The sunset was diffused and the Gulf of Mexico oily red. Unusual for December. The winter colours should have been sharper. Probably a volcano in Mexico, Christian thought, or wind dust from the central plains. The air looked the way it does in hurricane season, with the humidity. But hurricane season was over and it had been dry, unpredictable and turbulent. A phenomenon called El Nino off the coast of Peru, the papers reported. The dying throes of the Christ Child. Christ is a weather system. Christian was sliding into depression again. The weather in harmony. Too much talk of civil war. Renée. Revolutionaries and paranoia. A somber mood, like the red sky, was creeping over the villa. They drank warm rum and listened to the fish frying and the night sounds. The smell of fish and the hot olive oil, replacing the dust and tobacco scent of the dry night.

To the east, Fidel Castro Ruz and his guerrilla disciples were out of their jungle stronghold in the Sierra Maestra, moving like patient tigers through the mountains, preparing for the final assault on Santa Clara and the garrisons along the central highway to Havana.

"Señor Christ?...do you want to eat out here on the *terrace*?" Miguel pronounced terrace in English, the way Christian pronounced the word when Miguel had shown him around the modest villa that once belonged to a businessman from America. Terrace sounded more grand than patio. Miguel told him that the former owner, a Señor Bartuchi, had to leave Los Espiritos in a hurry because of certain *reasons* and that Juanita had acquired the villa, for certain other *reasons*.

"Yes, out here." Christian gestured to the bench, beside Maartyn. "Miguel, will you eat something with us tonight?"

"No, gracias. I have to look after my little sister. But first I must poison the Gringo."

"Should I inform Señor Maartyn of your mission?"

"It makes no difference. He's just another Yankee Imperialist pig."

Christian turned to Maartyn. "Miguel says, he's honoured that you will eat his humble blackened fish."

"Like hell he is!" Maartyn took his drink and stood at the stone wall, pretending to watch the last rose glow of the sunset. The low sun touched another bank of clouds spilling colours across the Gulf. Blood-red to dusty rose and violet. Cooking smells from the fishermen's homes mingling with Miguel's fish.

"Man, whole dumb place stinks of fish. Reminds me of the Delta. I ever tell you my ol' man worked shrimpers out of La Hache?"

"No, you never talked about your family."

"Didn't want to spoil the party."

"So, you want to tell me now?"

"Sure, there's no party to spoil. One night he got drunk an' fell overboard takin' a piss off the bow. Prop chopped him up good an' they pulled him out of the shrimp net in pieces. Ever see a steak go through meat grinder? Man!..."

"That must have been tough on your mom."

"Yeah. My ol' lady was real broke up about it. Married a Detroit nigger a week after the funeral."

Christian sighed. "Why do you still use that term for Blacks?"

"Hey, man, where I come from it's just a word, ya know? Like wop, dyke or spic, dig? Anyway, she an' this *Spade* split north. Detroit. Never saw her again. I joined the marines an' fought every *Spook* in boot camp."

"I can guess whose side you'd be on in the Little Rock thing."

"Little Rock, Arkansas? What about it?"

"The school desegregation movement? It's all over the American papers. Where have you been?"

"I never read, man. Makes you crazy."

"Governor calls out the National Guard and they stand around watching the Black kids try to get to school. The National Guard's supposed to protect those kids."

"Niggers, man! They want into everythin'. That Orval Faubus...A real good ol' boy. He'll put them uppity niggers in their place!"

"What would you call a black person you did like?"

"I got nuthin' against a black man. Want to hear the story or not?"

"Continue."

"One night a whole gang of...*black dudes*, got me behind the barracks an' beat me unconscious. So the marines kick *me* out because they say I was a *malcontent*. Like that word...malcontent? It's on my discharge papers. Dig it? The marines are trainin' us to kill Gooks an' Commies on sight an' they toss me because I get beat up by some of their underprivileged *African American* folks. How's that?"

"It's the attitude. Continue."

"I was born in a waterfront dive in Port Eades, Louisiana. Delta trash, dig? My ol' lady's part Creole or Cajun an' part Seminole Indian an' I don't know what all. My ol' man was Portuguese. But my last name comes from this Cajun whore who adopted me. She was the midwife 'cause my ol' lady was too drunk to get to the doctor in Pilottown. You wonder why I'm a little messed up?"

"Are you?"

"Why else would I be here?"

Christian didn't want to go down that long road. "What's Port Eades like?"

"We call it Port Hades...like in hell? 'Bout as far south as you can go on the Mississippi Delta."

"But what's it like?"

"Port Hades? 'Bout like this Lost Espirito. Short piss of a backwater fishin' village. A gang rape couldn't scare up a brain among'em, includin' the chick."

"Just your average, good ol' boy, all American red necks, right?"

Maartyn glared at Christian. "Y'all mockin' me, brother?"

"Sorry, you brought it up."

Miguel carried the kerosene lamp to the terrace. Christian carefully moved Lucille aside and Miguel set the lamp on the small table, the pool of yellow light falling beyond the revolver. Maartyn picked up the gun and pointed it at Miguel. Miguel ignored the gun and went back to the pantry, returning with a plate of crisp, blackened pompanos with the sliced onions on the side and the hot, frothy olive oil in a wooden bowl. Then he brought the bottle of wine and the half loaf of dark corn bread and two heavy china plates. "I'll go now if you don't need me, Señor Christ."

"No. Yes, go, thank you...and don't call me Christ."

"Okay, Señor Joyce."

"Not that either! Makes me sound like an old woman. Thank your mother for the bread."

Miguel eyed the bread for a moment, decided not to mention the account. "The pompanos are fresh. I kept them in sea water in the cold bag, hung in the shade."

"Good. Thank you." Christian used his fork to lift a section of blackened skin. "They look wonderful, under all that charcoal."

"I put on the pepper just as the Gringo said. Then I burned it."

"Fine."

"Should I open the wine?"

"That's okay. My favourite job."

"I hope the Gringo gets heartburn and his prick falls off."

"Miguel!..." Miguel retreated to the safety of the pantry. Maartyn stared toward Mexico, fingering the gun. He had understood one word. "Relax, Maartyn, he's just a kid."

Miguel left the house, closing the front door softly and then the gate. They could hear his bare feet just grazing the stones. The evening breeze from the hills rustled the dry acacia leaves.

"Thought Cubans're Spanish," said Maartyn, forking in a large chunk of fish.

"West Africans were brought here by the Spaniards four hundred years ago to work the sugar plantations."

"Slaves?"

"Yeah. They mixed with the Spanish but kept their traditions. If you paid any attention to the customs in the Islands you'd know the difference. The Africans were treated badly, of course, but they weren't push overs. In fact, the slaves created the first revolution in Cuba and the grateful Cubans have been at it ever since."

"Mother jumpin' Jesus! Can't get away from'em. I thought it was bad on Andros. An' that reminded me too much of Louisiana. Slow movin', slow talkin'."

"You have to admit Joseph and Trina were good to us."

"So? We're tourists, man. Spendin' money."

"Not yours...Renée's. And Trina wouldn't take our money, remember? I wonder what they must think of people like us?"

"None of their business what we do on their dumb little islands so long as we're droppin' greenbacks."

"You shouldn't hang out in the Caribbean if you don't like Blacks."

"I didn't say I don't like Blacks...Spooks. Spades."

"Then what?"

"It's just, the way I grew up, you know? In Louisiana the darkies know their place."

"Place?"

"Hey, man, back home we let them have their own restaurants an' schools an' things, for their own protection."

"Sure. You wouldn't even let them join the army in The First War but when you want real entertainment you go to Basin Street or up to Harlem to hang out in the jazz clubs. You even let Blacks play baseball now. It's all right for Blacks to entertain you."

"How would you know about our spooks, sonny? You probably never saw one 'til you got to the States."

"I grew up in Montreal. There's Blacks from the Indies and such. I never thought about 'place'. They never think of place either. Everybody's too busy surviving in that lousy, wonderful city. Too hot in summer..the humidity boils off the river and smells of sewage. In winter the icy wind rolls down Mount Royal and the streets are full of snow and slush. But everybody suffers the same. The French are more tolerant. Liberal is as liberal does. That's why I took languages and music. If you know languages and music, and some cultural history, you can go anywhere."

"I don't know, man. Somethin's wrong with all this."

"Come on, eat. Wine?"

"Is it cold?"

"Good red wine's supposed to be consumed at ambient temperature."

Maartyn made a face and wiggled his hips. "*Ambient* temperature. More big assed words!" He gave a finger salute. Christian almost laughed. Maartyn poured the dregs of his rum over the terrace wall. The stale rum splattered on dry leaves and a small creature skittered away. Christian cut the foil capsule of the Spanish Rioja. He had trouble pulling the old cork. Maartyn grabbed the bottle and pulled the cork in one fluid motion and handed the bottle back. Christian poured Maartyn's glass half full. The dark wine showed a hint of rust on the edges. He filled his own glass and sniffed, then drank. "If it makes you feel better, Miguel's a mulatto."

Maartyn tasted his wine and made a face. "Huh. Mulatto. Big deal. Back home we'd call'em half baked coons."

"Come again?"

"Half white, half nigga."

"I don't get it."

"Delta specialty. Swamp coon on rice. Bake in the sun until the coon rots an' the skin falls off an' the alligators get it, then feed the rice to the fish an' eat possum stew." Maartyn laughed in short snorts. "Oh, man!..." He drank off the strong wine and held out his glass.

"You really are messed up."

"It doesn't bother me!...Spooks. Black Brothers?"

"Now they're brothers?"

"Just skip it, man."

They sat in silence, drinking. Christian poured more wine. A pair of green moths flew around the chimney of the kerosene lamp until one flopped in, burst into flame, flared brightly, crackling, curling up in a spasm. The mate hovered a moment in mourning and escaped into the darkness. Out on the Gulf tiny white lights moved along the horizon. Fishing boats working the edge of the Yucatan Channel, or small coastal traders. Smugglers from Central America. The Yucatan Channel a busy highway of commerce and criminal activity. Below Christian's villa candles and lamps defined the village. The guitar players took a break while a mother was singing her children to sleep. They continued eating in silence, Christian feeling increasingly uncomfortable in the dead air that crackled like thunder before the explosion. He dipped his bread in the hot olive oil.

"More bread?"

"No."

"Wine?"

"Yeah, might as well." Maartyn held out his glass.

"So, your father was Portuguese?" asked Christian, draining the bottle into Maartyn's glass.

"I said he was."

"Right. How did he happen to settle in Louisiana?"

"I didn't say he settled in Louisiana."

Christian exhaled carefully. "Okay...how did you happen to have a Portuguese father?"

The strong wine was taking hold. "What d'y'all care?"

"Just asking. You know, small talk? Polite after dinner conversation?"

"A'right. Here's the story if you need it." Maartyn took a gulp of wine. "Simon was a deckie on a tramp steamer, when he met my ol' lady, her name's Lucille too, if that helps. They met in Baton Rouge. She worked the bars, know what I mean?" Christian looked blank.

"So, do I have to spell it out?" Christian shook his head. "A whore, she was, okay!? Ol' man's steamer got stuck up Big Muddy when owners went broke. Got tired of eatin' rats an' rice an' jumped ship. He an' my ol' lady ran for the Delta. You can get good an' lost on the Delta if you need to. Feds won't go near the place 'cause they turn up dead too often." He waited for this to sink in. "There was work on the shrimp boats. The ol' man fished an' Mommy turned tricks. I'm not sure Simon's my real father." Maartyn took a drink of wine. In the lamp light he was dark in that way.

"You look Spanish enough to be Portuguese."

"Thanks!" He took another swallow of the good wine. "He was okay, Simon. Liked to sing an' drink. Jesus, could that mother drink wine. He was good to the ol' lady though. It's just that she was a two-bit lay an' he was away on the boats. I liked the jerk, you know? Never hit me or nothin'. My buddies were always gettin' beat up by their ol' man. 'Specially on Saturday nights. They just had to beat on somethin', you know? They'd get off the boats an' get drunk an' start on the women, then the kids an' finish off on each other." Maartyn took a drink of wine. "Then one day he just never came back." He stared into the blackness of the night, thinking about home, the Delta.

"The accident?"

"Okay. You want more details? They packed what was left of'im in ice an' kept on fishin'. Brought him ashore over to Gulfport, up in Mississippi, you know?" He took another drink, not tasting the wine. "Left'im in a fish plant freezer. That's where we found the poor bastard, in the freezer. The shrimps, see? They had to sell the catch an' go out again 'cause the crew was on shares. They never knew who to call anyway, so we never knew for a couple weeks. Kept his share too. Wouldn't even pay to bury'im."

"That's a hard story." Christian raised his glass. "To Simon."

"Yeah...Poor ol' Simon." Maartyn drank to Simon.

"How old were you?"

"Twelve, I guess."

"So, what did you do?"

"Hung around the Delta. Worked the boats. Learned to fix engines. Love engines, man. Stole what I needed an' lied about my age. That's how I got into the marines when I was fifteen." Maartyn touched two metal dog tags on a chain under his T-shirt. He lit a cigarette and sat back, blowing smoke at Christian. It hung in the dead air.

"Doesn't sound like you, Maartyn. Why the marines?"

"The toughest, man. The best. Like a street gang but with machine guns." He patted the brass dog tags. They clinked softly.

"So, did you have a goal in life?"

"A what?"

"A plan?"

"Chris, man, y'all don't have plans on the Delta. You survive."

Christian tried to imagine Maartyn growing up on the bayous of the Mississippi Delta. "Any family?"

"What?"

"Family? You know? Brothers, sisters?"

He inhaled deeply, flicking hot ashes over the wall on the dry brush. Christian was tempted to say something. "Nah. I tore Momma up pretty good, I guess. Everybody was drunk. No more problems like me."

"Were you a problem?"

"Hell yes!"

"Did you go to school?"

"Are you kiddin' man? On the Delta you learn about bad whisky, mean women, alligators, snakes, stealin', gamblin' an' cheatin'. All the necessaries of life, brother."

"Then, where did you learn to read and write?"

"In the marines...mostly in the brig."

"The what?"

"The joint. The slammer. Jail? Damn, for a college boy you sure are dumb about some things in this life."

"Who said knowing the inside of a jail was a prerequisite to learning the art of gracious living?"

"There you go, just like you always did when Renée was around. Always talkin' like a big time intellectual. No wonder Renée thinks yer a jerk."

"Did she say that?"

"What do you think?"

"I think you're full of it."

"Full of what? Say it! You're such a nice talkin' boy. Are all you people from Canada so polite?"

"We're world famous."

"Sure."

"We're so polite you Americans can come in and take whatever you want and we don't say boo."

"Not me. I don't take nothin' from nobody with good manners. I only steal from asshole jerks like Paulo."

"Miguel will be relieved. I wish there were more Yankees like you."

"I'm not a Yankee!"

"Let's drink to politeness."

"Screw you, and Miguel!"

Christian sipped his wine. Maartyn pouted. "Miguel has another sister. Rosameralda. Student at the University of Havana...'til they shut it down."

"What was she learnin', Commie propaganda?" he said, sarcastically.

"No, not exactly. She wanted to be a lawyer and live in New York."

"Ever meet'er?"

"Nope. Miguel talks about her, like this woman's a goddess. She's into some political movement in Havana. The family's very disappointed. They made big sacrifices to educate her. Her older sister, Ezameralda, the prostitute, paid her tuition."

"That's weird. Lay'n'pay plan." Maartyn sniggered, back in mood.

"Why's that so weird?"

"Whores don't have regular families, do they?"

"Course they do!" Christian was also feeling the wine. "Fidel promises free education to all Cubans, even the prostitutes."

"I guess that gives the whores a break."

"It's not that simple."

"No shit! My ol' lady was a whore an' she never thought'a sendin' me to no uni-frickin'-versity."

Christian touched Maartyn's glass. "Let's drink to higher education."

"I'd get a whole lot higher if we had that Mexican grass Paulo lost."

"You set him up."

"The hell you say! Did he say I set'im up!?"

"Let's drink to Paulo."

"Paulo...the dumbass."

"Why is it you never told me about your mother and father?"

"Truth? Renée's a classy chick, right? Loaded, you dig? Even if she tries to be so, what did she call it?..."

"Bohemian."

"Bohemian...with her stupid poetry an' the weird clothes. Can you imagine wearin' that stuff in this heat?"

"Very cool, Renée."

"Too damn cool, man." Maartyn flicked away his cigarette butt and spit over the wall. "An' she has this superior attitude like I was some glob'a slime on the sidewalk."

"You like her though."

"I doubt it!"

"No, you do and it bothers you that she thinks you're just another loud mouthed American."

"Well, I goddamn am, an' proud of it! At least I stand up for what I believe."

"And what is that, Mississippi Delta Maartyn?"

"Goddamn right to be the biggest, loudest southern bigot, hell rais-er, is what!"

"Keep it down, will you. The fishermen have to get up early."

"Screw'em...Screw y'all!" he yelled at the village. "Fishermen I know on the Delta get off the boats an' party an' fight an' screw all night 'til it's time to go back fishin'."

"Sounds like a tiring life."

"Hey, Canada, you mockin' the American way?"

"No, no. I'm just amazed your country functions at all considering your penchant for self-abuse."

"There you go again! Every time you get goofed up you start usin' big words. Y'all like to mock people." Maartyn was as angry as Christian had ever seen him, even the night he and Paulo had the fight on Andros. "Just like Renée!"

Christian eyed the revolver. Maartyn followed Christian's gaze. Christian felt the familiar chill. "Did Renée really leave?"

"Dunno."

"You said she left."

"Can't remember."

"But you just said she went to Paris."

"She was hangin' out on the beach with Paulo's fag friends."

"You said Paris."

"I said, maybe."

"Did she or didn't she?"

"What?"

"Which is it?"

"Actually ol' buddy, I saw her get on a big white yacht with some fat Greek zillionaire headin' for Antigua. Gettin' laid all the way."

"Bullshit, Maartyn! You're just trying to make me mad."

"Worked."

"Didn't."

"Did so."

Maartyn drained his glass. Christian looked away. "Didn't." Maartyn held the glass close to Christian's face. He said, "and every time you drink you get mean and ugly."

Maartyn laughed. "Yeah, man, mean like a junk yard dog."

Christian could never resist his laughter. What was it about Maartyn? A very dangerous friend. He poured the dregs into Maartyn's glass. "That's it."

"Thank Christ."

The growing conversation gap became awkward. Maartyn studied the pictures on the front page of the Miami Herald; rare, grainy photographs of the elusive Castro guerrillas. Bearded young Turks in sweat stained fatigues. "So, this Castro dude. He's just another Commie too?"

"Not even a Socialist. The communists and the socialists don't agree with Castro's guerrilla tactics and he doesn't agree with their ideologies. If anything he's a fascist, like Mussolini...and Franco."

"Ah, they're all Commies. America's full of 'em too. That McCarthy guy, Senator Joe?"

"Heard of him," answered Christian. "He's holding hearings. Un-American activities."

"Good ol' Joe Mac. Right after them Commies like a mad dog. I can't believe some of the people he's chewed out. Charlie Chaplin for God's sake? How can they do that to their own country?"

"Chaplin's English. He came to America to make films."

"So? America's a good place to live, right? Right!?"

"If you say so," answered Christian.

"So what are we doin' here, man!?"

"The sun." Christian didn't want to get into reasons.

Maartyn stared into his glass. "This Castro dude ain't no democrat, that's for sure."

"I don't know, there's more to the guy than the papers say. He's a puzzle but Americans don't bother trying to understand the man. He's got a lot of good ideas when he's not talking like a fascist. Rights of the people and all that. Talks about having elections. That means he's a democrat."

"Shit, man! Democrats don't go around shooting things up to get their way and then have some dumb elections."

"What was the American Revolution then?"

"How should I know?" Maartyn looked uncomfortable.

"Skip it."

"Any more wine?"

"No," Christian lied flatly.

"Okay, don't get all prickly. Got any beer?"

"Nope."

"Goof?"

"Told you, I'm off it."

"Goddamn wine gives me a headache. I need a cold one."

"There's Juanita's Cantina."

"That's what I like about American beer. Drink all night, 'cept you have to piss more. Wish we had some music, man. Y'all dig Jerry Lee? Little Richard? 'Lucille'?"

"Never heard of'em," answered Christian, dryly.

"What!? Get out, man! Dig this..." Maartyn waved his hands over an imaginary key board. "Come on over baby, whole lotta shakin' goin' on. *Ba da da da, ba da da da...*" Maartyn rapped on the table making the glasses jump. "I said, come on over baby, whole lotta shakin goin' onnnn. We'll make it-whole lotta shakin' goin' on. I said shake, baby shake...shake baby shake, I said shake it baby shake...shake baby shake. Easy now, I said shake, baby shake."

"Great lyrics."

"Jerry Lee's the best, man!"

"Who the hell's Jerry Lee?"

"Jerry Lee Lewis!" Maartyn sank to his knees, mumbling. "Get real low now...Where have y'all been, man?...on the moon? Jerry Lee's about the hottest ol' Louisiana boy you ever heard. How 'bout this one?" He pitched higher." You shake ma head an' you rattle ma brain...a kinda love drives a man insane!"

"Obviously American music's going to hell in a handcart. Now you take Dexter Gordon."

"Who the sweet Jesus's Dexter Gordon?"

"Jazz sax. Very mellow stuff."

"Jazz? That shit you play's just nigger music."

"An acquired taste, like good wine. You play around with a tune until it begins to make sense. You know? First, you take a melody, then bend it until it sounds like anarchy, then these beautiful ideas come, but you have to wait for it. Play with it. Then you can really get in the groove. Jazz makes you work and sometimes it flows out easy, like, I don't know, it just flows."

"Like gull shit?"

"Very prosaic, Maartyn. Jazz is democratic. It's not like your Rhythm an' Blues or whatever, Rock'n'Roll."

"You mean Commies wouldn't dig jazz either?"

"Doubt it. Jazz is too expressive. Too, individualistic. Say a group's on stage, jamming. You have a lead sax. Side men; trumpet, baritone sax. Big bass. Piano of course, and when you get in the groove, it's just magic."

"Don't forget drums." He hit the table. "*Bam! Bam! Bam!*"

"Drums aren't essential to good jazz. In small combos..."

"No drums? Are y'all nuts!? Then you never heard Delta Blues. Drums keep it all together, man. *Wham! Wham! Wham! Crash!*" He was yelling again.

"Maartyn, please."

Maartyn slapped the table making the lamp and Lucille jump. "*Wham! Bam! Crash*! Get yer sax ol' buddy an' I'll beat the shit outta this table."

"Not tonight."

"Why not? Remember the fun we had on the beach?"

"This isn't Andros, Maartyn." Christian scanned the village for movement. "Listen, I don't want to alarm you, but, if you don't keep it down a delegation of my neighbours are coming up the hill and slit your noisy throat."

Maartyn grabbed the gun and pointed it into the darkness beyond the stone wall. "Let'em come. Come on Commie bastards! *Pow! Pow! Pow!*"

"Okay, look, if I go down to the cantina will you shut up and be good?"

"Maybe...maybe." Maartyn sat down heavily and seemed to slide into a stupor.

Christian sat back, head against the wall. The rough stones still warm from the heat of the day. He didn't want to move. He didn't want to go down the hill. If Juanita was drinking she'd be in one of her moods. He was tired of drunk talk and the politics. Tired of being careful around people who change personalities by the ounce. Maybe, if he just stayed still Maartyn would go to sleep. But Maartyn seldom gave out until he had finished all the booze and threatened everyone in the place. Christian asked himself again why he had a friend like Maartyn?

Of all the drifters and misfits he had met on his journey, Mississippi Maartyn was the last person he would have chosen for a companion. If he'd had a choice. Maartyn had chosen him when they met on the supply boat crossing from Miami to Bimini. Big hearted, mouthy and pushy. Insisted on sharing a bottle of cheap Island rum with Christian. That first night on Bimini, Maartyn started a fight with the locals just for fun. Christian escaped with his life only because Maartyn protected him, carrying him out of the place under one arm, fending off knife slashes with the other.

Christian looked over at Maartyn, expecting to see the goofy, intimidating grin and those wild dangerous eyes. Christian had never been able to look at them for long. Would get lost in the dark depths and never surface. Maartyn could pass for a mulatto. Perhaps that was why he was so sensitive about colour. Maartyn was sensitive about everything. A lightning rod waiting for the jolt. An emotional short fuse. But Maartyn's eyes were closed, breathing deep and slow. Christian put his glass on the table, carefully, and was reaching to turn down the lamp.

Maartyn seized Christian's wrist. "Ha! Gotcha!" He grabbed Lucille and pointed it at Christian. "Trying to sneak off, chump?" He turned Christian's wrist and pulled him down, pressing the cool barrel of the gun into Christian's temple. "*Pow,* you're dead! Trick they taught us in the marines. Listen and smell even when you're asleep. The Gooks're always sneakin' around at night, the bastards. Fix'em. Good thing you ain't a Gook. *Pow! Pow! Ra ta ta ta ta ta tat!* Machine gun. Head all gone. Blood everywhere, man. Guts in your hands. Eyeballs over the wall!" Maartyn relaxed his grip.

Christian pulled free and backed away. "You *are* nuts."

"Me!? Y'all went for Lucille."

"I was turning down the lamp!"

"No way! You reach for Lucille, she screams an' I break your arm. Marine training. Judo. *Chop, chop!*" Maartyn leapt into the air, slashing at imaginary assailants. "*Eeeya*!!"

"Maartyn, shut up! Jesus!"

"You swore. He actually said a bad word. Hot damn, Sally! I'll corrupt you yet ol' buddy. Now, y'all goin' down there for beer or do I have to shoot yer toes off?"

Juanita's Cantina was typical hot country architecture. A shambling, low slung, frame affair with sand-blasted pink and blue paint, rusting tin roof, and broken shutters. Fading soft drink signs. The ensemble held up by dying royal palms. The hand lettered sign over the door was bleached to a shadow. A smaller sign hung by old fishing line from a nail beside the door said, 'Closed'. The door was open. Christian entered cautiously. The wooden floor hadn't been swept. Mementos of Juanita's patrons still lingered. Cold white light from a gas lantern gave the empty cantina a hard look. The heavy odour of sweat, tobacco and stale beer an invisible curtain.

"Hello? Juanita?"

There was a body at the end of the bar propped up on thick arms. Juanita, a big woman of indeterminate age, with a wild mass of grey-black hair splayed out over her broad shoulders in a protective cupola. Spreading in all directions, like her body, which was covered by a loose print dress. Prints were popular with nightclub singers in Havana. Christian thought the dress might be purple and rose, like the sunset. She could have been a Haitian Priestess sitting at the end of a zinc topped bar, back lit by an array of flickering candles, under a mouldering moose head. The stuffed fauna incongruous in a Cuban bar. The antler rack six feet across and a haven for spiders. Behind her, amid the candles, a crude wooden crucifix with cartoon Christ, a chipped plaster statue of the Blessed Virgin Mary in that famous blue robe, and icons of pagan gods, completed the shrine. Christian felt a rush of religious guilt, being a lapsed Catholic verging on submersion in the cult of oblivion. He felt the urge to kneel down and bless himself, just in case.

"Juanita?..." One fleshy eyelid opened slowly, like a sleepy gorilla. The bulging eye was yellow-tinged, laced with red veins, where the white should be. "I'm closed," she said. The voice was deep and raspy.

"I know," replied Christian.

The other eye opened. "Then what do you want, pretty boy?"

"Ah, I'd like some beer. I have a friend, up there..."

"I can plainly hear your friend. The one who stumbled in here today looking for a 'good ol' white boy' who plays saxophone." She said the phrase in English. She continued in Spanish. "His ranting has kept me awake and forced me to drink alone."

"Sorry, Juanita. Ah, If I don't get him beer he'll break things."

"And as your provider I must be concerned. If you bring him more beer he'll get louder and break things anyway. My things. Am I right?"

"Yes, Juanita. You're probably right. But what can I do?"

"Have quiet friends."

"I wish. About the beer?"

"No beer."

"Ah, what about the *special* kind?"

"Oho, so you know about the special beer."

"Miguel told me that I could ask for the *special* beer."

"I see...Miguel has told you the way things are done in Los Espiritos. All right, for the special beer you must play saxophone for me tomorrow night."

"Play? You mean a gig?" He used the English word.

"Yes, 'gig', whatever you call it. Show. You're some sax man. I can hear you in the morning. Wakes me up."

"Sorry, I didn't realize."

"Are you any good at night?"

"I, ah, can groove, some," Christian said in English.

"What does it mean...to groove?" Juanita asked in English.

"Jam. Like in combos. Jazz clubs. Get in the groove."

Juanita closed one heavy eye. "Oh, to get in the groove. You don't look like a musician of the jazz. Wrong colour." She laughed. Bad teeth the price of bad habits.

"Is the *special* beer free if I play tomorrow night?"

"Of course not. Playing is just the tax on the special beer. If you have to drink when I'm closed, then you pay."

"Pretty stiff terms. You remind me of a club owner in Toronto. He charged us for drinks while we played for almost nothing."

"Chris!" Maartyn called over the villa wall. "Hey, Dick head! Y'all comin' er what?"

"Okay, how much for this special beer?"

"Do you have American?"

"No. Only pesos."

"Then it's ten pesos."

"That's expensive beer."

"It's very special."

"Is it Cuban?"

"No."

"German? German beer's good." Juanita shook her head. "Mexican? They make good beer in Mexico."

"No. Yankee beer. The special Budweiser."

"What's so special about Budweiser?"

"We're closed."

"I see..." Maartyn was screaming his name again. "Is the beer at least cold?"

"The electricity's out again and there's no ice until tomorrow night."

"Wonderful. So, how long do I have to play for the privilege of buying your expensive, warm Yankee beer?"

"For as long as I say. And you must have a band."

"Juanita, I don't have a band. They're in jail, in Havana."

"Soon everyone in Cuba will be in jail because Batista's scared of his shadow. Never mind. We need some fun. There's a man who plays guitar, Old Jocinto. He needs some fun also, before he dies. I have a drum. Get your loud friend to play the drum."

"Okay. One condition. We at least get to drink free while we play. That's pretty standard in clubs. Makes up for the lousy pay."

"Depends on how good you play."

"How good is your guitar player?"

"He's an old man, very sick. And mostly deaf, so you have to show him with your foot...the rhythm?"

"Great! Just great."

"You're just a boy. If Jocinto Alejandro Diez can play his instrument and not hear, you can learn to play and move your foot."

"I don't think this is going to work."

"You'll be a big hit. Tourists will come from Habana to hear you. Juanita's will be bigger than the Tropicana, no?"

"There aren't many tourists left in Cuba."

"That Castro!"

"You don't approve of Castro either?"

Juanita shrugged. "Would you like a beer or a rum? I don't like to drink alone. It's bad luck." She kissed her fingers and touched the nose of the moose.

"Ah, no thanks. I've got to get back...but, I've been meaning to ask about the moose?"

"The what?"

"Moose?" Christian pointed to the truncated animal above her head.

"Oh, him. There's no word like 'moose' in Cuba."

"Not many in these parts I guess. Where did he come from?"

"Sad, sad tale, Señor Chris. We need a drink to ease the pain." Juanita manoeuvred her bulk behind the bar. When she bent over to get the beer, a cascade of thick hair fell around her face and shoulders and framed enormous breasts in danger of escaping from the open front of the print dress. "A few years ago a rich man and this skinny blonde woman came in here off a big yacht. Very unusual, you see, because foreign boats never come to Los Espiritos. Too dangerous through the islands because of the reefs, but they had a local pilot, who, for a reason you will hear, jumped ship and disappeared into the hills. They anchored out in the bay waiting for another pilot and drank in my cantina." She handed him a beer and opened one for herself, drinking half before she set it down, mostly foam. Christian drank his too fast, the warm beer overflowing onto the bar. "She, the yacht woman, made rude comments. I hated her immediately. They got drunk every day, the yacht man and the woman. The woman was too mouthy. She sat there, where you are, and seduced my husband with her tiny tits and her white hair, but you could see the dark roots. The man was from some place called Minnesota and did something with trees in some other place called Canada. A big time hunter who bragged about these monsters with huge horns that charged around, knocking down his trees. My husband got very interested. Not in the monsters but in the little tits of the white woman who looked like she would devour him. Same reason the pilot left the yacht, see? The man said he would take my husband hunting in Canada if he would be the pilot on his yacht. I never saw my husband again but the next year this *moose* arrives. So this, Señor, is my new husband. Like him?"

"Yeah, I guess. It's a very big moose. A bull, isn't it?"

"Oho! Imagine how big this bull was. Too bad he sent the wrong end!" Juanita shrieked so loud it scared Christian.

"I, ah, should get back, my friend Maartyn's alone up there."

"Is he a child?"

"No, no. He's very grown up, I think."

"Then he should be all right while we have another beer." Juanita snapped open two more Budweisers.

He guessed her age to be forty. She had been a good looking woman and still had the handsome African features in profile, but had not aged well. Perhaps it was the hard life. She chain smoked little cigars and drank her profits. Ate nothing and stayed up all night. He couldn't imagine her as a child, unless the child grew up in a cantina sitting at the end of a bar.

Christian forced down a mouthful. She drank off the contents and slammed the bottle on the bar. Foam squirted out, rising up like a fountain.

"...What's to approve?"

"Pardon?" he asked, watching the foam splatter over the bar and draw into perfect circles. The bubbles coalescing to amber liquid.

"Castro? Batista? Tell me, is one going to fix the electricity? No! They will ignore the electricity and keep all the tourists in Habana."

"Americans are a little nervous about traveling in the middle of a revolution."

"It's not a revolution, yet. Let me tell you something, sweetheart, you beautiful, sax playing Gringo..."

"I'm not a Gringo. I'm Canadian."

31

"Same thing. Maybe you know my husband? Short, very skinny, moustache like this." She drew a thin line with a blood-red fingernail along Christian's upper lip. Christian shivered at the touch. "Always has his eye out for nice white girls with no ass and small tits, or nice white boys like you."

"Canada's a big country."

"Listen, Gringo, there have been these Communists all over the world telling us about freedom. Promising to get rid of the corruption. Every time there's a revolution in Cuba all we get is fatter dictators. And all those other poor people with their new communist dictators are equal only in misery. So there's no drinking, officially, and there's nothing to eat. And no freedom to do anything except starve and listen to endless speeches. That's all this Castro will do. Me, I prefer the Batista bureaucrats. You can at least buy them off."

Christian didn't have an argument for Juanita's logic. Cubans watched the world struggle with capitalist dictators and fascist tyrants and communist promises and socialist rhetoric and he knew she was probably right. He didn't bother to mention that Castro wasn't a Communist. He didn't have the energy to explain the difference between world socialism and Russian communism or the hypocrisy of the Catholic Church, or get into the manifestos of Marx and Engels or the powerful logic of Lenin and the endless suffering of the peasants at the hands of fascist and monarchs, oligarchs and popes. He just knew that Juanita was probably right.

Christian remembered the marathon debates at the university in Montreal. Latin rebels like Castro were heroes of the working classes. Intellectuals argued for world socialism while bearded young rebels in Central and South America fought against corruption and Imperialism. They watched the Columbians rise up and riot in Bogotá and Guatemala City. Cuban flags decorated student rooms and the rebels were cheered by the well fed children of Capitalism, full of youthful indignation, fuelled by wine, narcotics and immortality, comfortably removed from the reality of sweaty jungles and violent death, protected from the inevitable suffering that revolutions cause. Behind the stone walls of the university the outside world was divided up and reassembled in late night, wine-soaked marijuana parties pregnant with Bohemian attitudes and post-adolescent angst. Christian exiled himself from the university sump, retreating into the world of jazz and heroin, idling form job to job, but always drawn south to the Islands. Escape to Cuba was ironic. And Juanita's was just part of his education.

Juanita unbuttoned her dress, dropped it to the floor, stepped out of the limp cloth circle and kicked it away. "What are you doing? Juanita?"

She swayed toward him like a huge brown tree trunk whose roots have been exposed by the hot tropic wind. Her body surprisingly solid and in proportion, although not Christian's idea of proportion. Renée was Christian's ideal of a woman, he said. He thought. But he couldn't help staring. Those full breasts, the nipples like brown bottle tops and the areolas the size of saucers. Dark eyes, dark skin, and mounds of glistening, warm flesh. It was all wrong. Renée was blonde and pale as china and perfect. Juanita was a solid wall of womanhood standing before him, a dusky sculpture, mother earth, shining in the glare of the gas lamp. The flame was a hissing kettle. Christian's eyes glazed, light diffused, and he became detached, as if he were somewhere else. But the sound was still there; the hot, sizzling, frying pan sound, searing a chunk of dark game meat. The big-racked moose, skinned and hung by a campfire, blood draining into a ritual bowl. Juanita's husband in chains, on his knees, straddled by the skinny blonde while the cuck- olded husband held the shotgun to his head. The big game hunter was going to send his head back to Juanita to hang over her bar in Los Espiritos. Then the moose spoke...

"Hey, pretty boy, Gringo..." Christian looked up at the gaping mouth of the moose. A big Cuban cigar between brown teeth. It re- minded him of a comedienne. Groucho, no, Uncle Miltie...His own mouth was open.

"What's wrong with you, boy? Never see a real woman before?" Juanita laughed and grabbed Christian around the waist, strong arms drawing him to her.

"Yes, but..." Sinking into her flesh, between the mounds.

"You beautiful boy. Now you pay for the beer you just drank."

Christian didn't resist. There was no point in resisting. The act was inevitable and he was a reluctant but not completely passive partner. Juanita positioned him to her satisfaction. He was surprised how easily he became aroused. She handled him like a toy. Poured tequila with beer chasers to revive him each time. Christian had a vague recollec- tion of broken furniture...

Time was destroyed. Juanita smoothed Christian's hair. She noticed the needle marks on his left arm. "You are a bad boy!" She tucked a bag of Budweisers under one arm and his clothes under the other. "There, now you go look after your friend and when you need some- thing you come see Juanita."

"Jesus," he whispered, "are all Cuban women like you?"

"Of course. Only some have husbands and lovers who stand guard so they can't express themselves."

"May I have my sandals, please?"

"Sure thing, Gringo," she said. Christian's sandals somehow ended up behind the bar, one in the beer tub. She added them to the bundle under his arm, tracing his young body with her brown eyes and brown fingers. Slim and not muscled. Hairless except for the henna curls of his pubic area, the damp armpit mat and the bleached fuzz against tanned legs. "Not bad, but you need some meat on your bones and much practice making love with a real woman." Juanita squeezed Christian's slumping penis. It attempted to stiffen. He recoiled in pain. "Pretty good. Don't forget to bring your drummer."

Christian backed towards the door. Laughter exploded from the other side of the shutters and bare feet thudded away into the darkness. He recognized the ringleader's laugh. Miguel! How many village kids had been watching a Cuban version of sex education?

Maartyn was waiting at the door. "Man! What happened to you?"

"I was mugged."

"Y'all been gone two hours, ol' buddy. It doesn't take two minutes to get mugged."

Christian shoved the heavy paper bag at Maartyn. "The beer's warm and it's not paid for," Christian, said over his shoulder. "We do that tomorrow night at the cantina. You're my drummer."

"Drummer? Are y'all nuts?"

"Some dying, stone deaf guitarist from the village is backup." Christian eased his body down on the bench to finish dressing.

"You serious?"

"I can't wait for this gig."

"Man, who worked you over?"

"The woman of my dreams, if I was a masochist who craved being mauled to death by a sumo wrestler."

"Juanita? The big scary one, looks like a Zombie?"

"The same. Oh, God, I can't even sit."

"Man, if it was so bad why are you grinnin'?"

"Pain."

Maartyn opened a bottle with his teeth and offered it to Christian.

"No, thanks. Something about the memories."

"Y'all mean the mammalries?"

"That's mammaries. Very funny. Cute. I need a sauna."

"What's a sauna?"

"Steam bath."

"It's too damned hot now."

"I was kidding. Let's take a swim," he said, getting stiffly to his feet.

"Swim? Now? You are a looney."

The Gulf of Mexico crept softly up Christian's thighs to his throbbing crotch and rose like a cloud of silk, bubbling against his chin. He pushed off and glided, drifting in warm, black weightlessness. Gulping in and spitting out the salty water. Juanita's musk lingered. He rolled on his back, searching the night sky. The comforting sameness of the constellations anchored him to the earth whether in Montreal or the Bahamas, Europe or Cuba. Only The Bear was missing at that time of night. Wondered if Renée was looking at the same sky in Paris. Then he wondered if she really was on a yacht in Antigua. Damn, Maartyn!

A splash. Close. Sounded big. Chills making the hairs on his neck and arms stand erect. Miguel said sharks hunt inside the reef at night but seldom come into the shallows. Should he swim for it? Waiting for the razor teeth to slash up from the depths. Where would the first attack hit? Felt very vulnerable in the crotch area. Then he heard Maartyn laughing. Another splash. A beer bottle popped to surface.

"You moron! You almost hit me!"

"No way, man. If I wanted to hit you I would. I was the best grenade thrower in my unit. Lob one into a barrel from a hundred feet, every time."

"Yeah, sure."

"No, really. Every time. We used to throw bottles at dumb pelicans sittin' on channels mark. I never missed!"

"Good. I'm not a pelican."

"Hey, ever think what's in the water at night?"

"Try not to," breathed Christian, stroking carefully for shore.

"Weird things, man. Spiny little fish with poison darts. Sharks cruisin' for an easy lunch. Man o'wars with thingies this long. Snakes. Alligators."

"There's not likely alligators in the ocean." Christian dog-paddled hard toward the beach, afraid to put his feet down until his knees touched the sand.

"Sure, man. You heard about this guy in Australia, swimming in the ocean? Just floating along, an' this Jesus big alligator comes up..."

"Crocodile."

"What?"

"In Australia, crocodiles. Florida...alligators, don't like salt water."

"Crocodile then. Just a snack, man. Munched'im like a Frito."

Christian crawled for the beach, bumped another empty beer bottle and felt the panic race to his throat. He ran from the water panting and flopped beside Maartyn. "You just had to spoil it!"

"Have a beer, man. Y'all worked so hard." Maartyn sniggered and belched.

"Thanks." Christian accepted the bottle, and yes, he had worked for it, and was still indebted to Juanita. He sat on the cool sand drying his face with the musty shirt. Laundry. Should send his laundry down with Miguel. Only a few possessions besides his Madras shirt and tenor sax. Grey UCLA sweatshirt without sleeves. Faded blue T-shirt. Worn out cutoffs. Levis, thin and tattered. Dirty sneakers with the big toes out. A dog-eared novel by a Canadian, Jack Kerouac, *On The Road*. And the copy of Sartre's little book, *Nausea* that Renée forced him to read. His journal. Passport. A worn out picture of his mother. Musician's Union card. Swiss Army knife. Renée's black silk panties. And a black beret, like Dizzy Gillespie's. And Fidel's. Not much of an estate. Not much of a life either.

Maartyn chugged his beer and burped again, deep and long. "Warm beer stinks."

"You could use the bath."

"I can't swim."

"What!? You were practically born under water."

"Y'all don't swim on the Delta, man. You don't have to get in the goddamned water to fish."

"That's weird."

"No it's not. No fishermen I know can swim."

"That's really weird."

"Why? Y'all don't have to screw your brains out just because ya live near a whore house."

"What a dumb analogy."

"What's that?"

Christian took a cautious sip of beer. "It's, ah, like a comparison. Comparing one thing to something else, using examples."

"Why don't y'all just say it?"

"What?"

"Comparison."

They both looked at the Gulf. The moon wasn't up so the stars had

36

centre stage, floating easily on the surface. A long line of phosphorescence moving across the bay sliced the mirror in half.

Christian gulped. "What the hell's that?"

"Just a shark."

"Maybe a dolphin," said Christian hopefully.

"No way, man. You can tell by the way it moves. Jus' cruisin'."

"That's the last time I swim at night."

"Ol' shark's just sniffin' around. An' if you don't make too much noise they just go on, unless there's blood."

"Sharks eat people!"

"Yeah, but more people are killed by pigs."

"Pigs?"

"Yeah. Jus' swimmin' 'round the deep end of their shit pond."

They shared a thin laugh. "Where'd you hear that, about sharks?"

"Marines, man! Like in the movies, always up to their ass in sharks an' alligators. Okay, crocodiles. You seen all them Jap-killin' war movies. It's okay until some poor dude gets hit, then the sharks come in like flies on a dead fish."

"Lovely."

"Read this story in Man's Magazine once, about a navy ship that sank in the Pacific someplace. Thousands of sailors floatin' around an' at night the sharks came in an' started eatin' the poor sons'a bitches. Every night there was more sharks, until there was only a hundred or so guys left. When they picked up the survivors they were all crazy."

"Nice story."

"Like that one? There's one about piranhas."

"That's okay. But you said sharks don't hunt people. How come the sharks went after the sailors?"

"They were bleedin'. Sharks go nuts when they smell blood. An' if you've got Vee Dee, they bite off your ol' dick...chomp. Just like that."

"Yeah, sure." Christian was tired of Maartyn's stupid stories. Tired from the time with Juanita and tired of missing Renée. It wasn't a perfect love affair. He was confused by the new philosophy they talked about; accepting pain and suffering as man's reward for individual freedom from mass tyranny at the hands of the classical philosophers like Hegel and Descartes. Had experienced Renée's brand of Existentialism; struggled with the concepts of inner self, and the appropriate question, 'why is there anything, rather than nothing'? Concluding that he knew his own suffering was self inflicted by his existence, and beyond that was the void. Maybe Sartre and Kierkegaard were right.

Forces within the self destroy all optimistic delusions. That scared the hell out of him on perfect nights on white sand beaches, after making gritty love to Renée as waves washed around their bare, sweaty bodies. Then they would argue about existence and nothingness. Even the pain of repeated orgasms in paradise failed to convince Renée they were actually on that beach, post coital. He wished he were some place else besides a perfect beach now, with Maartyn, with a perfect little villa in a quaint seaside village in subtropical Cuba where guerrillas were creeping towards Havana and the military dictatorship of Fulgencio Batista seemed unable to prevent the collapse of his corrupt regime. He wondered if he should run again? It was anybody's guess what would happen to Cuba if the Revolution succeeded. Of all the islands in the Caribbean why did he end up in Cuba? And why Los Espiritos? Or why anywhere?...Jean Paul Sartre and Renée, Fidel Castro and Fulgencio Batista bore down heavily on his spirit.

Christian had been lured to Havana to join a jazz combo. The nightclub was just another back alley dive frequented by desperate musicians and more desperate patrons. The band was jailed for smashing up their crummy hotel room when the air conditioning failed and the water was turned off. Christian made bail with his diminishing stash and left Havana to visit Ernest Hemingway's finca. Hemingway, the American writer who had been with Sartre during the liberation of Paris, the clash of egos as resounding as the guns of the Battle of the Ardennes. Hemingway wasn't in residence at Finca Vegio. Christian was surprised to see the dilapidated condition of the house that had once been grand with wide steps, high ceilings and a writing tower designed for the great man by his wife Mary. Hemingway fled to a hotel in Havana, waiting for Sartre. The finca's shabby truth of domestic reality somehow diminished the myth. Christian hitched a ride on a farm truck to the Varadero Peninsula but was barred from that famous stretch of white sand and fabulous mansions built by Americans.

After the Hemingway disappointment and the Varadero rejection, Christian drifted west until he found Los Espiritos and was befriended by the ubiquitous Miguel. Why west? Christian reasoned that if the Americans weren't interested in Pinar del Rio it was the place to be. Miguel introduced him to Juanita who owned the small stone villa with a terrace and a view of the Gulf of Mexico. He paid the rent for two months in advance. His young real estate agent also became his cook, housekeeper and fishing guide. He dropped his knapsack and saxophone case and settled in. Why? He didn't know. For how long?

He didn't care.

Christian had a headache and a bad taste in his mouth. He left Maartyn asleep on the sand.

December 17th. *I wasn't ready for the day. I tried not to think about last night, but it wasn't easy. My dreams were visions of this huge brown bear pursuing me through a crowd on a street. I think it was Chicago. It was winter, with wind and snow. I was naked, naturally...In the distance I could see Maartyn. He was holding Renée. They were waving...I ran into a pool in the park because I was still naked but there was ice over the pool like a piece of glass and there were sharks and things under the ice. My foot went through the ice. The water turned red. And then I was awake.*

Morning: The large window looked over the harbour. The one with the shutters and the wooden grill work like elaborate bars on a cell. Miguel opened the shutters to punish him. Christian was awake but still tired and the headache was worse but he got up to punish *himself*. On good days he would play or write music in the morning. Hemingway wrote early in the morning and didn't drink when working and boasted that he never missed a sunrise. Christian had missed many. He would never be famous, but he could be good, with experience.

Miguel left the glass of salted water on the wooden box that served as a table. The bed was an imitation Mediterranean in English walnut, with carved headboard and four carved posts for a canopy. The canopy cloth was missing. The mattress was American and of some quality, though musty with dampness. There were no blankets and many stains. The rough, white plastered walls were bare. The tiled floor would be cold on winter mornings. What would Sartre say about his suffering? Maybe he should invite the Great One and his mistress to winter in Los Espiritos. Imagined the late night conversations on the terrace over mulled wine, or absinthe. Christian would be the waiter. The villagers helped themselves to most of the furniture and carpets when the New York man, Senior Bartuchi, left for *reasons*. The Mediterranean monstrosity and the American sofa remained because no one had room for such things in their tiny frame shacks. The thick planked monk's dinning table was recovered by Miguel from a fisherman who used it on the beach to clean fish. Miguel scrubbed it down with sand and salt water and left it to dry in the sun until most of the smell was gone. Christian paid a gang of Miguel's urchins to carry it back up the hill.

Christian used the latrine in the floor and dressed, pulling on the UCLA sweat shirt inside out so that he looked as fuzzy as he felt, rinsed his mouth with the salt water and wandered through the living room to spit over the terrace wall. On bad mornings he gagged if he bent down to spit into the toilet hole.

Maartyn was asleep on the floor beside the American couch, sprawled as in death on a straw mat. Christian stepped over him to reach the door to the terrace. Asleep he looked younger and less hardened. And less dangerous, even though Lucille lay close to Maartyn's twitching hand.

Miguel was in the pantry boiling eggs on the single gas burner. He sliced fresh corn bread to fry on the flat skillet with olive oil after the eggs boiled and he could set them aside to harden. The coffee was already hot. Miguel boiled the coffee at home in the red enameled pot and brought it up the hill with the eggs and the bread. He reheated the coffee when the bread was done. Sometimes he boiled the eggs, straight from the chickens, in the coffee to save time.

"Buenos dias, Señor Christ," Miguel chirped.

"Morning, Miguel," Christian replied flatly in English.

"How does Señor Christ feel this morning?"

Christian noted the sarcasm. Of course, Miguel witnessed the seduction of the innocent Canadian by Juanita the Moose. The whole village was there. "Who wants to know?" Christian snapped, then regretted his temper. "I'm very well, thank you," he said, less sarcastically. He felt cold, spiritually dry.

It was cool on the terrace. The light morning breeze was from the northwest, as the clouds had predicted. There would be a blow soon, that night or the next day, or the next. The Gulf looked grey and hard with the sun still low in the east. Christian assembled his saxophone and tried a few notes of a Dexter Gordon ballad. His fingers were stiff and his lips dry. The notes cold and hard. Miguel's mother sent Christian a Cardigan that belonged to her husband. He went back inside to get the sweater. It was about the same colour as Juanita's moose and just as moth-eaten.

Maartyn stirred when Christian stepped over him, curled up into a tight ball and tried to pull an imaginary blanket over his head. Christian put the sweater over Maartyn's bare shoulders.

"It will be colder soon, Señor Christ. You'll need wood for the fire."

"We need food."

"Yes, food would be good." Miguel looked worried. "They say

there won't be any food if Señor Castro defeats Batista. We can get American food on the black market. But for that you need Yankee dollars."

Christian, usually protective of his meager fund of cash, spoke before thinking. "I have an emergency stash."

Miguel brightened. "Yankee dollars?"

"Ah, some." Should he trust his house boy? "No...pesos is all, for now."

"Okay, Señor Christ, but Mother says that Papa heard the peso won't be worth shit if Señor Castro wins."

"Don't use bad language."

"Sorry, Señor, but sometimes I have to swear."

"Then don't swear in my house."

"I'll say three Hail Maria's." Miguel folded his brown fingers. "Holy Malaria, full of grease..." He said in English and laughed.

"Better make it six."

"Shit is worth only three Hail Maria's."

"The other three are for me.

"Why don't you say the beads yourself?"

"I don't pray, 'specially in Spanish."

"Then say them in English."

"Does English work in a Spanish country?"

Miguel laughed again and dropped the spoon. Some hot water splashed out of the pot on Miguel's bare feet. "*Oweee*, bastard-shit!"

"You'd better say the whole Rosary for that."

Miguel hopped about the pantry rubbing his foot. "For the whole Rosary I get to swear at least six more times."

"Since when do you stockpile prayers for sins in the future?"

"It's an old Cuban custom, Señor Christ. My sister Esa says the Rosary on her knees to the Blessed Virgin before she goes out to get fucked for money each night."

"I think we'd better change the subject. And stop calling me Christ!"

"Okay, Señor Priest, I'll pray for you before you go to Juanita's tonight to sacrifice yourself on the alter of lust..."

"Miguel, enough," he said firmly.

"But I think it will take many times around the Rosary."

"That's it. You're fired."

Miguel pulled a pout. "Who will fry the bread and show you where to catch the fish?" He shut off the burner and started for the door.

"You're right. You can stay. But cut out the stuff about Juanita, okay?"

"I promise..." Miguel smiled and skipped back to the pantry. "But, Mr. Christ, you were pretty good."

"Miguel!!"

"Okay, Mr. Christ."

"...And stop calling me Christ! It's Chris!"

"Okey dokey, Chrispy," he said in English under the hiss of the burner.

Maartyn opened his eyes to a yellow sun slanting through the east window, anointing his face. His tongue was swollen. He had red patches on his arms from sand fleas and his right cheek had the red imprint of the straw mat to go with red rims around his eyes and wild dark hair awry above the dark stubble on his chin. "Gawd, I feel like I was washed out from under a bridge."

"You look fine, except for the barnacles," said Christian, sitting at the table peeling an egg. "Miguel, doesn't Señor Maartyn look wonderful this morning?"

"Señor Maartyn looks worse than Juanita on Sunday morning, if Señor Christ doesn't mind me bringing up the subject."

"Señor *Chris* objects vehemently, you little bugger. Once more and I'll throw you down the hill."

"Okay, Señor Christ."

"Stop calling me Señor Christ!"

"Would Señor San Christophe like his fried bread and coffee now?" Miguel asked politely, almost bowing as he approached the table with the plate and cup.

"That's right, grovel."

"Perhaps the wonderful looking Señor Maartyn would like to join you on the *terrace* for coffee."

"What's he so whiny about?" asked Maartyn stretching his sore limbs. He had on greying underwear and the donated Cardigan. Miguel seemed interested.

"Servant training one-oh-one."

"Come again?"

"Never mind. Miguel's just being a pain."

"Smell coffee. Give."

"Let's take it outside. It'll be warmer now against the east wall."

"No shit!" Maartyn touched a sore hip. "I think I started out on that couch. This hotel sure has lousy beds."

"Yeah? Well, the price's right."

Miguel poured a second mug of strong black coffee and handed it to Maartyn without looking up. "We must go fishing, if you want to eat anything today," he said.

"What's the best time?"

"Same as yesterday. But you never get up before sunrise so as to be on the reef and ready when the sun comes over the Sierra and the shadows make hiding places for the big fish who come in from deep water. Then they take the bait we dangle just out of reach in the good light so we can hit them just at the right time."

"Thanks for the fishing seminar. We obviously missed sunrise."

"Noon is the worst time, when the sun is high and there's no..."

"Cut. When do we go?"

"Better to go now with a little time left or wait until just before sunset when the shadows are long again and we can fish the inside. But then you will starve all day and not have time to fish and cook dinner before your big date with Juanita."

"It's not a date! I have contractual obligations to resolve our indebtedness to the proprietor of the establishment known world wide as, Madame Juanita's Dive'n'Drill."

"Oh," shrugged Miguel.

"What are you two going on about, man?"

"Our big gig tonight. Up for it?"

"That's a joke, right? You made a joke. *Up* for it?"

"No," answered Christian, "I didn't make a joke. You and Miguel will probably drive me crazy. You first."

Maartyn walked into the garden and relieved himself on the dry weeds, returned to the terrace and sat beside the scaling stone wall, still wearing Christian's donated sweater. He sipped the steaming acid coffee and made morning sounds.

The Louisiana Delta waterman stood back and surveyed the battered skiff. "So this is the floating coffin that goes with the shack?"

"Hey, I didn't say it was a yacht."

Miguel arrived at the beach carrying the gear and some very suspect sardines in a rusty can. "Let the Gringo row today, Señor Christ. Rowing's for women."

"Hey, what did he say?"

"Miguel just offered you the honour of choosing to row this first class fishing vessel or handling the contents of that can."

Maartyn looked into the can. "I'll row."

"Good choice."

The faded blue-green and red skiff was left on the sand by the retreating tide. They dragged it down the gentle slope and into the water where it floated like a bloated goat.

"I'm going to swim out," said Christian, peeling off his T-shirt and wading into a patch of brown seaweed. "You watch for sharks."

"There's no sharks, señor Christ. Just barracudas today. See their signs between us and the reef, but they won't hit you with the sun so high." Another insult or just education? The brown fronds streamed behind his legs until he slipped free into clear water. When the water was up to his waist he plunged forward, like a seal, skimming the white sand that rose in puffs. A cloud of silver fish darted aside and Christian could see a long way. The sun slanted in shafts of lacey curtains like a northern aurora. He worked hard, resisting the urge to surface. If he was a fish he could propel himself down the gradual slope to where the water was cooler. The white, clean sand would continue until he reached the reef. Two barracudas swam effortlessly beside him. Curious. It is dangerous for a small fish in the open with the sun high against the white sand, and the shadows give them away, but he would risk it and hide in the coral heads until the sun went down. Then he would sleep in the dark unless the full moon was up. But that was also a bad time. Sharks and barracudas cruising along the reef could slam in for a kill. Sometimes the big fish mistake their own shadow on the sand and attack. He would avoid sunlight and moonlight. Swim and hunt smart and live a long clean life on the reef. But since he wasn't a fish he had to breath.

Christian pushed against the firm bottom, breaking clear like a dolphin, gulping the sweet air. He heard the splash of the oars behind him and rolled over on his back, blowing water. If he was a dolphin...yes, dolphin would be better. Breath air, play and hunt and get laid once in a while.

"Señor, Christ, we'll fish the other side of the reef this morning with the tide going out. There'll still be enough shadows and there's no waves coming onto the reef to bother us."

"Suits me, Miguel. You're the big time, expensive guide."

"A big time guide with my two American big shot spenders who come to Cuba to fish our biggest fish and steal our most beautiful women, like..."

"Don't you dare!"

The harbour of Los Espiritos was just a large cove formed by arms of rocks, palms and scrub, with a quarter-moon slice of white sand beach protected by a wide reef further out. Beyond that was the line of small islands, de los Colorados Archipeligo, running northeast to southwest all the way to Cabo San Antonio. There was a pass through the reef and many channels through the islands. It's possible, thought Christian, that once the foreign yachters who stole Juanita's husband were out of danger and the blonde was finished with him they slit his throat and tossed him to the sharks, sending the moose head to Juanita as a joke. Some joke. Something the Mafia might do...The Canadian Moose Mafia.

Christian drifted beside the skiff taking in the beauty of his Cuban paradise, shutting out Renée and Jean Paul for a few moments. The fishing boats were pulled up on the beach or left at anchor and could be trusted that way unless there was a hurricane or a really good blow from the west or northwest in the winter months. Beyond the narrow beach was the village. The jumble of wooden shacks, only silhouettes against the hills with the sun in the east and ragged palm trees in relief. The main road up to the hills from the village was hard packed red dirt. To the southwest there was the large, enigmatic white stone mansion with a red tile roof that belonged to someone called Escobar. Behind the village were the fields and hills of Pinar del Rio; tobacco country, still dark in shadows. The blue pines and domed hills of Viñales are very pretty but unspectacular, even though they are called the Cordillera de Guaniguanico. The locals referred to them as the Sierra del Rio. Maybe they say it as a joke because so much is said about the Sierra Maestra of Oriente Province where all the revolutionaries have held out since Spanish times, waiting their turn at saving Cuba. Only one rebel invasion took place in Pinar del Rio, a few miles northeast of Los Espiritos a hundred years ago, but that attempt was short lived. The lowland parts of Pinar del Rio are not flat enough to be called savannas such as the interior to the east, but the high humidity and the rich soil produce the best tobacco in the world. Pinar del Rio suited Christian because it is Cuba's orphan, only one step up the family hierarchy above the swamps of Zapata washed by the Bay of Pigs. Orphans require adoption and loving care. He would give Pinar del Rio and Los Espiritos a chance.

Christian tried to spot his modest villa on the first hill above the village. He needed a flag. Which flag? The Cuban flag or the Canadian flag? His own country didn't have a flag of its own and Cuba seemed about to change hers. Maybe just a big white banner with red lettering proclaiming, Surviving, Mom.

They anchored on the reef and let the skiff drift back over the coral fans and waving weeds with the weakening ebb tide. Miguel baited the rusty hooks with the evil smelling sardines. He slipped the baits and leaders over the side and handed Christian and Maartyn each a line.

"This shit's more likely to scare the friggin' fish," observed Maartyn caustically, testing the bottom, jigging the hook a foot above the sand in the shadows.

Miguel understood three words. "Suggest to Señor Maartyn that he not shake the precious bait like he's masturbating."

Christian laughed. "Maartyn, our big time guide suggests that you use more finesse with the bait fish."

"Tell the twerp-runt servant I was born in a leaky boat, fishin' with dead spooks like him for bait."

Christian sighed and shook his head. "Miguel, our honoured guest, Señor Delta Maartyn, says to tell you that, as much as he appreciates your very considered and expert advice, he has his own system that was handed down through his family from esteemed ancestors."

Miguel's turn to laugh. "Inform our Yankee guest that his mother is a filthy whore."

"Tell him yourself, if you want to be shark bait."

"Is he that dangerous and lacking in humour?"

"See that gun in his belt? He calls it Lucille, after B.B. King's guitar, or his mother, who he says, *was* a whore."

"Is that little gun for fishing, Señor Christ?"

"No. That's for anybody who calls his mother a whore, besides himself."

"Is Señor Maartyn's mother really a whore?"

"Actually, yes. By his own admission."

"It's considered the ultimate insult to mention one's mother in anything but reverence. I am guilty of insulting Señor Maartyn's mother, but he deserves it."

"We should stick to insulting B.B. King."

"What are you two saying about B.B. King?" Maartyn asked.

"Oh, nothing. Miguel just wanted to know what you called your gun. I said maybe you named it after B.B. King's guitar."

"No way! Little Richard's latest." Maartyn sang out, "'Lucille, oh baby is that true? Oh, Lucille...baby is that true? You better start-a-back doin' the things you used to do!' Dig it?"

"Never heard of Little Richard."

"Man, you have been livin' on the moon!"

"Yes, and it's been very peaceful. Until now," he said in Spanish.

Maartyn struck first, expertly landing a red snapper. Christian lost a pompano and an angry bone fish and gave his line to Miguel who took three nice bonitos and lost a big snapper. Then the sun was too high and there were no more shadows on the reef worth working. They rowed in on the beginning of the flood. Miguel cleaned the fish, rinsed them in salt water and then fresh water at the village well and went up to the house to make lunch. Christian and Maartyn stayed on the beach to swim and sleep in the sun.

Later they ate fried fish sandwiches on the beach and Christian and Maartyn went swimming in the shallows to get refreshed then talked about Paulo and Renée and Juanita. Maartyn said his mother would outweigh Juanita by fifty pounds of meanness. When the sun was low they walked up to the house, stopping at the well to splash fresh water on their bodies, getting interested looks from the women. They had supper on the rest of the fish with corn chapattis and some exceptionally hot salsa sent by Miguel's mother.

Juanita's Cantina was packed with farmers and fishermen, and humid with body heat and grey with smoke. When Christian and Maartyn entered the patrons respectfully moved aside to let the celebrities pass. Flashy, dark skinned women in a carnival of colours stood out like decadent flowers against the white and blue uniforms of the working men. Hand rolled cigars flared like tiny volcanoes. One of the perks of the poor farm hands. When smoking their own Pinar del Rio cigars they are on a level with tycoons and foreign kings. The men and women puffed and drank and made noise. This was a special evening. The word had spread that Juanita was presenting a big name American jazz player.

"Oho, look, my Gringos are here!" Juanita was dressed in a gaudy orange gown with ruffles, looking herself like something that fell off a Mardi Gras float. The gown was cut down to there, front and back so that either way the patrons got their money's worth. She was scrubbed and radiant, with hair piled dangerously high, held in place by a battlement of shell combs, topped with a big red bow that clashed. A fluorescent birthday present about to unravel. Above her coif the moose head's rack was covered with straw hats and gun holsters. Juanita's rules. Holsters had to be checked at the bar. The guns, however, were not in their holsters.

Juanita scrutinized Maartyn's body. He was wearing Christian's only clean T-shirt. Christian was wearing his long sleeved Madras shirt under the sleeveless grey UCLA sweatshirt.

"Juanita, you've met Mississippi Maartyn, the Delta Rhythm King."

"Yes, we've met, but too briefly. Buenos noches, Señor Maartyn Hardmuscle."

"Hi y'all," said Maartyn, grinning, perfect white teeth flashing like a beacon. Maartyn grew up so poor in the Delta that he was spared the sugar treats to which American kids are addicted. Juanita grew up in Cuba where sugar is King and about the only thing poor kids get are sugar treats; raw, liquid or processed. And years of rum and cola and tobacco also took their toll.

"Does he speak Cuban?" asked Juanita, not taking her eyes from Maartyn's thighs.

"A few dirty words. Nothing you haven't heard."

"Yes, every day of my life, Señor Chris. Every day and done it as often. That's all I can say about my life."

"I only blow sax."

Juanita threw her head back and laughed and jiggled. Her big breasts swelled and overtopped the gown. She laughed harder and tucked them away. "Later," she said.

The attentive crowd, three deep at the bar, cheered as if the best bull of the day had just been brought to his knees by a skillful matador. Then the joke was repeated. Laughter and cheers splashed around the packed cantina like slanting combers on a rocky beach. The atmosphere was hot and expectant.

"And tonight we have cold beer!"

Another cheer went around the room and orders flew. Juanita was busy again serving dripping bottles and shots of rum and collecting the American dollars fluttering like pale green moths through the dense air. Christian surveyed the room. He'd played every type of sleazy jazz club, notorious for crowds, but never had he seen anything like Juanita's. One low ceilinged, dingy room, filled with an aromatic haze so that the faces wavered behind a scrim cloth. A dozen sturdy wooden tables with invisible chairs did not come close to serving the mob. He guessed there were at least two hundred bodies squeezed in, sitting, standing, kneeling, maybe lying on the floor out of sight. And in the press he spotted Miguel hustling drinks, dancing through the crowd, tray held high, collecting empty bottles and glasses, wiping up spills and palming change. Their eyes met. Miguel's were full of laughter and mischief. Christian knew his sassy boy servant was also a survivor.

Fishermen got up a sea chantey in one corner, rowing out in the dawn to fight marlin and shark. Returning home to bed their women. In the other corner gnarled hands of farmers thumped tables telling the fishermen to shut up. A bottle sailed through the air and broke against the wall behind the loudest singer. Neither the singer nor Juanita batted an eye. The score was tallied and would be settled later. Now it was time to drink and get ready for the entertainment.

"Hey, I like this place," shouted Maartyn. "Reminds me of a little spot outside La Hache on a Saturday night. Built on stilts over a bayou so you can only get to it by boat. If we didn't like the band we just threw them out the window for the alligators."

"Remind me to never play La Hache."

"Hope you never get that desperate. What's the chances for a cold one, ol' buddy?"

"Probably have to play another hour," shouted Christian.

"I don't care. I'd give my left nut for a cold beer right now."

"I'll attempt to negotiate with the boss lady..."

A cold beer hit the bar beside Christian. Then another beside Maartyn. He looked around. Juanita, grinning and sweating, was talking to Miguel, taking orders and opening bottles but she had that look. "I accept your offer, Gringo-muscle," she said to Maartyn in English.

"Did she understand what I just said?"

"Of course, Gringo," she answered. "I worked the bars in Miami when I was younger. Waited tables. Sang with the band and fucked the customers, or the band, every chance. It's where I met my ill fated husband, God rest his Yankee soul."

"Your husband wasn't Cuban?" asked Christian.

"Oho, Jesus and Mary, no! Well, at first, yes. Later, after he moved to Miami, he was just another no good Yankee bloodsucking mosquito. His family is still in Cuba, including another wife I found out, but once he left the Island he was corrupted in America and became addicted to big cars and other people's money. Other people's blondes also. Some problem with the police sent him back here. Then next thing I know he's in that Canada. Los Espiritos is a good hideaway, no?"

"Yes, definitely," agreed Christian, wondering.

"My customers are thirsty!" Juanita motioned to Miguel and filled his tray with sweating bottles. Miguel danced through the crowd with his cargo over his head, placing bottles on tables and collecting money with the skill of a Flamenco dancer. But instead of returning to the bar when his tray was empty he darted out the door.

Christian and Maartyn looked at Juanita. Her trusted waiter had just fled with a pocketful of her money.

"Don't worry, he'll be back," she said, reverting to Spanish. "And yes, the beer will cost you one more hour of music."

"But you said the beer would be free when we're playing."

"You aren't playing, Señor Sax Man."

"Well, when do we start?"

"Hear my customers? If you don't start soon you'll be hung like a gutted fish or a hank of tobacco drying in the sun. Take your choice. Fishermen. Farmers. Depends which faction takes you first."

"I think that's called an incentive, Maartyn. Where's my guitar player?" he asked Juanita in Spanish, exchanging glances with a sweating fisherman.

"Old Jocinto? He's coming, if he hasn't died. The poor old man can hardly walk let alone carry his heavy instrument."

"Wonderful. I hope my life doesn't depend on the quality of the music."

"Oho, it might. You see, I have told my patrons that you're a very famous, big time sax man from New York."

"Do they believe you?"

"There is some question about your ancestry."

"Ancestry? I'm just a humble jazz musician."

"Yes, but the wrong colour. You see, in Cuba they think jazz players, at least the great ones, are black and come from America. Lester Young. Johnny Coltrane. Bennie Webster."

"You've never heard of Art Pepper or Zoot Sims?"

"Oh, yes, I have seen this pretty boy Zoot with my own eyes, but that was in New York City. And what of the Chet Baker? I could just crush this beautiful horn man." Juanita jiggled.

The cantina went quiet. A frail old man was standing at the door, dressed in the farmer's uniform of patched white cotton shirt and trousers, wearing dark glasses and a black beret. Miguel was beside him carrying a big guitar case. Chairs were moved this time. The old man held his head to one side and angled for the bar. Men tipped straw hats as the guitar player passed. He smiled or nodded, waving with a slight gesture.

Royalty, thought Christian. They treat him like a king and the old man is accustomed to homage. Something very special about the small, weathered person hardly larger than Miguel. A tingle went up Christian's spine and tickled the hair on the back of his neck, like it did the night before in the water. Jocinto was standing in front of him, acknowledging the crowd at the bar. Christian wondered if he should bow.

"Señor, Christ, this is my grandfather, Jocinto."

"Buenos noches, Señor," shouted Christian, holding out his hand. "Very pleased to meet you."

Jocinto nodded, studying Christian from head to toe. He looked at Juanita. Juanita handed Jocinto a glass of clear, oily liquid. He downed the burning liquor in a long, slow drink. The crowd followed every movement the way they watch the priest consume the sacred wine from a gold chalice. Jocinto handed back the glass and Christian studied his hand and bony fingers. The knuckles were red and swollen, the fingers, twisted. They were long and looked feminine but to Christian they were musician's fingers. Jocinto flexed his fingers and they seemed to grow longer, unfolding like a flower. The breathless spectators erupted into cheers and table thumping. Christian and Maartyn looked at each other. "Seems like an easy bunch to please," ventured Maartyn.

Christian pointed at the holsters decorating the moose. "See the bulges under their shirts? Juanita must have some rule about guns."

"Good thing I brought Lucille." Maartyn patted the bulge in his own shirt.

"Oh, God! You didn't!?"

"Never go in a strange bar without Lucille."

"Jesus!...Just forget it. These people get excited, you know, but they're harmless."

"Oh, sure, man. Then why did you mention the weapons?"

"I was kidding."

Juanita cleared a space on the bar. Miguel hefted the black guitar case and snapped the brass latches. Jocinto approached the case and bowed his head. Miguel opened the lid, easing it back, wiping away some water. Jocinto smiled as if seeing an old friend, then lifted the beautiful Spanish guitar above his head. Varnish immaculate, the fine wood glowing through like burnished gold. The rising sun. The room was hushed. Every perspiring face turned toward the hallowed icon, following the arc it made up and then down to nestle in Jocinto's arms like the Christ Child in the sepia print of the Madonna and Child hanging next to the wooden crucifix with the nicotine-brown Jesus drooping from the heat, above the wavering votive candles illuminating the shrine of the Virgin of the Tobacco Fields, beneath the moose head and a picture of the lost husband. Among the candles were straw crosses about to explode, terracotta figurines, grotesque wooden heads and colourful beads; red, white and blue Yankee souvenir necklaces and gaudy pictures of sex acts. The old man and big guitar dwarfed the icons of the Santeria religion. The Catholic and Santeria symbols melted together. An eclectic display of primitive artifacts, made small by the veneration of Jocinto. He made a C chord. C for Christ. A G for God. The crowd exhaled.

Jocinto nodded to Christian as if to say, 'your turn'.

Christian's battered, saxophone case was at his feet. His tenor sax was polished brass with mother of pearl inlaid finger pads but he refrained from competing with Jocinto for ritual honours. Instead he squatted down to assemble the instrument. He carefully moistened the reed, feeling the familiar flutter in his stomach. He worried if he didn't feel butterflies and the slight nausea, the nervous sweat. Being on the edge. Ready. He had the same sensation when the syringe was poised to strike, dripping the promised venom. The potion that would martyr Art Pepper and Chet Baker, so many of the greats and unknowns alike. He stood up, puffing the reed, feeling the seminal vibration. Controlling the instrument. Airing the tubes. Popping the valves. He cared for his axe more than he cared for himself. A condition common in the jazz world. He should never question Maartyn's priorities.

Christian ran his fingers over the valves, lightly grazing the keys. Hearing the notes in his head instead of playing. Not yet. The ritual of tuning the mind as important as tuning an instrument. He had to feel the music. Prep mind, prep soul, prep body. To Christian, playing Carnegie Hall or playing Juanita's Cantina was all the same. The venue was secondary to the needs of the audience. But even the audience was secondary to the music. As the body is less than the soul and the soul subservient to the master spirit. If Christian had a religion it was the mystique of the music, sent out to some unknown place like an offering. He was too aware of contradictions to question the mystique. It was the strongest conflict with Renée. Music had a divine purpose beyond mortal needs, and imposed a rational order. More than nothingness and chaos. Could Sartre be a musician and an Existentialist at the same time?

Christian ran a scale. Jocinto wasn't watching. Back turned, indifferent. He felt intimidated by this little guitar player who could barely walk, dwarfed by his instrument, but who exuded the power to silence a room full of drunken fishermen and sweaty farmers, the way an opera star commands simple aficionados who know more about the heart and soul of real music than trained conductors know about theory. What was happening? Christian ran another scale, imagining it to be off tone. Fumbling with the familiar keys as if his fingers too were stiff with age.

Jocinto turned, reached out and gently touched Christian's arm, imparting grace. Christian looked into the walnut face cracked by a toothless grin and relaxed. Then he remembered that the old man was supposed to be deaf. "I'm going to play ballads," he shouted. "Just slow, mellow stuff at first, okay? Watch my feet." He pointed to his feet, tapping the unusually clean floor. Juanita had gone all out scrubbing up the cantina as well as herself.

Jocinto nodded.

"Just hit a chord you want," continued Christian, as if talking to a child.

Jocinto nodded again that he understood, then said in high pitched English, "You should play slow at first. Ballads. I'll try to hit a few chords." The old man was toying with him. He could either hear well enough or he was reading Christian's lips. The old man said, "Maybe later, when we get well drunk, we'll play some hot jazz." Jocinto smiled. The toothless grin reminded Christian of Miguel's teasing.

"Where did you get that phrase?" asked Christian.

In very good English, Jocinto answered, "I wasn't always old and crippled and impotent. I was in Miami and Habana. Many important gigs. Played with Benny Goodman in Miami. You know Señor Goodman?"

"No, ah, but I've heard him play. Carnegie Hall."

"Ever heard him play? They say he played Carnegie Hall. In Miami I also was guest artist with Señor Paul Whiteman. Bix Biderbeck? Señor Skitch Henderson? No? I played with Señor Kenton when his band toured Cuba."

Juanita handed Jocinto another glass of liquor. He downed that in two measured drinks. He placed the empty glass carefully on the bar and continued, "I once played a duet with Jango Rheinhardt in Paris, France," he said, pausing, remember the good nights. "Very nice man. Nice town, Paris, France. Been there?"

"Yes, once..."

"Been there?"

"Yes."

"You should go. Very nice town for black musicians. Nice girls in Paris."

Christian felt small enough to climb into his sax case. "Juanita, I can't do this."

"You must. I told Jocinto you were world famous sax man. Or was that sexman? Never mind, he's looking forward to playing before he dies. So you'd better hurry up. One more rum liqueur could finish him."

"Better give me one of those," Christian said.

"For the expensive liqueur you play one hour more."

"No, Juanita! I've got my axe in hand and the gig's on."

"Okay, okay, Señor Chris, don't get mad with me. I'm just the owner of the drinks."

"Good, because I need one now."

Juanita half filled the glass. Christian tossed down the white fire. He'd spent enough nights on tropical beaches to handle island liqueurs but the liquid fire never goes down easily. At first. The first half of the bottle is the hardest. Chased with cold beer. After that it's experience.

Juanita carried a tall conga drum around the bar and placed it in front of Maartyn.

"What am I supposed to do?" he appealed to Christian.

"Think of it as a big bongo drum," answered Christian.

"I don't know, man. I never played in front of people."

"Just tickle it with your fingers whenever it feels right," added Christian. He had a feeling about the gig. Maybe it was just the alcohol.

Christian led off cautiously with a slow, 'Green Dolphin Street.' Jocinto eased in with some sweet chords, just a touch off time, but Christian knew it was on purpose, and they fit like parts of a puzzle. Maartyn ventured a few finger flutters on the conga drum, surprised by the effect. The crowd approved but Christian couldn't fathom this rough bunch getting into jazz. He obviously misunderstood the Cuban feel for music. 'Night In Tunisia' upped the pace. Jocinto took a solo. Christian was in awe. The notes were crisp and clean. The simple runs exciting. The melody flowed in and out and he recognized a dozen takes on the standards. And the old man's fingers remembered a time between the wars when life and music in the Caribbean were insepa- rable.

Jacinto finished his solo with a note that hung on the air like a mid- night chime. The mob applauded and whooped. Christian, still tin- gling, toyed with the melody while waiting for the place to settle down. Jocinto just stood quietly with his head bowed, perhaps re- membering the good times, the great nights when it seemed the music would last forever. He saw the wars come again, the music fade and change and his own country decline to the brink of anarchy. But for one more night at least, the music was King even if the venue was sweaty and humble. Christian watched the frail old man and imagined fabulous nightclubs, footlights and spotlights, white linen tables dripping with orchids, near the band, and the strutting dancers, all legs and feathers. Expensive gowns and flashing jewels. Hundred dollar tips and Champaign toasts. Deals and dark deeds in back rooms where gangster bosses met under cover of their club's glitz and brilliance. Limousines with long hoods and wire wheels waiting at the curb. It was Jocinto's world. And it was a world no longer innocent and he knew that soon he would have to face certain truths. For the moment, in Juanita's bar he could put off the future. There were no demons, just the music.

Christian finished 'Night In Tunisia' with his best take but it felt bush league compared to Jocinto's solo. Maartyn stayed within the fluid, moving limits of the music, although Christian could see him straining. Maartyn grinned and swayed to the rhythm as if in a trance. He hoped Maartyn could refrain from shooting up the joint for sheer joy.

Jocinto called a halt to give Juanita time to serve her guests who had been elevated to the level of patrons by the artistry of Jocinto's performance. Jocinto accepted a small shot of liqueur. Christian and Maartyn downed cold beer. After the break Christian opened with a very nice rendition of 'Darn That Dream'. Dexter would have been proud and Christian imagined Johnny Hartman stepping to the microphone, three spotlights cutting the haze, revolving around that velvet voice. Jocinto poured sweet chords all over the piece, helping Christian along, accenting but not taking, not even watching his feet. Jocinto's head was turned away and up as if he was getting divine inspiration beyond the stars. Feeling the music. Tears in his eyes. It may have been the cigar smoke.

That's it, thought Christian. Jocinto feels the music. The vibrations, and he's the sounding board. Himself a delicate instrument. Or perhaps he's really a messenger sent down to show the mortals how it's done.

Christian played his Dexter Gordon repertoire. 'Don't Explain.' 'Ernie's Tune.' 'Body and Soul.' Jocinto wove magic through the melodies and the tears continued. His fingers only left the strings long enough to wipe away the salty moisture from the beautiful guitar.

They played the classics. They did Cuban Latin rhythms. They jammed and laughed and cried. Even Maartyn felt the strong bond that forms when music is the language. They drank dark rum and cold beer chasers and every number was better than the one before. Rare moments in music are seldom experienced beyond the sacred confines of clubs and bars like Juanita's Cantina, but that too is common in the mystique of backstreet jazz. The finest moments in musical history shared by a few musicians and a small audience, seldom documented and never equalled, but it's enough to have been a part.

By midnight the show was just heating up. It was sometime later that Jocinto said goodbye. One short liqueur for the road. He shook hands with Christian and Maartyn. Miguel put away the guitar and led Jocinto through the crowd. There were no cheers or applause as the old man shuffled out the door. The silence as heavy as the heat. Jocinto didn't look back.

"Is he alright?" asked Christian.

"Who knows," shrugged Juanita. "Two days ago the priest came to give him the last rites. That's why I asked you to play. It's all that keeps him alive. Tomorrow he may be on his deathbed again. We'll light candles around his head and feet. The priest will come to hear confession. His breathing will be weak and shallow, with that peculiar sound, you know, a rattle, like dry cane. His mother will cry all day and all night."

"His mother!?"

"Yes, poor old lady, she takes his endless dying very hard."

"How old is she?"

"Who knows? How old is Old Maria?" Juanita asked a slumping farmer at the bar.

"Who knows?" the man shrugged. "Who knows? Maria Diez Garcia Martinez...Maybe one hundred. Maybe two hundred."

"Maybe the immortal Blessed Virgin herself, you stupid farmer! You're her son. Jocinto's your own brother and you don't know!?"

"Who counts anything but cigars and bottles of over priced beer?"

"That's right, idiot, make us look like ignorant peasants in front of this world famous musician I brought to Juanita's all the way from New York."

"New York? I saw the Gringo walking the road from Pinar, like a vagrant looking for a ditch to sleep in," said the farmer, dismissing the Gringo with a vague gesture.

"He's also a famous world traveller. Drink your beer, quajiro. Pay no attention," she said to Christian.

"He can play, but he's no Lester Young," said a slender, well dressed, white Cuban standing at the end of the bar. His age was hard to guess but there was a veneer applied to the pastry coloured skin covering much experience. He spoke English too precisely. The smile purely ensemble. Slicked down and manicured in a pale yellow muslin suit and downtown straw hat. Thin grey moustache that looked like it was drawn by a pencil. Yellow silk tie, socks to match. White leather shoes cut low like slippers. Elegant walking cane with a jackal's head in silver on the knob, handle hooked over the bar rail. Puff hankie. Monogrammed. E.E.

"And you know Lester Young, I suppose?" asked Juanita. She bristled noticeably when she spoke.

Where had the man come from? wondered Christian. He hadn't seen him in the crowd.

"I had the privilege to hear Mr. Young many times in Harlem. Very nice man. Very nice. And the appropriate colour."

"I suppose you can hear colour too? I'd put my Christian up against Lester Young any day!" Juanita turned her back on the man. "Pay no attention. That old fool was to New York once and never lets us forget. He has one suit and a pension from Batista and he comes in here to insult my musicians. I will throw him out!"

"No, that's okay. I'm not insulted. Are you insulted, Maartyn?"

"No, man, I'm not insulted. I'm not even a musician."

"You are now. In the groove," said Christian, grasping for a way to ease the tension.

Maartyn leaned close to Christian's ear. "I'll tell you one thing, ol' buddy. That guy's a raging fag. Queer as they come."

"Maartyn, promise me you won't start on him."

"Hey, you know me. I don't start nothin'. But if that guy comes on to me, so help me, I'll put a neat little hole right where that goddamned yellow hankie lives. Fags! What a place. Spooks an' fags. Man, there's got to be someplace a guy can go and not have to put up with'em."

"Maartyn, let me introduce you to the real world. I don't know what it's like on the Delta but you're going to have to live with it."

"Oh, don't start that bleedin' heart stuff again. Y'all make me sick."

"'Scuse me? What gives you the right to claim the territory?"

"'Cause I said so!"

"That's it? Because you say so?"

"Yeah. Want to make a big deal about it?"

"No thanks. I don't have a gun. But now I understand why the rest of the world feels the way it does about Americans."

That's good, Chris ol' uptight buddy. Because that's just the way it is an' if you an' the rest of the stupid world don't like it y'all can take a flyin' leap!" Maartyn turned away and leaned on the bar fuming. The adrenaline of the music still running hot. "Hey, whose got a smoke!?"

Juanita put a box of small, crooked cigars on the counter. "Help yourself."

"What're those things?"

"Hand rolled. Special."

"Look like constipated dog turds."

"Your friend's in a bad mood," she said to Christian.

"He's okay. Just a little emotional. We cooked tonight didn't we?"

"Yes, you cooked."

"We burned."

"You burned, indeed," she said.

"Righteous, eh, brother?" Christian said to Maartyn and laughed, hoping to ease the tension. Never in their short career as friends had the potential been so great. The place was an arsenal. The cultural gulf as vast as that body of water outside the cantina door. And the odds were extremely bad.

"It was very good. You must play again the next time Jocinto is dying. If you don't and the old man dies from a tragic lack of music these men will cut you into fish bait!" Juanita shouted for the ears of the drinkers around the bar.

"Jesus...Juanita..." Christian whispered. "Not so loud." Several hard looking men on the periphery also heard the remark. They were new faces. Working fishermen, or criminals. He hadn't seen them in the crowd. Christian scanned the room for a quick way out. The line to the door was blocked by a wall of bodies. The windows also. The back room, accessible only by a sprint around the end of the bar, probably had a door to the outside. But who or what was in the back room?

"What'd she say?" asked Maartyn, jabbing Christian in the ribs.

"Pardon?...Oh, they like us. Want us back."

"Then why are those ugly dudes looking at us like that?"

The group of men were standing near the end of the bar behind the well dressed man. They were staring at Maartyn. Dark, sweaty faces with hard lines and stubble and moustaches, like movie bandits. Accusing. Threatening. The life of their guitar master was in the hands of foreign musicians. Maartyn's hand edged toward Lucille. Christian moved to put himself in Maartyn's line of sight.

Juanita knew the signs. "Just some locals. Pay no attention. The pistols in their pants you can see well enough," said Juanita in English, smiling. "But they never use them in here. Knives maybe. It's when they take you outside you have to worry. That toy you have stuck in your pants, Mr. Hardmuscle, isn't going to persuade them. On the bright side, they always shoot for the legs. It's an old custom in Western Cuba. Everybody's related and it's considered bad manners to kill relatives or their guests. On the other hand, maybe for Yankees they would make an exception."

"Ah, Juanita, could you explain to them that I'm from Canada?" Christian said in English.

"Me too. I've just converted."

"Who in this place, besides me, has ever heard of Canada? Listen, my Gringo-Canada friends, some of these men are hiding out from their wives. Some are revolutionaries hiding out from Batista's secret police and some are just crazy drunk. They don't trust anyone. It's good as long as you entertain them, but don't talk to them. Most of all, don't ask questions. I tell you this only for your own protection."

"No problem."

"Man, this is too weird," said Maartyn, placing his hands carefully on the bar.

"How does it feel?" asked Christian.

"How what feels?"

"You know, being treated like a minority."

"Shut up!"

"Juanita? Ah, possible to get a last cold beer for the road?" asked Christian. The sweat was pouring down his face but it wasn't from the heat.

"It'll cost, Señor. You are no longer musicians, remember?"

"Sure. Fine. One beer and we go home, nice and quiet. Okay?"

"Beer coming up. Watch."

Juanita reached far down into the tub of ice below the bar. Her swollen breasts did their magic pop up trick. A ripple of cheers spread out from the hot zone. Two dripping brown bottles with the classic long necks and their labels dissolved away, rose into view and settled on the top of the bar. She snapped the tops and pushed the bottles slowly towards Christian and Maartyn. She held on to Maartyn's bottle forcing contact with his fingers. Christian took a sip of his beer letting the chilled liquid do its job. He held the bottle to his face, inhaling the cool wetness while he watched Maartyn wilting under Juanita's heavy gaze. Without shifting her gaze she said to Christian, "Tell your friend, if he's not a silly virgin like you, he can stay and have a...how do you American's call it? A nightcap."

"Thanks for the compliment," Christian said. He turned to Maartyn. "Juanita reminds you of your previous offer...your desire to offer up certain parts of your anatomy in exchange for favours, and says that if you don't stay and have several hours of wild, deeply passionate sex with her, that smiling hombre, her body guard, will cut off your left testicle with a rusty machete."

"Ah, Jesus, man! Chris, get us outta here!"

"Can't. Give me Lucille."

"No way!"

"Maartyn, use your head. Juanita will look after you as long as you do exactly what she says. Give me the gun." Christian moved close to Maartyn. Two friends talking over beer. "Give, or you won't leave here on your own legs." Maartyn reluctantly handed over Lucille. Christian put the gun in his pocket and pulled the sweatshirt band lower. The heavy weight of the snub nosed revolver felt odd and somehow thrilling.

"Take care of my best girl," Maartyn said.

"Sure. By the way, Juanita, where did you get the ice? It has a funny smell."

"In Cuba you can get anything for a price, Señor Chris. Everything your heart desires is under your feet, as they say. You just have to know the price and who to dance with. Don't ask about the smell. Don't ask about anything. Understand?"

"I guess. Well, thanks for the gig. It's been a slice."

Christian patted Maartyn on the arm, picked up his sax case and walked into the cool night. The well dressed man in the yellow suit followed.

Outside the cantina the night was dark and dense. "Señor Joyce, wait."

Christian stopped and turned to face the man. "What? What do you want?" He wondered how the man knew his name.

"Only to apologize for my rude comments. You are a good jazz musician, and I have heard many. I could perhaps do something for you. I have friends, in New York."

"Why? I'm not that good. Average, maybe, on a good night. It was Jocinto that made the gig work."

"Jocinto is a great master but he's finished. You have...style. You're young and very beautiful."

Christian remembered Maartyn's comment. "Thanks, but not interested."

"Wait. My name's Ernesto. Ernesto Escobar. You recognize the name?"

"Yes, you own the big villa."

"Escobars are well known in Latin America. Old family of Cuba and Espana. Politics. The arts. I could show you paintings."

"No thanks."

"I have jazz music. Many classics."

"I've had enough music for one night."

"Would you like to have a drink? Perhaps a nice bath?"

"No!" he said too strongly. "Look, I know what you want. I'm not into that, okay? I'm tired. I'm going home to bed." Shouldn't have mentioned bed.

"Christian...wait. I apologize. I meant nothing. Just wanted to offer my hospitality. I'm an old man. Lonely for culture. You can imagine, here in Los Espiritos, one does not find much stimulation. We could talk about the jazz or even baseball. I am a big fan of the Yankees and the Dodgers. Sometimes it is a problem when they meet in the Series. It's unfortunate there's upheaval in America. What do you think about the move?"

"Look, Señor Escobar...We can talk, sometime. Okay? Just talk. Right now I'm going home."

Christian walked out of the pool of light from the open cantina door into the anonymity of the darkness. Drunken laughter exploded from the bar and followed him up the hill, mocking every step. He felt the eyes of Ernesto Escobar burning on his back. He felt angry. Confused. But most of all vulnerable. And then some regret. Maybe Maartyn was wrong. The old man just offering friendship and a bath. One runs into these situations. Good Samaritans. A ride. A meal. A bed. The price, only company and some stories. Harmless, usually. Christian climbed the hill to his dark villa, more than the weight of Lucille pulling his spirits down.

December 18 1958: *And I thought yesterday morning was bad. Morning was bad enough but Miguel arrived late, and with bad news. I let myself get suckered into the funeral...I wonder what I'm getting myself into?*

Christian was on the terrace when his houseboy arrived, climbing the hill like the weight of the world was pressing down. "Morning, Miguel."

"Buenos dias, Señor," he answered without the usual smile. Miguel climbed over the terrace wall and went straight to the pantry.

Christian was sitting near the door to the pantry, reading a book of Spanish verse by the poet Rubín Martínez Villena. He sensed Miguel had bad news.

Miguel put a loaf of corn bread on the counter and took two eggs out of his pocket. He put the small brown eggs in the iron pot on the burner.

"Sorry I'm late, Señor Christ." The burner hissed to life. "Grandfather died during the night and I had to help my mother wash him and dress his body for the burial."

"Jocinto?"

"Yes. Very peaceful. Mother said Grandfather was ready to go to God and he was waiting for a good time."

"Jesus," breathed Christian, sitting down at the table.

"Yes, Jocinto's gone to play with Jesus. Do you think Jesus played music?"

"Yeah, sure. His old man was a carpenter. Probably made the little lad a set of bongo drums. How the hell should I know if he played anything!?"

"Sorry, Señor Christ...just asking."

"Stop calling me Christ!" Christian experienced the usual rush of regret for his short temper. "When's the funeral?"

"Tonight from the church. Jocinto was not religious but he wished to be buried with candles and music. There will be a candlelight procession through the village and up the hill to the cemetery, up there." He indicated the east window. "You can see the big cross."

Christian looked, wishing he hadn't snapped at Miguel. "Jocinto. What a way to go."

Miguel approached the table slowly. "Ah, Señor Christ?..."

"Look, I'm sorry I yelled."

"It's not that, Señor Christ. Mother asked me to ask you, if you would, ah, lead the procession, following behind the priest and the acolytes with the big candle and the incense and the cross on the long staff. And play your saxophone?"

Christian considered the request, the responsibility and assessed his standing in the village if he refused. But the last thing he wanted was to be the centre of attention. In the real world he avoided things that involved leadership and decisions. On stage in tiny walk-down jazz clubs was another matter. The smoke, the intimate crowd. Casual. Relaxed. He could be anonymous behind the music; the glass wall of sound. If he didn't like the crowd he turned his back and played to the band. Alone on a beach, the crash of cymbals like rolling waves, clarinet wails like sea birds. And the haze of the drugs. All his life he had avoided recognition. "Sure. Tell your mother it would be an honour. Just another gig, right?"

"Gig is a show, like at Juanita's?"

"Yeah, a show. Send the old boy off in style. In New Orleans, where Maartyn's from, they have these funeral bands. Marching bands, old dance hall musicians; jazz, you know? The real stuff. They hire out to do funerals during the day. Maybe a few 'Rock of Ages. Praise the Lord an' Turn the Pages' stuff, but they like to swing it, warm it up."

"Swing? You mean make hot, like Jocinto."

"That's it. Make hot. The old bugger. Mucho hot. Hot old bastard, wasn't he?" Christian felt a wave of guilt and doubt. The warning signs were rising. "I think we killed him."

"Oh, no, Señor Christ! Grandfather was ready to die." Miguel bent his head in reverence. "He just wanted one more, gig. He died with his guitar by his side." Miguel looked quickly to see how Christian was taking the story.

"He could play."

Miguel tried to sound indifferent. "There's a big argument in our home as to whether we should bury the guitar with Grandfather."

"Seems a shame," Christian said, seeing the big guitar shining like beaten gold.

"Yes?" Miguel brightened. "About Jocinto, you mean?"

"Well, yeah, and the guitar."

"The problem is, we have no money to feed the gang who will show up for the burial fiesta. They must be fed, it's the custom. A family feels great shame if there is no food, or money for the musicians."

"Your family doesn't have to pay me."

"It's a tradition."

"No money."

Maartyn appeared at the bedroom door. "I heard that. Non denaro. I know what that means." He wandered into the living room in his underwear looking tired and beat up. "We're not exactly flush for cash, right?"

Christian ignored Maartyn. "Look, Miguel, I know what the guitar's worth but I'll buy it for what I've got."

Miguel's eyes lit up "That's right, Señor? You have the 'emergency stash'?"

Christian wondered if Miguel had suddenly remembered the money. "Yeah, my contingency. A few Yankee dollars."

"If Señor Christ has some Yankee dollars I'm sure my mother would consider parting with the guitar, especially to one so worthy."

"Don't over do it. I've got a hundred dollars. That guitar's worth ten times that, but that's it."

Miguel held out his hand. "Give me the money and I'll get your guitar."

"Not so fast."

"What're y'all going on about?" demanded Maartyn. "Give'im what? This little runt's tryin' to shake you down?"

"Relax, Maartyn. It's the old man's guitar."

"What about it?"

"Jocinto died during the night. Miguel says some of the family want to bury the guitar with the old man."

"So what? Indians always do weird shit like that."

"They aren't Indians. I said I'd buy the guitar for a hundred dollars."

"Are y'all crazy, man!? We're starvin'…a dead man's guitar!?"

Christian opened the saxophone case and parted the felt liner. Miguel edged in for a closer look.

"Señor, Christ! That's more money than I have ever seen at one time, except at Juanita's."

"Where'd you get that?" demanded Maartyn.

"Emergency stash."

"We can eat for a month!"

"Can't let them bury a piece of work."

"No way, man! I'm not eatin' fish an' corn bread just so y'all can have a piece of work."

"Hey, cool it, Maartyn. It's my money."

"Cool it yourself! You asked me to come to this jerk off backwater. Y'all owe me, man!"

"Do not!"

"Do so!"

"Don't!"

"The hell you say!" said Maartyn, threatening with his eyes.

"What happened to that bundle you made selling grass to Paulo?"

"Well, I had some bad luck."

"What, dope deal go bad? Rolled by a hooker?"

"About right."

"Well tough on you." Christian retreated to the terrace, jamming the money into his pocket. "It's worth a fortune."

Maartyn followed. "...Not unless you sell it."

They avoided each other for the rest of the morning. Christian and Miguel fished the reef. Maartyn sulked around the villa nursing his ego and the wounds from his night with Juanita.

It was afternoon when Miguel and Christian returned, Miguel carrying a string of pompano. Christian was carrying a big guitar case. Maartyn went to the bedroom and refused to come out for lunch.

They ate a fried fish each. Miguel sat at the table cutting the rest of the fish into strips for drying. Christian sat at the other end of the wooden monk's table staring at the guitar case reclining on the sofa. Beyond was the bedroom where Maartyn sprawled face down on the bed.

"Your friend's acting like a spoiled child," said Miguel.

"I don't know. Maybe I shouldn't have bought the guitar."

"Jocinto would be very happy to know," said Miguel, hedging.

"Hundred bucks. Lot of moolah."

"We can go fishing if we're hungry. And I can get beer from Juanita's. She wouldn't miss a few."

"No! Don't ever do that. If I can't pay for something I don't want it. Hear me?"

"Okey dokey, Señor Christ."

"And stop calling me Señor Christ! It's Chris."

"Okay, Boss. I'm just your humble servant."

"Not that humble either."

"That's right, Boss. And when the revolution comes I won't be humble and Cuba won't be humble, especially to the Gringos."

"Does that mean you won't work for me?"

"Oh no, Señor Boss. I'll work for you because you are not a Gringo Imperialist pig, like Señor Maartyn."

"You think things will be different with Fidel Castro?"

"Oh yes, definitely. Rosameralda says that even without Fidel the New Cuba will be free of Yankee Imperialists who suck our economy dry and we will all be equal brothers and comrades and no one will have more than the other."

"Truth is, you'll probably have a lot less."

"Some of us for sure. The slavering dogs in Habana who are toe sucking twin brothers of the fat Gringo Gangsters who run Cuba now. But as you can see, Señor Christ, we couldn't have much less. You don't see fat Cubans when you look down from your terrace on Los Espiritos. Are the fishermen fat? Is my father fat? Only Juanita is fat.

One cannot get fat on the crumbs that fall from the plates of the Imperialists. The Capitalist Pigs must die!" Miguel made a fist around the knife and thrust it upwards. "Comrades unit!"

"Where do you get these ideas!?"

"Rosameralda."

"Do you have any idea what's been going on in Russia? Where, by the way, all the people are now comrades whether they like it or not?"

"Rosameralda only talks about Argentina and Chile and Guatemala, and Ecuador and Bolivia where the bastards who run things are friends of our own Capitalist bastard, Batista. Fidel Castro says they must all be turned away from the Pig's table. And we will be one family and must dine together on the fruits of a glorious revolution."

"Well, don't be surprised if Señor Castro doesn't come to dinner."

"If he does we'll take him fishing."

"Right. Fishing's good," he said sarcastically. "Fishing solves everything."

"Can you think of anything better than the reef in the early morning with the sun just coming up over the Sierra so that the shadows are long and the fish hungry and the heat of the day takes away the chill?"

Christian thought about the beautiful reef and the painted fish. Where in Canada could one sit in the sun drinking beer in December, watch dinner below, finning in the shadows of pink coral? There were other reefs and other islands but Cuba would have to do, Castro or no Castro. He opened the guitar case. A plump Spanish guitar lounged in the velvet lined case like a besotted pinup queen on a chintz bedspread. Perhaps it was the honesty of the mid-day light but the big guitar didn't look like the same lush instrument Christian had seen the night before in the dim yellow light of the cantina. The varnish looked dull and crazed. The top was cracked under the bridge. Many years of strumming had taken their toll. And the rosewood inlay between the frets was grooved by finger nails and cigarette burns.

Christian picked up the guitar. It looked like Jocinto's guitar. It was the right size and colour. He turned it over. There was a crack in the back board from neck to bottom. He sighted along the neck. His stomach tightened. The neck was twisted and bowed. Christian tried a chord. A flat buzz. He tuned the strings. Worse. "Damn!"

"Ah, something wrong, Señor?"

"This guitar's a piece of junk."

"It is very old, like Grandfather, bless his name."

"It's also very dead, like Grandfather!"

"But it makes beautiful music. You heard Grandfather play."

"Not this guitar." Christian ran simple chord changes.

Maartyn was in the doorway, arms folded, looking very superior in his grey underwear. "That's real sweet, ol' buddy. Play that one again."

"The Devil himself couldn't make this guitar sound good."

"You can say that again. Give me Lucille an' I'll put the thing out of its misery."

"I don't get it. Jocinto's guitar sounded great last night."

"We were pretty drunk."

"Does it sound like Jocinto's guitar to you?"

"It sure as hell don't! Sounds like horny cat tryin' to get out of tin box."

"But how, the hell...?"

"I'd say y'all got took." Maartyn looked directly at Miguel.

Miguel edged behind Christian pretending to look with amazement at the guitar. "Señor, Christ, I think it was how Grandfather played. He had the guitar a long time. It was his child."

"How could anybody play this thing?."

"Did you pay the money?" asked Maartyn.

"Yes, I did."

"Then get it back."

"I can't. The money's already gone for the taxis to bring the relatives from Havana. I saw Miguel's mother give it to Juanita."

"Juanita!? I suppose she drives the cabs too?"

Christian put the suspect guitar back in the case. He turned to Miguel. The look of innocence on his house boy's face was too angelic. "I owe his mother anyway. There's nothing I can do about it."

"Call Renée an' tell'er we're dying of starvation in a Cuban leopard colony."

"That's leper..."

"Who cares, man!? Call'er!"

"There must be another way."

"If there is you tell me. We're stuck in some dirt poor village, God knows where, in a country run by a bunch'a...What do you call those guys like Hitler an' Musselman, that Italian?"

"Mussolini. They were fascists," answered Christian.

"Fascists. The fascist dictator guy, Batista, is about to be run out of the country by a bunch'a Fascist Commies an' we haven't got the price of a goddamn meal between us! Have we? You got any more money stashed!?"

"No, well, a few pesos."

"Call your parents."

"Separated. I don't even know where they live. We didn't part on the best of terms. Last I heard, my dad was out west living with an ex nun from our Parish. Mom's in Toronto, maybe, or Ireland."

"Pity you. Y'all got a sister, put the touch on her."

"Montreal. Married some banker. She wouldn't be real happy to hear from me."

"Cut the ol' cord when ya left home, huh, chump?"

"I guess. Didn't seem important, then. I was off to see the world through the eye of a syringe. Can you blame them?"

"I blame you for spending a hundred bucks on some piece'a shit guitar! I'd like to break the thing over yer stupid head!" Maartyn made a move to the guitar. Christian stood in his way.

"Just back off, Maartyn!"

Maartyn, not fully recovered from his night of experience, was more interested in badgering Christian.

"Think yer way outta this..." He was about to threaten Christian with consequences related to revolvers and kneecaps but he remembered that Christian still had Lucille. "Ah, think about Renée. She's loaded. She's our ticket outta here."

"I don't want to get out of *here*."

"I can't wait!"

"Besides, you said she went to Antigua."

"No, man, I was just jerkin' yer chain. She went to Paris. Be back in Nassau by now. I swear. She said, by December and you were to call her if y'all wanted her to come to Cuba. So call her."

"You...You son-of-a...!"

"Yeah, I'm everything y'all can think of, includin' mean when I get hungry. Call her. At least get *me* out'a here."

"There's no telephones."

"Send a telegram or somethin'."

Christian considered their alternatives. "Miguel, is there a telegraph office?"

"Telegraph? You mean The Wire?"

"Yes, The Wire. Western Union?"

"Sure thing. We used to get the baseball scores during the World Series before radios. Esameralda's going to buy me a radio."

Christian sat down with his head in his hands. Feeling weak from the years of addiction. Stress pushing him back to the edge. "I hate this."

"You'll hate havin' broken knees a whole lot more."

"Maartyn, shut up. Threats are not very helpful."

"Oh, 'scuse me. I'll whip myself 'til I bleed."

"Where's the telegraph office?"

"In the back of Juanita's."

"That figures."

Maartyn changed moods. "Hey, that's perfect. Take one for the team, ol' buddy. I'll come on down an' cheer y'all on."

"No. I'll handle this myself."

"Hey, man, before you go, I want Lucille."

"No."

"Hey, she's mine!"

"She...I mean *it*, is in a safe place, if you want me to call Renée."

"Blackmail."

"Sure. I might be doing you a favour, okay?"

He was halfway down the hill when Miguel caught up.

"Señor Christ, wait."

Christian was still angry. "Tell me about Jocinto's guitar."

"There's things you shouldn't know."

"What 'shouldn't' I know?"

"Maybe you should give me the message. I will put it into proper Spanish for Juanita."

"Juanita speaks English. My Spanish is okay and my Cuban's getting there. Besides, I'm sending the message in French. Where's Jocinto's guitar?"

"Juanita can't send a message in French."

"Why not? She doesn't have to understand the message."

"Juanita will be very upset. She likes to know everything that goes on in Los Espiritos. She's the mayor. And she's also the Chief of the Police."

"And Justice of the Peace too, I suppose?"

"There's not that much justice in Los Espiritos unless Juanita makes it and there won't be any peace if you don't let me give the message, in Spanish, while you wait at the bar and have a cold Yankee beer."

The dirt road leveled out at a crudely paved avenue with buildings of the commercial centre and shacks on one side and the curving harbour on the other. The broken asphalt and cobbles had been laid down in a flurry of political activity after the war. It was appreciated during the brief rainy season, other wise it was a black heat sink. The commercial centre consisted of Juanita's Cantina, a store that sold dry goods and a bank that loaned money to fishermen and farmers. Juanita owned the bank which also doubled as post office and dry goods store. Beside the bank was the fish buying house. The fish buying house sold fishing gear, hardware and what lumber was available in the area. Some fishermen idled in the sun on boxes and barrels, drinking bottles of cola with rum. Beyond was the small church, it's stones plastered smooth and white washed. Frame shacks with collapsing garden walls and dying vegetation fanned out in either direction around the harbour. The cantina, held up by tall royal palms, was on the corner of the dirt road and the main road so that Christian and Miguel only had to turn left to enter. They stopped in the shade to continue the debate.

"What's going on, Miguel?"

"Nothing, Señor. Just trying to help. You know what happens when you go into the cantina to confront Juanita."

"That's not it. Tell me what's going on."

"And if Juanita's in a bad mood there's no telling what..."

"Miguel! We'll leave the missing guitar out of it for now. All I want to do is send a lousy telegram. Explain to me why I can't just walk in there and give Juanita the message, pay for it and walk out?"

"Because." Miguel looked beyond Christian as if the answer to an accumulation of questions lay somewhere across the Gulf of Mexico.

"I'm waiting."

Miguel was genuinely afraid. "Señor Christ, if I tell you honestly about the guitar will you let me take the message to Juanita myself?"

"That bad, huh."

"Worse than bad." Miguel looked at Christian, pleading. "See that boat out there?" Miguel pointed to a rust-streaked fishing boat anchored a quarter mile out. The white hulled vessel was one of the ubiquitous shrimp draggers so common between Texas and Florida, and up the East Coast, with the tall outrigger masts and a clutter of black shrimp nets hanging like funeral veils. There was a white dingy pulled up on the sand opposite the cantina.

"Where'd that come from?"

"It's one of the things you don't want to know, Señor Christ."

"Then why did you point it out to me?"

"It's one thing for a Gringo to come to Los Espiritos to live but it's another thing to know what goes on here. You see, last night, during the show at Juanita's, this boat came in, as it does twice a month, but something happened and it could not go out again before the sunrise."

"Okay. You don't need to spell it out. They bring something to Los

Espiritos. Juanita is the agent."

"You don't want to know that, Señor."

"Right. I don't won't to know. How do you know?"

"You don't want to know that either, because I may have to kill you."

"Miguel! You're joking, right?"

"Yes, I'm joking, but only about the last part."

Miguel studied his bare feet, making arcs in the sand with his big toe. "I'm waiting."

Miguel's shoulders sank in resignation. "Twice a month I take a limousine to Habana, but you don't want to know what for. Near Habana I take a cheap bus to the centre of Old Habana, near the harbour. I hang around the Malecon, play with the other kids and I fish. Then I go to the big boat part of the harbour to sell my fish to...certain people. I do my business, visit Rosameralda and Esameralda and come home. No one asks questions of a poor street boy in Habana."

A man's shadow crossed over Miguel. "Miguel! That's enough!" Ernesto Escobar was dressed in a white linen suit with Panama hat. He was as well groomed as the previous evening but looked tired, the pasty skin crinkled, like used tissue. He squinted against the sun and his expression changed when he addressed Christian. "Ah, young Christian. It's so nice to see you again." Escobar offered his soft hand.

"Buenos dias, Señor Escobar," responded Christian politely. He shook hands briefly, feeling even more exposed.

Two men emerged from the cantina behind Escobar. They had dark, wind-burned faces, thick, black mustaches and were dressed in the dirty peasant uniform. One of them wore a sweat stained straw hat. They looked at Christian with hostility. Christian recognized them from the night before; the group of men near the bar. Juanita said they were just farmers. They didn't look like farmers, even though the biggest, ugliest one wore the hat. Escobar nodded. They grunted something in reply and walked down the beach to the waiting dingy.

Christian was staring after the two men. "It's hot in the sun," said Escobar.

"Pardon?"

"Perhaps you would accept my hospitality today. I have just received some special food packages."

"Thanks, ah, not right now. Message to Nassau. Personal stuff, you know?" Why did he add the thing about personal stuff? Escobar had watery blue eyes. Odd, thought Christian. If Escobar were Spanish or Cuban...? The blue eyes wandered over Christian as Escobar stood squinting, waiting for him to go on. "Maybe another time."

"Very well. What is your wish?"

"I don't know." He played a hunch. "How about, tomorrow?"

"Oh, Christian, I am sorry. Unfortunately, tomorrow I have business that takes me to Habana."

A connection? "Ah, maybe another day then," said Christian, hoping fate would intervene again.

"The day after tomorrow? A late lunch?"

"Lunch? Okay. Lunch would be, fine."

"Miguel can guide you. I generally have a rest in the hot part of the day. Say three o'clock."

"Three o'clock. Miguel can stay for lunch too?"

"Of course, Christian my boy. Miguel is always welcome." Escobar winked at Miguel who looked embarrassed. Unusual for Miguel. Escobar collected the polished walking stick leaning against the wall of the cantina, waved his small hand like a dying monarch and picked his way along the pavement. Delicate, mincing footsteps more suited to an emperor's marble hallway than to the decaying political asphalt of a Cuban fishing village. His white mansion was as incongruous in Los Espiritos as Escobar's impeccable dress. Miguel was tugging Christian's shirt tail.

"Okey dokey, Señor Christ, we can go in now and send your message."

"Go in? Now?"

"Yes, we can go in, to see Juanita...as I just said."

The cantina reeked of sweat, cigar butts and spilled beer. The shuttered interior like a coal bin at midnight after the bright sunshine. The only light from sputtering candles on the shrine. Juanita sat in her place at the bar below the moose. A beer cap hit the zinc counter. Juanita was dressed in a shapeless shift of some light colour. The moose was as usual, but its eyes sparkled when Juanita struck a match to light a crooked cigar. The flare of the match rendered Christian blind again. The waft of invisible cigar smoke didn't help. "Juanita, it's me, Christian." Miguel eased into the cantina behind Christian and slunk around the tables.

"Well, well, look who's back. My Canada jazzman. Would you like a cold beer? There's still some ice."

"Ah, no thanks. I just want to send a telegram."

"Good. We can do business. We don't need Batista's electricity because the wire machine has it's own batteries."

"How much does it cost, to send a telegram?"

"Cheap for the service I offer. One peso for each word and twenty pesos for the batteries."

"That's pretty expensive, isn't it?"

"You can go down the street to another wire office if you think Juanita's prices are too high. However, the price does include a cold beer. It's special today only. But if you wish, there is another way to reduce the cost of a wire to, say, five pesos, flat rate, plus batteries. However, the batteries are free if you bring along Señor Maartyn Hardmuscle." Juanita snorted and heaved and coughed.

"Look, I'd like to send a telegram and that's all. I have enough for about twenty words. Now can we do this without negotiations?"

"Señor Chris, what do you think of me!? I'm just an honest, hard-working woman, who has had a sad and tragic life, what with no-good husbands running away to some Canada with a blonde with roots and small tits and having the responsibility to house and feed this animal, whose appetites are enormous."

"Juanita, you don't have to feed a stuffed moose."

"Oho, you would be shocked to know what expenses I have just to keep a roof over his ungrateful head. The taxes on stuffed heads in Cuba are exorbitant, but the price of staying in business is something you don't want to know about."

"I'm sure there are many things."

"And you should never know, so don't inquire of my innocent waiter. He's only a lazy urchin who I employ out of the goodness of my large heart, as I give domicile to this mangy animal."

"About the telegram?"

"Oho! That reminds me." Juanita disappeared into the utter darkness of the back room.

Miguel touched Christian's arm. "Sit down, here at the bar, Señor Christ, and I'll open a cold beer. Or perhaps a cola with rum."

"Miguel! Stay out of the rum!" Juanita's voice was loud but sounded as if she had her head in a cupboard.

"I was just getting the Gringo a cola. But the cola would taste better with a little rum in it. And some ice."

"Make a small one then. I'm not giving away rum to every stranger who wanders in to my cantina!"

"Beer's fine," said Christian.

"Rum is better, Señor Christ."

"Jesus. You people can't take no for an answer."

"I like to practice mixing."

"I don't want a rum!"

"Okay. One cold beer. I'm practicing to be a bartender, like Juanita."

"It'll take more than practice. It would take a miracle."

Miguel laughed. He popped the tops on two bottles. One bottle he slid smoothly along the length of the bar to Christian. "I saw that in a movie once in Habana," he said. "Esameralda took me to see this American gangster movie. The big time gangster owned a casino and for fun he would slide glasses of beer along the bar," Miguel took a quick sip, "and his friends would try to shoot the glasses as they went by. Sometimes they would shoot each other and that's how the gangster got rid of friends he didn't like. The cops couldn't do anything because the gangster said it was just an accident, and he had witnesses."

"Hollywood movies. Illogical and unlikely. On the other hand, maybe I just haven't been hanging out in the right casinos."

Miguel came around the bar and leaned close to Christian. "I can't cook for you tomorrow. I have to go to Habana with Señor Escobar, to fish."

"No matter. There's nothing to cook anyway."

"Just eat lots at Jocinto's fiesta tonight. You paid for the food. Eat enough to last two days and I'll try to bring something from Habana. I get a tip for my fishing trip."

"About the guitar?"

She returned through the swinging beads like a ship coming out of the mist. The Goodyear Blimp leaving it's hanger. "Here it is," said Juanita, waving a piece of paper. "This came for you last week."

"Last week? What is it?"

"Telegram, of course. It was sent to Habana. Whoever sent it thinks Los Espiritos is a casino. Habana sent it to me by the post. I'll add it to your bill." She placed the limp scrap of paper on the bar in front of Christian and lit the gas lamp. The flimsy paper stuck to a puddle of water. When Christian tried to pick it up the tissue disintegrated.

"What the?..."

"Santa Maria! Paper is so cheap these days."

"How can I read this?"

"I remember the message." She took a long pull of Miguel's bottle. "It said, *'Leave Nassau Friday, arrive Havana by boat…will find you Los Espiritos, stop'*." Miguel stole a sip. "Hey, I told your mother you don't drink when you work for me." Juanita took the bottle away from Miguel and cuffed him on the back of the head. She drank off the remaining beer. The belch sounded like it came from the moose.

"Who sent the telegram?" asked Christian.

"You don't know?"

"How would I know?"

"Who are you expecting?"

"Not sure. Why didn't you tell me there was a message?"

"I'm busy. I don't have time. If the message was important you would know."

"But, how was I supposed to know it was coming?"

"Everybody who gets a telegram in Los Espiritos knows. Then they come to Juanita's to wait. Sometimes the wait is very long and I have a good day and am very busy consoling those who wait for bad news. Sometimes its relatives in America. There have not been so many telegrams lately, not since Señor Bartuchi left. He's the gentleman who owned the villa. His name was Frank The Butcher. He wasn't in the meat business. As for myself, I have been waiting all this time for my husband, so the moose, as you call it, and I have to keep each other company."

"How long has he been gone, your husband?"

"Six lonely years."

"Long time."

"Yes...unfortunately the moose doesn't talk."

"Who sent the telegram?"

"Oho, the telegram. Not an American name."

"A girl?"

"How should I know?"

"Renée?"

"No, not Renée. Let me see. I think it was, Pablo."

"Pablo? I don't know a Pablo."

"No, no, wait...Pueblo."

"Paulo!? Oh God! That's all I need."

"Bad news?" asked Juanita hopefully.

"Sort of. This guy, Paulo, met him in Nassau. He was in jail when I left."

"Is he good looking?"

"Does it matter?"

"Not as long as he's a hardmuscle like your friend. Juanita likes a fresh one now and then." She shimmied and squealed.

Christian and Miguel stood in the blinding December sun looking at the decrepit fishing boat anchored offshore. The dingy now tied alongside. Nothing moved on deck but when the boat swung in the breeze Christian could see that the wheelhouse windows were shattered and the deck house had black holes in the peeling white paint and splintered planks above the waterline. "Some serious business here…" Christian said, but he couldn't help thinking of the villain's boat in the Popeye comics. Bluto's *Vile Body*. He wasn't Popeye. Life could be a joke but it wasn't a comic cartoon.

New considerations were crowding Christian's hazy horizon. He was hungry. The guitar was a fraud. Worse, they were now broke and he had just sent a message to Renée begging for money. Paulo was on his way to Cuba. Dangerous Lucille was in hiding and Maartyn was waiting at the villa for deliverance. Escobar and his precocious house boy were involved in something illegal and there was a new fear. The mysterious fishing boat in the harbour may be connected to the approaching socialist revolution; another dark shadow over the land. What else could be out of shape in paradise?

Miguel studied Christian's expression. "Señor Christ, don't think too hard about it."

"About which thing?" Christian could have added the growing desire for the means to escape temporarily. That was a more tangible fear.

"The fishing boat. It's not something you want to be involved with."

"And you do?"

"I have no choice. There's a problem with the boat."

"What's wrong with the boat?"

"Something to do with the engine. The man who works on the engine was…injured, and now the boat can't leave."

"They need a mechanic?"

"That's it! That's the hombre they need. The man who was injured was called the engineer but now they need a mechanic. Are you a mechanic too, Señor Christ?"

"No, but Maartyn worked on boats like that one. He talks a lot about engines."

"Wait here, I'll tell Juanita."

"Miguel!…"

Too late. Miguel darted back into the cantina. Another mistake, thought Christian. He had a guilty twinge about involving Maartyn. His first thought had been the faint hope that Maartyn might be taken away by the fishing boat. He was a big boy and could look after himself, couldn't he? His second thought was more practical and mercenary. Perhaps the owners of the boat would pay Maartyn. On the other hand, they might just slit his throat and dump him overboard. Other fantastic scenarios were crowding into Christian's imagination. Miguel was back.

"Juanita says to send Señor Maartyn at once."

Christian focused on the empty wine bottles as he gave Maartyn the news. Maartyn was already drunk, sitting on the terrace stones, legs splayed out as if he had been shot. The two empty wine bottles lay beside him like downed bowling pins. "Fix any goddamn diesel, man," said Maartyn defiantly.

"You sound pretty sure of yourself. What if it isn't an American engine?"

"That's a Gulf Shrimper," said Maartyn. He had been watching the vessel since Christian and Miguel left for the cantina. "They all have Jimmies or Cummers. Some have Cats. I can take one down with my eyes shut."

Christian had only a vague idea what Maartyn was talking about. "I take it a *Jimmie* is a kind of engine?"

"Right on, man! Detroit iron. Once took one ol' somebitch down that had twelve cylinders. We were driftin' in the Gulf an' there was a Jesus big hurricane comin'. The skipper cracked a wrist pin tryin' for one last pull. He figured if the somebitch was gonna take his boat he'd get a good pay day. It took me hours to take that Jimmie down. Then we pulled shrimp another six hours an' beat it into Bayou La Batre. Sold the load. Skipper ran'er on the beach. We all got paid off an' waited out the hurricane in a bar. Tore the roof right off the bar, man, an' I never spilled a drop. When it was over there wasn't a goddamn boat or dock left on the bay. All we could find of our shrimper was the keel an' this big mother of a Jimmie sittin' out there on the beach, man...oh, I feel sick."

"So I take it you could fix their engine?"

"Shit! What did I just say?"

"Juanita said they'd pay you but you have to keep your mouth shut and forget the boat was here."

"If they got cash I'm their boy."

"Look, Maartyn, I'm not sure about this. Miguel says these people are dangerous."

"Just gimme Lucille an' I'll put her in my tool box."

"You don't have a tool box."

"Well, ol' buddy, I ain't goin' near that boat without Lucille in my pants. My tool box...dig it?"

"Okay, I get it, but, I don't like the idea."

"Look, buddy, I ain't goin' down there naked. So give."

There was no point arguing. "Move over."

"What?"

"I said, move over."

Maartyn shifted, sending an empty wine bottle clanking across the terrace. It shattered against the wall. "I hate that lousy wine, man."

"Then don't drink it," said Christian angrily. He stepped on a loose terrace stone. The stone tilted enough for Christian to insert his fingers and lift the platter sized slab. Lucille rested in a shallow hole wrapped in Christian's T-shirt.

"Ahhh, sweet thang. Come to Daddy," Maartyn cooed. He unwrapped the revolver and kissed it.

"You're welcome."

Maartyn slept sitting against the wall like a street drunk, snoring and mumbling about gooks and commies. He left the villa late in the afternoon. After Maartyn had gone Christian sat on the terrace staring at the broken wine bottle's dark green shards. The heavy base was a perfect three pronged weapon. A ring of broken wine bottles strategically placed on the approaches to the villa could do some real damage, to bare feet. But if they came they would be wearing jack boots and carrying weapons. Molotov Cocktails...wine bottles filled with gasoline. Wicks of burning rags, his musty old T shirts, would be good. Machine guns positioned around the wall would be better, thought Christian. Maartyn's paranoia was spreading through him like a virus.

He dozed and when he woke the was sun going down. Christian was depressed and only wanted to sleep. From the terrace he could see the Spanish church with the rounded façade and the hole near the top for the bell. He would go when the bell sounded. Little of importance took place in the village until the bell summoned the faithful. He had never liked bells, of any kind. Reminded him too much of home. School, Sundays and family. Sundays usually started with church bells, then drinking and ended with the family fighting.

Since Maartyn's arrival his solitude had been shattered, his energy absorbed and the thin veneer of security worn away. Like the varnish on the fraudulent guitar. Miguel was keeping his distance. On the other hand there was nothing for Miguel to do. Christian could eat the dried fish or go hungry until the feast after the burial.

He decided to remain hungry. Remembered fasting for Holy Communion. The purity of the penance. Penance? What had he done wrong? He dozed again, head back against the wall. Warm sun on face. Pieces of masonry crumbling away, showering the dry leaves. Like rain on a tin roof. Dreaming of past sins; arm held tight by friend, tighter with strap, silver spear arching out of the sun, wounding with sweet expectation...then drifting in clear warm water, reef ahead in blue distance. Bells. Sunday morning, Montreal. The bells on Catholic churches never stop. Cold. Must be snowing. White, clean snow, hanging on trees like whipping cream, stretching away for miles along the avenue. Then the cars starting up and the snowplows and people marching through brown slush carrying umbrellas upturned to catch the white snow...Christian woke in darkness, shivering. The bells! Jocinto's dead. "Shit!"

Christian grabbed the saxophone and fit the mouthpiece and reed as he hurried down the hill in the dark, surrounded by fireflies of candle light. Surrounded by apparitions, lighted faces, noses, teeth and dark eyebrows. Tears. And straw hats. He didn't have a hat. Beret in back pocket. Pull it on. Sunglasses would be good; anonymous but almost blind in the dark, feeling his way. He fell in behind a family group carrying candles.

At the carved door to the church Christian slipped aside into a deeper shadow at a corner buttress. He sought the succour of the mouthpiece and sucked on the reed. Blew silently down its metal throat, like swallowing a snake. It whispered back, familiar. "It's okay," it said. "You've got me. Just tickle my linkage and I'll tell you the truth, or all the lies you need to get you through." Maartyn had gone on endlessly about linkage one night on the beach on Andros Island. He was drunk from tequila with beer chasers. Linkage had something to do with diesel engines. A stupid mechanic, he said, wanted to replace all the injectors but Maartyn insisted it was just the linkage and he saved the boat owner a lot of money by fixing the linkage, but got the boot when the owner found him in bed with his wife. So much for gratitude, Maartyn had said.

He wondered how Maartyn was doing with the new gig? Suburban family man, working the night shift, just like regular folks. Gigs are good, keeps the whole scene together...couldn't be more apart. He was hiding in the shadows of a Cuban church while his only friend was being tortured to death by psychotic drug smugglers before slicing him up for shark fiesta...the last candles were flowing by, swallowed up by all the candles inside. Smell of sweat, candles and death flowing out.

Christian peered around the heavy wooden door. The fat priest entered from behind a huge tapestry of a twistedly painful biblical scene; the Creation. In the pews bodies were rustling in black church-going clothes. Throats coughing. Now singing. A scruffy, tan and white rat-dog wandered into the church; tail curled over its back in a furry question mark. He sniffed at Christian. No comment. Ears perked. Intelligent eyes. Cynical rat dog goes to church.

The service was starting. The stench of burning incense drifting out the open doorway. Christian had been an alter boy and usually gagged, holding the incense burner while the priest spooned heaps of the stuff on the smouldering fuel blocks. Barbecue starters. Christian and Howie Martz, a converted Jew, joked about little Crispy Christs, charbroiled for Sunday dinner. Christian remembered the big church in Montreal. Westmount, where the rich live but the poor from Montreal West worship the bankers and doctors and lawyers, and touch the limousines, praying that the grace of capital and compound interest would rub off. Christian lived with his parents in a walkup apartment on Sherbrooke Street. Below was a flower shop that smelled of lilies. The shop sent lilies to the funeral parlour down the street. They had a fenced back yard and a small garden. They were poor Irish but he was sent across the mountain to school with the rich kids. He liked the rich. They were decent and fun and ambitious. Their only fault in life was being born rich and therefore had a separate reality.

Well, Christian old man, you're really in touch with reality now. Cuba 1958, on the verge of anarchy and can't buy a meal. Wonderful. And Howie Martz? Old man was a psychiatrist to celebrities. Howie, like his father, was about as screwed up as a kid could be. Howie was the one who turned him on to heroin. Screw Howie! Probably strung out in a chintzy mansion below Mount Royal. No, really, fuck Howie up the ass...Unusual thought for church, he said to himself, or perhaps he said it out loud. The rat dog turned to see.

The singing stopped. The fat priest was saying some nice things about Old Jocinto. Native son, good kid who respected his mother, blah, blah, blah. Born poor in Los Espiritos but worked hard and made something of himself. Blah, blah. Loved his family...Made it in America with his God-inspired music. Wonder if Old Jocinto did smack when he was touring with the bands? Marijuana at least. God knows there's enough shit floating around to hit up all the musicians, the audience and the bartenders for weeks. Sometimes it was the bartenders who fronted the stuff. Sometimes the waitresses. The managers. If not, there was always some smooth talking dealer sliding around the back door, hand in your pocket...Blah, blah. Jocinto came home to die, and...died poor playing his music and now he is going to be buried rich in love of family and friends, with his beloved guitar. "Guitar!?"

A smoky pond of black hair, and black clothing swam before Christian and beyond that, the alter soaring in glorious white on white tiers of carved wood, trimmed in gold leaf with silver ornaments. All the spare cash in the district gathered to make a stage for the shiny priest, gesturing, arms raised, like a marionette in rich vestments, eulogizing the dearly departed Jocinto Alejandro Diez, in a plain wooden casket. Open. Jocinto was propped up, half sitting, eyes raised to the clouds of incense that gave the place a jazz club feel. And the guitar...Jocinto's guitar! The fabulous guitar was in Jocinto's skeletal hands; fingers crabbed around the neck and splayed in mid strum. A hundred candles blazed off it's perfect finish. An explosion of light. "Miguel, you little buggar...!"

He must have said it out loud. A few mourners near the back turned to see. He stuck the mouthpiece between his lips and blew a sharp low E. More heads turned. The notes exploded, one-two-three. Too late to stop. It's not one's mistakes, it's the recovery. He added a scale. *Dah da da dat...Dah da da dat...Oh when the Saints...Oh when the Saints...Oh when the Saints go marching in*. He was beside the casket. People were clapping. They'd had enough eulogy. The acolytes abandoned candles and incense burners, crosses and statues of the Virgin, banners with painted pictures of Mother and Child, to clap. Only the priest objected.

Tears still streamed but smiles flashed brighter than the candles. Then in the front pew, one special smile. Oh, God! That face! Another. Oh, my God! Two pairs of dark eyes and two sets of red lips. Oh sweet Jesus! The eyes, hair, breasts, everything perfect! Black hats and veils and black dresses with jackets hiding the rest, but not successfully. The Diez Sisters of Doom. Which one was the Hooker and which the Revolutionary? Who cares? Christian lost his timing and missed a note. That nonsense about love at first sight, but then he had never been smacked over the head with a board either. Twice. Time to go.

Christian jived his way to the big double doors, the scruffy rat dog in the van, followed by the acolytes, then the casket bearers with Jocinto, then the family and the rest of the mourners. The priest, still protesting, brought up the rear.

Christian, in a heart pounding daze, remembered little of the procession to the cemetery. He followed the rat dog, who seemed to know where it was going. Maybe the dog was hired too, part of the ritual. Official guide dog of dumbfounded musicians. He played all the classics he knew; *Heart and Soul, As Time Goes By, Unchained Melody, Rock Around the Clock, Boogie Woogie Bugle Boy*. Why did he put that in? For Maartyn? What he did remember were the dark eyes, the red lips and those smiles. They were behind him, somewhere in the darkness, and he could still see the eyes clearly. One number he played for a reason. *Young Blood*. The Coasters...big hit the year before. He'd heard the tune on a truck radio, hitching to Miami. Low down sax with blues riffs. The dog whined a lot. It might have been criticism. He did a version of *You Ain't Nothin' But a Hound Dog*.

Tall candles with glass shields marked Jocinto's grave. An island of wavering light with a black hole in the middle. The dog sat down beside the open grave. Christian played Hoagy Carmichael's *Stardust*. The acolytes took up positions. The casket, carried by some dangerous looking hombres in white suits hired for the occasion, arrived out of the candle splattered darkness. Jocinto was still sitting up playing his 'beloved' guitar.

The family shuffled around the grave, heads bowed. Friends assembled. Christian continued to waft *Stardust* across the night, searching. There, beside Miguel, who was looking guilty as fraud, smiling through tears, the Diez Sisters. The notes trailed away in aimless pursuit of silence. The mourners started up on cue with the tears and wails.

The priest, imposing moral authority over all things to do with death and redemption, tried to nail Christian with a look. He picked up the eulogy from where he had left off and continued until the mourners were suitably punished. When he made the sign of the cross and nodded for the family to say their last goodbyes, a sigh of relief circled the site. Old Jocinto was probably as ready to go as the crowd were ready to make an end. A soft moaning wail rose up as two Diez brothers that Christian recognized from the bar, draped a piece of heavy canvas over Jocinto, extinguishing the fire of the guitar. The dangerous looking pall bearers pulled the supports and lowered the ropes. The casket, Jocinto, and the guitar disappeared into the black hole. Sobbing mourners began pouring spirits and throwing flowers, cigars and handfuls of dirt. Christian wondered how long the guitar would last under the tarp. What would happen to his soul if he dug up the grave?

Later, Christian and Miguel stood together on the periphery of the fiesta. Christian could not take his eyes off the two girls. Sunrise and sunset.

"Rosameralda and Esameralda." Miguel replied, without Christian asking.

"Man! They're something!"

"Yes, Señor Christ. Be careful."

Jocinto's burial feast began in the courtyard of the church and spilled out and across the road to the beach. Many more than had attended the burial. There was music and laughter and dancing on the pavement in front of the church. Young lovers slipped away to the shadows or the beach. The music was supplied by three guitars, accordion, trumpet, hollow sticks, maracas and an odd instrument that looked like a wash tub with a string on a long pole. It sounded vaguely like a bass. The result was musical anarchy but it worked in a Latin way. The rhythm infectious.

"She's...they're, beautiful." breathed Christian.

"My sisters are beautiful. That one's Rosa. She's younger, but meaner."

Christian watched his sisters dancing. Arms entwined, they made small circles inside a large circle, whirling past Christian in a rush of laughter and the fragrance of tropical flowers. He tried to catch Rosameralda's eye. The evidence of earlier tears only highlighted the inability of death to cloud the high-cheeked beauty of her dusky complexion. The black jacket had been discarded. The full figure a work of art. Christian thought Reubens. Renoir at least. The tawny colouring of her long neck, strong shoulders and high, rounded breasts, were toned by candlelight and shadows. Her skin smooth and firm. Luxurious amounts of shining hair, freed from the restraints of hat and veil, spilled over her shoulders in black waves. Christian felt weak.

Esameralda, a year older and less voluptuous, was as beautiful as Rosameralda but was overshadowed by her sister's stunning figure. But the eyes had that special flash of life.

"That's Esa. My oldest sister."

"Pardon?"

"Esameralda."

"Oh, yes...beautiful."

"She's a prostitute in Habana."

"You told me."

"Rosameralda's engaged. Her fiancé's a Castro revolutionary with the Habana guerrillas. He keeps a machine gun under his bed."

"What?"

"Machine gun!"

"Oh..."

"Maybe he'll be killed. I can arrange it."

"No!"

"Want me to introduce you?"

"No!"

"I told them all about you. How you are a famous musician who makes recordings and has mansions in Miami and New York. I said you were a friend of Señor Bartuchi and the Mafia."

"Miguel!

"It's okay, Boss. Rosameralda never believes anything I tell her."

"Smart girl."

"Yes, very smart. She was studying to be a lawyer but now she studies ways to blow up Señor Batista."

"I don't believe you either."

"It's true. Only last year the students attacked the palace. Rosameralda helped to plan the attack. Unfortunately the attack failed and many students were killed. Rosameralda herself was almost captured by the police afterwards, when the Batistianos tried to silence all students. Many were beaten on the streets in daylight just for being students."

Christian couldn't imagine the beautiful creatures involved in violent revolution or prostitution. The attempted assassination of a president? Terrorism? It just doesn't happen to real people.

Terrorism was a new term. Civilian terror. Far away. Israel. There was talk of a terrorist group in his own city, Montreal, but they were just clumsy young political thugs, making noise about freedom and separation. Terrorists made life miserable for the French in Indochina and in Paris. The Middle East had the Suez War and terrorists exploded bombs in Cairo and Beirut. Nobody actually knew terrorists. Back home it was American Rock'n'Roll, Chevy convertibles and American hamburgers, with a French Canadian accent. Proms and graduation. Even though he had left all that behind in the pursuit of indifference, it was part of his understanding of normal life. The girl next door suffered from acne too. But she wanted kids and a pink house in the suburbs. Christian wanted to look like James Dean and ride a Harley motorcycle like Marlon Brando. The most conflict he experienced was asking his father for enough money to take his acne-scarred little darling to a movie or bop to loud music in a sweat-box church basement while the nuns scrutinized thrusting cool, boney hands between dancers.

While Christian contemplated life and contradictions, the Latin rhythms slowed. Dancers paired off, drew closer and touched carefully under the watchful eye of the chaperons. Rosameralda and Esameralda were gone.

"I won't be able to bring breakfast, Señor Christ. I leave early for Habana. You eat something at the feast before these fishermen make it disappear."

"I'm not hungry."

"Some day you will be."

"Will, ah, your sisters be here tomorrow?"

"No, they're going to Habana with us. It's too dangerous for Rosa to stay in Los Espiritos. They watch her."

"Who does?"

"You don't need to know. Rosameralda has a revolution to plan and bombs to make. Esameralda has to make money with her pussy. Me, I go fishing."

"Should you be talking this way, about your sisters?"

"Everyone knows. Rosameralda's a student. It's expected. Esameralda's supported our family for many years but she fears the revolution will be hard on the prostitutes because Castro talks about Cuba becoming a moral country that believes in God and not Yankee dollars. It makes arguments in our family. You wouldn't believe the yelling between those two."

"And what about you? What do you do?"

"You aren't supposed to ask me."

"You go to Havana to fish?"

"That's it, Boss. Fish."

"I don't believe you."

"You aren't supposed to. By the way, Señor Christ, I'm sorry about the guitar. At the last moment the family decided that Jocinto's spirit would haunt us if we gave away his proudest possession."

"You weren't exactly giving it away!"

"Yes, and my family decided to give you Jocinto's old guitar that was worth more than what you paid. You just need to fix it up a little. I must go. Don't forget your date with Señor Escobar." Miguel dodged away.

"It's not a date!...Damn that kid!"

Christian walked across the soft, cool sand to the edge of the tide line, kicked off his sneakers and pulled off his shirt, laid his sax on it and waded into the water. The water now warmer than the sand. Invisible floating seaweed pushed against his bare legs like sea snakes. He felt the chill but kept going. His life not important enough for sharks. It meant his spirit was waning, like the moon. The low, crescent moon was just a slice of silver but there was enough light to see the outline of the white fishing boat. No lights showed on deck but Christian could see pin points of light lower down, just above the waterline where the navy gunners had aimed trying to sink the wooden boat. Must be where they keep the engine, he reasoned. The dingy was alongside. Maartyn was still at work. The night shift. Almost funny.

Christian absorbed the softness of the night and the music from the fiesta. The tits-up moon. The gentle, warm salt water of the Gulf. The sand was firm. The tide still going down, tugging at his legs. He should have been content with paradise but there were too many things leaning off centre. The fishing boat was one problem. And there was the new thing. The girls. Rosameralda and Esameralda. The breathtaking beauty of the dark revolutionary and the exotic mystery of the night creature.

Christian stood for a long time lost in thought. The tide crept further away and he didn't follow. The sand became softer. He ran the mental puzzle of his past and the present, and all the while he had a feeling there was something near, behind him. Felt the familiar tingles. Some new danger? He turned to look. Nothing. Just the fiesta and lights and the frenetic movement of dancers. He turned back to the harbour. Still there, the feeling. A noise. A small noise, a whine. He turned again and looked down. The rat dog was sitting behind Christian, tail curled in that question mark, looking up, waiting.

"What do you want? A payoff? I could've found my own way to the cemetery."

The dog made no sign.

"Food? The food's over there. It's mine, so help yourself."

Nothing.

"A friend? Are you a stray?"

Whine, was all the dog said.

"You need a home? No problem. Follow me. I'll call you Wolf and pretend we're in the woods, Northern Quebec, and you're a lost wolf cub that I've befriended, taking you home to raise as my trusted guardian, who would kill on command, or instinctively."

Christian picked up his naked sax, blew off sand particles and, carrying his shirt and sneakers, angled across the beach to avoid the fiesta mob. He was feeling neither hunger for food nor the desire to come into contact with another human being, except for one or two...or three. And that was a more serious hunger.

His dreams that night were chaotic and disturbing. Chasing figures dressed in black through a long night, up hills and down, through smokey bars, dry tobacco fields and thick scrub forests. Dry, gnarled trees slapped his face and scratched at his body. He pursued forms across alligator swamps and along endless hotel corridors piled with bodies and syringes. He woke up feeling a sense of loss, an ache around his heart and unknown fear. He was sweating even though the night had been cool. First conscious impressions were of too much light and something in the bed beside him. Small and furry, smelling like dead fish. Hand exploration revealed the sandy, damp rat dog. Next impression was normal hunger. Raw and gnawing but manageable.

December 19th, 1958. *I woke up with a wet dog in my bed. I felt hollow, like an old log neglected in the forest. Ignored by all the young trees standing high above, not even looking down, because all I was good for was growing fungus. I wondered if the girls were an illusion, induced by delusion, self-delusion that somewhere out there was a reason for all this. I should have stayed in bed but there was Maartyn returned from work and we had more problems...*

It was late. Sun already mid-morning high. Christian drank nothing the previous evening so there was no excuse for the way he felt, but the ache was deep inside and the fear not going away. Something was wrong. Rat dog was pacing back and forth from the bedroom to the living room.

He found Maartyn lying face down on the living room floor covered in blood. He looked dead. There was blood on the sofa. Blood on the straw mat. Blood on the doorway to the terrace. Massacre, he thought. Second thought was guilt...maybe he stepped on the broken wine bottle coming over the terrace wall, but Maartyn seemed to be bleeding from the face and head. Good sign, thought Christian. At least he's still bleeding.

"Maartyn?...Maartyn!" The wounds were superficial, except for a deep cut on the back of Maartyn's head where blood still seeped through his dark hair. Face had been punched or kicked. Eyes masked with ugly yellow-blue tones already turning green. Broken nose crusted with dry blood. Cheek split. Lips swollen. Greasy shirt torn. The usual signs of a brawl. "Can you talk?"

The body on the floor rolled over and moaned. "Screw you!"

"Thanks. Glad you're okay." No further response. "What happened?"

"What look like?"

"You got the worst of it, looks like. I'll get water."

Christian went to the pantry. The water pail was empty. "No water. Wolf, clean him up." Rat dog, alias Wolf, was already investigating the blood sources.

Maartyn reacted. "Hey! What the...?" The rat dog stopped licking Maartyn and sat down, tail in the question mark, head tilted to one side as if trying to figure out why Maartyn refused ministrations. "What's that?"

"Dog. I call him Wolf."

"Get'im away."

"Here, Wolf." Wolf cocked his head the other way.

"Oh, man. Where'd dog come from?"

"Followed me home. Another mongrel."

"How can feed it?"

"Don't know. Think he looks after himself."

"What name?"

"I told you, Wolf."

"Wolf? Why Wolf?"

"Los Espiritos already has a moose."

"Shit. Man, what a mess."

Christian put a T shirt in his hand. "Hold that to your head. I'm going down to the well. C'mon, Wolf."

Wolf didn't understand the command in English but Christian was going away so he followed.

When Christian returned Maartyn was sitting up against the couch. Christian put the bucket down and went to the pantry to get a bowl. Wolf began drinking out of the pail.

"Hey!...dog!" Maartyn kicked at Wolf. The rat dog jumped away and in a flash had a death grip on Maartyn's big toe. "Owe! Shit-dog! Get off." His instinct was to kick but another instinct said, stay absolutely still. "Owe! Chris!"

"Wolf!" Christian yelled in English. The dog held its prize. He spoke in Spanish. "Wolf, let go. Sit. Stay. Heel. Let go!"

Wolf sat down looking satisfied. Maartyn fumbled in the pocket of his tight chinos for the gun. "Teach you, you little...!" The gun wouldn't come out. "Son-of-a-bitch! Kill that sorry mutt!"

"No! Maartyn! It's your own fault."

"Want poison me?"

"Relax. Dog's cleaner than you are." Christian scooped water with the wooden bowl. He wetted the bloody T shirt, scanning Maartyn's battered face. The head area first. The head wound still bled. Maartyn wasn't clotting. He dabbed and scrubbed, ringing the shirt. The water in the bowl turned red. "What happened? The guy's on the boat do this?"

"Man, you wouldn't believe."

"What? Don't tell me...You mouthed off? Picked a fight?"

"No. Didn't. They understood English, but only talked about the job. Fixed their lousy engine. Foreign junk. Rusted piece'a shit...Owee, that's a bad spot."

"Sorry." Maartyn's lips were badly swollen. Front teeth loose. Another bad spot. "Sorry. Then what happened?"

"Stop Juanita's for one lousy beer!"

"Sure, just strolling home from the job, hard working young mechanic stops at the corner bistro for a brew with the boys."

"Shut up!"

"...Hockey game on the television. Argue about The Rocket or Stan Makita. You piss off a Chicago fan. Argue. One thing leads to another."

"Will you shut the fuck up! Juanita's fault. Other night she said what would happen if ol' man dies."

"I think she was kidding."

"Oh yeah? Mindin' my own business. Ouch!...Two beers. Leave. Jump me outside. Son-of-a-bitch hit me from behind."

"No kidding. That wants stitches."

"Get me down. Can't get Lucille out or I'd done those mothers, man! Woke up under palm tree."

"Just as well. You only have to heal instead of stand trial for murder."

"Self defense."

"Right. Headlines read, 'Gringo thug plugs local'. Quick trial. Gringo hangs from nearest palm tree at sunrise. Probably the same tree. Local justice. Who ever knows?"

"At least have satisfaction doin' bastards."

"Great last thoughts."

"Screw you! I go out my way, you go yours. Stupid junkie musician. Die slow death blowin' spit in some horn an' shit up yer arm. No thanks."

"At least you got paid for your pains."

"Yeah, well here's good part. Took wallet, money an' passport."

"Oh, great!" Christian stopped daubing Maartyn's face. There was some improvement but the rest of the colour arrangement was fixed. "Back to zero."

"Passport's fake, but I need it to get into Mexico. Shouldn't boy hustler be here with breakfast?"

"He's not coming today. Errand to Havana."

"Has to do with that boat, doesn't it?"

"I wouldn't know."

"Real screwy, man. Those guys watched me like a hawk. Got nervous if I'm snooping. Man, I'd go for a spanner an' this one dude'd go for his gun. Made me more nervous than takin' down that Jimmie in a hurricane. Up to some evil an' I know what."

"Really?"

"Yeah, your favourite flavour. Smack."

"No. A real Sherlock. What was your first clue?"

"Must be friends of yours, huh, buddy? Now I know why they call them fishing smacks." Maartyn tried to laugh. "Owee! Hurts to laugh."

"Then don't. It's not that funny. You don't know what it's like to be hooked and your friends make it too easy."

"Shit. Tried that stuff too. Take it or leave it, man. All in head. You got to be tough, man. Join the marines. Teach you how to take pain. This's nothing, man. I used to get beat up regular, but always took one down with me."

"So, what happened last night?"

"Waitin', like they knew I was comin' out. Wham, from behind. Bushwhacked. Juanita, man, she set me up."

"Doesn't sound right. Why would she set you up?"

"Y'all tell me. Whole place's weird. I'd get outta here in a minute. Listen, Chris, I'm serious. This's bad news. I've never seen a place so messed up. Can't speak the language so the bastards set you up right while they're smilin' in yer eyes. I don't trust any of'em, specially the slinky kid."

"Miguel?"

"Yeah, that little bastard. Rips you off. Sets you up with Juanita. She's a scary one. Then lines you up with some fag. Those guys out there probably smugglin' dope. The stupid country's fallin' apart an' the Commies comin' out of the hills. Man, y'all sure know how to pick'em. It'd be safer in the ghettos. I'd take Miami or Orleans any day."

Christian wrung out the bloody shirt and handed it to Maartyn. "Hold this to your head until the bleeding stops. I don't know what they do here for medical emergencies."

"I'd be afraid to find out. Juanita's probably the local quack."

"I'll talk to her." Christian looked out the window. Wolf got up and wandered into the pantry. "By the way, your boat's gone."

"So's my fifty bucks."

Wolf trotted into the living room trailing a long strip of dried pompano. "And there goes your breakfast," Christian said.

"Who cares? What's there for real food in this joint?"

"Dried fish. Olive oil."

"Oh, man!..."

Wolf lead the way to the cantina and stood guard at the door. Lucky dog, thought Christian. The simple life. "Juanita? You in here? Juanita!?"

Juanita was asleep on her arms at the end of the bar. "Wha?...Who's there?" She lifted her head slowly, eyes half shut, blinking through strands of hair at the rectangle of light around Christian's silhouette

"It's me. Chris."

"Oho, Señor Chris, Sorry. Late night."

"Juanita, can we talk?"

"You sound too serious this morning. Want a cold beer?"

"We've got a problem."

"And who doesn't? Should I tell you my problems?"

"Bartenders are supposed to listen."

"Are you a paying customer?"

"No. I'm flat broke. There's not a thing to eat at my place and there's no prospect of money. The money Maartyn earned is gone, and he got beat up. Do you know anything about that?"

Juanita shrugged, the picture of innocence. "There was a little incident, nothing unusual. I don't know what Maartyn do with his money. He come in here for a beer or two. Juanita doesn't escort her customers home."

"He made it home, but without his pay."

"You have a friend coming? This Paulo?"

"He's just more trouble."

"Your woman?"

"I don't know if she got the message. Did an answer come?"

"No. Nothing. In this case I would have told you."

"About last night?"

"You were great, Señor Chris. Everyone said what a wonderful thing you did for Old Jocinto. And the fiesta was a big success, yes? You had fun?"

"No, but I got a dog out of it."

"That little one with tail like a bush pig?"

"Yeah, I guess."

"There, you see? That's the best dog in all of Cuba!"

"We can't eat the dog."

"You would if it came to that."

"About last night..."

"Yes, you met our girls. Miguel told me what a great effect they had on you. Such beauties, no? Such spirit, but watch out for Rosa. I should say no more."

"I only saw them from a distance. About last night."

"What is this about last night? If it wasn't the music and it wasn't the most beautiful women in Cuba, besides Juanita?"

"Maartyn. It's about Maartyn."

"What about Maartyn?"

"Somebody tried to kill him."

Juanita looked shocked. "No. He fixed the boat. He got paid. He came in here for a beer. He didn't insult anybody. He didn't shoot anybody. He had one free beer and one he insisted to pay for and went away. There was a little incident outside I was told."

"He got beaten up pretty badly, and they took his money and passport."

"Who did that? Who would do such a thing in Los Espiritos without Juanita knowing about it?"

"That's what I'd like to know. And we're out fifty bucks."

"Fifty dollars!?"

"Everything he had."

"Santa Maria! I told Santoz-forget that name-I gave the captain of the boat two hundred dollars to give to Señor Maartyn, one hundred to fix the boat and one hundred to keep him silent. When I asked Maartyn if he got his money he just made a sign like a zipper across his sweet mouth."

"Well, his mug doesn't look so sweet right now."

"Madre de Dios! That Santoz! Wait 'til I get my hands on him. But Santoz didn't beat up on Señor Maartyn, that I can promise."

"You didn't double cross Maartyn?"

"Double cross? You think I would do a thing like that?"

"Just asking. What are we going to do?"

"Wait."

Juanita slid off the stool and lumbered into the back room, obviously still angry about the turn of events. Rummaging noisily in the darkness, grumbling about ingrates like Santoz. She returned with a large slab of something wrapped in old newspaper and thumped it on the counter in front of Christian, beaming with beneficence.

"What is it?" he asked suspiciously. The odour wafting up from the paper announcing a presence he recognized. The fish market near the Victoria Wharf in Old Montreal.

Juanita peeled back the dusty newspaper. Inside was a slab of something brownish that resembled old cardboard covered with sand. "Salt fish," she announced proudly. "It was left as a present. It comes all the way from some foggy codfish place near Canada. You know this codfish place I mean?"

"Yeah. Newfoundland. It's to cod the way Cuba is to sugar."

"That's the place! I had this sailor from that Newfound Island. He called himself a Newfie. Oho, what a man he was, my Newfie. Fifteen children at home and I found out why. Must have something to do with the fish." Juanita laughed and shimmied.

"What am I supposed to do with this?"

"Eat it of course, you silly boy. What else would you do with a salt fish? Besides, it's a great gift. The last of my Newfie. Such memories, and it's all I have after five years."

"You have the moose."

"What use is a moose, besides to hang hats?"

"Juanita, if this fish was given to you five years ago, and God knows how old it was before that...?"

"That's of no consequence my hungry Chris. It was in a lead box so the rats could not get at it and I don't think anything would eat it besides."

"For good reason. Couldn't you lend me some money, just until Renée gets here?"

"I have no money. I send all my cash with Señor Escobar to deposit in the American Bank in Habana. I don't trust the bank here, even though I own it. Too easy to rob and it's been robbed more than once, by the Batista police. They call it business tax. Some day I'm going to burn this cantina down and go looking for my no good husband and when I find him I'm going to..." Juanita began to cry. Big, salty tears flowed down her brown cheeks like a flash flood. And her face screwed into a mask that would scare a Haitian witch doctor.

"Juanita, please...don't do that. Don't cry. Juanita?"

Maartyn was sitting on the couch holding the bloody T shirt to his head when Wolf and Christian returned from their mission to Juanita's Salt Fish Emporium. Christian tossed the slab of salt cod on the table. It didn't sound like food.

"What's that?"

"Food."

"Smells like fish."

"Good guess. Lunch. Dinner. Breakfast. Take your choice."

"That's it? That's all you could find to eat? I'm not eating any more goddamned fish!"

"It's not like I had a big selection." Christian sat down at the table and unwrapped the prize. He sliced a chunk of the hard flesh and tossed it toward Wolf. The fish never reached the floor. "Juanita sent it with her compliments. She tried to soften it up with her tears so treat this particular codfish with respect."

"What a generous woman."

"What a strange woman. Anyway, she claims she knows nothing about the mugging, but the captain stiffed you. She was pretty pissed, especially since she told Santoz to give you two hundred bucks. Did he give you two hundred bucks?"

"He sure as hell didn't! It was a big deal to come across with fifty. I put in hard hours down there, man. With those creepy dudes breathing cigar smoke in my face. And stink! Man, those guys have been at sea too long. I'm tellin' ya, man, we got to get off this crazy island."

"So, do you think it was Santoz and his boys who mugged you?"

"No, Chris, ya know? When I think about it, the guys who did this didn't smell right. I mean, they didn't stink of cigars an' sweat, ya dig? More like that bottled piss water they use in barber shops, ya know? Palm oil or something."

"That stuff? I remember the last time I was in a barber shop. My tenth birthday. Mom took me to get a brush cut. Last time I ever went near one of those hair butchers. The barber shaved the back of my neck then came at me with the red stuff."

"That's it. Man, I could smell that stink when the first guy grabbed me. Then another guy hit me from behind. I think there was a third dude. He had pointed boots. We call'em studs. Last thing I remember now, the smell of shoe polish. Then I was out."

"Studs?"

"Like cowboy boots but low cut."

"Sure doesn't sound like our sailors." Christian lopped off another chunk of fish and tossed it to Wolf. Instead of laying down to chew, Wolf trotted out the open door. "I thought getting ripped off for the guitar was my biggest problem. Man, some things in Los Espiritos just don't add up. The fishing boat's in the thick of it, I'm certain. Miguel knows what it is, and so does Juanita. Smuggling's big business." Wolf was back looking for another piece of fish. "No you don't. I know that old trick."

"Just wants to leave it around so it'll stink more, if that's possible. He'd love that shrimp boat."

"...Pardon?" Christian had been thinking about Jacinto and the buried guitar. Decided he wasn't going to dig up the grave.

"I don't know what else those dudes do, but they had a load of shrimp in the last few days, among other things."

"You sure?"

"Oh yeah. A load'a shrimp on ice all right. I got a look in the hold. Hadn't cleaned it out, or hosed it or nothin'. Same with the deck. There was shells an' junk fish in the corners an' around the gear. An' the nets still had junk in'em. They were in a hurry."

"But why? If they're running dope why would they fish?"

Maartyn shrugged. "Cover? Coast Guard doesn't take long to clue in when they board a boat in the Gulf that ain't carryin' fish or ice or at least the smell."

"Makes sense. Then why'd they get shot up by the Coast Guard?"

"Not the Coast Guard. The Cuban navy was waitin' for'em is my guess an' the engineer, see? They were shootin' for the engine to stop'er."

"Any idea where they came from?"

"Stateside for sure."

"Running dope from the States? That doesn't sound right. It's usually the other way around."

"Maybe they pick the stuff up here. Who knows? But I'm pretty sure they came from the States."

"How do you know that?"

"Cigarettes an' booze. All good American shit. Garbage all over. They might make a fortune runnin' dope but they live like a buncha pigs. Smell like it too. There was something else in that fish hold, ol' buddy, jus' to round out yer day."

"What?"

"A body."

"Oh, Jesus!"

"Packed in ice. Probably the engineer. Does that explain where Juanita got the ice for our little shindig?"

"Miguel said we shouldn't ask questions."

"So don't, man. Don't need more trouble. What we need is some way outta here. I don't care about the money. I don't care about the beatin'. I just want out."

"Fine. Next time Captain Santoz' in for the night ask him to take you along. If it wasn't them who jumped you what's the problem?"

"Right, so's I can get shot up by the goddamn navy? There was blood all over the engine room."

"Escobar fits into this someplace," said Christian. He looked in the direction of the white villa. "Rich old man, living in a far out place like Los Espiritos. Makes business trips to Havana and Miguel goes with him to fish. It's a cover."

"What are you talkin' about, man?"

"Everybody's into something illegal. Juanita's just a front for the game, and I'm not convinced it's as simple as running dope, even by the boat load."

"Maybe they do small packages," suggested Maartyn. "Like diamonds."

"Heroin comes in small packages too."

"Is it worth runnin' from the Cuban navy?"

"Some days. I don't know." Christian walked to the west window. The morning-blue Gulf, so deceptively calm and innocent. The image of paradise. Wolf watched every move. "I'm invited to Escobar's tomorrow. Late lunch with art tour. I'm taking Miguel as a witness."

"That's a joke. He probably set you up with the old fag. The little bugger's just a pimp."

"Jesus, Maartyn, do you have to see everything from a snake's eye level?"

"Well, Chris ol' buddy, y'all tell me. All I know is what I see an' what I see is nothin' but weird an' bent, know what I mean?"

"I'm beginning to think your paranoia isn't misplaced."

"My what?"

"Paranoia. Call it, survival instincts."

"Yah, I got that all right. But I didn't get this far by livin' in a goddamn drug dream."

"I told you I'm off the stuff. That's why I like it here. Quiet, at least it was."

"Don't y'all start on me with that 'wreckin' paradise' bullshit. All this shit goin' on's got nothin' to do with me, man. I just get here, an' first thing I know we got guys droppin' dead an' shot up, an' crazy, over-sexed women, an' fags'n' goddam drug runners an' Commies, an' who the hell knows what's next!"

"Okay, Maartyn, I get the point. You're the proverbial innocent bystander who carries a Rock'n'Roll gun just in case such things happen."

"Lucille's my best girl."

"Just keep her in your pants, okay? If we play it cool this will all go away."

"Wanna bet?"

"No."

"I'm tired, man."

Christian helped Maartyn to bed, closed the shutters and went to the pantry. There were a few strips of dried pompano hanging from a string, the ones Wolf couldn't reach. There was a part bottle of olive oil on the shelf and the rest of the good vintage wine in the hiding place. Nothing to take the place of hunger.

He went out to the terrace with his saxophone. The air was cool, with a light breeze from the north. The sun wore a veil announcing a weather system. He sat on the terrace wall and tried to play but there was no magic. He leaned against the wall of the villa so that the weak sun could warm his face and fingers. Wolf scouted the corners and cracks in the stones, finding small crunchy bugs. Christian shut his eyes and listened to Wolf snuffling, wondering how long the dog would stay. He liked the independent little scrounger who seemed to have life figured out. He had a dog when he was a boy; a mutt spaniel that wandered into his life one day, a stray with questionable credentials. His parents didn't want the dog but relented, with conditions. Then it got run over by a garbage truck. He remembered that as the beginning of the breakup of his family, his alienation, a punishment for indifference. "C'mon, Wolf."

They walked down the path to the beach and across the sand to the skiff. Wolf leading. It was an effort to get the heavy boat launched but once afloat Wolf jumped aboard and took up the bow position. Up front, guiding. "What a dog."

With no destination Christian just rowed. He didn't watch where he was going, just pulled, and became angry thinking about his crumbling paradise. He pulled harder and harder until an oar skipped and he fell backwards off the thwart and lay on the bottom boards. Sweat filled his eyes. The salty fluid distorted the sun and the puffy clouds building out of the haze looked like they were under water. The sun was warmer now and he lay in the tepid bilge water soaking up the heat. Wolf curled up in the bow to sleep.

He dozed, he dreamed, but he woke up not remembering the dream, just images and confusion. Appropriate, he thought. He hauled himself up and looked around. The tide had carried them to the reef where the coral rose up like a wall from the clear, blue depths. There was no wind. There should have been the offshore trades. The harbour was a mile astern but at least he had stayed on a line so that it was a straight row back. Wolf was awake, standing on the bow with his tail curled, looking toward the land. His polite whimper said, 'far enough'. Time to go back. You don't go beyond the reef alone in December. Hurricane season was passed, but it isn't the big storms with lots of cloud warnings, it's the sudden, clear air winds that sweep in from the north to carry boats away, with rowers who don't know enough to run with the wind and tide and try to make a landfall further east along the coast. Instead they beat against the wind until they are too weak to row and are carried to Mexico or Central America and usually arrive dead.

Wolf whimpered again and paced the bow. There wasn't much room to pace so his antics looked more like impatient stomping. "Okay...I get the message. But I'm going to take a swim first." Christian plunged over the side into the clear water. Eyes shut tight against the first stinging onslaught. Down, straight down into the cool depths, stripping away surface worries until his lungs began to burn. Then he opened his eyes. He was near the bottom. Something moved. A dark shape like a statute standing erect, arms akimbo and waving slowly. He was looking into the wide bulging eyes and cheesy-white face of a man.

He was screaming when he hit the surface. Lungs bursting for air. Coughing and choking on salt water, flailing wildly for the boat and hanging on to the rough gunnel. There was the awful feeling that the thing was going to grab his legs. He kicked out and pulled himself aboard the skiff, skinning his knees, and lay on the thwart, panting and heaving from fright.

When the bow of the skiff touched the beach Wolf hopped over the side and went off to see what the tide had left behind. Christian sat on the rowing thwart with the oars in his swollen hands, staring back out to sea. During the long row to shore he had calmed down enough to put logic to what he had seen but it only added to the confusion. Fear was replaced by thirst. The village well was a short walk across the beach. He had to move, to do something but he sat, staring, unable to gather the strength to get out of the boat, the shell of wood a protective cocoon. Something tangible that he could hold on to and manipulate. Nothing else in his narrow world was under control. Too tired to beach the boat higher he tossed the anchor and let the skiff look after itself.

It was almost dark when Christian and Wolf returned to the villa. Maartyn was sitting at the long table toying with some pieces of salt cod. Christian went to the pantry, lit the kerosene lamp and carried it to the table.

"Did you sleep?" he asked Maartyn.

"Yah."

"You look better," said Christian.

"You don't." Maartyn saw a different friend. He knew the look. Fear and denial. "This salt fish ain't half bad. Try some."

Christian accepted a piece that Maartyn pushed across the table. "Thanks."

"Where ya been all day?"

"Out, rowing."

"Yah? What?"

"Went for a swim..."

"And? Somethin' happened, right? Y'all look funny."

"I saw a man standing on the bottom."

"Uh huh."

"Out by the reef."

"Uh huh, an' what was this dude doin'?"

"Just standing there."

"Uh huh."

"No, really, standing...like this." Christian held his arms akimbo.

"I was the one who got whacked on the head an' you're seein' things."

"Well, say what you want, I saw this guy standing on the bottom, eyes open, looking right at me, I swear to God. Why would I bother making up something that stupid?"

"That's right, Chris. Y'all don't need to entertain me. Did he say anythin'?"

"Course not, he's dead."

"How could y'all tell?"

"Don't be an ass!"

"Just standin' there...dead?"

"Very much dead."

Maartyn looked away, a wry grin distorted by swollen lips. A superior, I know-it-all grin. "The engineer. Our friends on the boat pitched'im over the side on the way out, is my guess."

"Makes sense, in a screwed up way. But why wouldn't they wait until they got further out?"

"Think about it. Didn't want to take the chance. Too much to explain, what with bullet holes an' all."

The sweep of headlights slashed across the room. An automobile stopped outside the gate. Wolf was instantly at the door. Christian and Maartyn looked at each other. Maartyn covered Lucille with his hand and eased the gun under the table. Christian was tense, rehearsing in his mind an explanation. For what?

The door opened without a knock. Miguel ambled in wearing a big smile.

"Oh, it's just you," breathed Christian.

"Buenos nochos, comrades. And Pietro!" He bent down to stroke Wolf. "Hello, little one."

"This dog's a friend of yours?"

"Pietro's the Village Scoundrel. He's a very good dog but not so loyal. He'll hang around for a few days then find a home with better food."

Maartyn got up to check the door. The car was still idling by the gate. "Wow! A Lincoln. Man, the kid rides in style."

"Are you with Escobar?" asked Christian.

"We just this moment arrived from our trip to Habana." Miguel turned to the door and waved. The car backed away, crunching heavily over the gravel, down the narrow path to the main road. Maartyn limped back to the table and eased himself down. "Did you have something to eat today, Señor Christ?" he asked looking at Maartyn's distorted face.

"Oh yeah, we've been dining on some excellent salt fish provided by Juanita."

"That's good. Juanita's been trying to get rid of that awful fish since I was a little boy. What's the matter with Señor Maartyn?"

"Long story."

"I brought you something." Miguel unrolled a paper serviette to reveal a shrunken wiener in a dried up hot dog bun. "I carried this all the way from Habana because I thought you Gringos needed special food. Señor Escobar took me to a baseball game."

Mustard and salsa had soaked the serviette. Sickly green relish still clung to the wiener in isolated lumps, like barnacles on a log. Miguel placed the treat on the table and arranged the soiled paper. He stood back beaming.

"Ah, Maartyn, would you care to indulge your taste buds in a hot dog that looks like it walked all the way from Yankee Stadium?"

"Right now I'd eat the pig on the run that gave birth to that dawg."

"Shall I carve?" Christian opened the Swiss Army knife.

"Much obliged, Amigo."

"You've decided to take up the lingo."

"Yah, for when I escape to Mexico."

Miguel watched proudly as Christian sawed the hot dog in two pieces and offered one half to Maartyn. Maartyn carefully stuffed his half between his swollen lips.

"Mawfh, umph."

"You're welcome."

"Phumph youph."

"Thank you, Miguel, it was good of you to think of us, but I'll save mine for later. Not much appetite."

"That's okay, Señor Christ, you probably ate very well at the fiesta and you've had the salt fish. Things are going very well, yes?"

"No, to be perfectly candid. Things aren't going well. We can talk about it in the morning. Do you think you could find coffee?"

"It will give me great pleasure to serve my Gringo friends. But I have news that can't wait until morning. Today, when I was selling my fish I saw two people get off the boat from The Bahamas. One was a very skinny but interesting looking señorita with long hair, straight like sugar cane and the colour of sun dried tobacco and with a very pale complexion. The other was a tall hombre wearing a jacket of leather, white hair, with a handsome face but hiding his eyes behind dark glasses. He looked around as if he was expecting the secret police."

"That would be Paulo. Was the girl wearing black?"

"Yes, she looked very tragic in a black funeral dress with long black stockings you could fish with, that went all the way up, like the prostitutes wear only at night because of the heat of the day. And she had her long hair wrapped together like a rope and she was wearing sunglasses and a black beret like yours."

"Yes. That's Renée."

"The one to whom you sent the wire only yesterday?"

"She was already on her way. Where are they now?"

"I overheard them asking directions. Obviously they do not know the difference between a casino and Los Espiritos, but Señor Christ, they asked the wrong person. The man they spoke to pretends to be a bum on the Malecon but he is a Batistiano who watches all the boats for people who come to join the Revolution. So if they ask more questions and come to Los Espiritos the police will be driving the taxi. The woman is wearing this beret, like the one Ché wears. It is like a sign saying, I'm here to make a revolution."

"Oh, God!...It only gets worse."

"What's up, man?" asked Maartyn. "What about Paulo an' Renée?"

"They're here and they've already attracted the police."

"Y'all gonna eat that?"

"No."

"Give."

Christian pushed the hot dog across the table. "How will they travel?"

"Depends. If they go to a hotel and ask the desk clerk, he'll ask them if they have enough money to hire a taxi. The taxi will belong to a friend of course. If not they can take the bus and it will bring them on the Central Highway to Pinar del Rio and from there they can get a taxi or they can take a ride with a farm truck, or they could walk, but it is a long ways."

"I know."

"Yes, Señor Christ, but you did it for the experience and to enjoy the peace of the country. Your friends do not look like they would enjoy walking even from your villa to the beach."

"You're a perceptive little bugger."

"Thank you."

"Any idea which hotel?"

"The Batista bum advised them to go to El Nacional, that's so the police can watch them or kidnap them in their sleep."

"This isn't happening. The whole thing's a dream. I'm going to wake up in the hospital in Chicago with the shakes..."

"Is that all he brought to eat? One lousy hot dog?" interrupted Maartyn.

"It's the thought that counts."

"I have to go now, Señor Christ. My mother likes me to get to bed early after a day in Habana."

"Yeah," Christian said in English. "I guess running dope or whatever, would tire out a wee lad." Then he spoke in Spanish, "When do you think Paulo and Renée will get here?"

"Depends on many things. The man, Paulo, was holding her arm when they walked away from the Batista bum. Maybe they'll linger in old Habana and see the sights as lovers do. Sorry we couldn't give them a ride, Señor Christ, but to approach them would be to give myself away and I must be very careful not to be anything but a poor fish monger, and at that time I had no fish, having just finished my business and was about to get a bus to go and meet with Señor Escobar and take in the baseball game. The Habana Stars beat a team of professionals from America. Although the Americans were only minor league players and two big time players in Cuba for the winter baseball to recover from injuries. It was a good game though. Fidel's a baseball player, did you know that? A pitcher. I wonder if he'd rather be playing baseball than fighting in the Sierra Maestra making Señor Batista very nervous? Well, good night, Señor Christ. I'll come as early as I can. I have some other news...Bye, Pietro. Be a good dog."

Miguel was out the door after saying goodbye to Wolf, or Pietro. Christian, left to contemplate the news, dissolved into a deeper mental sink hole. What did Miguel mean by lovers? And what other news?

December 20th. *There's only one reason why I got up this morning; It's morning. Yesterday was bad enough; the man under water, Maartyn's beating, the mysteries that just keep happening, not to mention the news about the revolution. Paulo and Renée. Things are getting a little tense around here...and on top of that, Maartyn has taken over my bed!...*

The morning sunshine didn't have it's usual intensity. Christian was in a blue funk and hadn't slept. Eyes were open when Miguel arrived and he listened to morning sounds from the pantry. Christian occupied the American couch. It was comfortable enough, except for certain springs, and he should have slept. Reasoned that Maartyn's dislike of the American couch had more to do with mobility than discomfort. Maartyn threw himself off the couch regularly during violent dreams. Maartyn's problem. Sounds became breakfast smells. Miguel was heating up coffee. Then the familiar hiss stopped. Miguel uttered a soft oath...

"Señor Christ?...You awake?"

"Forever."

"I'm afraid the gas has run out."

"Why am I not shocked?"

"I could go down to the gas place and exchange this worthless bottle that gives out at the worst time."

"No money."

"I could ask Juanita for credit. She owns the gas bottles too."

"Don't want credit. Is the coffee at least warm?"

"Yes, it's warm, but that's all you can say about it. I boiled it at home, as usual, and it was still hot but it cooled off while I boiled your egg and fried the bread."

Christian rolled off the couch and sat at the end of the table, bare arms hugging his slender frame. It was cooler during the night and he had only the Levi jacket for a cover. The jacket had slipped to the floor. The rounded depression and bunched configuration of the faded, tattered jacket said that a small animal had slept comfortably. "The little bugger, probably pulled it off me. Where's Wolf?"

"Pietro? Out hunting lizards or cockroaches for breakfast. Maybe he'll bring some home to his new master."

"That would be a swell treat. By the way, why do you call the dog Pietro? That's an Italian name."

"Señor Bartuchi named the little bandito. He said Pietro was a special breed of rat dog from some place called Sicily. It seems our little one has special talents that certain families need for protection. I didn't understand everything Señor Bartuchi told me about his family in Sicily but it must be a very big family if they have their own breed of dog."

"Ah, yeah, very big. It's like having your own wine. Or army. Is Maartyn awake?"

"No, Señor. I could hear him still breathing badly when I came in. But now he sleeps peacefully like a baby. You need blankets and the fire wood I mentioned. It will be colder after the Christmas festivals."

"Situation the same, only worse. I may freeze to death in subtropical Cuba before I die of malnutrition."

"Never mind, Señor Christ, eat some fried bread with the egg, and think that later we will go to Señor Escobar's and there will be many good Yankee things to eat."

"You sure about that?"

"Oh, yes. Señor Escobar loves to be the host and I know some things arrived on the boat, the one you don't want to know about, things that you are very familiar with and will find quite amusing."

"Are you playing with my head?"

"I don't think so. Is your head a baseball? I have a baseball and a glove. Maybe we could play catch later or get a game on the beach with my friend Jésus and the others."

"Wonderful. I can be your Big Brother and take you all to the zoo," he said sarcastically. "Maybe feed you to the lions."

Miguel put the plate of fried corn bread and a hardboiled egg on the table. Christian regarded the oil soaked corn bread with revulsion. His stomach was giving him mixed signals. He cracked the tough brown egg shell on the table. Miguel put down the coffee mug and stood in silence watching Christian lift the broken shell fragments away from the rubbery egg white. Christian's stomach rolled all the way over. The coagulated albumin looked too much like the cheesy, milk-white face of the dead engineer standing on the bottom of Paradise Cove. Christian dropped the egg. It bounced and wobbled across the table and a came to rest against the base of the dead oil lamp.

Miguel retreated to the pantry. "Is something wrong, Señor Christ?"

"Just about everything."

"You should eat."

"You talk like my mother."

"Your mother's Spanish?"

"Yeah, she was Columbus' housekeeper. That's how I got named Christopher. I didn't like the way the Americans kept insisting that Columbus discovered America so I changed it to Christian, they were martyrs in the old days."

"Then you are the bastard son of a great man, if you will excuse my meaning."

"He wasn't that great."

"But Columbus discovered Cuba."

"Columbus didn't discover anything. He bumped into Cuba trying to get to Asia to make a fast buck by stealing other people's gold."

"You mean he wasn't the Great Navigator?"

"Nope. Basque fishermen told him how to get here. They all thought it was Asia. The Spanish were really pissed when there wasn't gold lying on the beaches. They hadn't invented casinos yet. For amusement they slaughtered the natives."

Miguel sidled from the pantry and stood balanced on one foot, swinging the other in wide arcs across the tilled floor. "Señor Christ is in a very bad mood this morning."

"When you stand like that you want something."

"Ah, I have a message...my mother asked me to ask you when you could pay for the bread and the coffee?"

"Now it's official, everything's wrong,"

Christian sipped the tepid coffee. It's acid strength matched his mood so he hardly noticed. With the pencil he sketched a face on the peeled egg. Scruffy hair. Wide, comic mouth with moustache. Odd teeth blacked out. Large nose. Eyes wide in surprise at being dead, shot while tending his beloved engine. He remembered another feature of the standing corpse; the arms outstretched, floating, so that the figure looked like a dancer, bobbing to the rhythm of the tide, or a crucifixion candidate waiting for the heavy wooden cross to arrive. Christian wrote in his journal, speaking the words aloud. *"The guy was probably thrown against the engine by the force of the bullets and died that way, arms out to break his fall or holding on to the engine. Hot metal, inside and out, was his last sensation, and throbbing of the engine his last sensation as his own life forces ebbed away. Maybe he jumped around in agony, flinging his arms out because he was pissed off about being shot and bleeding all over his engine. Maartyn said the engine room was covered in blood..."*

"What did you say, Señor Christ?"

"Nothing. Talking to myself."

"That's not a good thing."

Wolf wandered in from the terrace looking for the source of the new smell. Christian scooped the Levi jacket from the floor. Wolf pretended to know nothing about the jacket and sat down beside the table. The nose twitched and the intelligent eyes stared at the plate. Christian put the plate on the floor. Wolf sniffed the oil soaked bread and headed back out to the terrace to continue his hunt for bugs. Christian shrugged and put the plate back on the table. "Maartyn'll eat it."

"Maybe you need to go for a swim, Señor."

"That's the last thing this down child needs." He looked at his house boy. "Miguel, come here." Miguel stood before Christian like a schoolboy. "Sit down. I need some answers." Miguel sat on the bench looking out the terrace door, watching Wolf sorting through the shards of the broken wine bottle for cockroaches. "The other night, during the fiesta, or maybe later, did you happen to notice some strange men around Juanita's, dressed too well, with hair slicked down, wearing black leather shoes, like cowboy boots?"

"Cowboy? Like in the western movies?"

"Well, sort of, but black, low cut, dress up boots."

Miguel just stared ahead, no longer watching Wolf. He was silent for a few moments. They could hear Maartyn breathing. "Yes, Señor. This has something to do with Señor Maartyn, I'm afraid."

"And I think you know."

"I begged you not to ask."

"Miguel, there's things going on here."

"What could be so bad?"

"There's illegal stuff happening."

"If it's bad, why would you want to know?"

"Is it about to get worse?"

"Well, Señor, I can tell you about those men, but that's all."

"That's not all, but it's a start."

"The men who beat up Señor Maartyn are Batista police."

"Police!? Jesus, it's worse than I thought. Why would they do that?"

"To explain that I would have to tell you everything."

"Try just explaining why Maartyn got beat up. The police weren't just out to rob him, were they?"

"No, Señor..." Miguel looked very uncomfortable. "You want to know where Pietro came from?"

"Wolf? No. About the police. Why would they attack Maartyn?"

"Pietro first. You see, two years ago, about the time the University was closed, the students were calling for Batista's resignation. They were in hiding. Some here. That's when Pietro came to our village."

"Miguel, damnit! I don't care about the dog."

"Pietro came with the police."

"What? Wolf?"

"They were looking for Rosameralda and her fiancé. One policeman had this dog, but he treated Pietro very badly and the dog escaped and waited under Juanita's until he went away. Rosameralda and her fiancé hid in the caves up in the hills. There are some very big caves with lots of places to hide. No one can find them, even I could not find them. But Pietro could find them and that's why the police want him back. He's a famous police dog, decorated by Batista for finding a bomb in the palace. A bomb that Rosameralda made. They also followed Rosameralda here the night of Grandfather Jocinto's burial. Rosameralda must have seen them in the crowd and that's why they left so suddenly. Rosameralda and Esameralda were very sorry that they did not get a chance to meet you."

"Really? You're not just saying that?"

"No, Señor, they told me on the way back to Habana, how disappointed they were that you did not ask one of them to dance, but they agreed that it was just as well because if the police saw you together then you would become Rosa's accomplice and they would beat you up too. Or kill you."

"Me? Jesus! But what has that got to do with Maartyn?"

"Aha, Maartyn is now an accomplice of the other thing. The thing you don't want to know about. They must have seen Maartyn coming ashore from the boat and they take him for a Cuban."

"That explains why they took his passport."

"Now they know he's a Yankee, but that won't tell them anything unless Señor Maartyn is involved with the law."

Christopher felt the familiar chill. "The American cops are looking for him too. I don't know why, he'd never tell me. I think it's something simple like murder or bank robbery."

"Yes, that would not put him under any suspicion. As long as he was not involved with the military or the socialists, or a mercenary."

"Oh, God. It never ends. Maartyn was in the marines. He got kicked out for bad behavior."

"That's unfortunate, if the Cuban police ask the Americans about him."

"Standard procedure between two friendly governments."

"Batista and the Yankee Imperialists are still family I think, despite the fact that the Americans say they refuse to sell Señor Batista more guns."

"I think you're right."

"Then Señor Maartyn is in great danger. No doubt the police will be back. You see, they watch Los Espiritos because, of certain things."

"It has to do with smuggling. Drugs. Am I right?"

"Señor Christ, I beg you again not to ask. You have not been seen coming off the boat, like Señor Maartyn. You have not been seen with Rosameralda. You have only been seen fishing with the village urchin. You play jazz with a dying man. That's nothing. If you were seen visiting Señor Escobar it could be trouble, but we'll go a way that the police could not suspect."

"Wait. You're saying that if I visit Escobar I'm in danger?"

"It's just a connection."

"Are the police still here in Los Espiritos?"

"It's possible. They come in disguise, but like the hombres that beat up Señor Maartyn, they do something stupid like wear the Habana whorehouse hair oil in a fishing village, sometimes they even wear white suits and black boots. Very stupid those police. And Pietro will know even if they looked and smelled like fishermen."

"Why do they sneak around beating people up?"

"More questions. Okay, it's because they are afraid of us. I can say no more."

"Us? Who's us? The Mafia? This guy, Frank The Butcher Bartuchi? He's Mafia, right?"

"I can tell you honestly that he is Mafia but that is not to say it has anything to do with what you're asking me. Please don't ask any more questions. And don't ask Señor Escobar questions. He just wants to have a nice visit and listen to some music, and perhaps talk about, other things."

"What other things?"

"Nothing. Eat something. Drink good wine. Look at pictures."

"Why don't I believe you?"

"Why should you not?"

"Rosameralda doesn't believe anything you tell her."

"She knows when I am telling a truth."

"Are you sure you're only fourteen?"

"I swear, but I've been corrupted by a brilliant sister who teaches me the ways of revolutions and corrupted by another sister who teaches me the ways of people and religion. When the Revolution triumphs I'm going to be with Fidel and Ché and run the whole of Pinar del Rio for the glory of my people and the Revolution. If I was older I would walk to Oriente Province and join Fidel in the mountains. But my mother needs me."

"The Revolution's involved in this?"

Miguel shrugged. End of interview.

He took his cold coffee to the terrace, passing the saxophone case by the door. It was the first morning since he took up residence in Frank The Butcher's villa that he didn't play in homage to the wind and sun. It meant his spirit was ebbing. It also meant he was vulnerable. The danger would depend on what forces swirled through the dry December air. He had levels of fear and each level demanded some response. Stage fright was vanquished by getting up on stage and blowing tunes. Raw fear, like the shock of coming face to face with a dead man, caused flight. Survival. Fear of failure was not a problem or he would have chosen a different course. Fear of the unknown was handled by avoiding the unknown. Wandering the Caribbean or strolling into a village like Los Espiritos didn't count as facing the unknown because it was known from experience that there was food, a place to sleep and music. Fear of concepts and ideologies simply meant he avoided the twin prongs of the bull that gores intellectuals. He would not have pursued the Existentialists, if not for Renée. The World According to Lenny Bruce was American Existentialism, but without a name. Sartre came with the love making. Fear of love was hidden beneath the mist of the fear of losing, so love was controlled by running the opposite direction. Similar to the reaction to raw fear but more subtle. It was fear of his own weakness that caused Christian real problems. Fear of being weak and vulnerable heaped fear upon fear until there was no resolve. He feared Paulo's arrival for those reasons. The timing was critical. If his visit to Escobar didn't reinforce his resolve then he was at risk. Paulo was the grey-eyed devil of his nightmares, one of the reasons he had run to Cuba, but only one. Renée was another...

"You gonna eat that?"

"What?...Oh, morning, Maartyn."

"Gonna eat that friggin' bread, man?"

"No."

Maartyn sat down at the table beside the window with his back to the wall so that he could cover both doors. Patches of blood made him look like a prize fighter just home from work. The yellows, greens and blacks beginning to blend with his dark complexion. He placed Lucille on the table near his right hand and devoured the fried corn bread.

"Why mess up good egg?"

"Want the egg?"

Maartyn held out his hand. Christian placed the penciled egg in his palm. Maartyn's fingers closed like a machine and transferred the egg to his mouth. "Kaw-hee!" Maartyn demanded.

Miguel brought a mug of cold coffee and placed it on the table near Christian. "It's cold, Boss. Please explain to Señor Maartyn," Miguel said timidly. "I don't want to die because of gas failure."

Maartyn swallowed the dry egg. "Put here." Maartyn pointed to the spot in front of him. Miguel slid the mug carefully across the table. "Bring more food." Maartyn took a gulp of cold coffee to wash down the egg.

Christian chuckled despite his mood. Maartyn reminded him of the giant in the story of Jack and the Beanstalk. Miguel brought the rest of the fried bread and the other egg. Maartyn cracked and peeled the egg and stuffed it whole into his mouth, some falling on the table and the floor. He held the corn bread in his other hand, ready to load.

Miguel took away the empty plates. "I should have put it on the floor. Señor Maartyn would make a better dog than Pietro."

"You'd better watch your mouth, he's learning the language," Christian said. Maartyn just being Maartyn made him feel better.

"Talkin' about me?" The corn bread disappeared.

Christian watched the food being processed. "I thought you swore off corn bread?"

"Y'all can beat me to death...but you ain't gonna starve me too."

"I'm glad it didn't spoil your good humour."

"I'll humour ya with a good pistol whippin'."

"That would make my day." Christian motioned for Miguel. "Miguel, I have to ask you another question."

Miguel shuffled back to the table. "I hope it is not one of those questions."

"We've already touched on the subject."

"What subject is that, Señor Christ?"

"The reason Maartyn was asked to fix the boat. The engineer?"

"We didn't discuss that man other than to say he was not on the boat because he was injured."

"He was injured severely, wouldn't you say?"

"Yes, he suffered badly," said Miguel, hedging.

"He suffered enough to be dumped over the side when the boat left."

"You know about that?" asked Miguel, alarmed. "You've been asking questions, Señor?"

"No, no. I bumped into him, you might say, out by the reef. Maartyn saw the body on the boat packed in ice."

Miguel seemed deflated. "Please don't say anything."

"It doesn't make sense. They preserve him, then throw him overboard for the sharks. These men are ruthless and desperate."

"No...it was necessary," sighed Miguel. "We'll bring our comrade ashore and give him a decent burial, when the time's right. But Señor, I must beg you to say nothing. If the police find out they'll connect it to the boat. And you're right, Señor, it's not as simple as drugs."

"I wish it were."

"I'll tell you one more thing, since you have probably already guessed. Juanita pays off the police so that they'll think it's as simple as running drugs. That's why the police did not kill Señor Maartyn. If they find out he's more than a simple Gringo Mafia gangster there could be real trouble, for all of us."

"He *is* just a simple gangster, I mean, he's not even a gangster. Just a crook or a murderer."

"But he's also disgraced military. It's one of the things Batista fears. He can deal with hot-headed Cuban students but he fears foreign mercenaries above all. Especially former marines."

"This explanation is supposed to clear my mind?"

"I'm sorry, Señor Christ, it's the best I can do. We should go soon for your date with Señor Escobar."

"It's not a date!"

"As you wish."

"We're not due at Escobar's until three o'clock. His place is less than a mile away...Oh, I get it. We're not going directly."

"No. Today we go fishing on the reef, as usual."

"I'm not fishing for that body, Miguel!"

It was a familiar routine. Down to the beach in the morning when Christian was finally ready. The smelly bait that Miguel caged from the fish buying house. The sun hot because they never made it to the beach to fish at sunrise. Go for a swim before rowing out, although Christian had reasons to avoid the deeper water.

That morning Wolf was on the foredeck, testing the air like a direction finder. They rowed straight for the reef, sitting side by side. The village idlers on the steps in front of Juanita's speculating that the skinny Gringo would be drowned if he caught a real fish. Or that a clear air squall would blow him away. It would be a shame to lose the dog. Other topics, such as the cock fights and the lottery, would need careful dissecting. The chances on the lottery not good. The Havana lotteries were crooked, since no one in the province ever won the big one. But if they did win, the casinos, the women and the booze would take a terrible beating. So by the time the lottery had been spent the skiff was gone from the eyes of even the policeman disguised as a travelling salesman chatting up the fishermen.

Christian began to get the warning chills. Hair bumps rose on his arms, a sure sign. He expected the body to pop to the surface. Even Wolf was alert, expectant, remembering Christian's panic when he surfaced.

"Put a line over, Señor Christ."

"No. I told you."

"It's only for show, in case they are watching with the binoculars. We'll pretend to try our luck here and then over there." Miguel pointed toward the headland that formed the southwestern arm of the cove. "I hope you aren't too hungry."

"No. I'm fine," Christian lied.

They moved to within a few yards of the shore, Miguel rowing slowly along the headland. Christian lounged in the stern watching the sea birds and the easy waves rolling into the rocks, Wolf asleep on the bow, rocking with the easy motion, the high blue sky with humidity cloud building over the tobacco fields inland. Seaward the sky was ultramarine blue falling off to indigo of the Gulf outside the reef. Air soft and tropical between winter depressions. It should have been a pleasant boat ride.

"Hungry now, Señor Christ?"

"No. I'm used to it."

"Señor Christ is off the bad drugs?"

"I hope so."

"Los Espiritos is a good place for you, no?"

"You know, Miguel, this would be perfect if it wasn't that just about everything is completely screwed up."

"I'm sorry that things have become difficult."

"Figures. Every time I find a place like Los Espiritos, some jerk has to spoil it."

"Are you referring to your friend Maartyn?"

"No, no. I invited him. It's not his fault. I mean, he's just an animal of instinct. Maartyn does what Maartyn does. Doesn't even think about it. Problem, *bam*, straight ahead. Wall, punch through or over the top. Never questions the damage. Never counts his casualties. That's Hemingway talk."

"Who is this Señor Hemingway?

"Just another Gringo writer. If I tried to explain Hemingway to Maartyn he'd probably take me outside and thump me just to show me what a real casualty is."

Miguel laughed. "You like Señor Maartyn?"

"I guess. It's not easy. But he's uncomplicated. And I'd rather have him at my back in a bar fight than the charming Mr. Paulo, who, unfortunately, you'll get to meet."

"And you're not looking forward to this Paulo?"

"Not really. He's one trouble I do understand."

'What about the woman? She's your lover?"

"You know, I don't really know."

"Love is a problem for you?"

"Listen, you're just a kid, right? Back home kids your age are still playing war games with toy soldiers. You're part of this revolution, somehow...and I won't ask how. I think you also have an opinion about women. I mean, and no disrespect, your sister Esameralda is a prostitute; a common whore so to speak, and to accept that your family has to understand certain realities."

"Since I was a child I have understood certain *things*. Esameralda learned to fuck for money very young. At first it was just with the local boys for candy. But she protected Rosameralda and wouldn't let her do it. Rosameralda and Esameralda would go into the hills or to the caves to play and I would bring the boys. Sometimes young men, the married ones whose wives had babies. When my father found out he made us go to work in Pinar del Rio. I was seven, she was fifteen. We got a ride on trucks or walked so as to be there for festivals and when the farmers came to town for market. I made friends with the desperate hombres and took them to Esameralda and collected the money and watched to make sure the desperate ones didn't hurt her. Some of them were like animals, worse than Señor Maartyn was with Juanita, and I also mean no disrespect, but he would use a whore badly and leave her suffering, not because he's bad, but because it's just his nature."

"Yep, I was right. You've got this figured out. Okay, then tell me. Renée's beautiful, even if you think she's too pale and tragic...she's intelligent and sophisticated when she drops her Bohemian persona, and rich and very hungry. We're, were, lovers. You know what I mean?"

"I know what you mean."

"I should be in love with her, right?"

"Esa says you don't love just because it seems right. You love because you love in the heart."

"Right. Then I see your sisters, who I know nothing about other than what you have told me. I see these creatures, and, at first, I don't know who is the bomb maker or who is the prostitute. Rosameralda's devastatingly beautiful. A man could die for her."

"That is possible, with Rosa, Señor. But there's also Esameralda. She is more tragic and more passionate but also more woman. You just don't see her for Rosameralda. Between the two, you would chose Esameralda."

"But that's my point. Rosameralda's beautiful. But I've never talked to her. So how could I know what I've never had; never close, touched. Or tasted."

"A true mystery."

"It's a mystery all right. So can you answer the question?"

"I did."

"What's the answer?"

"It's a mystery."

"That's not an answer, that's the problem."

"No, Esa says, you accept the mystery. If you question the mystery you spoil it. When I was a child I loved to be afraid of the caves where we played and I could only go in a little ways. Once I stopped being afraid, the caves were not as much fun. And then we went there only for business and it was nothing. Juanita also uses the caves, but that's another mystery. It's why the priest says, when someone questions the mysteries of God, 'Do not question Him or you will be cast into ever-lasting ignorance and burn in hell'."

"You believe that stuff?"

"Of course not. Esa says, you can't be ignorant if you discover the truth, but it's easier to accept mysteries than to question them, espe-cially if it is harmless and will not change the way heaven works. If you love Rosameralda or Esameralda or your Renée, you love one or all of them, and all the questions you could ask or I could answer, would not make it so. Rosa is the shinning sun of morning that blinds you."

"Is that why I don't see Esameralda as clearly?"

"You will. It's like trying to look through a candle to see the moon."

"Heavy."

They glided in silence, the old skiff framed against the headland rocks, but invisible to the village. The haphazard paint job as good as camou-flage. It was mid afternoon when the bow of the skiff touched the rocky beach below Escobar's grand villa. It reminded Christian of a fortress. An attack from the beach would be bloody. Christian pre-pared to face whatever new reality waited. Why did he feel like a lamb being led to the slaughter by a fourteen year old shepherd?

The location of Escobar's villa wasn't chosen for the beach, which was narrow, with a fore shore strewn with rocks. The place where the flotsam collects in mounds and windrows. The history of itinerant ships and local fishing boats coasting between the Yucatan Peninsula and the Western Cuba.

"There's your winter wood supply, Señor Christ."

Christian eyed the tangle of driftwood, fishing nets and oil drums. He didn't see the comforting warmth from a crackling fire, only the work required to move even the small pieces. "Great. A memory of my youth. The family went camping in the mountains once. It rained, endlessly. We spent half the weekend burning wet wood. My sister had asthma and we had to rush her to a hospital, and I got a poison ivy rash on my balls."

"That's okay, Señor Christ, you'll think better of this place when you are shivering in your villa and the winter winds blow through your broken shutters."

"This's subtropical Cuba. How cold can it get?"

There was no entrance to the villa from the beach. They scrambled over rocks and through underbrush to the main entrance off the narrow gravel road.

Escobar greeted Christian in the grand main entrance dressed in a silk bathrobe with straw slippers on his feet. Thin bare legs, white and hairless. The design of the bathrobe was oriental, Japanese that reminded Christian of a Monet painting; a kimonoed-figure with a fan, dominant reds and blues in support. In one hand he held his walking stick, the other was poised with a Cuban cigar. If Maartyn was here he'd compare the cigar to a horse's dick. Great start, Christian said to himself.

"Good afternoon, Christian. Welcome to Buena Vista de Gulfo." Escobar looked older, with less veneer, so his features were more natural. Hatless. Thin grey hair slicked back, as if he had just stepped out of a bath, curling at the ends. Moustache trimmed too fine. Those watery blue eyes absorbing, probing Christian's young body. The Escobars were white, but not pure Spanish white, mixed European perhaps. He wasn't there to compare ethnic backgrounds.

The villa was bigger than he imagined. The wide veranda itself was larger than Christian's villa, but he wasn't there to compare villa's either. Beyond the dark entrance, tiled with grey-blue marble, was a large courtyard surrounded by pillars and arches. The courtyard itself divided into gardens, stone paths and reflecting pools, could have contained the entire burial fiesta with room left over for muggings and beatings in the shadows of ornamental citrus trees and classic statuary. "I said, welcome to my villa..."

"Ah, yes. Thank you." Christian was relieved that Escobar didn't offer his hand.

"Miguel...amuse yourself in the kitchen while I give our guest the grand tour."

"Yes, Señor Escobar."

It was an order. Miguel disappeared into an annex; a room very different from the rest of the villa. Christian felt panic lurking behind his own applied veneer. He had been hoping to escape to the neutral ground of the bright courtyard but Escobar blocked the way.

"You must be thirsty after your long journey. Wine?" He indicated a silver tray on a Japanned table and put his walking stick into a Chinese porcelain stand. He poured dark red wine into heavy blue goblets, the colour of the Gulf Stream.

"Thank you," said Christian dryly.

"Do you like Port? Best Portuguese."

Port, a heavy choice for a warm afternoon, he thought. Escobar wanted to get him drunk quickly. The black-cloaked character on the label looked menacing.

"Let's begin shall we." Escobar carried the wine bottle in his left hand. The goblet and the cigar in the right. At least his hands are full, thought Christian. "Like the goblets? Mexican sodalite. Very rare in the south. Mined in the Yucatan and refined in Spain. Blown especially for me in Toledo. The wine is Sandeman's '48. Sent by our family agent in Oporto."

"Very nice, impressive."

"Drink up, son."

Christian sipped on command. "Very good. Strong."

"A bit heavy for the climate but if one waited for the right conditions one would never enjoy excellent Port in Cuba."

They passed through an arch into a long gallery with windows open to the courtyard. Typical Spanish architecture with high plastered ceilings and heavy timbers. Christian noticed several beds against the walls; hospital beds, with white sheets draped over them. Coloured light splashed over the white sheets from the narrow windows, like gun slits. Glazed with leaded glass in reds and blues and earth tones, like Escobar's bathrobe. The motifs religious; saints and monks and bishops with tortured, elongated bodies in perpetual agony. On closer inspection Christian was dismayed to see that the figures were engaged in contorted sex. Escobar pointed to a window with the cigar. "Like this one? Commissioned. The Spanish master, Eduardo de Flores? A very tragic man. It's interesting, this one, most poignant. The artist rejected by his lover, the Archbishop. It's a prediction of Flores' own death and Assumption into heaven. He committed suicide before the Archbishop could have him hanged for revealing their *special* relationship."

Christian felt a flush of embarrassment as he viewed the naked Flores slipping skyward, eluding the grasp of the Archbishop. "I thought suicide was a mortal sin."

"Of course it is. For some. You're wondering about the contradiction of suicide and heaven. Art transcends the silly rules that apply to mere mortals. God accepts certain weaknesses in his glorifiers. Rewards must be commensurate with achievements."

"Not very democratic."

"Ha! God before democracy, Christian. The means to maintain control of the misguided peasantry is not the same thing as the transcendental nature of pure art. Art is glory above the mire. The ends and the means?"

"Then why is it artists always live in garrets and die of some horrible disease?" he asked, hoping to move the subject to safer ground.

"Ah, the artist is not important. All part of the grand plan. You would not admire an artist who was rich and successful in his own time. The rich must feel superior to the petty bourgeoisie; especially destitute artists, by being able to acquire them at inflated prices. Would you, if you were the Sultan of Arabia, want to sit down at a table with the artist who adorned your sumptuous palace? Of course not. You would want your rich friends to envy you your expensive acquisitions. Have you ever heard anyone brag how cheaply they acquired a work of art by a master? For his part, the poor living artist himself would care nothing about the art, only the amount of food and wine he could consume."

"Some artists were successful in their own time, like Rembrandt..."

"Yes, the great illustrator, and he died fat and miserable and alone. It's much more appealing to know that one's artistic gods died emaciated and penniless of some common brothel disease."

"I don't know. Seems to me artists deserve better," said Christian in self defense.

"Nonsense! If artists want better they should become directors of international companies. Eat extravagant French food and die of heart attacks while fornicating their concubines. No, great artists should simply starve to death, brush in hand. You are an artist, you should understand the necessary hunger."

"I wouldn't call it that."

"Don't belittle your art. Did you choose jazz to become fabulously wealthy?"

"Not a chance."

"Then you chose poverty and anonymity."

"I don't recall *choosing*."

"But you did, subconsciously, because, in reality, no one chooses anything freely. Now look here..." Escobar directed Christian to a small painting in a flaking gilt frame. The frame too ornate for it's size. "What do you see?"

"Ah, not much. Grey sky, clouds. Dark trees, black, maybe green." Unimpressive to say the least, thought Christian. The small lake or river in the foreground looked flat, uninteresting. A poor reflection of a row of Lombardy poplars. A deformed boat on the shore.

"Very European, isn't it? The sky in particular. You never see a sky like that in Cuba. Too drab. Lifeless. But that obscure little painting is worth this villa."

"Really?"

"Delacroix. From his time as an art student with Guérin. It's not very good. I doubt anyone even knows it exists."

"Then why is it so valuable?"

"You tell me, Christian. What's the value of art?"

"The name, I guess."

"Perhaps. There is great appeal in owning a name. But if I hadn't drawn your gaze to the little piece would you have known to value it? No. But look..." Escobar poked the small masterpiece deliberately. His sharp fingernail penetrated the canvas as if it were tissue paper. "The humidity rots the linen canvas. Tragic. But I have more." Escobar shuffled along the gallery. "This one down here, however..." Escobar steered Christian with the wine bottle to a much larger painting. "What do you see?"

"Bigger. More colour. Sunshine." Large field with red poppies. Two women with umbrellas and two kids playing. Big sky with bright, puffy clouds. Optimistic but not exciting.

"Did you study art history in school?"

"Some."

"Without looking at the name, could you tell me who painted this picture?"

"Ah, probably Impressionist...Monet's style, I'd say."

"Certainly looks like Monet. But the artist is Giuseppe De Nittis." He pointed to the name in the lower right corner. "Italian. Died young of a stroke. Contemporary of Monet and that Impressionist gang. As good as Monet? Perhaps. But it has no value, other than I love this painting. Bright, breezy colours. Could be Northern Spain or Italy as well as France. However, it was painted outside London. What does that say?"

"To me? Nothing."

"Exactly. If Monet had painted it, the piece would be worth ten times more. What's in a name? Who has ever heard of De Nittis?"

"Beats me."

"The De Nittis is a forgery, but sadly will rot away like the Delacroix. I keep it to remind me of certain realities. I wanted to be famous. Not as a painter or even a doctor. I studied Churchill and Hitler, but, alas, the world was not in need my theories in post war Europe. More wine?" Escobar refilled Christian's goblet. "Now, drink

119

up...come along. Here..."

Christian was face to face with a piece very familiar.

"Stand back and look carefully. What do you see?"

"A van Gogh! Anybody would recognize that...but?"

"But what do you see?"

"A guy walking through a purple field." Christian recognized *The Sower*. The gaudy sun coming up. Black birds. Rich texture and heavy brush strokes.

"A work of art?"

"I guess, if you like van Gogh."

"What if I said that isn't van Gogh's 'Sower' but is a Cuban farmer planting his tobacco field? And what if that was a sunrise over the tobacco fields of Pinar del Rio? Is that not a palm tree to the left of a Spanish house like your villa?"

"Could be..."

"Another forgery. Now, through here..."

Christian followed Escobar into the next gallery. A dinning room, with a long table set with dusty linens and plates and upturned glasses. A flash of Miss Havisham and the eternal wedding banquet, never consummated. And more linen draped hospital beds lining the walls. The walls themselves were filled with Impressionist Era paintings.

"Jeeesus!..." Christian whispered reverently.

"Impressive?"

"I'll say!..."

"Renoir! Gauguin! Cézanne! Caillebotte! Degas!" The whole gang. Their biggest, brightest, splashiest works. Big skies and rolling waves and sun splashed meadows. Women in dappled sunlight. Women in long flowing dresses drenched in sunlight. Gardens in riot. Poppies smeared across green and yellow fields. "I have more. This way."

They strolled from gallery to gallery. Every room was filled with paintings. And more shrouded hospital beds. Christian was becoming fuzzy-headed with the strong wine, and the swirling colours.

"Like my little collection?"

"These are in museums."

"True. This indulgence has cost me a great deal. All fakes, of course. But what of it? I'm happy to surround myself with beauty and who cares if they are real or not? My family in Spain keep a collection of very good originals. Worth a great deal. But here I have all the paintings I like and I don't mind them being, not exactly what they seem? They serve their purpose. Understand me?"

"I think so."

"European paintings cannot live in a climate like Cuba. Hot and humid, the salt air blowing in constantly, the risk from hurricanes. I commissioned all my favourite paintings done with this new paint on a plastic board...?"

"I've heard of it."

"So, I'm misrepresenting the art treasures of the world. What a vulgar thing to do. Are you ashamed of me? Drink up, my boy."

"Ah, no...I mean. If you admit to, ah..."

"Faking it? Yes, in many ways. Actually, few get to see these paintings. I wander the halls, night after night, with candles when the electricity is out, gazing at my beauties. We're all living a fantasy."

Christian was feeling light headed. Nauseated. "Señor Escobar, could I have some water?"

"Oh, yes, how rude of me. A few more. I keep the very best in my chambers; the nudes. Reuben. Renoir. Van Eck, so I can fondle them before I go to sleep, so to speak. My bedroom is just beyond that door."

"Truth is, the wine's strong?"

"Of course," he said, apologetically. "I've laid out some things. This way." Escobar guided Christian through a door to the annex. He stepped into a bright, modern kitchen that could serve a small hotel.

Miguel was sitting on a high stool at a preparation counter, mouth covered with chocolate. He grinned at Christian like the sad clown.

"I seldom eat, and since I no longer entertain I keep very little in the way of food, but twice a month I get a delivery, ah, from a source. Here, please, help yourself."

Christian blanched. On the serving counter was a row of serving trays. Each tray was piled high with a selection of American snack food in clear cellophane wrappers with gaudy graphics. The mainstay of American school lunches.

"Since you would already have had lunch before you left your villa I thought you might like a diversion. All boys like snacks. Take some for your friend Maartyn as well. I am sorry that I cannot offer you milk, or a cold soft drink, but since we cannot depend on the electricity I stopped operating the refrigerators. Look here."

Escobar opened a heavy wooden door. Inside was a room about the size of a large bathroom. A dank, musty smell rolled out. "This is the walk-in freezer. I had it shipped from the United States. And here..." Another door and another room of shelves and smells. "This is the cold room. I had it filled for a festival once and the electricity stopped and all the food spoiled! Now there is a generating machine that runs by a diesel engine. It might be useful some day."

"Ah, that's a shame, about the food." Christian picked up the nearest cellophane encapsulated cake; a round, flat chocolate confection called a Moon Pie. "I'll save this for later."

Escobar reverted to Spanish for Miguel's benefit. "Now, Christian, I must tell you another truth. Although I can't tell you everything. It's the reason I asked you here. No doubt you are curious about some things, Miguel tells me."

"Well, I think I have the right."

"Of course, my boy. You have every right. But it's my duty to warn you not to snoop."

"I haven't been! Things just keep happening."

"You arrived uninvited, and Miguel befriended you. He should have known better, but, well, the truth is, Miguel suffers from a weakness that sometimes clouds his judgment. He took a special interest in you."

Christian looked at Miguel. The grin had disappeared and the chocolate outlined mouth looked pathetic. "I know what you're saying, Señor Escobar, but Miguel's been..."

"Christian, that's only a complication. You were allowed to remain in Los Espiritos when others would have been shown the road. Once established we had to accept your presence in the hope that you would tire of our dull little village. We didn't realize you were fluent in Spanish or could pick up the Cuban dialect so quickly. For one reason or another, and I blame Juanita, who is also a very weak person, for encouraging you and your guest to stay."

"But, I don't see what..."

"What this has to do with your life or death?"

"Life or death?"

Escobar was calm, almost cold in his delivery. "I asked you here, not for gratuitous sex, as you so obviously assumed, although I admit my preferences for the male of our species, but my desires run to more interesting partners with experience and culture. You are neither experienced nor are you schooled in the arts sufficiently to amuse me. Even though you are young and musically talented, breakfast would be a dull affair. And there's the drugs."

"How'd you know about that?"

"Juanita has indulged in every form of debauchery known to mankind. Even Miguel knows the signs. He could get you all the illicit drugs you could imagine in Habana, but his love for you makes him pathetically protective."

"Jesus Christ," Christian whispered hoarsely.

"You think you know the dark secrets of Los Espiritos, but you're ignorant of more than you know. I would like to keep you that way, for our sake. Unfortunately, I also hear you've been exposed to our lovely girls, Rosameralda and Esameralda. Another potentially tragic mistake made by my little collaborator who should be taken outside and horsewhipped."

Miguel's eyes went wide. "But, Señor Escobar, I was only thinking that Rosameralda or Esameralda..."

"Silence, Miguel!"

Christian felt tapped. The room swimming when he stood up. "Excuse me, I'd like to go."

"No. You're here to be educated. Sit." Christian sat down obediently. "You may have wondered why Miguel took you on such a circuitous route to my villa."

"He explained about the police."

"The bumbling police are a reality. If they connect you to me in a certain way you'll be eliminated like a tobacco slug. They cannot touch me yet because of my connections. Yes, I do receive a pension from Batista, for past favours, a stipend really. Juanita likes to make me sound like an old eccentric. But my immunity from Batista's paranoia won't exempt me much longer. You are another chink knocked out of my protective wall. I don't blame you. Now, to heap misfortune on misfortune, you have imported more foreigners to become part of your mob."

"I made contact with my girlfriend, because we're broke, although it seems she was already on her way." He felt compelled to tell all truths that mattered.

"These foreigners? Are they coming to take you away?"

"No, I hadn't planned on leaving."

"You must."

"Why? I'm not involved. I'm not on drugs. I don't have anything to do with your smuggling racket, whatever it is?"

Escobar circled the kitchen deep in thought. Christian watched his face. Why the theatrics? "Frank The Butcher Bartuchi. Does that name mean anything to you?"

"He owned the villa."

"Señor Bartuchi and I had a business arrangement in America and I unwisely introduced him to Los Espiritos. He wanted a quiet place, away from the pressure of the casinos, he said. Instead of choosing Cojimar or Varadero to be with his rich American friends, he built the small villa. He wasn't in residence a month before the first boat arrived from Central America. They brought the contraband ashore in broad daylight! This man, this small time gangster from New York, with connections to the casinos in Habana, assumed we were such stupid Latinos that he could run his operation openly. Even had he operated discreetly we would not have allowed him to defile our village with his corruption. At first I tried to reason with Señor Bartuchi. He laughed at me. Said they didn't call him Frank The Butcher for nothing. He was a very bold but stupid man. His stupidity was dangerous for us. We had to take certain, measures." Escobar let the inference wash over his listener.

Christian, spirits sinking, said, "I get the point."

"We also have many friends in America. It wasn't necessary to do anything to our neighbour so as to draw attention. Let's say, he received certain information from home. Family matters. We never saw him again. And his name is seldom mentioned, unless by mothers of difficult children, 'Remember Frank The Butcher', they say."

"Señor Escobar, can I go now?"

"Christian, I like you. You're not Frank Bartuchi. I could teach you many things about life, the arts. My family connections allow me to range over the world, meet the best people. Open doors you could not imagine. As my protégé you would be given all the courtesies and the opportunities young artists like you only dream about. Name an orchestra. Goodman? Ellington? Who do you want to meet? Marilyn? Marlon? Live in Paris? Record in New York?"

"I don't believe you."

"Then you don't believe my warnings either. Very well, I insist you leave Los Espiritos. I will provide the means."

"I can't leave."

"You don't belong here. There's no future. But there's a good chance that if something goes wrong, all this..." Escobar indicated the surroundings and stood gazing at the expensively appointed kitchen as if saying goodbye, "...will become mere fodder in a larger conflict and you'll be only a smudge under the boots of the Batistianos."

"It's more than drugs?"

Escobar turned on Christian, his expression hard and his voice threatening. "Much more than you can imagine."

During the long row back to the village he tried to coax more information out of Miguel. The boy was hurting inside because Escobar had stripped away the thin shroud of his little secret. He couldn't blame Miguel, a fourteen year veteran of the sexual wars. A boy shouldn't have to pimp for his sister to survive.

They fished the reef in silence and caught three pompano in the afternoon shadows. Other than the late hour of their return, there was nothing to arouse suspicion, but many eyes in Los Espiritos followed their movements as they beached the skiff and unloaded their gear. It might have been Christian's increasing paranoia but even Miguel seemed ill at ease. Miguel made a point of explaining to an old man sitting on an over turned boat that the fishing had been slow. The old fisherman waved his cigar and said that there was a change coming. The old fisherman smiled, eying Miguel, then Christian. The old man was right about the change, thought Christian. Their was something over the horizon about to make his life more complicated.

They lounged on the beach watching the sun set over the islands and Christian ate the pompano Miguel cleaned and cooked wrapped in wet palm leaves on a charcoal fire. Wolf ate his fish raw and after checking out the beach and all the boats for dried bait he slept beside Christian, smelling like his discoveries. Miguel ate Moon Pies from the canvas bag Escobar had pressed upon them, along with more warnings. Miguel continued his pouting silence. They parted on the main road; Miguel non committal about arriving the next morning with breakfast. There was the question of money for food. There was also the other questions that Miguel was avoiding. All Christian had to show for the day was a canvas bag of American junk food.

That night Christian occupied the American couch again because Maartyn refused to give up the bed. Wolf insisted on laying beside him. Despite Wolf's distinctive odours Christian stroked the damp fur until the dog went to sleep. Christian's sleepless thoughts wandered through the events of the day. Wolf and Maartyn made night sounds and stunk up the house.

December 21st 1958. *It just gets worse. Bodies. Mysteries. Threats. Warnings. Escobar practically ordered me to leave. He did order me to leave. I'm tempted, and now the weather is turning against me...and I'm slowly starving to death. This morning I saw Miguel in a boat with five other men going out to fish up the dead engineer...*

Christian slept a little before dawn, awoke early and went out to the terrace with his saxophone. The hunger was becoming a problem. He felt weak and confused, but not just from the lack of food. The 'something' over the horizon was the impending arrival of Paulo and Renée and the revelation that Paulo was Renée's newest lover. Miguel could be evasive but he wasn't given to outright lying, was he? But worse, Paulo would bring heroin. Hashish at least. And there was the nagging doubt about Escobar. If only it was as simple as Maartyn's first reaction to Ernesto Escobar, a truth that was confirmed by Escobar himself, but so what? The problem was that the old man lived alone in a sprawling villa that had too many beds.

Christian stood on the terrace, hands in pockets of patched Levis. The saxophone lay in its case beside the wall as Christian tried to fathom Escobar's warnings.

The northern sky was building a large, grey-bottomed cloud bank smeared red by the rising sun. Something else was coming. The atmosphere heavy and bleak, like his mood. The horizon a brooding messenger. Then the morning sun was doused like a snuffed candle by the leading edge of the storm. Christian escaped inside as the first cold drops splattered the dry palmettos. Heavy rain swept in and the temperature plunged. Line squalls tore across the bay in increasing gusts; royal palms bending and rebounding. The harbour driven white with spume ripped from the young wavelets. A small waterspout swung across the bay leaving a shattered mist and confusion. When the squall passed he spotted the large skiff heading out. Four rowers, a man in the stern steering and a smaller figure in the bow. Christian was sure the bow rider was Miguel. It meant no breakfast. What else? They were going out to drag up the body of the engineer.

Christian closed the shutters, tip toeing around in his bare feet. Who was he going to disturb? Maartyn was like the dead. Wolf didn't care. The stone villa was cold and damp and now dark. The rat dog was asleep on the warm spot Christian had left on the American couch. He sat at the table toying with a chunk of salt fish, wishing he had asked Miguel to cook all the fresh fish. At least he would have the taste of cooked pompano instead of the tough flesh of an ancient codfish resurrected from a lead-lined box. The wind increased. The shutters rattled as if a hand was shaking a toy house. He wanted to look out, to watch the big skiff. Instead he opened his journal. But the words, like the music would not come. He dozed, lulled by the drumming rain.

Christian was bored waiting for the hard rain to stop. "Wolf, want to go for a walk?" The rat dog yawned and got more comfortable.

"Man's best friend. A true blue dog should be ready to follow his master through hell or high water."

Wolf looked up at Christian, blinked and tucked his award winning nose under his tail. Christian looked at the dead fireplace, imagining a crackling fire, warm light dancing across the tile floor. "Miguel's right. Miguel's always right. Everybody's always right!" He looked around for something to burn and thought of the bogus guitar. "Wolf, do you know that back home we could get a truck load of firewood for a hundred bucks. Hard maple from the Eastern Townships. Enough to last a whole Canadian winter and all there'd be by April is the ashes." The dog was not impressed. "Every night I had to carry firewood up the stairs from the shed and every morning my old man made me dump the ashes on the snow over the garden, and in the spring I'd dig the stuff in. That's all I ever knew about gardening. He'd say, 'work for your food'. I didn't see food. Just sweat and dirt with all this mucky, grey ash. In a few months there'd be things growing and mom would put a bowl on the table with spinach or carrots and my old man would say, 'behold the fruits of your labour'. I never cared where the food came from, dog. Maybe I should have paid more attention."

The wind pitched higher, driving the rain against the shutters until it was running down the inside walls and across the tiles. Christian shivered. Blankets. Wood. Pesos. Food. Future. He wasn't about to go scratching in the overgrown garden for roots. He wasn't that desperate, yet. He chewed a chunk of salt fish. "Not bad. Want some?"

Wolf roused himself, stretched, and sat waiting for Christian to feed him. "You certainly know how to humiliate a guy. Might as well be your servant."

Christian assessed the low points. Like a bottom feeding fish, he nosed about in the sediment of his brief history, turning over memories. Awkward with girls. A loner. There was the high school prom. The shared a mickey with Howie. The faked high. The clumsy attempt at sex. The fumbling failure, although the girl was willing enough, and the ultimate humiliation. There was some small compensation. His date reacted badly when he pledged respect for her as the reason for his retreat from the game. The Westmount bitch! "Who could blame her, Wolf? She was really very nice, just too mature." He rummaged about the family's values. The family slowly dissolving in bitterness. Music a retreat of another kind. There was the first jazz gig. He froze. It was humiliating, but the leader picked up the solo and Christian dug in hard and learned his trade, but ran from Montreal, falling into the narcotic haze, escaping the boredom of the road until the day he realized he was a junky. He could shake it, he told himself. Not that day, but some day. He spent another year strung out, in a fog of music and drugs of every kind. The day finally arrived in Chicago after the Lenny Bruce concert. Had to break the cycle by running south to the Islands, to cheap booze and warm beaches. He'd been cold in Chicago. He'd been hungry on the run. But he had never been cold, hungry and depressed at the same time. "At least on the junk you don't have time to be depressed, dog, no matter how cold you are." The most important thing was the next hit. "A fix a day keeps the blues doctor away." Now he was cold, hungry and tired. Depression hovering. Waiting. He wished Maartyn would wake up. "Must be bad if I need Maartyn to save me from myself, eh, dog? Hey, Maartyn!"

"What?" from the bedroom.

"You awake?"

"Who talkin' to?"

"You."

"Must be awake then."

"Good."

"Miguel...with breakfast?"

"No. He's gone fishing for the engineer. Want to know what's on the menu?"

"I'll come out an' break...face!"

"You don't know how glad I am to hear your sweet voice."

"Crackin' up. Where you last night?"

"Beach party."

"You dick head!"

"Hum, right."

Maartyn stumbled into the living room pulling on clothing, his own and Christian's. "I'm freezin', man!" His colour and temper had improved. More flesh tones and less yellows. Scabbing over nicely. Nose almost back to normal except for the angle. Maartyn was a healer. Strong and healthy. Interesting, considering how he abuses his body, thought Christian. "Why the Christ so dark in here?" he asked.

"Rain."

"Can plainly hear rain!"

"Wind."

"Hear that too."

"Open the shutters and experience both."

"Okay, get it. What's to eat?"

Christian tossed the canvas bag. "Room service."

"What this?"

"Pony express. I sent a telegram to Wild Bill."

"Yer a regular riot." Maartyn opened the bag and rummaged the contents. The cellophane packages crackled like the flames that should be in the fireplace. He dumped them on the table. "Hot damn! Look at this. Twinkies. Debbies. Moon Pies! Holy shit, the works! Where'd y'all get this stuff?"

"Escobar's idea of a late lunch."

"Off shrimper, man. Those guys must live on Moon Pies an' Wagon Wheels."

"Miguel thrives."

"Coffee!" demanded Maartyn as he ripped open a package with his teeth. The big round cake thing called a Wagon Wheel. He took a big bite. Gooey white filling oozed out and dropped on the grey UCLA sweatshirt.

"Could you watch it..."

"Wash whaph?"

"Skip it. No coffee. Miguel's on strike. Wine?"

"Are you nuts!? You can't drink wine with this stuff?"

"Would it make a difference?"

"Well, yah, I mean, beer's okay. Six pack'a Pearl an' a box'a Twinkies an' go out fishin'. Twinks too fresh. Spread'em out on seat. Nothin' goes down like a Pearl an' a sun dried Twinkie, dig?"

"I take it Pearl's a kind of beer?"

"Cheap an' deadly."

"Did you ever think of eating the fish?"

"No way, man. Sell fish. Buy beer an' Twinks. Got that from dear ol' Mom. About all the ol' lady could get her head around, you know? She wasn't big on cookin' an' things like washin' clothes."

"Pity you."

"Never had to go through all that shit, know what I mean? Like eatin' meals. Clean clothes. Church. Was real lucky that way, man."

"Regular Huck Finn."

"Who he?..."

"Just a kid that hung out on The River."

"Mississippi? Where...know him...from?" Maartyn asked between gigantic bites, opening Twinkies and laying them out, like a chain smoker.

"Ah, a book I read...Mark Twain?"

"Oh. Never heard of 'im. Wagon Wheels. Twinkies, man. Great! Have one." Maartyn tossed a Wagon Wheel across the table.

Christian shook his head. Maybe if he never touched food again he would just dry up and blow down wind, like autumn leaves and dande-lion seeds.

"So, Escobar come on to y'all, or what?"

"No."

"Bull, Chris. Tell."

"He showed me some paintings."

"Paintings? You mean like pictures...an' shit like that?"

"Yes. That's all."

"Try to get ya in bedroom?"

"No! Well, yes, I guess he did, to look at paintings."

"There, see? What I tell ya? An' all ya got for a day's work is a buncha cupcakes?"

"Maartyn, for Christ's sake! I said, nothing happened! I was dying of hunger so he took me to this kitchen that looks like something out of the Ritz Hotel. I couldn't believe it. Then he tells me we have to get out of Los Espiritos."

"He's right. Start packin'."

"And go where?"

"Anywhere, man."

"I'm not walking around Cuba broke and you with no ID. If we get picked up we'll be thrown into some lousy jail and never see the light of day."

"You mean it could be worse than this?" Maartyn waved his hand around the cold, dark room. Pieces of Twinkie flew away. Wolf pounced, sniffed and resumed his place on the American couch. "At least they'd feed us."

"Probably not. If you were just a common criminal, maybe. But they don't treat political prisoners all that well in Cuba. 'Specially Revolutionaries working for Castro."

"No way, man. I know dick all about Cuban politics."

"The police think you do. Check this list. You were spotted coming ashore off a blockade runner. You look Cuban. You have an American passport. You hang out in Juanita's. You're an ex-marine with a crim-inal record and that makes you a mercenary. And, from what I can tell, just being in Los Espiritos makes us both suspects."

"What are you talkin' about, man? Suspect of what?"

"Like Miguel says, you don't want to know, Señor," said Christian with a wry smile.

"Got to be drugs or booze. What the hell else?"

"Guns. There is a revolution going on."

"Maybe. Most of'em just cowboys."

"I wish it was something simple like booze," said Christian.

"Nah. I'd bet drugs," said Maartyn.

"Too obvious. Escobar said they ran Frank the Butcher out of town for bringing drugs in from Central America."

"Christian, you dummy, look at it this way. If you were Escobar, and you were runnin' drugs, would you want some Mafia dude cuttin' your turf?"

"That fishing boat comes in twice a month from a Gulf State, probably Florida. You said so yourself. Who would run drugs from Florida to Cuba?"

"Maybe they sell the shit in the casinos."

"If that was the scam Batista's police would meet the boat at the dock and help unload the stuff into army trucks. If Frank The Butcher Bartuchi was bringing in drugs it was probably to ship directly to the States and cut out Batista. And another thing...Escobar's villa is full of hospital beds."

"Beds? I told ya, man. Naked old men an' little boys running around grabbin' asses an' shit like that."

"Maartyn...Maartyn, pay attention. Hospital beds. With wheels."

"Wheels!? Weird, man, just weird."

A stronger burst of wind slammed the shutters. Rain squirted in. The wind shrieked, then the drumming stopped. The wind sighed off as quickly as it came. Christian opened a shutter on the Gulf side. The storm clouds were low, ragged and disorganized. Soft rain still fell over the village making the dry palms look shiny new. Further west the sun was already making bright pools of blue out on the Gulf. He looked for the skiff. The bay was swept clean. Just waves confused by the sudden lack of wind. Remembering the trick Miguel used to reach Escobar's villa he scanned the shoreline. He knew what he was looking for so wasn't surprised to catch the flash of an oar as the sun broke through, buttering the red rocks and painting the cove a mottled blue and grey. A casual observer might have missed the signs. "The skiff's headed for Escobar's villa." Christian imagined the body wrapped in a shroud. Remembered the cheesy face and bulging eyes. He felt the chill again. "This is not paradise," he said, feeling very vulnerable. Los Espiritos was becoming a dark little sewer of deceit and intrigue. He shivered visibly. "They're almost here."

"Who? The cops? What?"

"Renée and Paulo."

"How know that?"

"I can feel it."

"Can y'all feel the money too?"

Later that afternoon Christian was hauling a load of firewood in the skiff. Wolf stood on the narrow bow, as always, testing the air. Christian beached the boat and began carrying dead branches up the hill. Wolf ran ahead, nose to the ground, excited by a new scent. At the gate to the villa he turned in and shot straight through the open front door. Christian heard the warning snarl, like a short tempered rattlesnake. Then a curse, loud and profane, in French. The next sound was Wolf's yelp of pain.

Christian dropped the load and ran for the gate. The sound of battle increased. A woman screamed. Renée. And over the chaos of Paulo's curses and Wolf's snarls was Maartyn shouting encouragement.

"Get'im, Wolf! Shred'im!" And Maartyn's laughter.

Renée was standing on the American couch screaming at Maartyn. Paulo was backed into a corner by the rat dog, who seemed twice normal size. Tail pointing forward over his back like the deadly end of a scorpion.

"Wolf! Stop! Back off!" Christian commanded in Spanish.

"Get that dog off me!" Paulo yelled. His white hair awry, grey eyes wide with fear. Wolf could smell it. Wolf the savanna lion moving in for the kill.

"Wolf!...back off." Christian was afraid to touch the dog. The snarls became bubbling sounds. Blood foamed from Wolf's nose and mouth and splattered the tile floor. Blood ran down Paulo's leg. The combatants were in a standoff, both wounded, each waiting for the other to move.

"Man, I hope that little bugger's on our side when the commies come," said Maartyn. "Get'im dawg!"

"Maartyn, stop, please," Renée pleaded. "Christian, do something!"

"Hey, Paulo, want my gun?" Maartyn asked, grinning. Maartyn waved Lucille wildly, pointing it at Wolf, then at Paulo. *"Bam! Bam!"*

"Give me gun! I'll teach the little swine..."

"Hey, man, yer wounded! Should put y'all out of yer misery."

"Maartyn! Put the gun away!" said Christian.

"Maartyn!...Christian, please stop them!" Renée was in tears, blonde braid shaking. She looked ridiculous, like a cartoon heroine terrified of the mouse. Wolf was poised to leap and Paulo desperate to escape. Christian only wanted to avoid more bloodshed. What was going on in Wolf's mind? Wolf advanced a step. Renée reverted to screaming. Wolf snarled and coughed up blood.

"Look there, man...blood. Both wounded. Put'em down before the sharks come. Who's first?" He pointed the gun at Paulo.

"You idiot, Maartyn!"

"Maartyn! For Christ's sake...Wolf, back off!"

Renée sobbed. Maartyn laughed insanely.

"Wolf!..."

Wolf reluctantly backed down, turned and walked stiffly out the terrace door. He stopped at the opening to the garden and retched up blood. They could hear him choking in the tangle of weeds. The four people in the house melted into silence, the way survivors of a car crash are left dazed by the violence. Paulo moaned.

"You kicked the dog?"

"Little bastard! Look at my leg..." Paulo undid his pants and dropped them to the floor.

Renée stepped down from the couch and went to Paulo, kneeling to get a better look at the wound. She was still sobbing, so was of limited use as Nurse Jane.

"I'll get water," said Christian. "A lot of bloodshed recently."

"Want me to shoot the dawg before I shoot Paulo...?"

Miguel appeared from the terrace. "Señor Christ? Is something wrong?"

"Miguel do you have iodine? Detol or something?"

Miguel shrugged. "My mother has quinine for fevers. There's leaves in the garden for bleeding. What's happening, Señor Christ? We could hear the noise all the way down the beach."

"Nothing. We were just fooling around."

Miguel eyed Maartyn and the gun and inspected the newcomers. "These are the Gringos I saw in Habana. Why did you try to kill them so soon?"

"No one's being killed!"

"They were at the cantina asking directions. Juanita told them you were out in the boat for fire wood, like I told you, so they said they'd wait here...Juanita's coming."

"Miguel, go and head her off. That's all I need."

"Juanita will be very disappointed. She has been talking about a new one..."

"I'll send him down when he heals. Go."

"Okay, Señor Christ." Miguel backed to the door, not wanting to miss anything. "She's pretty, but very pale and skinny, nothing to Esameralda..."

"Go!..."

Miguel turned and fled.

"That boy. In Havana, he was watching us," said Paulo, forgetting his injury.

"Who's Esameralda?" asked Renée.

Christian felt dizzy and nauseated. The four friends were awkward. Paulo with his pants down. Renée wiping away his blood and her own tears. Maartyn still holding Lucille. Renée looking at Christian in that way. Christian too upset to be the perfect host. Paulo shuffled to the couch. Maartyn put the gun on the table. The revolver wasn't exactly a conversation piece.

"Well, nice to have us all together again," said Maartyn. "Like old times."

"I, ah...have to go," said Christian suddenly. "Find Wolf."

"Hey, what about my leg?"

"Christian?" Renée said softly.

Christian turned his back on his puzzled girlfriend. "Wolf?" Christian waded into the weeds. He found the spot where Wolf had retched up dark blood and followed the speckled blood signs across the garden to a dense patch of trees where he was stopped by a wall of vines. In the tangle Christian touched a rusting link fence with razor wire strung along the top. Vines mimicked the fence so that the fence and whatever it enclosed, were invisible from the villa. At the base of the fence was a well used depression in the soil, big enough for a dog.

The fenced compound was about sixty feet to a side, with a gate at the corner, secured with a trip latch but not padlocked. He had to tear away vines to open the gate. In the centre of the compound, huddled in the shadows of scrub brush and palmettos, was a small building, with stone walls similar to the villa, but with a hipped tin roof. There were no windows. A heavy wood door stood half open. He pushed through the vines and approached cautiously.

"Wolf?..." The darkness was complete except for the rectangle of pale, diffused light that fell across a dirt floor with his shadow. He heard the dog whine. If Wolf was in the building there was nothing to fear.

Wolf was laying on a pile of burlap bags against the back wall. "Wolf? You okay?" Christian felt his way over rotting bags and what felt like a platform. The place smelled of dust and tobacco. "I know, boy. Take it easy." Wolf whimpered, raised his head and coughed, long pink tongue hanging in the dirt. Christian put his hand on the dog's shoulder, smoothing the wet fur. The wetness was sticky. He held his hand under Wolf's mouth. There was a trickle of fresh blood and saliva. The dog licked his fingers. "Just lay still. Off course lay still. You know exactly what to do. You'll lay here because it s your choice, and you'll get better. Right? Am I right?"

Wolf continued licking Christian's hand, as if the dog was consoling his friend, saying, 'Don't worry, Chris, I'll be fine'.

"What hurts, Wolf? Ribs?" Christian felt what areas he could reach without moving him. Ribs seemed out of place, with sharp edges. "Punctured a lung? I don't know what to do for that. I think that old bastard, Escobar's a doctor. Notice his hands? Like a surgeon's, Wolf. Maybe he experiments with people. Cuts them up and makes new ones. A friend of Batista, see? Maybe Batista died and Escobar made a new dictator out of spare parts. That's why Escobar gets a retainer from the government. Too weird to be a theory, right? Hey, dog, anything's possible in Los Espiritos," he said in a whisper. "I'll bring you some water."

Christian entered the living room through the kitchen. His friends a tableau in the darkened room. Maartyn and Paulo were sitting at the table. Renée perched on the couch like a frightened bird. "Is the poor dog badly hurt?" Renée asked.

"Internal bleeding. Some ribs broken," Christian answered rather coldly.

Renée felt the chill. "Oh, I hope he'll be all right."

"Christian," said Paulo, cutting short Renée's concern. "Christian...about the, dog."

"You kicked him pretty hard."

"I didn't mean to hurt the thing." His expression didn't show remorse. "The dog came at me like a wild beast...through that door straight for me. I had to protect myself, otherwise I'd be a dead man. I shook him off and he came for me again. Self defense. Believe me, Christian."

"Okay, let's forget it."

"Why did your dog attack us?" Renée asked.

"Did he go for you too?"

"No. We only just arrived. We were talking to Maartyn, when the dog came running, like the wind, and went straight for Paulo."

"Odd. Wolf doesn't do anything without a reason. Paulo, have you ever been to Cuba?"

"No! And I am never coming back."

"Maybe he mistook Paulo for someone else," offered Renée.

"I don't know. He was on the trail from the beach."

"He was crazy, vicious," said Paulo.

"Well, he recognized something."

Renée touched Christian's arm. "Do you recognize *me?*" Renée asked, her pale lips curled in a perfect pout.

Christian really looked at her for the first time. The same Renée, now that she had stopped screaming; the sun-streaked, golden hair like a braided baguette. The child's bangs dusting sun coloured eyebrows. The perfection of pale skin unaffected by the sun. Almond shaped face and eyes, a touch of Eurasian blood in the structure perhaps. Small nose turned up. High cheek bones. The perky breasts he had sucked greedily when they first made love. The long, slender body sheathed in the black jumper and black roll neck jersey, black stockings hiding the long, smooth legs, unshaved and soft with down. Her spicy crotch, with oriental fragrance. Had sucked that as well when she commanded. Everything about Renée was perfection. He thought of Esameralda's dusky, rounded features...

"Christian?..."

"Oh...sorry. I was thinking about, Wolf." Not accustomed to lying, he felt awkward. Confronted by Renée without his defenses intact made him long for protection, something warm. His adult teddy bear. There was nothing within reach, except Renée. But in his emotional confusion he might as well be stripped naked in a cold interrogation room. The probing eyes and hands just out of reach. He wondered if Paulo was carrying drugs. "I was bringing fire wood."

"Is there anything to drink in this dreary little hacienda?" asked Paulo.

Maartyn snorted. "Rot gut wine."

Renée looked puzzled. "Is something wrong? I detect an atmosphere."

"You might as well know." Christian sat down on one end of the long bench. Paulo sat on the other end. Renée could choose to sit between them, or beside Maartyn or she could sit on the straight backed chair near Paulo. She chose to sit near Paulo. Christian felt the space. "We're broke. We haven't had a decent meal in days, other than dried fish. And there's no prospect of anything in the near future."

"Hey, man, don't forget the Twinkies!"

"But, Christian, I thought you were here to play?"

"Some dive in Havana. Long story."

Maartyn spat out the window. "But, Christian the jerk, blows our last hundred bucks on a piece'a shit guitar."

"My hundred dollars!"

"An' then he brings home this rotten ol'fish that died about a dred years ago. Welcome to Villa Urinales. We aim to please, so you aim too, please."

Paulo laughed. 'Villa Urinales. That's good, Maartyn. Cuba agrees with you."

"Ya, I jus' love it here, man!"

"That's obvious."

"So, y'all got some mula for el flopa, Amigos?"

Paulo stopped grinning. "Tell them the bad news, Renée."

Renée hesitated. "Our luggage was stolen...Paulo's passport. Most of our money..."

"Friggin' great," said Maartyn flatly.

"Luckily I was carrying my dope," said Paulo.

"My clothes. Books. I have a few things in my knapsack. Fortunately my passport's sewn into a special pocket. I had the bag custom made, Moroccan leather, as you know, but I am a poor girl now so I have taken a vow of poverty."

"Hey! yer ol' man's loaded. Put the touch on him," said Maartyn.

"My father threatened to disown me if I didn't stay home, marry the boy of his choice and take my degree at the Sorbonne. He has a career in the Diplomatic Service all arranged. Of course I said no, and that was the end of it. I am, how do you say? the black lamb, until I come to my senses. My senses were freezing in Paris so I used my return ticket to Nassau and went to visit Paulo in jail to get the news, since no one writes or gets in touch." She looked at Christian. He looked guilty enough. "Paulo could get out of jail if I would say I was his wife and we promised to leave the Bahamas. Maartyn had told him to come to Cuba. We took that filthy island boat thinking you were working in Havana and we could manage, as always. So here we are.

Christian let that news sink in. "You had enough money to stay in a good hotel in Havana."

"That boy told you?..."

"You've got some things to learn about Cuba," said Christian.

"Yes, it was probably him who stole our luggage!" offered Paulo.

"No, not Miguel."

"Our hotel room was locked."

"Servicios Especiales..." There was a commotion on the path outside the gate. "Now what?" Christian went to the windo. "Miguel's fighting with some boys, swinging sticks at each other, kinda like road hockey back home. It's over. Miguel now has all the sticks."

Miguel clattered in loaded down with sticks at odd angles. "You

should not leave precious firewood lying in the road, Señor Christ."
Miguel dumped the sticks beside the fireplace and began breaking
small bits for kindling. "I'll break that Jésus' neck one day." They all
stared at him. "How is our poor little Pietro?" he asked.

"Wolf's, well to be honest, Miguel, I don't know. He's in that old
stone building."

Miguel turned, eyes wide. "Señor Christ!...The warehouse? You
have been in there?"

"I followed Wolf. Wait, don't tell me, let me guess. It's the secret
hideout of the Cuban chapter of the Buck Rogers Space Cadets."

"What did you find?"

"Find? Wolf. I found Wolf."

"Señor Escobar will be furious. The warehouse is to be avoided.
Everyone in Los Espiritos knows that."

"No one told Wolf!"

"Did you go inside?"

"Yes, I told you. I followed Wolf."

"What did you see?"

"Damnit, Miguel!...I saw Wolf. Dirty rags. Okay?"

"You must not go there."

"Why? Tell me why the hell not!"

"The tracks. You make tracks in the garden."

"If everybody in Los Espiritos knows, what difference does it
make?"

"It's not for someone outside of Los Espiritos to know. Especially
the police who are surely coming now that your friends are here. I
should have warned you. Now Señor Escobar's going to beat me for
sure."

"Hey, kid, light the fire," said Maartyn, impatient with the foreign
banter. Renée and Paulo were trying to follow the heated conversation
but did not have Christian's facility with the local language or the his-
torical background.

Christian didn't need the fire for warmth. Everything was coming
apart before his eyes. He turned on Miguel. "Tell me about this goddamned warehouse right now or I'll beat the crap out of you myself!"

"Señor Christ is truly angry?"

"Truly! Now tell."

Miguel went to the Gulf side window and opened the shutter. The
late afternoon sun had finally dropped into view below the cloud base
and the room was flooded with optimistic light. Miguel then went to
the opposite window and opened that shutter. Resigned to tell some of

the story, even truthfully. "You already know about Señor Bartuchi. His boat would come in the harbour and anchor. They'd put their goods in a small boat, row to shore and carry them up to the warehouse, where Wolf now licks his wounds."

From the villa window the compound was just a dense thicket of dead palms, weeds and vines, indistinguishable from the untidy vegetation that banked the plateau to Escobar's villa.

"Okay, so it was narcotics or something, so what?"

"Purest opium. Señor Bartuchi shipped his goods to Habana in bales of Pinar del Rio tobacco. There the goods were made up into special cigars and sent to America. It was a very good business until Señor Escobar encouraged him to leave Los Espiritos."

"That's it?"

"Yes, that's all."

"That's not all, Miguel. There's more."

Paulo grew impatient. "Christian, my friend, you are not being the perfect host. I need something to help the pain."

"Okay." Christian went to the pantry and returned with a bottle of wine.

Miguel returned to his fire making. "May I have your knife, Señor Christ?"

"Sure." Christian tossed the utility knife to Miguel, leaving the bottle of wine unopened. "Don't cut yourself."

Paulo picked up the bottle. "Not as good as from my side of the Pyrénées. Rioja, '48. That was a vintage year even for Spanish reds but how will we know if you don't open it."

"It's vintage rot gut," offered Maartyn. "So, how was jail, pal?"

"I've been in worse," replied Paulo grandly. "Nassau's a resort compared to some. In Turkey they loose the key, they beat you and they don't feed you. You either do tricks for food, if you know what I'm saying, or you have someone on the outside. But, Afghanistan's very bad. Never go there to do business."

Renée was watching Christian who stood in the middle of the room, hands in the pockets of his ragged jeans, adrift, alone among friends. "Christian, you don't look well. Have you been ill?"

"Working on it."

"You should eat something."

"Grocery money's a little scarce."

Renée was puzzled by Christian's distance. She sought comfort in another direction. "And what happened to you, Maartyn? You have been in a fight too?"

"Sucker punched, man. An' it sure ain't a fight when you spend the whole time on the ground gettin' yer face kicked."

"But why? You made somebody very angry?"

Christian intervened. "Ah, we don't know why. Some guys jumped Maartyn outside the bar and took his wallet."

"What? Here in Los Espiritos? I would have thought Havana..."

Christian's chuckle was dry and sarcastic. "At first glance Los Espiritos is just your average one fish town. After you've been here awhile you'll think you're in a bad movie."

"Do we want to stay that long?" she asked.

"Well, I wouldn't have said this a week ago, but, I think you shouldn't stay here longer than it takes to leave."

"But, Christian, you invited us."

"Maartyn invited Paulo. You came with Paulo."

Renée was stung. "You said you were going to Cuba to make some money, and that I should come when you get established. Paulo said you were probably making good money and spending all day on the beach drinking Cuban rum with beautiful women. I never expected to find you like this. And now this distance. I thought you'd be happy to see me."

"Question is, are you happy to see me?"

"Of course. When you left Nassau we said certain things."

"And now?"

Renée looked embarrassed. "Can we go for a walk?"

"Actually, my friends, we need to carry up fire wood if you want to be warm tonight. Paulo?"

"Sorry, Chris, I'd like to help, but with this leg, the pain."

"Maartyn?"

"Still pretty sore, ol' buddy. You an' Renée run along an' I'll fill Paulo in on the gruesome details."

"Don't be too explicit. Wouldn't want to ruin his first day."

Renée caught up at the gate. Christian's mind was whirling with the events, amazed that even in the eye of the storm he could feel jealousy. Convinced that his affair with Renée was over. What could he expect? He and Renée had often discussed the current sexual revolution rampant in Europe and America, spurred on by writers like Sartre and Camus. Pain and anguish to be confronted. Life is meaningless and love should be for the moment. No ties, accepting the other's need to be free. The notion spread through the network of young idealists, free to rebel, safe from war and poverty. It seemed to make sense when Christian and Renée were falling into bed. It made sense when it was in Christian's favour. But he was having trouble making the leap from working class Catholic values, to the new philosophies of Allen Ginsberg and crew. The Kama Sutra. The confusion of Camus. Sartre's Existentialism. Hedonism. Playboy Magazine....and this new guy, Jack Kerouac, *On The Road*. Freedom from guilt and morals, and his personal road trip of recovery didn't help. They walked down the hill in silence.

She took his hand. "Tell me what's wrong, Christian." Renée said, breathing deeply, looking up through her bangs with those devastatingly cool, blue-green eyes. He saw dark eyes and full Cuban lips.

"I won't be trite enough to say nothing's wrong. Ask me if something's right." Christian turned and continued down the path.

"I don't understand, I thought you'd be happy to see me. What could be so wrong in a place like this? You have a nice house, it needs some things. It's warm here, compared to Paris. You've been down before and things always worked out."

They reached the bottom of the hill and stood facing the beach, and beyond the burning sunset over the Gulf. The tourist-perfect picture, but it was like looking at a scene on a wall, flat and static, framed in phony gilt. Like the fading prints in hospital rooms that are intended to ease the suffering. He thought of Escobar's galleries. Colourful fakes and shrouded hospital gurneys. Stained glass windows with iconic figures of Bishops fucking priests and children. Escobar's warped idea of the erotic revolution.

"Are you sleeping with Paulo?" he asked abruptly.

"Not if you don't want me to."

"So, you are."

"Should I stop?"

It was not the answer he expected. He wanted a reassuring denial so that he could pretend she wasn't sleeping with the jerk. How could he be angry if Renée insisted on being perfectly honest? "I don't know," he admitted.

"Why don't we sleep together and see?"

"What about Paulo?"

"What about him?"

"He's more dangerous than Maartyn."

"Would you rather I sleep with Maartyn?"

"Renée, this isn't very helpful. Life here is, well, confusing. No, it's more than that...it's warped, okay? Imagine everything that can go wrong."

"What does that have to do with who I sleep with?"

Christian walked out on the beach. He had to do something. He could control firewood. Carry firewood up the hill, where his servant is laying a fire in the stone fireplace. Where his friends are about to take turns laying his girlfriend. See? Fire is the only activity. No, there's Wolf. To hell with worrying about making paths that Batista's soldiers can follow to machine gun the terrified villagers who are hiding out in the compound. Why? Who knows? Take some water and maybe some fish broth. Cook fish in fireplace. Warmth. Drink good wine while watching fire. Sing camp songs. Life's not so bad. Then he remembered how much he disliked camping.

"Christian...wait!"

He was standing in the water beside the skiff . Renée couldn't approach without taking off her sandals and stockings. He realized how ridiculous her Beatnik uniform looked on a beach in Cuba. She looked like a sexy nun. "You should be in a convent."

"Christian, you're being childish."

"Just making up for lost time," he said, stacking pieces of drift wood in his arms. The pieces were irregular shaped and wouldn't lay still, attempting to jump away in all directions. He waded ashore and threw the load down on the sand.

"Temper," she teased in English.

"Look, Renée, you sleep with whoever you want, okay?"

"No, it's not okay. I don't need your permission, but if you continue to act this way it certainly won't be with you."

"Fine. I'm so relieved."

"You're being an ugly beast and I should hate you. I've come hundreds of miles on a flea infested boat just to be with you, and you treat me like a whore. Like I sleep with every boy who talks to me."

"You weren't suffering a drought on the way, apparently."

"So what, Cheri? So what if I fucked every boy I met in the last two months."

"Did you?"

"Don't be boring, darling." The American darling. "I wouldn't have had time to eat or sleep!"

Christian didn't have the energy to fight. "Renée, I'm sorry. For what I don't know exactly."

"Don't be a martyr. I hate it you when you feel sorry for yourself."

"Then hate me. It would make it easier."

"Do you really love me, Christian? Or do you just want to fuck me?"

Unfortunate questions, he thought. For one thing, Christian wasn't used to girls talking so bluntly. He preferred the nicer game, in which boys only said 'fuck' when they were doing stupid boy things. Nice, well bred girls never said 'fuck', did they? At least not around boys. Renée was a revelation. The hard core jazz scene didn't count because he was still a fringe player and not that far removed from the façade of the urban family, being strung out on heroin aside. On the junk there wasn't much time to learn anything of life besides scoring the next fix and making the gigs. But it was the late fifties. The barriers were coming down, and he had no idea how far they would tumble. But for the immediate questions, his only answer could be..."I don't know. I honestly don't know."

"If it makes any difference, Paulo's gay."

"You're kidding?"

"Very sexy, handsome and very queer. We are just play acting, making love for fun. There were lonely nights for both of us."

Christian sucked in his breath. "Jesus...Juanita's going to be very disappointed."

"Tell me about this Juanita."

"Juanita? Where does one begin?"

"You've slept with her," she teased. "Yes, you have, I can tell."

He couldn't bring himself to lie. "I wouldn't call it that..."

The trip back up the hill was completed in frigid silence. Christian staggered under a heavy load. Renée towed a gnarled, sun bleached branch that she said was too nice to burn, leaving a wavering trail in the red Cuban dirt. He wished she would stop dragging the stick. Trails. To hell with trails!

Miguel had vanished. The remains of a fire flickered in the hearth, the room otherwise dark. A sharp snap sent sparks shooting across the tile floor. Christian dropped to his knees to ease the load. Renée toyed in the embers with the end of her stick. Christian built the fire with the salty wood which gave off interesting hues. The fresh blaze painted the cold room in moving oranges, greens and blues. With no glass in the windows the shutters could only slow the air being sucked in to feed the fire. Most of the heat shot up the chimney but the visual effect was rewarding. It could have been a nice evening except for certain, things. One was the snoring coming from the bedroom. Christian wondered what Maartyn would say when he found out about Paulo, unless he already knew.

There were two empty wine bottles on the table. That would explain why the boys were in bed early. Two more bottles of the precious vintage wasted. Cellophane wrappers were scattered over the table. The empty canvas goodie bag drooped over a chair like a drunken sailor.

Renée sat on the bare floor, hugging her knees. A dusting of fine sand around her feet. A thin resemblance to a beach, but then their relationship was that way at the moment. Christian sat on the floor also, feeling the cold tiles through his thin Levis. He should get cushions from the American couch. Should have offered one to Renée first, instead they both suffered in silence. The distance could have been that of Cuba to Andros, or earth to moon. Renée looked first.

Christian felt compelled to speak. "Cushion?"

"No. Thank you."

"Okay, just asking."

Christian wondered why relationships were so damned difficult? Perfect strangers can pour life histories out like emptying a bucket. A slop bucket, some of them. His life was sloshing across the floor, running down hill, in many directions and him saying, 'Look, Renée, there goes the reason I'm so uptight about sex. And over there, my parents fighting. My father drunk and smashing things. There's the episode with Howie that got me on the junk and there's the day I decided to kick the junk, and the thing that made me move toward the place where I found you'.

"Do you remember the first time we saw each other?" Renée asked.

He wondered if she was reading his thoughts. "So, we're going to do the sentiment thing?" he asked sarcastically. Her answer was an angry pout. Only Renée could accomplish that. "Sorry," he said. "That wasn't called for."

"It wasn't."

"Yes, I remember."

She waited awhile to punish back, then continued. "You were sitting on the beach watching Maartyn wrestling with Paulo in front of those tanned bovines with the huge breasts in their new bikinis? I watched you sitting alone, skinny and pale, detached. Like you weren't really there."

"Maybe I wasn't."

"You looked like a typical American. But you know, I saw you as different. You were cute, rather than good looking, in a juvenile way, but I thought, I would rather meet you and have you make love to me than either of those two silly, muscle flexing morons. I concentrated on making you look."

"I know."

"I was almost exhausted from the effort, and only had enough left to give you one good smile."

"It was enough."

"It took you a long time to come to me."

"Why didn't you come to me? I mean, you're very free and uninhibited, even for a French girl."

"True. But there's still something about making a boy come on to me, like I am a magnet. It worked but you were resisting strongly."

"I'm just shy."

"Yes, it's one of the few things about you I liked. Did you know that Paulo came on to me while you were at the café getting our wine. He asked me if I wanted to sleep with him?"

"I thought you said he's gay?"

"He is, but he goes both ways. And he told me then that he was a homosexual, standing there over me with this big penis pushing through that tiny bathing suit. He said I looked like a boy."

"Did that turn you on?"

"Yes, it did. How could it not?"

"But you said no?"

"Reluctantly. He persisted." She paused to let the implication sink in. "It was an experience. I had never been with a gay person before, male or female."

"So, you still have one to go?"

"That's my business."

"Did you sleep with Maartyn?"

"Don't be bitter, Christian. I can't help how I am. You went away. And now you are even further from me."

"Things change."

"You mean people change."

"No, I mean things...events, crazy things happen, bad things. Then people change. I came here for a reason, remember?"

"Yes, you needed to get away from me."

"I didn't say you."

"Not in so many words," she said.

"That's not fair. You're judging and accusing."

"Cheri, I could have protected you."

"I didn't see that wonderful shield. What I saw was every guy on the beach looking at your long legs and perfect derrière in the string thing you call a bathing suit, and your long blonde hair and your perfect face..."

145

"Don't forget my perfect tits," she mocked.

"No, and what I also saw was you looking back and wondering what it would be like to sleep with that one or all of them at once."

"How would you know what I'm thinking?"

"Because, every time we talked about relationships the subject got around to free love. You seem so sure it's the way to save the world. You said that if everybody slept with every body else on impulse there wouldn't be time for wars."

"Hah, you're such a baby sometimes. You're so delicate I had to be careful."

"Careful!? Jesus, I'd hate to think what my mental state would be if you did act on every impulse."

"Christian, that's so sweet, you're jealous."

"Only about twenty hours of every day. The other times I was sleeping."

"Oh, and how nice it was to lay with you in the heat. You have nice breath and a nice smell. You said I had a nice smell too, even when I pushed my love hair into your mouth you were like a hungry young goat."

"Goat!? That's a good one. Little goats…kids."

"You're acting like one."

He wanted to touch the hand that moved closer as she stretched out on the floor. She waited too. The fire crackled. Sparks leapt about.

Christian retreated from the gesture. "Wolf. I should have taken him some water."

The brief pyrotechnics died down. Renée sighed and rolled on her side, knees drawn up. She rested her head on her arm and studied Christian in profile. He was complicated. Not her idea of a great lover, but there was something reassuring under his immaturity, a promise for the future, after she had experienced men and boys, and queers and lesbians, and explored the philosophies of sexual freedom, the postwar Bohemian nihilism rampant in Europe. She was aware that when the lust burned out like the fire, a relationship would depend on many things.

"We could go now," she said.

"It's too dark."

"You have a lantern?"

Christian didn't answer. To answer he would have to explain the compound. It was easier discussing their fractured sex life. He thought about the living room of his Montreal apartment and the first time he had a girl alone. Wine, candles, condoms and the forbidden marijuana.

146

He had everything going except an erection. Too many possibilities and complications, not the least of which, his parents arriving unexpectedly. They often fought at their bridge parties and returned early in a silent rage. His father taking out his frustrations on the bathroom mirror, or on his son. Does Fulgencio Batista or Ernesto Escobar count as a father figure?

"Christian?"

"What?"

"Lantern?"

It was easier to just go. There was also the nagging resentment that Miguel said he shouldn't go. "Yeah, okay."

Christian lit the kerosene lamp and filled a wine bottle with water. They crossed the terrace to the garden, the kerosene lamp throwing light in all directions except at their feet. The tangle of weeds and vines tripping them up with every step.

"Why don't you turn off the lamp."

Christian turned down the wick and blew into the chimney. The wick smoked, spreading an oily stench over the soft night. "Damnit!" he whispered.

"What's wrong?"

"Forgot the matches."

"I brought them."

"Can you take the bottle?"

"Yes. Did you bring some of that awful fish?"

"No. He won't eat."

"How do you know?"

"Dogs don't eat when they're hurt."

"Did you bring a bowl?"

"No."

The moon riding above the hills cast enough light to make out clumps of weeds and the spaces. The low vines were tricky but the palmettos with their dangerous spear points were easier to avoid by moonlight. Christian made a looping approach to the dark wall of vines. They found the fence by running into it, worked along the perimeter to the corner. Once inside the gate, in the shadow of the overburden, they were in darkness again.

"Matches?" he whispered.

Renée handed him the box of matches. Her long fingers were cool and dry. Christian pulled the chimney off the lamp. It slipped out of his fingers. Instead of the crash he expected, the fragile glass chimney was cradled by a mass of ground creeper. "I'm not cut out for this spy stuff."

"What spy stuff? You're just visiting your injured dog."

"*Shhh,* not so loud."

"And why are we whispering?"

"I'll explain later."

Renée sighed. "Boys."

He lit the lamp and replaced the chimney, shielding it with his hand. Was the compound watched? Renée followed him closely, her hand on his arm.

"Wolf? It's me."

"Will he attack do you think?"

Wolf answered with a low whimper and tail thumping, sounding like a drum. Christian noticed the odd sound. They moved cautiously, feeling along the ground with their feet. Renée cringed at the organic touch of the scattered burlap bags. Invisible clouds of dust rolled up. She began sniffling. "I'm allergic to something in here."

"Dust."

"Tobacco. When I tried to make cigarettes for my German boyfriend I broke out in this awful rash."

"You won't like Pinar del Rio."

"So far I don't like Cuba."

Wolf was lying on a pile of bags. Probably where the dog lived between homes, Christian said to himself. The floor was hard packed dirt, but under Wolf there was wood planking. Christian set the lamp down on a clear patch of wood. The heavy lamp made a hollow sound, like a drum again. He stroked Wolf's head and neck. The blood had dried but there was a pool near his mouth, thick and black.

"Easy, old boy. Don't move. We brought you some water." He poured water from the wine bottle into his hand and held it close to Wolf's nose. The dog flicked his tongue, catching up a few drops. He coughed. He poured more. Wolf flicked his tongue again, as if he was doing Christian a favour. On the third try Wolf took a few drops but the water just ran back out of his mouth mixed with blood.

"Okay, fella. I'll bring a bowl tomorrow with some fish broth. Your favourite. Salt fish. Like that, eh?" He could do nothing except stroke the little dog.

Renée became bored with dog nursing and looked around the room. Nothing but rough stone walls, bare beams, a rusting tin roof and dirt floor. Fine dust drifted over the lamp, rising with the heat, spreading out like the anvil top of a thunderhead. She traced the structure of the wood platform under Wolf. "A door," said Renée. "Look, hinges."

"Jesus!.." breathed Christian.

"What's under there I wonder?"

"I don't want to know."

"Trap doors always lead to dungeons where they imprison the beautiful maiden in heavy chains until the hero rescues her by fighting hideous creatures. Let's look."

"We can't move Wolf."

"He's not very big."

"Renée, I'm not moving him."

"But..."

"No!"

"It's a door."

"Let's get out of here."

"Christian, you're such a poop sometimes."

The convoluted walk back was made in tense silence. He built up the fire and put the pot of water with chunks of salt fish into the coals. Renée sat at the table smoothing cellophane wrappers with the utility knife. The noise grated on Christian's nerves.

"Must you do that?"

"That fish's smell's putrid," she said flatly.

"Would you care for some wine, Renée? They say it's a very good year."

"Oh, so formal."

"May I?" Christian took the utility knife, opened another bottle and served the wine in a chipped, dirty mug. The irony was not lost on Renée, thinking about her Parisienne roots and the crystal-glutted dinner parties with pompous dignitaries and groveling dictators looking for handouts from France. She sipped the wine too nicely, to make the point. Christian almost laughed. He had watched her drink Madeira from the bottle; two handers, alternating tokes on fat joints of Acapulco Gold or Asian hashish from water pipes. At the same time yelling obscenities in four languages at unenlightened tourists, loudly damning bourgeois customs. They would argue for hours about American values and society's hang-ups.

They both focused on the pot. When the water was bubbling and the fire banked up he tumbled the cushions from the couch.

"Would you like the floor with the cockroaches or the sofa with the bad springs?"

"I would like that big bed in the other room with someone who cares for me."

"Well, in there you have your choice."

Renée laughed into her mug. The wine helped. "Maybe I should take both of them and watch *you* boil."

"Fine. Feel free. I know you do. And in the morning you could tell me all about the fantastic experience so that I won't be a stupid child all my life."

"Oh, Christian, I love it when you pout, but you *are* being like a child."

"I thought you hated self pity?" He pouted in turn. "I'm too tired to do this. Go to sleep."

"It's too cold to sleep."

"Take my jacket."

"What will you use?"

"I'm fine. I'll keep the fire going."

"My noble darling." She stretched like a cat and sat on the couch. "Feeling sorry for yourself again?"

Christian smoothed the Levi jacket around Renée's shoulders, hesitating for a moment. With her right hand she reached across to touch his hand. "Thank you, Cheri. You really are very sweet, you know. I could love you." Christian pulled away gently, reluctantly.

Renée unwound her long braid, letting the golden cascade flow over her shoulder. In the fire light it was burnished copper. Even her pale face had colour, like Doris Day in a fireside scene with Rock Hudson in the days of innocence and necessary lies. Their adoring world unaware of certain ironies. She made a pillow with her knapsack and curled up, shaping herself to avoid the worst springs. She smoothed her jumper until her hips were in perfect outline, patted the knapsack and closed her eyes. An angelic smile on her lips. At home in a strange bed. Although she was born well, her free spirit had already taken her to exotic places and many strange beds. Renée was one of those easy explorers of life who adapt. Capable of base wildness but never far from grace. She despised people who were set in their ways so the ideological collision with her parents was unavoidable. At twenty Renée was, like Christian, a Beat Generation orphan. And the beat was only beginning.

Christian poked at the fire, trying to lose himself in the flames, but every flame was a shape that grew into a body and head with features, then vanished before the faces revealed themselves, to be replaced by another, and another. Wondered if Renée was really asleep or if she was trying to reach out with her power. She knew he could not resist.

He turned. Her eyes were closed and her breathing steady. Firelight played over her smooth features. Perhaps he was spiritually chilled and not receiving. He assessed his new feeling for Rosameralda or Esameralda. Nothing there at the moment but that could not be relied upon because he had no history of clinging, sweaty closeness with the Cuban girls, only a vision. But the vision of Rosameralda was not as clear as it had been the day after the funeral. Esameralda was there too, getting stronger. Renée's face in sleep, although she was only a few feet away, was not as clear as either, or maybe it was just a trick of the firelight. Softening the edges, toning the fine sculpture so that the subtle shades of the pale marble skin were suddenly set aflame or in deep shadow and the upturned nose wobbled about.

Christian amused himself, poking the fire and making flames shoot up, manipulating Renée's features. Making her vanish or making her grotesque. He was toying with her and moulding her, in a way he could not when she was not pretending to be asleep.

"What are you doing?"

"Nothing."

"Then why are you watching me?"

"I'm not...only looking."

"Come, lay down here beside me. I'm frightened with you so far away." Which distance did she mean?

Christian laid more logs to the back of the hearth. Organizing the firewood, watching it catch, waiting a few minutes, just to put some space between the command and the execution. He wanted to lay close to Renée but did not want to be told, even though they both knew who was in control. Only the first few times they made love was it spontaneous. After the first wild nights Renée directed the passion the way her mother might organize a diplomatic banquet. Everything had to be in place. Protocol was everything. Play acting. It was still great sex but not free love. He wondered what married life would be like.

He lay on his back on the cushions, hands folded over his chest, staring at the rough hewn beams. Very old world. Very Canadian also. Like the beams in a ski lodge in the Laurentian Mountains. His father decided the family would take up skiing. The Canadian family that does things together on snow breaks things together. First it was his father's wrist, before they reached the chair lift. Mother stayed behind to nurse. Then his sister fell getting off the lift and had to be helped down the hill by the entire ski patrol. Only Christian made it to the top. He chose a suicide run, straight down the hill, and fell just before crashing into the chalet's ski rack. He took off his skis, placing them in the rack very carefully, pole straps looped over tips, just like all the others. He took off his boots, placed them beside the skis and walked to the lodge in his stocking feet.

The family spent the rest of the weekend in the bar. It was the only time a family outing didn't end with a fight. That night he lay on the floor of the room he shared with his sister, gazing at the ceiling beams, because his sister needed the twin beds pushed together. It was the weekend she lost her virginity. He couldn't decide if his sister was really dumb, really cool, or just desperate, to bring her ski patrol bum into their room and do it while her little brother pretended to be asleep on the floor. He was sworn to secrecy of course, under pain of death. She also got pregnant that night. Christian thought it fitting. Heavy wooden beams always reminded Christian of deception and consequences. Nothing's changed.

"What are you thinking about?"

"Skiing."

"Do you think Fidel Castro's skiing in the mountains? The radio said that the guerrillas...isn't it interesting that they always call the jungle fighters guerrillas, but if they're fighting in the streets of American cities they're called hoodlums...they said that Castro has left the mountains. I think they mentioned Santiago de Cuba?"

"In the east. Other side of Havana."

"Christian, will the Revolution come here?"

Revolution? No, but something's going on, at least a side show. Escobar's involved. And Wolf's warehouse probably has something to do with it. "No, the Revolution's just a bunch of toy soldiers in Oriente Province. They might scare Batista out of the country or he might crush the rebellion, with the help of the Americans. Either way, nothing ever happens in Los Espiritos."

"No? Then what about Maartyn? You said things were not as they seem. Your exact words, 'You've got some things to learn.'"

"Well, I was exaggerating."

"And your boy was very upset about the warehouse. And the trap door?"

"That's not related to anything. Miguel just meant that I shouldn't be snooping around."

"Christian, you aren't telling me the truth."

"Right. I'm not, and I'm not going to stop."

"Not stop what?"

"The less you know the better."

152

"That's sweet, Cheri. But you're being too gloomy."

"Is that what you think?"

"No, I think you're just being selfish and want to keep this secret to yourself, so you can pretend to protect me."

"Renée, this isn't one of your life affirming experiences. There's nothing going on here. It won't advance your knowledge of the world, free love or existentialism."

"Why are you so negative? Sartre would say that you are the existentialist who doesn't believe in Existentialism."

"No, he'd say that I'm a realist. Truth before essence."

"Fatalist."

"Whatever."

"You're more than gloomy. You're pessimistic. You're a clumsy fatalist."

"I always thought that, on a good day, I was an optimistic realist."

"What's that, Cheri? Something new?"

"My own logic. I'm a realist enough to know that everything goes wrong, but optimistic enough to assume that it will all work out."

"So, we're all in danger. But, since you're an optimist, we need not worry because it will all end beautifully. Really, Cheri."

"I didn't say that. We might all be killed, but the end will be good."

"Christian, that's crazy. How can being killed be good?"

"Somebody will benefit. Look at all the soldiers who died in the war, your people and my people, the Americans, even the confused Italians. Some of those poor slobs must have known they were going to die a horrible death but it was for a good reason."

"You said the Revolution was way over there. Now you are talking about dying for a good cause. You're just a tourist, my darling, not a terrorist."

"No, I'm not a tourist, or your darling."

"I toy with you."

"We're innocent observers of something weird that may be nothing more than a bunch of drug smugglers. Nothing to excite you, or Jean-Paul Sartre."

"Sartre would find some reason."

"I'm too tired to get into the Sartre thing tonight."

"But I want to know what good my death would serve?"

Christian sighed, determined to put his stamp on the discussion. "If we die we become food. Wolf and his pals..."

"*Aaagh!* You're disgusting."

"A disgusting optimist or a disgusting pessimist?"

"Stop it. You're making me depressed."

"No, come on, tell me. Sartre would say my optimism is based on negatives attacked head on by the will and beaten by positivism, right?"

"Yes, Christian, he'd possibly say that, but are you that thing? That tough optimist?"

"I'm working on it, but I'm pessimistic enough to think it won't happen."

"Then it won't."

"That's pessimism on your part. But I'm too much of a realist to think otherwise."

"You're just trying to confuse me and make me mad at you. Are you punishing me for something?"

"Yes, for bringing up Jean-Paul Sartre at a time like this."

"I didn't bring up Sartre, you did."

"Well, I knew you would eventually."

"No, I knew you would."

Renée rolled onto her stomach. She always did that when she had won her point and wanted to up the punishment. If they were on the beach his hand would eventually trace the curving line of her back to her hips and along the edge of the bikini to the hallow where the roundness and firmness of her perfect derriere caused the material to stand above her smooth skin, the line between her light tan and her white skin. He'd slip his hand in. Then, forgiving him, she would reach down and pull the string ties. It would end with her on top and they would make love with only a towel or blanket over them. It was daring and dangerous. Renée loved to shock the adults and amaze the children. Once an irate mother poured a bucket of water on them and kicked sand, screaming furiously about disgusting degenerates. Renée shouted back that the ugly bitch was just jealous and should go and jump on her poor husband. Christian saw the husband agreeing but as far as they knew it didn't happen. What a pity, Renée had said later.

"Where is your hand?" she asked.

"Where should it be?"

"Exactly where you are thinking it should be and if you don't have it there soon I'm either going to fall sleep or find a boy who will make hard love to me."

No way out, he thought. "Renée, why do you do this to me?"

"Do what? I'm offering my exquisite young body openly and honestly. Should I squeeze my ass tight and make you beg?"

Christian thought of a come-back that attacked her confusion be-

A Novel of Cuba: 1958

tween offering herself and giving ultimatums. It was pressure diplomacy. Her father was right to try to push her into the Diplomatic Service. She could be devastating dealing with weak-willed ambassadors.
What would Sartre do in this situation?

He wanted her from hunger but wanted to resist from pride. If they
were alone, without Maartyn and Paulo as the threat, it would have
been simpler. He would hold back by will power. She would punish
him more the next time. But in the current impasse he believed she
would go to the bedroom and Christian would have to deal with the
consequences. A philosophical call. The horns of a dilemma. Or a
classic situation in psychology. Approach-avoidance. But he wasn't
sitting in a lecture hall at the University listening to some doctoral
candidate drone on about Jung and Kant or Skinner. The creature who
could torment him with her body was only inches away. He knew
what the silky skin was like between the tops of her stockings and the
edge of her white panties. His hand was already on the back of her
knee pushing the hem of her jumper upward in soft folds, making little
black waves. She didn't move or make a sound. Holding back.

The first border crossing was the elastic of the stockings. He lingered at the brink, wanting to feel the delicious bare skin. Soon she
would make the delicate sounds that were the signal to keep going, but
he feared that she might withhold the signal and force him to commit
himself further, pushing the buttons recklessly without a chance to recover graciously if she called it off. Cautiously his fingers crept over
the edge of the elastic, then, free to fall, touching silky smooth thigh,
like a child jumping from the brink of a grassy sand dune, pausing to
savour the hot sand before exploring the space between the dunes and
the warm, salty ocean, there to plunge into the mysterious depths.
Then, finally, Renée's muffled squeals of delight, or triumph, like a
startled sea bird taking flight. The white bird, wheeling over an indigo
sea against a pure blue sky with towering clouds in the distance,
screaming in protest at being disturbed. The young couple walking
along the beach, arms around each other, hands exploring shyly the
comfortable zones of hips to the mounds slowly undulating under their
hands with each step. Teasing. Not requiring immediate action or a
conclusion, but a promise. He, slender, white and blonde. She volup-
tuously rounded and dark...dark!?

"Well?..."

"What?"

"Are you going to or not? You can't just leave me like this. What
are you thinking about?"

155

"Nothing...making love."

"You stopped just at the worst time. Where are you?"

"On a beach."

"Who with?"

"You of course."

"Untrue. I'm here on this terrible couch with your hand up my crotch, except your hand is not connected to your brain, and you're on a beach with someone else!"

"Sorry. Must be the lack of food."

"You'd better make love to me right now," she warned.

"Come down here then."

Renée sat up, pulled the jumper off and slid over the edge of the couch, placing her Vogue Girl legs astride Christian and covering him with her slender body. She looks like an Oreo cookie, thought Christian. Black sweater, white panties and long black stockings. Christian's mental image of his Oreo cookie days caused him to take a looping flight to do with childhood practices; eating the filling first.

"Do you want to take off your sweater?" he asked, resigned to the act, as he had given himself up to the irrepressible Juanita.

"No. It's too cold."

They made love in their way, from hunger. He did all the required things. It wasn't exciting enough to describe.

Later, they lay together on the cushions with Christian's jacket and Renée's jumper for a blanket. The room was silent. Outside the villa night sounds were muted. Renée and Christian were close but their thoughts were in different parts of the world. There wasn't anything to say. They just lay in each other's arms, watching the last of the fire. Just before they fell asleep there was a sharp but brief commotion in the bedroom.

"...Hands off, man!"

"Oh, merd, sorry. I, ah, thought you were someone else."

"Just keep yer hands to yourself..."

"I said, sorry..."

"...Break yer stupid neck."

"Fuck you, Yank..."

"Hey! What smells out there!?"

"Fish broth," he said and closed his eyes.

December 22nd 1958. The sun was already high. Sea birds cried warnings as they circled the returning fishing boats. Christian awoke with

Renée lying on top of him. He was stiff and sore and had slept just enough to be groggy, roused from a disturbing, but already forgotten dream by the sounds of cooking. The aroma of coffee and the familiar hiss of the gas burner and Miguel moving about the pantry. The morning sun was streaming through the east window and for a moment Christian's paradise was in order; then one by one, the painful realities returned. Christian slid out from under Renée and covered her up.

"Morning, Señor Christ."

"You're back."

"I made a deal with Juanita for a gas bottle and my mother sent some rice and beans with the eggs and coffee. She even made a special bread with white flour from America."

"Uh huh, and would the occasion be our visitors with American dollars?"

"The thought had crossed my mind."

"I hate to disappoint you, Miguel, but you might as well feed breakfast to those seagulls." Renée stirred.

"It's not a problem. Mother's keeping an account, just like Juanita. I told her that you would be good for a generous tip."

"Really smooth, Miguel. We'll discuss this later."

Dressed in Levis and Madras shirt, since Maartyn wouldn't give up the sweatshirt, he went to the terrace without his saxophone. The art forgotten. The sun felt good but the sight of the compound tangle reminded him that Wolf was waiting.

The guests were rousing themselves from their sleepy beds with visions of breakfast all fresh in their heads. 'Twas the night before Christmas and all through the villa,' he thought with a wry sense of humour...He didn't want to face the mob. Let Miguel feed them and take responsibility for their happiness, for a price. Renée was speaking to Miguel, asking if there was cream for the coffee. Miguel could get cream, he said, for a price. Perfect.

Paulo was Basque, but raised on the French side of The Pyrénées in Bayonne, near the Biscay Coast, so he had French, a working knowledge of Spanish, good English and spotty comprehension of the Cuban dialect. Renée translated what he missed. Maartyn was up also. He spoke only Louisiana American. Renée, who spoke private school English, also translated for Maartyn. The conversation was chaotic and amusing. Christian wasn't amused.

Christian threaded his way through the garden, careful to avoid the route of the night before. Still, he could already see traces of their trips to the compound. It wouldn't take much to establish a path. His paranoia was developing. At the gate he stopped to look down at the village. A few tin roofs on the hillside, but nothing but the stubby tower of the church was visible from the beach level. No obvious vantage point to see him enter the compound, except for Escobar's villa on the same level a mile away. But the distance would require binoculars.

"Wolf?" The answering whimper was immediate. Wolf had moved to the back of the trap door and was half way to sitting up. When Christian entered Wolf tried to get to his feet.

"No, Wolf. Easy, boy. I'll get you some water." The water bottle, which Christian had left at the edge of the trap door, was lying on its side. There was no sign of a puddle. "If only you could talk."

"And, if the dog could talk? What could he tell you?" The voice startled Christian. He recognized the cultured English.

"He'd tell you to go leave Cuba."

"Señor Escobar."

"You may ask what I'm doing here. I could ask you that very question. Although I know, because Miguel informed me."

"Informed is right."

"Necessary."

Escobar emerged from the deeper shadow. "This must be a pretty special place," Christian said.

"It's only a dirty, disagreeable place, don't you think? Not fit for espionage and skullduggery."

"I didn't come here to..."

"Snoop? Of course not, dear boy. Purely humanitarian instincts and I admire your concern for this reprobate. No doubt Miguel has told you more of the disgusting history of this building, but since you are perceptive, I assume you believe there's more to this than meets the eye. Unfortunately the dog has led you here and now I'm forced to make a further explanation. By the way, the dog will be fine. He has cracked ribs and the stomach lining may be torn. A little water but no food for a day or so."

"You're a doctor?"

"Was. And may be again, but that's of no consequence in our present discussion. Your guests didn't take long to make an impression."

"The thing with Wolf and Paulo? It was..."

"Their arrival is the problem. Miguel tells me the dog attacked the one called Paulo."

"Yes, it was pretty weird."

"Your friends arrived by car from Pinar del Rio. Did they not think it unusual that a total stranger would offer a ride?"

"They did mention a ride."

"The driver was one of Batista's police. A man called Carnero. In fact, Carnero was the trainer of this dog. Miguel told you about the dog's history and how it happened to be in Los Espiritos. Your friend Paulo picked up the scent of the one man this dog stalks with a vengeance. The attack was pure instinct. The dog is trained to kill, among other interesting skills. Señor Paulo's fortunate."

"He's aware."

"This is no ordinary dog. He's the village guardian. We always know when the police are about. Probably the same men who beat up Maartyn. Pietro, who you call Wolf, doesn't usually attack the police. He just alerts Miguel. This policeman's presence is a warning. Are you beginning to see the picture, Christian?"

"Vaguely."

"Miguel told you that Señor Bartuchi used this building for his narcotics business."

"Yes, he told me."

"That's all it was. A depot. After that it's of no consequence to our story."

"Oh, really? I happen to know where some of it ended up."

"It's of no concern of mine. You see, I have no sympathy for human weakness, including my own. What the individual does is done with knowledge of the consequences. If a person cannot overcome their weakness then they must learn to live with misfortune. But that's getting too far from our topic. I came here for two reasons. One was to see to the dog. He's too valuable. Also, I knew you'd be coming to visit him because one of your weaknesses is caring for the unfortunate."

"What's wrong with that?"

"It's perfectly fine to have compassion for dumb things. It's why you allow a person like Maartyn to be your friend. A low class hoodlum from the dregs of American society."

"That's a bit harsh..."

"The Paulo character. What is he? A cheap narcotics pusher who feeds on the weak. Unfortunate that Pietro didn't rip his throat out. Tell me about the woman."

"Renée? We met in the Bahamas."

"I know that much already, from Juanita. But who is she in the great scheme of things?"

"What does it matter?"

"What can she do for you when this blows up in your face?"

"Blows up? What are you talking about?"

"Haven't you been using the information you've acquired in the last few days?"

"I've given it some thought."

"Then by now you should have taken yourself and that gang of misfits to another island where you can indulge in your cheap, childish games. Continue to be the irresponsible children of the glorious war veterans...what do you call yourselves, the Beat Generation? Do any of you have a cause?"

"No, not really."

"Fidel Castro Ruz and his followers are going to wrench Cuba out of the hands of Batista and his American cronies. This is not play acting, Christian. This is not something you do on the beach. This is a deadly serious business. You disciples of the so called Beat prophets, like Ginsberg and that French phony Sartre, you know nothing of suffering and tyranny, except what is self inflicted out of boredom. You've grown up spoiled and protected by your parents and lied to by politicians who use democracy as a tool, the same as a dictator uses tyranny to fill foreign bank accounts, and if a small portion of the riches spill over to the masses, you're drooling and grateful enough to keep the bastards in power."

"I have studied this...in school."

"We're fighting back, Christian. But not in schoolyards. The children are in the hills. Soon in the streets. Cubans are being killed as we speak and Fidel Castro's preparing to take Santiago. General Batista continues to resist. It's only a matter of time until his own army turns on him, but in the meantime the army and the police play their games, and will stomp the life out of anyone who threatens them. Your friends may seem like insignificant tourists but if the police see fit to shadow you, the next step is arrest, because they believe you are here to help the Revolution."

"I was getting to that point."

"Good. When are you leaving?"

"I told you, I can't."

"And I told you I would provide the means."

"I'll think about it." Christian felt a sharp pain in his stomach. He knelt down beside the dog. "Bye, Wolf. See you later."

"Christian, don't come back to this place."

His guests were sitting on the terrace drinking coffee as he picked his way across the garden. The stomach cramps, that had only been a gnawing ache the day before, were no longer hunger pains. And he was feeling light headed, slightly nauseous. He assumed it was just the stress.

"Nature boy returns," said Paulo.

"Y'all find anything interesting out there in the jungle?"

"No."

"Is your dog all right?" asked Renée.

"He'll be okay."

"We saved you some coffee," she said.

"It wasn't hard to do," said Paulo, grinning sardonically. "It's about the worst coffee I've ever tasted."

"There's rice and beans and bread. The coffee I can take, but that bread! A true Parisienne would choke. Honestly, Christian, what is the attraction of this place?"

"It doesn't have any, that's why I like it."

"What's that supposed to mean?"

"It means, nobody would want to come here and spoil it."

"Oh, prickly."

"Easy to see why," said Paulo sarcastically.

"Paulo, you were in jail a few days ago, how can you criticize?"

"It goes with the business. To be the drug King you have to pay some dues."

Maartyn had a mouthful of beans and bread. "Yer not fuphin' king of anyphin', man, you queenie. I set you up wiph deal...front you the goddamn shit, an' what you do? Y'all blow it."

"And who are you, big time Yankee gangster? Too scared to make deals yourself. If you hadn't talked so much..."

"I didn't say one word."

"You were too drunk to remember. Big time crook in America. It was easy for the cops to put it together and they stop me because I was seen with you, you low life."

Maartyn shot back, "Hey, pretty boy, how'd you really get out of jail? Huh? They wouldn't believe you're married, y'all'er queer as daylight."

"I'll show ya some daylight, right through that big mouth and out the other side."

"Boys, boys," interjected Renée, "Breakfast hasn't improved your tempers."

Paulo grabbed his crotch. "You want queer? I'll stuff Dick down your throat and you'll choke! You phony American cocksucker!"

Maartyn jumped to his feet. "Ya? An' I'll ram Lucille so far up yer ass I could load'er through yer eyeballs!"

Paulo knew enough to back down, but did so with a gesture of dismissal. It was ridiculous and over played on both sides.

Absurd, Christian thought. So absurdly funny. Christian sat on the terrace wall and laughed through the cramps. He laughed until the tears flowed down his cheeks. It's all so abstract. His friends a blur; like objects seen through cracked glass. Fractured and unreal. He wanted them far away but they were all rooted in Los Espiritos unless he accepted Escobar's offer. He could make the announcement but decided to wait. To punish them. He was surprised that he didn't feel guilty. Maybe just a little. And who would care if they vanished? An insignificant casualty of a rebellion. Blown about by war like the dust from the wheels of passing army trucks. None of them would add a thing to the moral stock of the free world. Maartyn had a death wish. Paulo? Should be punished for his sins. Renée? What about Renée? Her beauty transient. It's all she has and when it's gone she will have nothing. That's unfair. What of himself? He looked into the future. Cold, grey nothingness.

The stomach cramps became a seizure. Renée helped him to the bedroom, smoothing the damp hair around his burning face.

"Get me a clean serviette out of my bag," she said to a figure hovering on the periphery. "Christian...Cheri, I'm right here."

The figure left the room and returned.

"Bring me some water."

"Is he dyin'?"

"No. He needs rest."

"He's in pain," said another. "Look at the convulsions. Withdrawal. He needs a good hit. I'll make up a syringe."

"No!"

"Hey, I know what Christian needs, Renée. A hit to get him over the top."

"No! He'll want more."

Paulo dropped his bag on the bed and dug into his personal things, coming up with a black leather shaving kit. "I know what I'm doing, Renée."

"Paulo, if you do this to Christian, I swear...!"

"What are you two yellin' about?" Maartyn demanded, entering the room with a crash.

"Paulo wants to give Christian heroin. Shoot him for me, please."

"Sure thing. Where first?"

"Left leg. The dog has taken care of the other one."

Maartyn held the gun low, pointing it at Paulo's knee. The wide grin on his face was comical, but Paulo had no doubt Maartyn would shoot. "Maartyn, take it easy. I'm only trying to help. Christian needs this, believe me."

"Bullshit, buddy. Y'all can stick that in yourself."

Paulo tried on a smile. "Maartyn..."

"I mean it. You just get busy an' cook that shit right up. Nice big dose, now."

"Maartyn, you're just having me on."

"I'm not kiddin', Amigo! Get the bonfire goin' an' toast up a big one. I'd jus' love an excuse to do you. Who the fuck d'ya think y'are? Queen Marjo?"

"I said I was sorry. I was half asleep, honestly."

"Yeah. Doesn't mean I wouldn't kill ya, just for the fun of it."

"Would you two stop! Just keep Paulo away."

"Okay. Nurse Jane's on duty. A'right buddy. Let's you an' me go outside for a little Louisiana barbecue."

"Maartyn, I can't...don't do this."

Christian drifted in and out of consciousness. The wracking convulsions became less severe. Renée held Christian's hand. His hands were cold and his face flushed, perspiration beading out like raindrops. Renée was reminded of the government limousine that arrived each morning to take her father to the Secretariat. The chauffeur polished the black Citroen while he waited, unless it was raining. Then she would watch from her window as the rain made silver beads, trying to guess which one would swell and break away. She pretended to be a bead of rain, growing larger, stronger, and when she was large enough she too would run. She didn't stop to consider that the raindrop's real glory was it's milieu, the shiny auto, and became common the moment it mingled with the mud between the cobbles. It was enough for a twelve year old to escape from cloying privilege. Too impatient for life to begin to accept that privilege comes with responsibilities, but sophisticated enough to know that privilege also comes with restraints. One reason for her easy adoption of the philosophies of the self; existentialism and nihilism.

Christian's eyes opened.

"Would you like a drink of water?"

Christian shook his head. "Wolf...Escobar's got him."

"Pardon? Who's Escobar?"

"Madman. Wants us off the island."

"Please take some water." Renée held the wine bottle to Christian's lips. He took a sip, like Wolf, out of courtesy.

"Don't go to the tobacco place."

His condition frightened her. He was sweaty but chilled. And now delirious. She had nothing but water, a cool cloth and her hands. Maybe Paulo was right. Heroin is just another medicine, like morphine. She knew about morphine. The drug her father clings to. She pushed the guilt away. "Are you in pain?"

Christian pondered the question. Paulo had narcotics. His body needed nourishment, but his subconscious reached out for an easier way. The endless battle being waged beneath the surface. It was the thing Christian feared most. If he gave in it was a fast trip to the dark regions. Had almost forgotten the morning he awoke in Chicago over the jazz club, burning up, freezing, sick enough to know it was time. The next morning he woke in a County Hospital emergency room. Band members had dumped him off at the ambulance entrance. One of the lucky ones. The worst of the nightmare was, he didn't know why he was screaming. He hadn't been a junkie long enough to be of two minds. One, the rational junkie, take it or leave it. The other, the dependent junkie who'd do anything for a hit.

It had been a long, tormented climb back. Near the top but not yet there when he arrived in Cuba. Tender, vulnerable. "Don't let him..."

"No, Cheri. I won't let him."

Then he slept, secure in the vague awareness that Renée was near. He was hooked on a new chemistry. He just wasn't aware. Renée knew but she too had a long way to go in her own emotional journey.

It was dark inside the bedroom. A glance at the shutters told him that it was also dark outside. Renée was asleep, arm over his chest. Wolf was curled up beside his leg. He was hungry. It was the hunger that occurs because one eats, not because one starves. Another person had been present. Maartyn. Not Paulo. He vaguely remembered Escobar's voice also but couldn't tell if it was a dream. The hunger would have to wait. Renée stirred, got more comfortable and slept on. Christian drifted, the last sound was Maartyn's familiar wheezing snore from the living room.

The next time he awoke it was mid day according to the light flooding through the window. He was ravenously hungry. Sounds came from the pantry. The hiss of gas. A pot being moved. Water splashing. Comforting sounds, like home.

"Renée!?..."

Wolf wandered slowly into the bedroom.

"Hey...How are you, dog?"

"Question is, how are you?" Renée asked from the door.

"Oh, man, I slept for hours."

"Cheri," Renée said softly, "you have been away almost two days." She helped Wolf up on the bed. He whimpered when she touched his stomach. "So long that poor Wolf has had time to recover. See? He's happy to see you too."

Wolf stood over Christian looking deep into his eyes. Satisfied, he curled up and went to sleep.

"Two days? That's impossible."

"Not in your condition. Señor Escobar said you're lucky to be alive."

"Escobar?"

"Yes. He brought Wolf because he had to go to Havana. He said to prepare for anything. When I told him what had happened he was concerned because you allowed three strong powers to invade your body. Those were his words."

"He's a doctor of some kind."

"Well, Cheri, he's not conventional. He said that you starved your body at the same time adding stress, which, taken together wouldn't be a problem, but, because you were not eating, you had allowed your body to cleanse itself. He meant the drugs. The three elements combined are too powerful. Your system tried to shut down to stop the process. That's what he said."

"So, how did I survive?"

"Chicken broth."

"Then I wasn't hallucinating."

"With herbs Escobar sent Miguel to find."

"Wow, chicken soup. Howie's mother used to make him eat a gallon of chicken soup if he even got a pimple. Where'd you get the chicken?"

"Ah, Maartyn borrowed a chicken or two from the village."

"Borrowed? You mean, 'May I please borrow that chicken to make soup and I'll bring it right back'?"

Renée laughed. "Not exactly. When he tried to 'borrow' another one he was nearly caught, so the chicken loan business has come to an end. Maartyn's much better. He and Miguel are out fishing. Fish broth is even better than chicken but no one can stomach the salt fish, except Wolf and he ate most of it. So, you see, everyone is healing nicely."

"You're a fantastic nurse."

"Thank you. And what about my cooking?"

"I don't know. Did I really eat?"

"You ingrate! I've spoon fed you my best chicken broth and you have the nerve to say you never tasted it?"

"Whoa, easy. I could smell it and it smelled great."

"Liar. I hate the smell of chicken boiling. Makes me want to throw up."

"Me too. I dreaded chicken soup day. During the war Mom would buy these old hens from a man who came around with a cart. They were so old she had to boil them for a whole day. Man, I did everything I could to stay out of the house."

"I know. My mother made the cooks boil chicken out in the carriage house. Even then I'd be too sick to eat. My maid warned me when chicken was on the menu."

"You had your own maid?"

"Of course," she said.

Again, the wide economic gulf between them. His mother cooked over a wood stove in their small apartment, the sweat running down her arms, the frizzy hair hastily piled off her neck. The worn out dresses and aprons that Renée's maid would use for dust rags. "It must've been hard, to make the broth, I mean."

Christian and Renée looked at each other. There was an understanding that neither could explain. Renée curled up in the crook of his arm, head nestled against his face and shoulder, fingers teasing his damp hair.

Christian studied the strands of her blonde hair gathered in folds across his chest. "I dreamed I was in a lecture hall. Jean-Paul Sartre was standing at the lectern looking sweaty in a dark suit. He went on and on about Ontology and Dialectics. Existential Ethics and Meaning. I interrupted him in front of hundreds of students and said that I thought it was all a bunch of crap. He agreed and shook my hand. Said he was glad someone finally had the balls to say so and he could now go home to Paris and fish in the Seine because that's all he wanted to do."

Renée laughed. She spoke English to make it easier. "I agree. It's been a great weight to carry; understanding all the words just to sound intellectual." She turned to look into his eyes, holding him tightly. "I never really understood all that he was saying, except about not being if being was being without love."

"That doesn't sound like Sartre."

"But he had Simone de Beauvoir. A person at home is not always the same as the public image. That's me too."

"It doesn't sound like you either."

"Not the person I am in a discussion about philosophers and Bohemian ways."

"It's all an act?"

"No, no! I am me...the wild child of the Beat Generation and I believe all the important things we talk about...sexual freedom and self expression, it's just that, I don't need Sartre or Camus to say it for me in complicated ways. It's so much talk, talk, talk. I think they must talk in their sleep instead of making love."

"They don't seem the type. But you'd have to ask Simone."

"I've known this since I was a little girl. My mother taught me. She knows Simone. You see, my mother made the mistake of falling in love with my father who's the opposite. Because of her great love for him she has suppressed all the things that made her free. She wanted to be a dancer. Adored Isadora Duncan. Weeps when she watches expressive dance. You'd be surprised at how it breaks her heart just to see our horses run free. She never rides. Told father that she can't stand horses but the truth is she cannot stand to see them led around and have people tell them when to go and when to stop. It makes her think of Indochina and the repression. She thinks all wild things should be free. Yes, my mother is responsible for me running away, although she pretended to be horrified by my behaviour. If she didn't father would probably beat her."

"Beat her? You don't mean that literally. That's not the way important public figures behave...is it?"

Renée pulled away and sat on the side of the bed staring at the Gulf, braiding her hair. "Christian, my naive lover, you would be shocked to know what goes on behind tall doors. Some of the most exalted leaders are so bestial that we should bring back La Guillotine. My friends at school, from the best families and the Colonies, we'd compare our parents. It was rare that a person I knew wasn't scarred by brutality, molested by fathers or even worse, by emotional and spiritual neglect. Even a beating followed by wild love making is preferable to being completely ignored while your man goes to the whores."

"That's not just in the best families."

"I know, it's why we are who we are. We run from that reality. Our parents were brought up to accept it. I didn't need Maupassant. I don't need Ginsberg to educate me on sexual freedom. No, my mother set me free. She warned me to fly from relationships. All the money in

167

France is not worth living in a coal cellar of the mind and spirit." She turned to face Christian to emphasis her belief.

"Yeah, I dig. I guess I spent too long figuring out Lenny Bruce."

"Why do you worship Lenny Bruce?"

"My real father. If *father* is the one who teaches. I caught him in a little club in Chicago. Your mother taught you to be free...well, I never learned a thing from the man who screwed my mother, but Lenny's teaching me how to say *fuck* so that my tongue doesn't go funny. Lenny's over the line and they'll break him for it but in the meantime all the constipated geeks like me are getting a voice. I'm just not there yet."

"You've made a good start, even since we met."

"Thank you. I thought jazz was my escape but it wasn't enough. Then I thought, it's cool to break the law, use drugs, see? Lenny says I was just plain stupid. He's trying to break through the moral lies. Expose the phonies, the bigots. But they'll get him."

"Who, the priests?"

"Lenny pisses off just about everybody. The moralists. The suburban drones. Right wing hypocrites. Teachers. Censors. When all he's doing is showing us how small minded we are. He talks like a bigot to expose bigotry. He talks about sex in public to expose the phony moralists."

"And gets away with it?"

"Not for long. You know what, I think Ernesto Escobar would like Lenny Bruce."

"Monsieur Escobar gives me the creeps. Something's wrong..."

"The dude's plugged in when it comes to things like dictators and power. He makes fun of the Batista government to expose government corruption."

"Such hypocrites, those politicians. All of them," she breathed with disgust.

"I know," agreed Christian.

"I don't want to be like them."

"What do you want to be when you grow up?"

Renée got up to look at something on the water. "I'm twenty years old, Christian! That's supposed to be grown up. According to my father I should have been married already, with babies. I wonder how he thought I could get a degree, have children and look after a husband who is just like him? He should've had boys."

"My father had a boy but he didn't know it." Christian watched Renée, but his thoughts were in Montreal and he was a kid, confused

by life. "But then I wasn't much of a son. I think he ignored ...
cause I was interested in music and art instead of baseball and hockey.
I was a big disappointment so I never had to measure up."

"It wasn't just you, Christian. Parents are always disappointed.
Their kids never are what they planned or what they fantasize as the
little embryo grows in mommy's tummy. They develop this false hope
that the embryo will be something other than a monster. It scares
them. Adults are all failures and they want their offspring to succeed
so they have something to be proud of. When we fail them they're
twice disappointed and take it out on us. Instead of letting us be our
selves and make our own mistakes they either ignore us or try to guide
us to the right shining path. It's so pathetic."

"You have to feel sorry for them though."

"Even if they're bastards?" Renée turned and asked with a smile.

"I guess. Jeez, when I think of all the stupid things Howie and I
did. It's a wonder my old man didn't leave home sooner."

"Obligations. Church? That's changing I think. At least in France
because the priests are loosing their hold and more people are thumbing their noses at the Pope. Living apart and living with the guilt. It's a
big burden if they still believe in the Church. I don't want that."

"Me either. My parents never divorced. They just got tired of the
game."

"You think love is just a game?"

"No, I mean, the game...staying together."

"The obligation."

"What's the difference between obligation and responsibility?"

"That's easy. One you accept and one is forced on you."

"Which is which?"

"You figure it out."

"Mind's not up to it." Christian was tired but didn't want to stop. It
was the first time he and Renée had talked honestly and plainly.
"Where's Paulo?"

"He went to Havana with Monsieur Escobar."

"Is he coming back?"

"I don't know. He was very angry with Maartyn for forcing him to
take the heroin. He and Maartyn had a fight. Maartyn was going to
carve Paulo up with a broken bottle. Those were his words."

"Oh, God. What happened?"

Renée, suddenly animated, crossed to the bed and held her arms out,
hands together as if holding a pistol. "I got Maartyn's gun and said
that I would shoot both of them if they didn't stop. So, they stopped.

They had no idea I couldn't have pulled the trigger. Then we had this big argument about what to do. Paulo's very angry at you for bringing us to this crazy country...I know...you didn't. It was a vague invitation, but that doesn't satisfy Paulo. It would be better if he didn't come back but I'm afraid for him, Christian. He is such a fragile person."

"Havana isn't the place for Paulo."

"Escobar said he could get him a passport."

"Escobar...always Escobar. What is it about that guy?"

"I know, he scares me."

"Escobar's scary, but he may be our best hope."

"You look tired. You should sleep. I'll make a big pot of Momma Renée's broth. Miguel brought onions and herbs."

"Get to know Miguel. If there's anything you need, it may have a price but he can deliver."

"He's teaching me Cuban. I think Miguel likes you a great deal."

"Yeah, I know...Should I be worried?"

Part Two

Renée's Redemption

Renée and Maartyn were seated at the table eating soup and grilled fish by lamplight. Escobar's car purred to a stop outside the gate. When he let himself into the villa, Miguel's sisters were with him. Maartyn gaped, mouth open, still chewing. Renée's social instincts were immediate.

"Maartyn, we have guests!"

"Señorita Renée, Señor Maartyn...I present to you, Rosameralda and Esameralda Diez," he said in English for Maartyn's benefit. "Miguel's sisters. They'll be staying with you for awhile."

"I see," said Renée, in French. "Can you tell me why?"

Escobar answered in Spanish. "All in good time. I can tell you only that the girls are in great danger."

"So you bring them here so we'll be in danger also?"

"No, no. They're in danger only if they go home. If there's any trouble they'll simply vanish." He indicated the terrace.

"What are we to do with them in the meantime?"

"Miguel will see to their needs." The three girls eyed each other.

"Where is Miguel?" asked Escobar.

"I don't know. I'm not his mother. He comes and goes like a ghost."

"Yes, that's Miguel. And the dog?"

"He went with Miguel."

"That's good. And what of Christian?"

"He's sleeping."

"See that he's not disturbed. He'll need his strength in the days ahead. You and Maartyn must be ready to go with Rosameralda at a moment's notice. Don't ask questions and don't hesitate. Christian must be left alone."

"Why?"

"It's very simple, really. A technicality. Señor Maartyn has no papers. You've been identified as mercenaries. Christian's not directly connected to the Revolution, as yet..."

"Revolution!? Us...?"

"By association. The police know you're here. Christian can weather the first assault but not if you're found here as well and I can no longer protect him."

"This is absurd," said Renée.

"As you say. It has elements of the bizarre."

"Where's Paulo?" she asked.

Escobar sighed. "Very tragic. The young man was beginning to interest me. Not as cultured as I would like, but there were compensations...Paulo was arrested at the airport. The police found drugs in his luggage, and, unfortunately the passport was not a good fake. Your friend tried to run." Escobar shrugged Paulo out of existence.

"But where is he!?" Renée demanded impatiently.

"My sources tell me that he's in a hospital. That's all I know. Good night, Señorita."

Escobar whispered something to the girls and left, closing the door softly. There was an awkward silence as Escobar's leather shoes shuffled along the stone path. Every sound amplified by the heavy atmosphere. A car door opened and closed with metallic precision. The Lincoln crept away, like a big cat stalking the night. Rosameralda looked at Renée, sizing her up. Renée felt the eyes like hot probes, passing over her. The warm tingle and chill of fear were confusing. "Por favor, would you like to sit down?" offered Renée, in Spanish.

"Thank you," answered Rosameralda, surprised by the pale Frenchwoman's poise.

Rosameralda and Esameralda took places at the table opposite

Renée. Maartyn sat at the end of the table, back to the corner, window to his left and the pantry door to his right. Had the girls and the exits covered. He could size them up without making eye contact, unless they looked.

"We interrupt your dinner," began Rosameralda apologetically.

"Not at all. Would you like to join us?" Renée asked.

"No, thank you," replied Rosameralda.

Esameralda shook her head. "Thank you, no."

The Cuban girls surveyed the dinning room, windows and exits. Maartyn remained silent, awe struck by the glowing beauty of Rosameralda. But Esameralda would dominate any room that she didn't share with her younger sister. One of them was wearing a sweet spice oil. Talk was not easy for Maartyn. He understood action, or violence. And the girls were speaking another language. There was more than a language barrier. Rosameralda's glances were superior. She looked through Maartyn, as if sensing the transparent veneer of tough American thug; exposing the little boy from the Delta who, like them, grew up too fast. But Maartyn's emotional self hadn't kept pace. He could smell that mulatto musk; an exotic essence of sweet body oils, road dust and sweat and his senses vibrated. He spooned at his soup self consciously, looking away each time Rosameralda's eyes returned to his. Esameralda's look was less haughty, but unavoidably superior, as one who has learned about men and waits to see how things turn out. Of course the girls had been briefed by Escobar so there would be no surprises about Maartyn. Renée was another problem.

"A glass of wine perhaps?" asked Renée politely.

"Yes, please," answered Esameralda.

"No," replied Rosameralda. "Fidel has declared we must abstain from alcohol because it diverts one's attention from the cause. He says that one cannot make a revolution looking through a bottle, only through the sights of a rifle with a clear vision."

Maartyn looked at Renée for a translation. Renée was preoccupied. "Fidel Castro's probably right. Are you in favour of the Revolution?" she asked Rosameralda.

"I belong to the student section of the Acción y Sabataje which is a wing of the Resistance Civicio Movemento. My fiancée is a Castro fighter. He has gone to the hills of Las Villas to join Raul."

"Rosa..." Esameralda said softly, as a warning.

"I should not say too much. You might be spies. Señor Escobar says that you arrived in the automobile of the Servicios Especiales."

"We weren't aware of anything political, at the time. This man offered us a ride to Los Espiritos. We were unaware what was happening with your local politics. We knew that rebels were fighting in the hills. But that's going on all over Latin America so we thought nothing of it. Havana seemed like any normal big city. So did Pinar del Rio. Then we came here and things seem oddly, confused. I still don't know what's going on."

"Maybe it's better."

"Everyone keeps telling me that." She looked away with difficulty. "Maartyn," Renée said in English, "would you get that bottle of wine and some clean glasses."

Maartyn obediently got up and went to the pantry. The Cuban girls watched him carefully, noting his movements and strength of body, for practical reasons; survival perhaps, as well as the normal reasons.

"I speak some English," said Esameralda to Maartyn's back. "Most of my clients are Americans. Sometimes they talk to me, the nicer ones."

"Your clients?" asked Renée innocently. "What do you do?"

Maartyn returned with a bottle of the Rioja and two glasses. He put them on the table in front of Renée, clumsily arranging the glasses.

Renée observed their scrutiny of Maartyn and was not surprised to discover the girls exploring her openly, with equal curiosity, imagining how she looked in their eyes. Felt pale and inadequate in the presence of the dark, burning intensity of Rosameralda. Wondering what it would be like to make love with such a beautiful creature. She looked away, finally, to Esameralda and felt more comfortable in her warm gaze. She would flee to Esameralda for conversation or comfort but she wanted to experience the other's heat, like Cuban sunshine. Understood what it must be like for a man. She thought of Christian gazing at this vision in army fatigues. The battle jacket open, revealing the wonderfully rounded breasts beneath a man's white undershirt. Has Christian seen them? she wondered. Jealousy the first emotion. Then the demon envy rose up pushing aside jealousy. She flushed more. Then remembered the wine. "Excusez moi," she stammered, then switched to Spanish. "I am distracted, thinking of my poor Christian." The Cuban girls looked toward the bedroom door. She poured the wine with slightly trembling hands.

"I'm what you would call, a common whore," said Esameralda bluntly.

"Pardon me?" said Renée, spilling wine on the table.

"You asked my profession." Esameralda reverted to English for effect. "Common whore? Prostitute. Hooker. Call girl. Tramp. Rag doll.

Slime Sister. Mattress. Cum Cup. Pin cushion. Back Walker. Thump-er. Bounce. Shag Rag. Jump. Stab. Dick Pad. Virgin Mary. Midnight Flyer. Dog Bed. Zeed. Those are just some of names."

Renée's face was on fire but Maartyn was transfixed by the litany. Many words painfully familiar from his childhood. Adolescent hard knock school. He knew about Esameralda's profession but Renée had not been forewarned. But she was French, a child of experience and certain realities. "I see, and you're not happy with your chosen profession?" asked Renée, recovering.

"I wanted to be a nun," Esameralda answered simply.

Maartyn went from transfixed to amused. "I've heard those names for whores but what's a Zeed?"

"Zeed, is the last resort. End of the road when you come to me."

"You're being too hard on yourself," said Renée, reverting to Spanish. "Much too beautiful to be used like that."

"Beauty has nothing to do with it, Señorita. I've been a whore since a little girl. I'm too ashamed of my life to expect more."

"But, I don't understand. Being a prostitute doesn't mean you can't be a good person. In France it's a noble profession, even for the low class girls who hang out with criminals."

"It's because I refuse to be associated with criminals. I work where the Cuban gangsters can't find me. And also the police. And I won't be some rich man's mistress. So I go where the men are Americans or desperate losers. You do a lot of things that aren't worthy of a human being and so I cannot think of myself as high class, like the others, who are on the payroll of the casinos."

"When Fidel triumphs you won't have to work as a prostitute," said Rosameralda sharply.

"When Fidel and his ragged heroes stumble into Habana we'll both be out of a job!" retorted Esameralda. "She thinks the coming of Castro will be some kind of magic and all the poverty and crime will vanish over night."

"It will. Just as Fidel and Ché predict...."

"She's dreaming, as usual. Too much talk about revolution and socialism..."

"The Revolution *is* for you!"

"For the idealists, you mean!" The conversation went too fast for Renée. The argument seemed to be the difference between the way the revolutionaries see things and the way things actually are in Cuba. Rosameralda insisted the revolution was for the people, the poor Cubans committed to the muck of the city cesspools and the swamps of the barrios. About corrupt Cuban politicians and greedy American capitalists. The ones Rosameralda and her compadres will expel from Cuba to save Esameralda from her life on the streets. Esameralda vehemently objected to being patronized by her fanatical younger sister. Social justice got lost in the rhetoric of ideological revolution and the hard facts of the eternal struggle on the streets of Havana. And every city and town and village. The politics of poverty.

Renée diverted her attention to what they were wearing. Both girls were without adornment other than colourful scarves holding back luxurious amounts of dark, shining hair, captured in thick bundles for travelling. The severe hair style made their faces stand out clearly so that their beauty was in the natural, high cheek bone structure. The test of real beauty. Rosameralda was the same age as Renée but looked older. A maturity of experience far beyond Renée's Bohemian rebellion. What would Jean-Paul Sartre make of Cuba and these girls? wondered Renée. Experience and reality, in the flesh, she said to herself. The loose khaki battle fatigues could not camouflage Rosameralda's stunning figure, further complicating Renée's assessment. She could only console herself by thinking that Rosameralda would probably get fat and show veins and stretch marks.

Esameralda was wearing a simple blue and beige dress with white floral patterns. Colourful, but would not be out of place in church. It didn't hide her figure but would not label her as a prostitute. She could have been a very pretty teacher or an office girl home from work. There was something about her also that said too much experience for her years, but her bright eyes looked hopefully for the future...The argument suddenly ended in a panting draw. Renée was drawn back to Rosameralda like a moth to fire.

"Why are you dressed like a soldier?" she asked.

"Señor Escobar says that you know too much already so it won't matter if I tell you. I am also a member of the July 26th Movement. I make bombs to kill tyrant pigs like Batista. Our own guardian dog, Pietro, was responsible for foiling one attempt when he worked for the Servicios Speciales, but we don't hold that against him. After all, many of Batista's military are joining the Revolution. We missed Batista last time, but next time..."

Renée was struck again by the stark reality of Cuba. Her own journey of self indulgence on the fringe of reality seemed shallow and pointless. William S. Burroughs knows nothing of real life, she thought. Only a self destructive journey in his own mind. Kerouac should have travelled more in Latin America, she decided.

"Can you tell me about the July 26th Movement?"

"Soon the whole world will know." She smoothed her hair and straightened her fatigue jacket as if preparing to deliver a speech. "In fifty-three, Fidel Castro and a small band of courageous fighters attacked the Moncada military garrison in Santiago de Cuba. Are you familiar with our country?"

"I must admit, only vaguely."

"East Cuba. Santiago de Cuba is a very beautiful old city in Oriente Province, the first capital of Cuba, and the place where all the revolutions have begun. The army dare not enter the hills. Three times since eighteen sixty-eight, the people have risen up against corrupt dictators like Batista, and meddling foreign governments like Spain and the United States. Each time the revolution has failed. But this time Fidel will be victorious. But in fifty-three the small, brave band of fighters were cut down by Cuban soldiers armed with American weapons. Many were killed, even in their jail cells after they surrendered, and Fidel and others were captured and imprisoned on Isla del Pinos. The disastrous attack took place on July 26th and Fidel vowed that the next time it would not be just Moncada." Rosameralda was not in the villa at that moment. Renée believed her heart, like many Cubans, was with that band of poorly armed but determined rebels in the jungle. "Fidel languished in prison for two years. He wrote a manifesto and when they released him he went to the United States and then took part in the rebellion in Columbia. He met Ché in Mexico. In fifty-six Fidel and Raul and Ché and eighty of his brave fighters made a heroic voyage back to Cuba on a small yacht and landed on the beach in Oriente. With only a few weapons they fought their way into the mountains. Since then Fidel and his Comandantés have been recruiting people and establishing the revolution so that now Fidel controls all of eastern Cuba and most of the central Provinces. The 'next time' has come, and soon the banner of the glorious 26th of July will fly above the palace in Habana. At this moment Comandanté Camilo Cienfuegos is marching toward Pinar del Rio to establish a Western front in preparation for the victory in Habana or to die fighting to the last man for Cuban liberty!"

Renée gasped. For the first time she was aware that the Revolution was not hundreds of miles away. A revolution she knew almost nothing about. She could only look with awe at Rosameralda. But at the same time she detected a falseness, as if the story were a recitation, not from the heart but a practiced sales pitch.

The Cuban girl had charisma and a cause. Renée felt small and immature in her presence. What had she done with her life except run away from home and waste her youth in pursuit of a fantasy called Bohemia? Christian was an artist, also confused by life. Would be considered a dilettante had he lived a century earlier. Maartyn, the macho thug, was an itinerant misfit. The Cuban girls, although at opposite poles ideologically, were immersed in a struggle for the survival of their country. Poised at a crossroads, a rare moment in history. It had nothing to do with Renée, she was certain, but somehow she had been thrust into the vortex...She was still holding the glass of wine.

"Pardon, mademoiselle. Vos vin...Excusez moi..." She pushed the glass toward Esameralda. The heavy wineglass tripped on a crack and fell over, shattering, propelling the liquid in a purple-red fan across the narrow table. Rosameralda and Esameralda jumped up, fleeing in opposite directions to escape the flood, bumping the table, knocking the bottle over. It rolled toward the edge. Maartyn dove for the bottle, slamming the table against the wall. He held on to the bottle but his weight pulled the table back and he fell over the bench. The bottle smashed. The table ended up on top of him. The three girls were shocked by the sudden violence.

Rosameralda was the first to recover. She giggled nervously. So did Esameralda and then Renée. They lifted the heavy table and helped Maartyn to his feet. He was dripping red wine and bleeding from glass cuts on his arms. A piece of green glass stuck in his hand.

"Are you all right, Maartyn?"

"Yeah, I guess."

"You're bleeding."

"A scratch."

"And glass...let me look," said Renée.

"Renée?...Renée!?" Christian was calling.

"Oh my, we've disturbed Christian." Renée called, "I'm coming, Cheri! Au moment, Maartyn's bleeding."

"You go," said Esameralda. "We'll see to Señor Maartyn."

"Thank you."

Esameralda righted the bench and sat Maartyn down. He was like a wounded child, submitting to the tender ministrations of Mother Esameralda. Rosameralda, less interested in nursing and more in tactical surveillance, wandered out to the terrace to challenge the air. The cool night breeze had replaced the earlier calm. A fresh, dry northerly was blowing in across the Gulf. It would be cold by morning.

Christian tried to sit up. "Don't get up, Cheri," said Renée, closing the shutters. "It was only a small accident. Maartyn tipped over the table. Has a few cuts. Esameralda Diez is looking after him. How do you feel?"

"Esameralda?"

"Yes, she's here. Her sister Rosameralda also. Monsieur Escobar..."

"Rosameralda!? Here?"

"Yes, as I was saying...Monsieur Escobar brought them. He said they are to stay here and you are to get more rest."

"Why?"

"Because you're not well"

"No. I mean, why are they here?"

"Oh...that's not so simple. Why don't you sleep now and I'll tell you all about it in the morning." Renée smoothed his forehead, gently tracing the hairline, tucking longish strands of blonde hair behind his ears, drawing a wandering line down his neck, fingers fanning out over his chest, rubbing and soothing. She rubbed lower over his tight belly. Claiming her territory, the Alpha female.

"Where's Wolf?"

"With Miguel."

"He's all right then?"

"*Shhh...*

Christian was groggy with sleep. Still weak from days of tension and deprivation, lulled by the familiar hands and soft, comforting accent, so the confusion of emotions caused by the nearness of the Cuban girls, remembered mostly in his dreams of candles, dancing by firelight, surfaced briefly and then subsided. Replaced by a desire for Renée...aware of warm lips, he was aroused...and then he was asleep.

Renée returned to the living room to find order restored and an awkward silence. Rosameralda was on the terrace. "He's sleeping," Renée said. "Poor baby, so exhausted." Her own heightened sensuality was problematic. It would have to wait.

"I think this clumsy boy will live," said Esameralda in English. She had removed the glass shard and made a bandage with her scarf but the bleeding continued. Her loosened black hair tumbled around her shoulders. It made the sleeping problem more difficult for Renée.

Maartyn grinned shyly. "This place is more like a fu...friggin' hospital every day."

Renée yawned. It was a signal. "Someone can sleep on the floor. And one on the couch." Now for the difficult part. There was room in the Mediterranean bed for three. The choices were Rosameralda or Esameralda or Maartyn, plus Renée. Christian would be in the middle for practical reasons. "It is cold tonight," she said, trying to sound calm and efficient. Rosameralda was the dangerous fire, sensuous and magnetic. A condition Renée understood. Esameralda was tropical sunshine and spiritual warmth, with flashing eyes. But she was also a whore, used to men's bodies. Perhaps the nearness of Christian, the patient, would be nothing more than clinical. There was still the tawny body and that damned luxurious hair, like a shinning black tidal wave. Perhaps Maartyn? No. "Esameralda, you sleep with us. Rosameralda may want to keep guard, I think."

Esameralda was amused, as if she knew the thought process Renée had just gone through. "As you wish," she said simply.

Rosameralda entered, closing the terrace door against the wind, drawing the thin fatigues close to her body, emphasizing the wonderful curves of her hips. Renée thought she had made the right choice.

"Rosa," Esameralda said in Spanish, "you lose. I get to keep Renée's man warm. You get to fend off the clumsy American." Esameralda giggled at Rosameralda's expression.

"At least the American boy can protect me," she shot back.

Esameralda looked at Maartyn slouched on the bench holding his bandaged hand, like an injured player on the sidelines. She spoke in English. "My sister asks if you can protect her from the dangers of the night?"

"Goddamned right!" Maartyn said, as if his manhood had been challenged. He reached across his body with his good hand and worked the small revolver out of his pocket. He showed the gun to Rosameralda proudly.

"What's that toy?" Rosameralda asked in Spanish. She undid the straps of her field pack and drew out a brown leather holster that matched her skin. She slipped a large pistol out of the holster and laid it beside Maartyn's revolver. It was blue-grey, cold and streamlined.

"Holy shit! A Browning."

Esameralda explained in English. "My sister takes a gun as a lover. An American pistol that was pointed at her by a desperate Batista officer. The cop was very disappointed that all he got was a knee in the nuts for his efforts."

Maartyn winced. "Man, I'd give my left nut for one of those babies." He immediately regretted the statement, remembering the night with Juanita. "Don't y'all tell yer sister what I said."

Esameralda laughed, white teeth flashing. Suddenly Renée realized she was too beautiful to take to bed. "...And her fiancée sleeps with a machine gun so she thinks sex has to do with triggers, calibers and muzzle velocities."

It was Maartyn's turn to laugh at the typical army barracks humour he understood.

"Someone must keep watch," Rosameralda announced. Esameralda translated for Maartyn. "Comandanté Rosameralda orders that a night watch be kept. The police are probably looking for us."

Maartyn grinned, thrilled by the approaching danger. Renée felt her skin crawl. The stark immediacy of their situation flooded back. Yes, the villa was like a field hospital in the Spanish Civil War, an army outpost in a Hemingway story. Also a hideout for desperate revolutionaries. The enemy was pressing closer and it wasn't the least bit romantic.

"I guess that's me," Maartyn said.

Maartyn attempted to make a fire but was having trouble breaking the larger pieces of drift wood with his damaged hand. Rosameralda stood by the window looking at the turbulent Gulf, visible by the light of the stars and the phosphorescence in the tumbling waves. She knew the moon would be up in an hour to make the night vigil easier. The cool wind was blowing her loosened hair like battle pennants. In defiance of the wind she removed her fatigue jacket. The goose bumps on her tawny arms stood out in the lamplight. Cotton shielded breasts thrust against the cold, the taught nipples like twin wind sensors. Chilling her body down to normal. Maartyn tried not to stare, cursing his inability to break the kindling. Rosameralda crossed to the fireplace, took the branch from Maartyn and broke it across her knee. She broke a half dozen more branches and returned to the window.

"Ah, thanks...muchis gratius."

Rosameralda smiled indulgently. It took Maartyn many tries to fire the kindling. The wind whistling up the chimney from the open window kept blowing the matches out. He wanted to tell Rosameralda to close the shutters.

By the time Maartyn had the fire producing respectable flames Rosameralda was feigning sleep on the American couch, the 9mm cradled in her arms. He closed the shutters and put the fatigue jacket over her bare shoulders and Christian's sweatshirt over her hips, taking a few moments to appreciate the impossibly round firmness. He swallowed hard and eased the sweatshirt into place, fingers grazing the coarse drill of her military fatigues. The merest trace of a smile curved her lips.

Maartyn kept the night watch diligently, in his element. Patrolling the terrace, making regular circuits of the villa, and tending the fire. Eying the 9mm automatic cuddled into the bosom of the exotic revolutionary curled up on his couch.

Sometime after midnight he caught a glimpse of Miguel and Wolf crossing the far edge of the garden. The moon was hidden by a cloud and only sharp eyes could have seen the pair skulking through the underbrush, heading for the compound. Nothing else moved during the night except the dry palmettos scrapping together in the wind like arthritic crickets. The dry northerly blew itself out before dawn, leaving behind the sharp cold, tinged with the smell of tobacco. Los Espiritos and Western Cuba were deceptively calm at sunrise.

While the village slumbered the tempo of the Revolution was picking up in the east. But Ernesto Escobar seldom slept. At night he shut himself in his empty villa with a powerful radio, monitoring the progress of the Revolution. In the morning he gave Miguel messages to deliver to Escobar's key personnel before attending to the needs of his Gringos.

The messages were brief, but the meaning significant to the cause. The rebels were on the move and Batista's army was unable to stop them. One indication was the increasing denials by the government. Rebel radio, on the other hand, maintained its daily gush of revolutionary slogans, Latin music and coded messages to the Provincial Comandantés and recorded speeches by Fidel Castro to his fighters scattered about the countryside.

Castro was somewhere in Oriente Province. Ché Guevara and Camilo Cienfuegos continued to control the rural areas, harassing small garrisons, increasing their supply of weapons and all the while adding young fighters. Cuban peasants openly supported the rebels, cheering as the small columns rolled through a village on its way to the next garrison, or fed them when they stopped for a brief rest in a roadside ditch. Braving the strafing runs of the Cuban Air Force B-26 bombers making lazy figure of eight passes over the countryside. The air force gunners fired from a safe distance at anything that moved. Many innocent civilians were killed.

The rebels were under orders from Castro not to steal from the people, therefore the farmers fed them willingly and protected them as they slept. In two years the revolution had gone from a few desperate mountain guerrillas to two thousand hardened fighters facing forty thousand reluctant soldiers of Batista's army. Outnumbered but seldom out fought, the guerrillas moved at will between the towns and villages. Batista's army rarely ventured out of their garrisons to challenge the rebels. The rebels, in turn, never gave the army an opportunity to fight in the open. They were now seasoned hit and run experts; bearded young Turks, and some too young to grow beards; Cuba's ragtag heroes, in grimy, sweat-stained fatigues. Escobar noted all this carefully for the future. For the present he assessed Castro's and Batista's chances.

It was apparent to Fulgencio Batista, that the majority of Cubans supported the 26th of July Movement. What he continued to deny was the inevitability of the Revolution, so it was business as usual. The corruption and the brutality of the crumbling regime continued, or increased, as upper level Batistianos consolidated their wealth and moved money to bank accounts in the United States and Europe.

Castro had his own priorities. His goal was the ideological as well as the practical takeover of Santiago de Cuba, the heart of Cuban rebellions and the scene of too many failures. Castro had a personal score to settle in the east before he moved on to Havana in triumph. The old city of Santiago was about as far from Los Espiritos as one could get in Cuba but other forces were growing in Pinar del Rio Province to challenge the 26th of July Movement.

December 24th 1958: Rosameralda awoke before dawn and indicated to Maartyn that he should sleep. The firewood was used up but the morning felt softer after the passing of the northerly and the day promised clear skies and more Caribbean sunshine. Maartyn sat on the American couch watching Rosameralda preparing for her watch. She brushed her hair, leaning to the side to let the masses of shinning ebony fall down and away, cursing the tangles under her breath. When the thick bundle had been subdued she tied it back with a purple silk scarf. The long, arching pony tail made her look like any gorgeous, dark skinned teenager getting ready for school. Then she poured water into a bowl, stripped off the white top and splashed water on her face and upper body, massaging the cold water into the mat of dark hair under her arms. She cupped cold water to her breasts, shaping and kneading, enjoying the firmness of her own body. The dark, distended nipples stood erect and hard. Maartyn nearly feinted.

Rosameralda toweled off with the undershirt and hung it on the rack beside a last strand of dried pompano. Next she took a brass tube, that looked like a rifle shell, from her pack and casually applied red lipstick, using a hand mirror she kept in her Spartan cosmetic pouch. The pouch had once contained .303 calibre shells for the American rifles. She did that curious thing with her lips that women do when applying lipstick. Then smoothed and fine tuned the colour at the corners with her baby finger, then did the curious thing again. Patted a few strands of loose hair into place. Front view. Side view. With Rosameralda all angles were wonderful and she knew the effect it would have on Maartyn. Her fatigue jacket was beside Maartyn on the back of the couch. She walked into the living room and reached across Maartyn for the jacket. He could have touched her breasts with the slightest movement of his hand. Her morning smell was intoxicating but it was no more than her natural musk. Maartyn inhaled deeply for many reasons. He could detect a hint of a smile on her lips, then she was gone, automatic pistol stuck in her belt. How could he sleep?

Christian awoke lying on his back, Renée's arm over his chest and one bare leg over his, as they had been on previous mornings. Her sweet breath brushed his face like a feather. But there seemed to be another arm over him and another naked body close to his. It wasn't Maartyn. He turned his head and to the darkest eyes and brightest smile he had ever seen up close. The other reason why he felt so warm and protected. The three bed partners were covered by Renée's jumper and Esameralda's dress. Esameralda moved closer. He could feel the warm, moist mat against his thigh, her smooth, bare skin the length of his body. Esameralda slipped her hand under the ersatz bed cover and stroked the fine golden hair on Christian's chest with delicate finger tips, gliding expertly down to his thigh. Christian held his breath as the inevitable happened. He glanced the other way. Renée was still breathing easily, lightly. His own breathing was becoming erratic. He feared he was still too weak to survive the ecstasy. How to stop the process that was going to cause big trouble?

Esameralda's hot, wet breath caressed his ear. "It's all right, Christian. Renée and I made a pact that whoever woke first would see to your morning needs."

Christian swallowed carefully and whispered. "I don't think she meant..."

"*Shhhh...*"

Renée stirred and snuggled closer, her own hand began kneading his chest, pinching his tiny but stiffening nipples. A reflex, something she often did in sleep, dreaming or whatever. And usually she continued down over his stomach until she was rubbing his penis. It drove Christian crazy, especially if she refused to wake up. Or worse, stopped rubbing.

"See, she knows what you need," whispered Esameralda.

"Oh, God!..."

"*Shush*...boy, we know what to do."

Soft hands drifted over his body, one conscious, the other unconscious and searching. The hands danced around each other, an erotic game of keep away. Christian, locked in a sweet dilemma, realized there was only one thing to do...or two things...

Renée awoke tingling, damp and smiling. "Oh, Christian, you are feeling better." Esameralda was damp and smiling also, but pretended to be asleep. Diplomacy of the highest order.

Miguel was in the kitchen preparing breakfast when Christian, wearing only Levis shorts, weaved into the living room and sat down at the table. Maartyn, still clutching Lucille, was sound asleep, sprawled on the floor having flung himself off the couch again. The demons pursuing him in his dreams, or maybe it was just the nearness of Rosameralda, who had covered him during the cool of the morning with her fatigue jacket. Maartyn stirred and the gun was pointing in Christian's direction. Christian gently moved Maartyn's arm so that Lucille was pointing harmlessly at the wall.

"Feeling better, Señor Christ?"

"Some...what's for breakfast?"

"Fried black beans with rice. Corn bread with butter and sugar. Café con leche. Oranges. All sent by Señor Escobar. But for you I have orders from Señorita Renée that you should only have the chicken soup and maybe an orange."

"I see. Regular fascist dietitian."

"What is a 'dietitian'?"

"A professional food person."

"Is it like a cook?"

"Not exactly...it's who cooks are supposed to consult when they prepare meals for sick people."

"I get it. It's like not serving too many fried things the same."

"Yeah, that's it. Like not serving Twinkies with Moon Pies after starting a meal with Wagon Wheels. Dig?"

Miguel grinned. "Señor Christ was not impressed with Escobar's lunch?"

"You could say that. Where is everybody?"

"Your woman and my sisters have gone swimming."

"Swimming!?..."

"It's okay, Señor, Pietro's patrolling, and as you can see, Señor Maartyn's sleeping so he can do no harm, as long as he doesn't pull the trigger. Besides, the ladies have gone to a secret place up in the hills, known only to the village. The children go there to swim. My sisters will take care of your woman and maybe show her the caves. I think they like your skinny woman."

"Okay." One problem solved for the moment, he decided. "Tell me about the body?"

"Body? Who's body?"

"You know...the dead engineer."

"Oh, we found our comrade okay. I mean, he wasn't okay, but we found him in the same place. The floats were just below the surface."

"That would explain the arms waving."

"And so they scared off the big fish. Crabs got his feet and he was swollen up like a long dead pig, but he wasn't too bad otherwise, except for the colour, and his missing eyes..."

"Miguel, I didn't ask for details. What did you do with him?"

"The smell was pretty bad too, by the time we got to shore. Señor Escobar has those big freezers and the electricity's restored so we have the unfortunate engineer on ice, as they say."

Miguel placed a bowl of chicken soup in front of Christian. He picked up a spoon and pushed at the oily, grey contents. Things floated up and disappeared, like dead things in a spring flood; goosebumpy flesh and chicken grease. Something surfaced that looked like the dead engineer's missing eyeballs. Although he was hungry when he sat down, his appetite vanished. "How about just coffee."

"Sorry, Señor Christ. Orders. Señorita Renée said, no coffee for her poor convalescent."

"More orders. Is this my home or a concentration camp? I feel like I've been away about a month."

"Only two days, Señor Christ. Much has happened. I brought you the papers, but they mostly lie because they're controlled by the Batistianos or the Americans. However, Radio Rebelde talks about victories in the East. Señor Escobar says to believe rebel radio because you cannot lie to the people. Oriente's under Fidel's control, except for Santiago, but Fidel's just waiting for the right time to move. Ché and Camilo and Raul have made great gains in Camagüey and Las Villas. The Comandantés are moving toward Habana. And there'll soon be another front, ah, near here. It's only a matter of time now before *He* leaves."

Christian missed the brief reference to their geography. "Who's 'He'?"

"Batista of course. The great General Batista who's too afraid of his own people to go from the Palace to Camp Columbia without a hundred armed guards."

"Camp Columbia, huh? Sounds like a Boy Scout Jamboree."

"Camp Columbia's the reason Batista and his gang have remained so long. They keep the best soldiers and big tanks and things at this huge compound outside of Habana. He even has an air force. Señor Escobar says that if Batista would let the army out of Camp Columbia to help the cuartels, Fidel would never make it to Habana. But lucky for us that Batista is too scared to give his own generals power."

"Yeah, I can see his point.'

"It's happened before."

"You've had a coup d'etat the odd time."

"Oh yes, Señor, Batista himself did this, twice. It's how he came to be president. He fears mostly his own generals and mercenaries but soon the tyrant pig will learn to fear us."

"You really hate this guy don't you."

"Really do, yes. All Cubans hate Batista, unless he owns them. But most are afraid to criticize. He sends his special police around the country to beat his citizens or steal their money. And all the time the brave Batista army is hiding in their cuartels, shivering that Fidel and the Comandantés might select their garrison. But Fidel's very clever. Now he tells his Comandantés that it's better to shout at the soldiers and sing the anthem all night until they shit their pants from fear. They don't want to kill them, only the evil ones like Batista and his generals."

"I see, I think..."

"Señor Escobar says that many soldiers run to the arms of Ché and Camilo, begging to become revolutionaries. Señor Escobar says, wait until the Revolution is declared and see how many Cubans suddenly become proud members of the 26th of July Movement. He says that in Habana lawyers and judges are letting their beards grow and buying uniforms like Fidel wears so they will not be accused of supporting Batista. But the difference is that Fidel and all the fighters will have dirty uniforms. The lawyers will look too clean, even if their hands are dirty. And all the Batista gangs will fall on their knees before Fidel, begging his forgiveness for not joining him sooner. There will be a big fiesta and much killing."

"Killing? After the Revolution?"

"Many scores to settle, Señor. The Batistianos have beaten and murdered us for so many years. It's one thing to try to kill your enemies, but this Batista dog, and I mean no disrespect for dogs, sends his police to kill innocent Cubans, children and women too. And those they don't kill, they beat and rape. The ones who only starve to death are the lucky ones. And many young men and students are imprisoned just because they ask for free elections and an end to the corruption."

"Is it really that bad? I mean, I walked around Havana. I didn't see anything like that."

"Of course not. You only saw one Cuba. Esameralda says that Habana is a happy place. We've been so long under one tyrant or another, that to weep in the streets would waste our precious time." Miguel put a half cup of coffee in front of Christian then sat quietly, looking out the window at his poor village while Christian tasted the illicit brew. Christian ran his own history of the Cuban struggle.

First it was the Spanish kings, then the Spanish grandees in Cuba, then the generals who enslaved their own peoples. The Spanish brought slaves from Africa, Miguel's ancestors, and anybody who was a worker was a slave to the system. So there were many bloody rebellions against the Spanish until Cubans finally threw them out and when they did the Americans took the credit and enslaved Cubans in a different way.

"Esa says that the Americans just made money easier but it was they who kept the money and my parents are still slaves. Even Esameralda's a slave of the Americans. My parents and their parents, work and plot to one day be free of them, all the time being happy in the streets. So you see, it's why we like to dance and sing."

"What? Because you're treated like slaves?"

"Sure. It's a custom of our African ancestors. The more we are beaten the louder we sing and the faster we dance. It's all we can do to forget.."

"I think it has something to do with the weather," mused Christian. "It's easier to be happy when you aren't freezing to death."

"Is it that cold where you come from?"

"Canada? Only about eight months of the year. The rest of the time we keep warm swatting kamikaze mosquitoes."

"It can't be so cold if you have mosquitoes. We have mosquitoes."

"Cuban mosquitoes wouldn't last a day. Canadian mosquitoes are born with fur coats, just like Juanita's moose, only smaller, but not much."

"Señor Christ is pulling my leg?"

"Sure. Do you know what a glacier is?"

"Ah...I think it's some kind of ice, yes?"

"Yes. Lots of ice. Any idea how big Canada is?"

"I remember a picture in a book once. Canada is pink, like Bermuda. United States is green. Canada is about twice bigger than the United States."

"Not really. It depends on the angle. But imagine all of that pink covered with ice. Ice about five miles thick."

"How thick is that?"

"See that island way out there?" Christian pointed to the nearest small island of Los Colorados Archipelago. Miguel looked out the window to the Gulf. "About that far, only straight up." He pointed to the ceiling.

"You mean your country is under that much ice?"

"Not at the moment. But it used to be and the ice is coming back soon so I'm staying right here."

"Santa Maria! Juanita could keep a lot of beer cold when the electricity is off and the boat's not coming."

"It would solve her problem."

Miguel sighed. "You should try to explain that to Señor Escobar. He may suggest that you go to South America if ice is your big problem."

"It's not my 'big' problem." Christian was lost in thought for a few moments. "So, what's been going on in cuartel Los Espiritos?"

"Oh, not that much, of any importance."

"Miguel...I can tell when you're being evasive. Your sisters are staying here, for a reason. Maartyn kept walking around the house half the night and then your sister, Rosameralda, did the same until after dawn."

"Señor Escobar's orders."

"Orders?"

"Suggestions."

"You mean, like an officer gives suggestions to his soldiers?"

"Something like that."

"Is Escobar some kind of officer?"

"I can say no more."

Miguel clammed up. But pieces of the puzzle were falling into place. Christian was unaware just how big the puzzle would be. "May I at least have an orange?"

"Sure thing, Boss."

"I'm not your boss."

The first hint of the girl's return was a shrill squeal. Christian rushed for the window. Maartyn rolled over and jumped up, Lucille at the ready. There was another squeal, followed by feminine laughter. When Christian and Miguel reached the gate they saw Rosameralda, Renée and Esameralda arm in arm, swinging down the dirt road. Three school girls, their long hair still wet, sharing a joke. Renée was the filing in the Oreo cookie. Christian slumped against the stone wall with relief. Maartyn was standing hands on hips shaking his head. Miguel looked for Wolf and headed back into the house. "My sisters are just loco," he said over his shoulder.

"Hello boys," shouted Renée. "You should have come swimming. It was wonderful!"

Christian and Maartyn looked at each other. Maartyn shrugged. "I guess secrecy ain't a big thing today," he said, sounding disappointed.

"So what was all the creeping around last night?" Christian asked.

"Picket duty. Her gun's bigger than mine so I didn't argue," Maartyn said.

"I'll never understand this place."

"Me neither. Rosie's somethin' though."

"Rosie is it?"

"Y'all try pronouncin' her name."

The girls swung through the gate still giggling. Their damp hair beginning to curl. Esameralda was dressed in loose green fatigues like her sister. The jacket unbuttoned. Renée was wearing only Christian's long sweatshirt that barely covered her derriere, which was not a problem for her. They looked at Christian and Maartyn and burst out laughing again. Both boys blushed. This caused the girls to double over with laughter until they could barely stand.

Christian had recently been the filling between Renée and Esameralda feeling the excruciating pleasure of their touch. Had Esameralda told Renée? If so Renée was showing no jealousy. Even more awkward. Esameralda's image had finally taken the place of the lingering, firelight fantasy of Rosameralda. And a dilemma. He regarded the trio with a new fear.

Maartyn walked out on the dusty path and looked toward the hills. The land rose from the harbour in ragged steps of royal palms, palmettos, scrub and tobacco fields. The path looped and curved away between red fields until it lost itself in the white rocks of the Pinar hills. The beauty was subtle, accented by the soft air of a Cuban morning that was giving way to a hot and humid day with the heat mist rising inland. Nothing moved but the shimmering waves of heat from the sunbaked ground. Heat bugs clicked and rustled sporadically. The countryside was calm and peaceful. Too peaceful for Maartyn who had been trained to suspect calm. Trouble came over hills. By stealth or in hordes. The carefree actions of the girls, especially Rosameralda, who was so serious and alert that morning, unsettled him. He needed a target, something tangible to justify the growing tension.

A flock of small birds suddenly broke cover, loudly protesting. The heat bugs fell silent. An unmistakable movement in the scrub just off the road. Some one or some thing was creeping through the undergrowth. The scrub rustled again. More birds rose up, clattering away.

"Inside everybody!" Maartyn closed the gate and pushed the mob ahead of him. Rosameralda resisted, straining to see what had spooked Maartyn. He herded them inside and slammed the door. Rosameralda pulled her pistol out of her pack, snapping the slide and chambering a bullet.

"What's happening, Maartyn?" asked Esameralda. "What did you see?"

Miguel came running from the pantry. "Esa? Did you see Pietro?"

"I think so, once," she said.

"Somebody's in the bushes by the road. Five, maybe six," Maartyn said to Renée. Renée translated for the girls. Rosameralda moved carefully to the window. "Everybody, keep down and away from the windows!" she said in a harsh whisper.

"Are you sure?" Christian asked Maartyn.

"Well, I didn't actually see the Gooks, you know, but y'all can tell. There's half a dozen at least."

"Who?" asked Renée.

"Don't know. Who was we watchin' for all night?"

Miguel peeked cautiously over the window sill. "Look! Pietro's with them!"

"The little traitor!" hissed Rosameralda.

"Wolf?" asked Christian.

"I just saw him run out on the road," answered Miguel.

"Oh my, what are we going to do?" Renée clung to Christian. "Why would they be sneaking around like that?"

"Is it the army or the police?"

"Are they armed?"

"We should make a run for it."

"We could go down to Juanita's."

"No, they'd connect the Movement to her."

"Too late to run for the compound."

"We'll fight to the death," said Rosameralda.

"Not me," said Christian.

"Monsieur Escobar said, whatever happens, Christian was to stay behind. I'll stay with him," said Renée.

"No, you can't, Renée. It's too dangerous." Christian said.

"We can't make it to the compound. We stay and fight."

"Wait!" said Miguel. "There's Pietro. He's chasing something." Miguel uttered an oath and flung open the door.

Rosameralda made a grab for him. "Don't go out there, Miguelito!"

Miguel ran along the road shouting, picking up stones. "Pietro! Come here you little bandit!"

Pietro popped out of the bushes and trotted towards Miguel carrying a stick. Miguel ran past him, shouting at the bushes. A dark skinned boy wearing only faded shorts broke from the bushes and ran up the road. Miguel flung a stone at him. Then another terrified boy broke cover, closely followed by two more boys and two little girls. The girls were laughing and pointing at Miguel. Miguel hurled one last stone at the lead boy, Jésus. Pietro sat down beside him, watching the retreating children. "Pietro, you son of a Yankee cur!"

Miguel was still scolding the dog when they reached the villa. "And you were supposed to be on patrol, not playing with the village urchins."

The silence in the villa was embarrassment, and relief. Pietro slunk under the table and lay down.

"What were those children doing?" asked Christian.

Rosameralda and Esameralda smiled. Miguel blushed. "They were spying on your woman at the pond. We used to do the same to my sisters. But this little bandito was with them playing chase the stick!"

"Maybe it was his way of watching over us," suggested Renée. Crisis over but the tension hung heavy on the darkened villa. Miguel and the dog left on some business he did not share.

The girls lounged on the terrace in the sun brushing their hair, painting toenails, and making small talk. Christian, worn down by the commotion, went back to bed. Maartyn said he was going for a walk in the hills and look for the pond.

Renée followed him to the gate. "Go to where the main road turns at the rocks. Take a path to the right and then leave the path when it comes to a big rock that has a nose like Charles De Gaulle."

"Who's he?"

"French General. Big war hero. He's the President of France...Just go over the rocks when you see a big nose. The pond is beyond some pine trees. Don't get into trouble."

"Not me." Maartyn patted Lucille and swaggered up the road, checking left and right.

Renée rejoined the Cuban girls on the terrace. They traded cosmetic tips and talked about the boys. Miguel returned shortly with a basket of mixed fruit and prepared a bowl of sangria with the fruit and sugar and another bottle of the good wine. He put it under the preparation table in the cool of the pantry, covered with Esameralda's bloodied scarf to keep the lazy flies away. Then he went to the terrace and sat in the shade to listen to the girls.

"...And what did you do before the Revolution?" Renée asked Rosameralda.

"The endless Revolution," Rosameralda sighed, as if the burden of Cuban freedom was on her shoulders. "I was studying to be a lawyer. It's unusual for a girl from Los Espiritos to go to university. My family insisted so that perhaps one of us could grab some of the money the Batistianos steal from us. Being a lawyer is the only way, unless you want to be a politician or join the army and they don't let girls do that. We couldn't wait for Miguelito to grow up and it seemed like the little savage was fit only to play the fool. He likes to hustle for Esa and Juanita and since Esa was already working I was next in line. Señor Escobar used his influence and I owe Ernesto more than you could imagine. I was only sixteen and naïve when I left for the big city. The first thing that happened in Habana was this gangster tried to grab me off the street. The first of many battles I had for my virginity. It was easier for Esa. She was already a prostitute but she was smart enough to stay away from the gangsters and the pimps."

"We call them procurer. But it's the same thing," said Renée.

"The difference is the way they treat their girls, I think. Fortunately Esa had warned me. I was a prisoner at the University. Afraid to leave the campus. I had no social life except with the activists. There were many socialist and liberty groups, even the communists, all yelling at each other about justice. I studied law but what I learned was that if you yell loud enough you can annoy the politicians. But then we annoyed the politicians too much and they sent their police thugs. It meant danger. Then I met a boy who was a follower of Fidel Castro. He took my mind to the rebels in the hills as he took my body to bed. This was exciting as well as dangerous. I was captivated by the idea of a real revolution. But because my family depended on me to be a lawyer I didn't go to the hills. I stayed behind to study and cause trouble for Batista. Then they closed the University. So I did what I could for the Revolution. Now women are in the hills with Fidel. I was going too but Señor Escobar convinced me to stay here and help create the Western Front."

The notion of a Western Front did not register with Renée either. "Do you regret missing out on a degree?"

"There wasn't time unfortunately. All our great revolutionaries were lawyers. Our spiritual leader, José Martí, was a lawyer as well as a poet. Fidel was a law student in forty-seven when he and some other students tried to invade Dominica to overthrow that pig Trujillo. They were stopped at the last minute by the Cuban Navy. Fidel swam ashore with a Tommy gun around his neck and became a hero. And then in the next year Fidel became the president of the Student Law Society and went to Bogotá for a big meeting of the Anti-Imperialist Student Congress."

"So, Fidel Castro really is a Communist?"

"Oh no, never think that. The students resisted the Communists who wanted to take over all our activities. Fidel studied socialism and Marxism, before he became a lawyer, but he's much too smart to fall for the Communist's ideology. He believes in the rights of the people and wants only to be rid of Batista and the dictatorship and all the American corruption that goes with it."

"We have a lot of enemies," said Esameralda, baiting her sister.

"I fear the Americans most of all! They'll do anything to keep us down, but that doesn't mean to say that we are anti-American," she added quickly. "Well, some are, but I would like nothing better than to be a lawyer in New York City. America's a wonderful place. We have nothing against the Americans. Just the capitalists and their politician lackeys who support Batista."

"This is so confusing," said Renée. "The newspapers say Castro and his followers are Communists. You say they have nothing to do with communism."

"It's well known that Americans want desperately that Fidel be a communist so they have some justification for what they do. The American people should not believe what they hear, only what they see. The Capitalist Imperialists lie."

"It's still confusing but you make it sound so important. I wish I had something to do with my life besides wander around looking for a good beach and a great lay."

Rosa laughed. "Join us then. Fight for justice and rid the world of tyrants. France must have tyrants."

"She looks for tyrants under her bed," interjected Esameralda.

"We've had our share," admitted Renée "And our own bloody revolution, for much the same reasons. Innocent people died. I don't think I could do it. I like my world peaceful and poetic."

"Peaceful and poetic?" scoffed Rosameralda with a toss of her ebony mane. "First you must rid the world of the criminals. How can you be safe to read poetry if you fear for your life and have no freedom except to be poor?"

"You're right, Rosa. I managed to avoid the awful things. Mind you, I heard about them first hand. I know some state secrets that would make you shiver. But, you know, those things always seem to be happening someplace else. Algeria, Indochina, East Africa. Places they don't even teach you about in school. I know disgusting dictators and their disgusting crimes. And politicians from a succession of troubled little countries who come to our home begging, usually for themselves. I was forced to sit at the same table, for my education. The suffering of their people is never mentioned. Only the politics, the money and what France should do to save some despot's corrupt government. But here you people are the real names and the real faces."

"I'm glad you think that way. You could be one of us."

"I lack your passion. It would be just another adventure. No, I need to find my own way. What will you do when the Revolution's over?"

Rosameralda was obviously uncomfortable with the question. "I should stay here, and work to make sure Cubans have justice." She changed the subject. "Did you know that Fidel was going to run for Congress before Moncada? Yes, and just before the election Batista seized power again and the election was a farce. That was in fifty-two. The next year, after the disaster of Moncada, Fidel was a fugitive. He was caught and there was a big trial in Santiago. Fidel and another lawyer, Haydée Santamaria, convinced the judges that Batista's own police murdered rebels in jail. Fidel went to jail instead of being executed, and it was a small victory for the Revolution. Batista was trapped, you see. If he had executed all the rebels, Cuba would have turned on him. So Fidel was sentenced to fifteen years on Isla del Pinos along with the other rebel survivors. Batista grew too confident with Fidel in exile. But Batista's big mistake was giving Fidel amnesty." She paused to brush her hair.

"What happened to Castro and his movement then?"

"Then Fidel went to Mexico where he met Ché and formed the 26th of July Movement. Fidel and Ché trained guerrilla fighters and made the long, heroic voyage on the small yacht *Granma* that I told you about, all the way from Mexico to the East of Cuba, but they were betrayed. Batista's army was waiting. Many were gunned down even after they surrendered. Only by a miracle the survivors reached Pico Turquino in the Sierra Maestra, all the time being chased by the army and shot at by the Air Force. Every step of the way was a near disaster but Fidel and his brave Revolutionaries never wavered. They survived sea sickness and hunger and swamps, traitors, informers and the brutality of the army. Only twelve of the eighty two rebels survived to reach Turquino, our highest mountain."

Although Renée had suspicions about the practiced rhetoric she was fascinated by the story. "Why would he climb a mountain to start a revolution? Revolutions usually start in the cities."

"Fidel's strategy, worked out during his exile. It's significant that Fidel chose to start there. I believe it was more than just a strategy. It was his spiritual destiny. But they arrived hungry and without weapons. First they had to win over the poor guajiros. This they did with kindness and generosity. Fidel reads all the books about revolutions and knows that he can only succeed if he has the help of the peasants. It was always thus. The rebels pay for their food, never stealing from the guajiros, and Ché, who is a doctor, started clinics to treat the people that Batista ignores. The people love Fidel. They will do anything to help him defeat Batista. Now Fidel and the Comandantés, like Camilo and Ernesto...I mean Ché," she corrected herself, "are ready to take over Cuba and finish off the Master of Corruption."

"*Phew!*..." breathed Renée, ignoring the fragmented, perhaps accidental reference to Escobar. "That's an incredible story."

"It's not half of Fidel's story. He's a figure from mythology, but that's not to say only Fidel can save Cuba."

"I've heard this story over and over," said Esameralda. "She tells it so well it even makes me want to join the Movement."

Renée tore her gaze from Rosameralda. "And what will you do when the Revolution's over?"

"Me? Well, since Rosa insists there won't be work for prostitutes, I guess I'll have to become a nursing nun." She laughed.

Rosameralda scowled. Renée couldn't help smile at the off handed way Esameralda switched roles. An interesting leap of faith. "You're serious aren't you."

"Yes, I'm serious. It's what I have always wanted. So, if Señor Fidel can make this miracle happen then it's God's will. And if God is such a big person, the guardian of the poor, then he can forgive me, a poor, insignificant sinner. He's done it before."

"Of course! Mary Magdalene."

"The most famous whore in history."

The two girls laughed. Rosameralda remained strangely aloof and said, "You can laugh, but why was Jesus Christ able to forgive Mary Magdalene? Because he was a free thinking revolutionary, like Fidel and José Martí."

"Come, come, Rosa...You can't compare Fidel to Jesus," chided Esameralda.

"Why not? Are not both tall and passionate?"

"And have beards?" quipped Esameralda.

"So do pirates," laughed Renée self consciously.

"And they are devoted to the poor and the oppressed. Jesus Christ didn't bow to the Roman generals, or sit at banquets with dictators. He spent his time with fishermen and farmers. And He, like Fidel, was condemned by those who feared His growing power as more peasants joined His rebellion. And now look...the words of Christ and His disciples still command the lives of half the world."

"Yes, and the other half try to silence them," answered Esameralda.

"So the disciples must fight."

"And even the disciples fight amongst themselves out of ignorance."

"Does your family want you to be a nun?" asked Renée, afraid the conversation was going to leave her behind again.

"Our family does not agree on everything."

Miguel, who had remained quiet in the shade, spoke up..."Señor Escobar says all religion is a waste of time. He says we would be better off if we had one less thing to fight about. The Revolution has nothing to do with what Christ said or didn't say, only inhumanity."

"Señor Escobar!" scoffed Esameralda. "You see what he has for art? Priests and bishops fucking each other in coloured glass. The old pervert! He's no better than..."

"Wait. What did you say?" interrupted Renée.

"Escobar's no saint. I wouldn't trust him with a sick goat."

"Aren't we at the mercy of Monsieur Escobar?"

"Worship Escobar and you are at the feet of the Devil!"

"That's not true!" protested Rosameralda. "His sexual appetites have nothing to do with what he believes. He is a great patriot."

"He's a morally corrupted old man."

"I don't understand...He seems only a little eccentric, and somewhat scary," offered Renée.

"You call perversion eccentric!?" asked Esameralda.

"What is his sin?"

"He brought your friend, Paulo, to my apartment in Habana. He got the young man drunk and tried to seduce him."

"Oh, that," said Renée. "I wouldn't feel too sorry for Paulo. He was using Monsieur Escobar too. It's Monsieur you should feel sorry for. I think he really likes Paulo."

"It is a lover's dilemma," interjected Miguel in Escobar's defense. "Besides, Señor Escobar's very upset about what happened. He talks of ending his own life."

"What's this world coming to?" lamented Esameralda.

"I made sangria. Maybe you should eat something and forget about Señor Escobar and his wounded friend."

Miguel darted inside and returned with the big bowl of fruit and wine and put it on the small table. The girls gathered around and inspected the sangria, tasting it with their fingers. Miguel passed out the spoons.

"Rosa...the wine? Fidel's watching," taunted Esameralda.

"I'll try very hard to taste only the fruit."

Paulo's problems and Escobar's appetites were forgotten before they were half way through the bowl of rich fruit and strong wine.

"Christian should eat some of this," said Renée, feeling guilty.

"Should I go and wake him up?" asked Miguel,

"No, I'll go."

"But I have a message for Señor Christ, from Juanita. She wants to see him right away. It's about another gig."

"I'll tell him."

Renée sat on the edge of the bed holding Christian's hand. "How do you feel now?"

"Better," said Christian, sitting up.

There were no pillows to fluff. "We've been having a girl's time, although I must admit it's the most unusual conversation I have ever had with 'the girls'. The topic was mostly about revolutions, dictators and the plight of prostitutes, but it was nice to sit in the sun and just talk as if we were in the south of France," she said dreamily. "Rosa and Esa really are very nice, if you accept their professions as just average, which they are not. Are you hungry?"

"I'm not sure."

"We saved you sangria. Miguel made it with powdered sugar. Has a citrus taste. Very unusual."

"Probably stolen from Juanita's bar."

"That reminds me. Juanita wants to see you about a gig?"

"With Juanita it could mean many things. Old Jocinto's dead."

"Maybe he came back to life."

"Anything's possible in this place. But I'm pretty sure we buried him, along with a guitar that's worth more than this villa."

"What a shame. Well, try the sangria. The wine might do you good."

"How much wine's left?"

"One bottle."

"I'd like to save it for an occasion."

"What occasion?"

"I don't know yet.

"For us?..."

He couldn't answer. "Do I have to come out?"

"Don't be shy. The girls won't bite, unless you want them to."

Christian sat in the sun of the terrace, eyeing the fruit swimming in red wine, imagining the girls starring at him, whispering. The wine looked too much like blood and the fruit resembled body organs.

"How are you, Christian?" asked Esameralda.

"I'm okay," he answered untruthfully. There wasn't much to choose between the two Cuban girls, but when Esameralda smiled the feeling went deep. He looked at Renée watching the interplay, bemused. Did she notice that Christian wilted in the intense heat of her smile? Had she really remained asleep during their morning tryst? Putting aside the bowl without tasting he announced, "I'm going down to Juanita's."

"I'll come with you," Renée said. "She seems interesting."

"That's an understatement." Christian was about to offer objections but decided he would like the company.

"No," said Rosameralda firmly.

"Pardon me?" said Renée, taken aback by the command.

"You cannot leave!"

"Why not?" asked Renée, not used to being told what to do.

The relaxed mood of the morning vanished. "It is not safe, if they come."

"Who?"

"The police. We must be prepared to run."

"Run? Where?"

"To the warehouse."

"Does it have something to do with the trap door?" asked Renée, more curious than afraid.

"You know about a trap door?"

"Only that there is one."

Rosameralda looked away to the blue Gulf. There was something out there, out of sight beyond Los Colorados Archipelago. Was it, she wondered, the beginning or the end? "The boat's coming tonight, Christian. You must do your best."

He was about to ask then changed his mind.

He entered Juanita's Cantina with a heavy weight pressing on his spirit.

"Christian, my beautiful Canada jazzman!" Juanita exclaimed at his thin silhouette in the open door. She was as usual. The inevitable beer in one hand, crooked cigar in the other. Hair piled up precariously, pins askew, wearing a bright print dress of ample proportions but crumpled as if she had slept in the gaudy confection. He wondered if she was a permanent fixture, like the derelict on a street corner, in any weather. The actual bodies interchangeable but there is a continuing thread. You can leave, and return, but the static one, or a replacement is always there. A comforting logic to root the itinerant in advancing time. "I need you tonight."

"I know."

"I know you know. Unfortunately. We warned you. Now I must tell you that if you do not help us you will be...detained."

"Against my will?" He asked, incredulous. She nodded sleepily. "I see. Thanks for being blunt."

"I believe Señor Escobar was?"

"He was."

"And you didn't take his suggestion."

"Correct."

"Welcome to the Revolution. Beer?"

"Is it free?"

"The least I can do."

"Thanks. This may the most expensive free beer in history. What do you want me to do?"

Juanita opened a beer. Christian took the chilled bottle and thought of the body of the engineer in Escobar's freezer.

"Play your sax tonight. We need a loud, long show."

"I've been sick."

"Do you remember how frail Old Jocinto was? Miguel practically carrying him?"

"Okay, no pep talk. I'll do my best."

"I know you will. You have your woman to think about. Much depends on the boat coming in as usual."

"The show's just a cover, right?"

"When did you figure that out?"

"Nothing specific. Things just began to make sense the more they didn't make sense."

"Los Espiritos' the core of the Western front," she said simply. "Señor Escobar is our leader, as well as our contact with Castro."

"That's pretty straight forward too."

"The fishing boat is our link with the outside world. That's why it was necessary for Maartyn to do the work. He could not have been compromised by the Batistianos."

"You used him."

She closed her eyes. "The beating was unfortunate."

"He's suspected of being one of them, I mean...the Revolution."

"Consequence of being in Los Espiritos," she said with a wry smile.

"Los Espiritos? A rebel camp?"

"All things in good time. They could still torture you for that information."

"Great. And Renée?"

"The same. They'll torture Paulo for sure, if he's still alive. What a shame. He could connect Señor Escobar."

"I don't understand. Apparently the police drove Renée and Paulo here from Pinar del Rio. Before that it was probably the police who robbed them in their hotel. Why didn't they take them in Havana?"

"Hoping to follow Castro sympathizers to the Western Front. They know it's happening."

"At least clue me as to how the show helps."

"Simple, my beautiful Gringo Revolutionary."

"Wrong on both counts."

"Juanita's is the only game in town, so, when I have a big night everyone comes. If they don't they must have a reason. If one is a traitor they are exposed. It also gets everyone indoors so it is hard for the secret police. No crowds to mingle with. The noise covers any gun play if it's necessary. And there are less people to see what the boat crew bring ashore."

"I see. Can I ask what?"

"No. It would be difficult even for the Batistianos to execute you for playing jazz. Unless you play very badly." Juanita laughed and jiggled.

"Very funny. Ah, is there a band? Some backup?"

"There are any number of musicians. Old Jocinto was the best. God rest his soul. But you must bring Señor Maartyn to tickle my drum."

Christian couldn't help being amused. Maybe it was the beer, or the heat, that made him lightheaded. Or maybe it was just Juanita. He was amused also by his own attitude, as if the revelation of more parts to the puzzle made things easier, peeling away layers of mystery. He was feeling better just thinking about the music; when the music's hot and the band's in a groove. So it was a shock when he entered the villa and was confronted by a man with a white Cuban complexion and a thin dark moustache, wearing Paulo's leather jacket.

"Christian James Joyce?"

"Who're you?"

"I ask the questions."

Christian glanced at the terrace. The empty sangria bowl was on the table.

"Your friends?"

"Well, they probably went...fishing."

"In Cuba women don't fish."

"Who said anything about women?" asked Christian, his denial sounding hollow.

"At least one of your guests is a woman," said the man smiling ingenuously. One gold tooth gleaming. He was very sure of himself, Christian thought. Young for the secret police, but his smug, swaggering coolness placed him in a position of power. And there was the problem of Paulo's jacket. He was staring.

"You recognize this jacket?"

"No."

"I could break you. Where are your friends?"

"I don't know. They were here when I left."

"Where did you go?"

"For a walk."

"You don't go for walks."

"I've been...sick. Needed exercise.

"Don't try to be clever with me, Socialist scum!"

That answered Christian's question about limits. They were narrow. "I have to sit down."

"I'll tell you when to sit!"

Christian ignored the threat and sat on the American couch. There was nothing to be gained by being afraid of a bully. "If you plan to beat me up you'll find an excuse. Right?"

"You are close to the edge."

"Ask me the questions."

"You're too brave."

"I'm too weak to be brave. So, what do you want?"

"Your papers."

"Knapsack. Bedroom. Help yourself." Christian was very tired. He wondered how he would manage a gig that night, provided the police didn't beat him senseless first. It was so stupid and pointless. Life under a tyrant. Open threats and no regard for rights. Intimidation visits by the police. He was learning human reactions first hand and felt the gnawing, sweating fear of the innocent accused. The cop came out of the bedroom with the passport and his journal.

"How did you know my name and where to find me?"

"Airport records. The nightclub. The hotel incident. Your trip to Señor Hemingway's Finca. The truck and bus ride to Pinar del Rio. We lost you there."

"Sloppy."

"Where are the others?"

"Which others?"

"Four of you have eaten. Maartyn St. Jacques, the American mercenary. The French woman," he looked at a note book, "Renée Terésa Jalobert. We have her accomplice, Paulo Merichault, alias, Pascale Martinez, alias, Pablo Malibu, in a cell in Habana. You have one other comrade to account for."

One other, thought Christian. Then the cop doesn't know Rosameralda and Esameralda were at the villa. Maartyn's in the hills. Where did the girls go? Miguel must have warned them, or Wolf. The compound. The trap door.

"The fourth conspirator!"

"What? Oh...me. I'm the fourth."

"No...you are the third. Who is the fourth?"

Think fast, Chris. Who can squirm out of accusations? "Ah, Miguel, my houseboy. He ate with us today. Then I went for a walk...

The cop tossed Christian's passport on the table, sat down on the bench and began leafing through the journal. He stopped at the entry date for November 3rd. The first day of his Caribbean rehabilitation. The day he left Miami on the supply boat for Bimini. The same day he met Maartyn. Just a coincidence but the timing could be incriminating. Otherwise, the entries were innocuous enough. Boring, except for the part when he first made love to Renée. The cop was reading that part slowly. Other wise, trip records, partying on beaches and soft drugs. But mostly the effort to get off drugs. He could be accused of being a degenerate. That shouldn't bother the Batista regime. A national pastime for the generals. But surely there was nothing to link the four of them to a revolution.

However, there was Maartyn's police record. A fugitive. And unfortunately, Paulo tried to leave Cuba with a forged passport. Renée's passport had a diplomatic stamp. Obviously Christian was harbouring trouble makers who had come to Cuba to plot against Batista.

The cop continued reading. Was the guy going to read the whole journal? Then Christian realized the cop was stalling. Waiting for someone to stumble through the door. He should do something. What? He could play his saxophone. What songs had warning messages? *Lover Get Away from My Door.* Too obscure. *Take The A Train.* Not specific enough. *Thief of Baghdad.* Not even a song. Think. "Mind if I play while you read?"

Christian got up to get the saxophone case which was behind the couch, beside the guitar case. When he placed the saxophone case on the table the cop pulled a pistol from a shoulder holster so quickly Christian jumped.

"What are you doing!?"

"Sax. Play?"

The cop threw open the case. He grinned, flashing the gold tooth. The beautiful brass instrument glinted back. The cop picked up the sax, turning it over and over in his hands as if admiring the craftsmanship. He smiled again, looked at Christian and then swung it over his head, smashing the horn down on the heavy table. The bell crumpled. He turned the defiled thing end for end and smashed the valve pads and delicate linkage on the edge of the table. Pieces of brass flew about the room, clanking across the tile floor like broken glass. He threw the ruined saxophone back in the case. Christian was transfixed by the mindless violence.

"You bastard," he whispered.

"Sit down!" the man ordered. Christian remained standing, as mute as his ruined instrument. Many thoughts flashed through his mind. One was revenge. He didn't know how long he remained standing. The cop went on reading. Finally the cop said, "There's nothing for the last three days."

"Pardon?..."

"Your diary. Three days are blank."

"Yeah, that's why."

"What is why?"

"Blank. I told you I was sick."

The cop was momentarily at a loss. "Maybe. I think you're hiding something."

"Nothing to hide. What's your name?"

"Why do you ask?"

"You know my name."

The cop decided to try another approach. He'd read a book about police tactics in America. "Yolando Justo Carnero. Good Cuban name. I'm a white Cuban. The best. The rest are trash."

"Wait. Your Boss' a mulatto, right?"

"El Presidente is an ass as well as a mulatto. My middle name means The Way."

Christian realized he was dealing with a very big ego and possibly a psychopath. How to use that information?

"So, Yolando, may I call you Yolando? Or would you prefer Yo Yo?" he asked in English. "You don't exactly approve of your President Batista?"

Carnero hesitated. "The man's an ignorant peasant who should still be cutting cane. A sergeant clerk in the army, a secretary, when he seized control of our country from Señor Machado."

"You were young."

"I was two. My family were great friends with Machado."

"That would be Gerardo Machado, the dictator?"

"You know the heroes of Cuba?"

"Just the notorious ones. And your family was doing very well with Señor Machado as President?"

"My father was an administrator in the government of Señor Machado. A trusted friend, and advisor."

"What happened to your father when Batista took control?" Christian asked carefully, unsure how far to probe.

"Everything went *ffzzzt*! Just like that. My father was imprisoned. My mother was forced to beg in the streets. I and my brothers were raised by my grandmother. My grandfather was a veteran of the Great War of Independence against Spain. You know of this war?"

"Yeah, they call it the Spanish-American War."

"The Americans call it that. The Gringos came into the war when it looked like Cuba was about to win her independence. They blew up their own battleship in Habana Harbour and then had a few battles and took the credit when Spain gave up. Then the Americans dominated us. My grandfather was wounded and tortured by the Spanish. And do you think he got so much as a pension? Not a peso. Nothing!"

"I don't understand. You're a white Cuban...Spanish, but you hate the Spanish."

"No! I don't hate the Spanish. The Spanish are a great and proud people. I hate the Spanish kings and governments for their ignorance and their bad treatment. Just like we love the American people and hate their governments who try to make slaves of us."

"Okay, so you hate Batista, but you work for him."

"Okay, okay, Señor...Let me explain. In Cuba you either are a Batistiano or you're a guajiro. I spit on being a guajiro because my family has a proud tradition. Because my family had no standing after Batista took over I had to do something. There's no prospects unless you're a Batistiano, you understand? No one gets anywhere unless a Batista man okays it and then you have to bribe him. I looked around when I was growing up. I wasn't about to cut sugar cane like Batista's old man. I didn't want to be in the army and get stuck in some dirt floor cuartel in the Provinces. But there's always jobs for someone who doesn't mind getting their hands dirty. So I became a policeman and worked my way up. I worked very hard for this."

"How hard?"

"What do you mean, how hard?"

"I mean..." careful, Chris, he said to himself, "what did you have to do?"

"You ask, Gringo!?" Yolando Carnero flashed his dark eyes. "I know what you want. You think I use brutality because I'm a Batistiano. You think that if Castro seizes the government that you'll denounce me to save yourself and your criminal friends!"

"No, no. I'm just curious, you know?"

"I kill people like you!" Carnero pulled his automatic out again and pointed it at Christian's head. He tried not to look at the small black circle. The gun didn't seem as big when seen from head on but the black hole was immense.

"Whoa, no offence. Maybe you could tell me what it was like growing up, ah, as a kid in the city."

Carnero slid the pistol back in its holster with such precision that Christian knew it was a reflex, wondering how often it went off? "We didn't live in the city. My grandfather scratched the dirt of poor farmland not far from here. He couldn't even grow tobacco because to grow tobacco you have to have permission. I had to start far from Habana. I used to take vegetables or a sick chicken to the city. I wanted to stay in the city so I beat up a shoeshine boy, took his box and his corner. It was necessary to fight every day just to stay in business. I was tough. I got to know the police. I'd tell them things, you understand? When I got older they paid me. You understand what I'm saying, Gringo?"

"Yes, perfectly. You were like an apprentice." He wanted to say, asshole bully rat fink.

"No! I was an informer. Good at my job. So good they trained me to be an undercover cop. I was so good at that they asked me to report to the Head of the Servicios Especiales. The big boy who plays cards with Batista himself. I had a clear road. I was going to get to the top. I was going to move up by being the best Batistiano and when I had the chance I was going to kill that Gringo loving fucker, Batista, with my bare hands! You hear what I'm saying!?"

It wasn't hard to hear Yolando Justo Carnero. Christian backed away a pace. "Yes, I hear...Loud and clear."

"Then Castro and scum like you come along and wreck my chances because there is no way Batista can stop Castro."

Christian saw an opening. "Then why don't you go over to Castro? Join the rebels."

"You stupid Gringo shit! Do you think the rebels don't know who I am!?

Christian was losing ground too quickly. Back peddling is dangerous when you don't know what's behind you. He tried a desperate ploy. "Would you like to get out of Cuba?"

"What?"

"Ah, we happen to know Batista's planning to leave, soon." Christian didn't know, but things were deteriorating and his only other option, other than to lie, was to run.

"Who's *we*, Gringo infiltrator?"

"I, ah, we're with a secret organization based in Canada. We're here to help the Revolution, as you already know...for a price. We bring in guns an' stuff and take people out who want to escape so they can't be tried for war crimes." He wished he hadn't said the last part of the lie but if Carnero didn't go for the whole lie it wouldn't matter. "We kind of play both sides, like the Americans, but, hey, it's for the money. You understand about the money."

"I knew you were involved in such a thing."

"Well, you are a pretty clever guy."

"How can you do this?"

"I have no morals or scruples. I belong to no..."

"Shut up! I meant, how can you get me out?"

Christian needed time to think. "Could we go out on the terrace? I need fresh air."

"Of course. What do you have to drink?"

"Ah, nothing...much."

"I don't believe you."

"I'll look."

"I'm watching, so don't try anything out of the movies."

"No, not a chance. I'm cool."

Carnero followed Christian to the pantry. "By the way Gringo, I regret about the saxophone. I sometimes get excited."

"No problem, Yo. I never played it much anyway." He remembered the gig that evening. How would he explain this to Juanita? On the other hand, what was a gig to an execution?

Pulling aside the preparation table, Christian uncovered a heavy wooden trap door. The door was about two feet by three feet and had a handle set into the wood. He lifted the end and peered in. Carnero had his pistol out again, shuffling behind Christian to get a look into the black hole. He produced a small flashlight from the inside pocket of Paulo's jacket. The hole was about two feet deep. A cold locker built into the stone. Intended for storage of vegetables and meat. There was a wooden case with one forlorn bottle of the Spanish Rioja. "Okay...Last bottle," sighed Christian.

"Hand it up, slowly."

Christian drew it out reluctantly. He had a fleeting, terrifying notion to break the bottle on Carnero's head, considered his chances and handed over the bottle, lamenting that he had missed out on most of the excellent vintage. He'd been saving it to celebrate Maartyn's departure. Or share it some evening with Renée, in front of a nice fire, or...with Esameralda. Or perhaps to toast the Revolution. Why, he wondered, would a humble Irish Canadian lad from Montreal be toasting a revolution in Cuba? If his university pals could see him. Those endless, wine-soaked debates about Socialism, Marxism and Capitalism. And the main characters. Never dreamed he'd be this close to the legendary Fidel Castro. Well, he was in the same country. Castro was only seven hundred miles away, at the other end of the island.

"Rioja! Good. Señor Bartuchi's. I have shared more than one bottle with this fine gentleman. It's too bad what happened to his family."

Christian didn't ask. Pretended to know nothing about Frank The

207

Butcher Bartuchi. Didn't want to know about the family. He could imagine. Reality was a large, breathing entity sitting on his chest. He felt
the dangerous end of the automatic against his spine.

"Move. Terrace. Now. We'll have a drink and wait for your comrades and you can tell me about our business deal."

Out in the sun Christian felt only marginally less at risk. There was
no chance to run. No place to hide. "Sit down."

Christian sat on the small bench behind the table, so that his back
was to the wall of the villa. Carnero had his back to the garden. A stra-
tegic lapse, thought Christian, then reasoned there were probably a
dozen cops hiding in the bushes. Had they discovered the compound?
And if they did would they find the trap door? A sixth sense told
Christian that Renée was down there. The Cuban girls as well. Maybe
Maartyn, Miguel and Wolf. Maybe all of Los Espiritos and he was the
only person left to face the wrath of the police. He would pay the
price. It was no longer a fantasy. His girlfriend was missing. Paulo
was in a coma, dying or about to be beaten to death. The boat was
coming back with God knows what on board. The Revolution was on,
approaching a climax. A maniac with a gun was sitting across the table in the Cuban sunshine, grinning like a...maniac, gold tooth glint-
ing, waiting for him to open the last bottle of good wine. And he was
expected to reveal a plan to spirit the psychopathic killer out of Cuba...what next?

"Open the wine."

"Right." Christian produced his utility knife. Carnero tensed. Christian held it so that the auger accessory was visible. "Just an opener."
Carnero nodded. Christian pried open the blade tool, fingers trembling, cut the lead foil wrapping, closed the blade and opened the auger, inserted the point into the cork and screwed it down, experiencing
momentary panic. What if he lacked the strength to pull the old cork?
Why should he care if he was a weakling before this maniac? It mattered, for whatever reason. Christian tugged. The cork resisted at first,
then pulled smoothly, with a satisfying pop. A wisp of white vapour
spiraled up. "I'll get some glasses."

"Never mind." Carnero snatched the bottle, smacked his thin lips
and took a long chugging drink, red wine running down both sides of
his chin. He wiped his mouth with the sleeve of Paulo's leather jacket.
"Very good stuff." He downed another long pull then ran his tongue
sensuously around the top, making love to the wine. He belched. "Yes,
very good." Then he cleared his throat and spit into the bottle. The
hork pearl glided down and spread over the wine. He thumped the de-

filed bottle on the table and shoved it toward Christian. "Have a drink with me, Gringo." Christian bolted to the wall and was sick. He didn't care if Carnero shot him. "Oh, Gringo, what is the problem? Drink and we'll be brothers." Carnero was laughing in snorts. "That was wonderful! I just want you to know how dangerous I can be. Now, tell me about this boat."

Christian, head thumping, sat down, holding his stomach. The awful taste in his mouth was caused by the stomach acid eating into his teeth. He worried about his teeth. Hadn't been looking after them for two years. Surprised they were still white and cavity free. Cavities made him think of black holes. Small round holes in his stomach, heart, head...right between the eyes. He felt weak and on the verge of passing out. Worse than not being able to perform cork rituals...or sex. Don't go down that road. Focus on the lie, Chris. "Boat?"

"For what other reason would your headquarters be in Los Espiritos? It's why Señor Bartuchi was in Los Espiritos."

"Right. The boat comes in. We disguise you as a mercenary or a messenger, and take you to Florida. For a price."

"Yes, I expect there would be a price. Negotiable as usual. When is the boat due?"

"Ah, there's a boat in...about three days, I think."

"Lie! You know exactly when the boat is due!"

"No...Ah, I've been sick...missed a day or so, had to think for a minute. Three days, maybe two."

"Lies!!" Carnero jumped up, brandishing his pistol. He picked up the wine bottle and thrust it in Christian's face. "Drink!"

"No!"

"Drink it!!"

Christian was staring into the black hole again. This time he imagined he could see the bullet. It had a tiny headlight, like a train coming out of a tunnel...Maartyn vaulted over the wall and in two steps had his revolver in Carnero's back. "Drop it, buddy!"

"Don't shoot. Easy...!" the cop gasped.

"Take his gun, Chris."

"Jesus!...Do I have to?"

"Take the damn gun!"

Christian gingerly reached up and removed the automatic from Carnero's hand. They were face to face. Carnero looked into Christian's eyes, almost pleading. "I hope this doesn't mean the deal's off, Gringo. I have plenty of money."

Maartyn stepped back, the revolver wavering as if he wasn't sure where to aim. Christian was holding Carnero's pistol by the barrel so that it was still pointing at himself. The three men shuffled their feet, eying each other, waiting for someone to relieve the standoff.

"Chris, give me the gun."

"What?..."

"The gun!" Christian thrust the gun at him. "Who is this guy?"

"Ah, Yolando Justo?" he asked in Spanish.

Carnero nodded. "Yes. Yolando Justo Carnero. The Way."

"Yolando Justo Carnero," repeated Christian nervously. "He's the head of the Secret Police or something."

"Holy shit! Are we ever in trouble now, ol' buddy."

"No kidding. What the hell's going on?"

"Y'all tell me," demanded Maartyn, motioning for Carnero to sit on the ground. Carnero sat down against the low wall of the terrace, hands in the air, still holding the bottle, watching Maartyn who seemed undecided and nervous. Maartyn switched the guns in his hands, checking to see if the safety was off the automatic. Carnero was sweating, unused to being on the receiving end. "Well?"

"I don't know," answered Christian. "He was in the house when I got back from....a walk. When I left...ah, Renée and Miguel were here."

"What about Rosie?"

Christian tried to warn Maartyn off. Carnero perked up, obviously following some of the English. "You don't know either." Christian made the question a statement.

"No, I was up in the hills."

Christian took the wine bottle from Carnero. Maartyn backed away, keeping the pistol leveled at Carnero's head. "He understands some English, so don't mention names," Christian whispered, putting the wine bottle on the table.

"I dig. Okay, what do we do with this cop?"

"He wants to get out of Cuba."

"Right. Me too."

"I told him we were a secret organization running guns for the Revolution and helping Batistianos escape from Castro."

"Oh, man, that was clever!"

"It's all I could think of at the time. Now he wants to make a deal. Says he has plenty of money."

"Money? Let's search him."

"No. We have to play this cool. Get his confidence."

"Are y'all nuts!? This guy's a cop."

"Worse than that. I think he's a psycho."

Maartyn studied Carnero. "Hey, I recognize that jacket."

"Yeah, it's Paulo's. He's in jail. Been shot."

"Bastards! Let's shoot this one now."

"No! There might be more, out there."

Maartyn looked beyond the garden to the dense bush. "I don't think so. I reconned that area. There's nothin'."

"Are you sure?"

"Yeah, Marines can smell Gooks."

"They aren't Gooks! Did you see the compound?"

"That place with the fence an' all?"

"Renée and the girls went there. There's an underground room or something. Miguel freaked out about tracks."

"Okay, y'all got this figured out."

"I don't have anything figured, but we should tie him up."

There was a sudden commotion in the garden. The guttural snarl was the only warning as Wolf flew over the wall. Carnero barely managed to drop his arms in time to save his throat. Wolf clamped on to the sleeve of Paulo's jacket; an expensive Italian suede. Sharp teeth sunk through the leather. Carnero scrambled to his feet with the dog dangling from his arm. Curses and screams of pain, and snarls of joy from Wolf. He finally had his man plus Paulo's coat. Double revenge. Carnero danced around trying to shake the dog loose. He peeled off the coat and flung it down on top of Wolf, fleeing across the terrace to hide behind Maartyn and Christian. Wolf continued his attack under the coat. The sound of battle increased. Wolf freed himself, then seized the coat and shook it, holding it down with his paws, tearing out long strips. Then Wolf remembered his other target and turned on Carnero. Backed him to the wall, snarling, assuming the proportions of a rabid German Shepherd.

"Wolf...Stop!" demanded Christian.

Reluctantly Wolf backed off.

"Up...Get'em up there!"

Christian spoke to the panting dog in Spanish for Carnero's benefit. "Wolf, good boy. If he moves rip his balls off."

"Too bad about the coat," said Maartyn. Wolf never blinked. Carnero watched the dog, both of them trembling. Christian, in the middle, tried to organize their options. He didn't notice Maartyn beside the table reaching for the wine bottle. "No point wasting this stuff."

"Maartyn!..."

Maartyn took a long drink and wiped his mouth with the back of his hand. "What?"

"Never mind."

"Ya know, I'm startin' to like this stuff."

Carnero was too terrified to appreciate the moment. Christian felt his stomach turn. "Yours to enjoy."

"Okay, what now?"

Carnero looked pathetic cowering from a small dog, but he knew the dog too well. He spoke softly, pleading. "Good Marlon. Nice Marlon. We're still pals? Good boy...take it easy, precious. Don't hurt Daddy, Marlon."

Christian and Maartyn looked at each other. "That's disgusting," said Christian.

"Marlon?" Maartyn asked. "Did y'all hear him...Marlon?"

"That's what the man said. Marlon. Marlon? Here boy."

Wolf wagged his tail and moved over to sit beside Christian.

"Marlon Brando?"

Carnero perked up, jumping at the chance to reestablish communications. "Yes, Marlon Brando. You know this movie? I saw it at the cinema while training this ungrateful dog. It seemed like a good name at the time."

Christian translated. "He says he trained the dog. The movie was in Cuba, I guess."

Carnero interrupted. "No, Gringo, not in Cuba. The United States by me for the CIA. He's a CIA dog. Special assignments."

"He says Wolf was trained by the CIA, in the States."

"What for? Ride motorcycles?"

"Assassinations and bombs."

"Jesus!" Maartyn put his hand to his throat, "I've been livin' with a killer." Carnero sensed a commonality and lowered his arms. "Hands up. Get'em up there. Higher!"

"We can't keep him," said Christian, scanning the village.

"Let's give'm to Juanita."

"Don't mention names! Think."

"Let's take the bastard out in the boat an' dump'im."

"We couldn't."

"Look, man...this dude's a killer. I say we put'im out of action at least."

Christian assessed their situation. "I don't know...It's not the way I was brought up."

"Are y'all nuts!? Nobody's brought up for this shit. It's like bein' drafted. One day you're walkin' down the street mindin' yer own business, looking for pussy an' the next day they ship you off to Korea to kill Gooks."

"I couldn't do it."

"The hell you say! His buddies come in here, they'd do us, just for laughs!"

"Maybe we could trade him for a way out?"

"Sure, man. We'd never make it to the airport. Come on, Chris, use yer head. It's us or him."

"Okay, I have to think."

"Then think fast."

"What if we let Wolf kill him? No! No. I never said that. Wait, he wants to leave Cuba. He'll pay." Christian whispered in Maartyn's ear. "The boat's coming in tonight. Juanita could turn him over to Santoz."

"Yeah, good idea. They can slit his throat an' dump'm in the Gulf for the sharks. Nice an' clean."

"No! Damnit! How did I ever get into this mess?" Christian sat down on the wall, shaking his head. The fatigue catching up. Adrenaline subsiding.

"Look, Chris, first thing...we have to tie 'im up."

Esameralda's bloody scarf had blown under the table. Christian fetched the scarf. "Here, tie him up with this."

"Right, an' I suppose you're goin' to keep a bead on'im?"

"Well, I suppose I could."

"An' if he moves you'd probably shoot me."

"Okay, you're right. Ah, how should I do it?"

"Tie a goddamn knot!"

"I don't know..."

"Can you tie your shoes?"

"Yes, yes...I can tie shoes." Christian spoke to Carnero in Spanish. "Ah, Mr. Carnero, put your hands, like this." Christian made a prayer pose.

Carnero lowered his arms, bringing his hands together.

Maartyn was loosing patience. "Chris, behind. Behind him, man! He grabs you an' I shoot past yer head. Want me to shoot past yer head?"

"No, not shooting...Hands behind."

"For a special agent you seem very nervous," said Carnero.

"Well, I'm not used to this, you know. Non combatant, as they say."

"Is our deal still on?"

"Ah, yeah. It's on. I have to make arrangements. Please, put your hands behind your back."

Carnero put his hands behind his back. Christian moved around so that Carnero was between him and Maartyn.

"Tell'im if he moves I'll drop'im like a hot stone," said Maartyn, waving the guns around.

"Ah, Maartyn, could one of those?..." stammered Christian, wrapping the scarf around Carnero's wrists, trying not to make contact with his skin, "Could a bullet go...you know, right through him?"

"The nine millimeter. Frags might come out, who knows where?"

"Ah, if you have to shoot, use the little gun, okay?"

"If I have to shoot this mother y'all better just drop 'cause I'm pullin' both triggers."

Christian was sweating again. "Jesus, if I ever get out of this."

Carnero flinched when Christian pulled the knot. The silk scarf fibers as strong as rope.

"Aiyeee! Señor...That is too tight. My hands will drop off."

"Sorry...ah, can't seem to, loosen..."

"What's the problem, man?"

"Knot's too tight."

"Good, leave it."

"But, he's in pain."

"Even better. Sit down, Amigo." Maartyn motioned. Carnero eased himself down, facing the compound tangle. "Okay, but watch those feet. Better take off the boots. I think those're the Studs that kissed my face. I'll return the compliment."

"Maartyn, no. This guy's just a scared cop whose in line to face a firing squad."

"Good deal, Lucille! Where do I sign up?"

Christian carefully removed Carnero's boots and carried them to the pantry. Wolf watched every move, still panting from the battle with the coat. Ears alert, impatient for Carnero to move. Carnero cast quick glances from Wolf to the terrace door. Maartyn caught the glance.

"This guy's waitin' for'is buddies."

Christian stood beside Maartyn, hands in his pockets, looking down at Carnero. He finally made a decision. "Take him to the compound."

"To the compound? Then what?"

"There's a trap door. A tunnel or something."

"Okay. If he tries anything I can shoot him, right?"

"Yes, Maartyn...you can shoot him, wound him. And Maartyn, take the long way around."

"No tracks. A'right, Amigo, you an' me are goin' for a walk." He waved Carnero to his feet. "Nice an' easy. Tell him nice an' easy 'cause I'd just love an excuse to do'im."

"He has a flashlight, in the coat. I'll get it." Christian gingerly reached into the coat for the flashlight. Maartyn pocketed the revolver and took the flashlight. "Ah, Mr, Carnero, my friend wants you to walk that way. Wait, Maartyn, maybe we should blind fold him."

"No way, man. Then I'd have to lead."

"Okay, but be careful. I'll come as soon as I can. Wolf you stay with me."

Maartyn pushed Carnero toward the garden, pressing the 9mm hard into the small of Carnero's back. Wolf paced uneasily, whining as he watched his prey getting away.

They watched Maartyn and Carnero make a looping circuit of the perimeter, pushing past overhanging vines and low ambush palmettos. Carnero was having trouble in his sock feet, the yips of pain and the lurching progress a satisfying torment, but Christian had other things on his mind.

The sangria bowl had already caused trouble. He dumped the dregs over the wall and stashed the accessories in the pantry. The wine bottle he left on the table. He scuffed at drops of Carnero's blood on the terrace stones until they blended with the rough textures. He picked up Paulo's shredded leather coat and flung it into the thick brush below the west wall.

Artifacts of the destroyed saxophone were scattered over the living room floor. Christian, on his hands and knees, handled the brass pieces as if they were precious gems, identifying each note, toying with melodies. Some day he would write it down as his memoir of the day, if he survived.

Christian dumped the junk into the saxophone case and stashed it behind the couch beside the guitar. The gig was still on. He dragged the case out and opened it on the couch. The old guitar didn't look as bad in the aftermath of the violence done to the saxophone. He scanned the room for other details. Renée's personal belongings. The police already knew she was living at the villa. There was nothing else amiss so he was about to return to the terrace with the guitar when Wolf caught a familiar scent. The growl was a deep, almost purring signal meant only for Christian.

There was a noise at the east window, then a sharp whisper..."Chris!"

"Who's there?"

"Are you alone?"

He recognized the unmistakable accent of the French Basque region. Christian experienced many emotions; relief that it was not the police and then fear..."Paulo?" A battered straw hat rose slowly over the window ledge, then the cold grey eyes and the white hair plastered across the forehead with sweat and red soil, but the thin face was barely familiar or the thin body wearing a peasant jacket. "Any cops?"

Wolf went into a choking paroxysm but Christian had him by the scruff of the neck.

"They're everywhere. What are you doing?"

"Hold that goddamned dog!"

Paulo slipped past the window to the terrace and stood in the doorway. He was dirty, emaciated, with a scruff of a blond beard and obviously in pain. Christian clamped Wolf to his side with one arm and took Paulo's bony fingers and eased him down on the bench. Paulo was holding his right side.

"Do you want to lie down?"

"No. If I lay down I won't get up."

"Jesus, man. Escobar said you were in a hospital." Carnero had told him that news also but Christian didn't want to explain.

"If that was a hospital I wouldn't want to be in a jail. Just a dirty cell. Anything to drink?"

"Water?"

"No. Something strong...been drinking out of ditches."

"Ah, there's a part bottle of wine, but..."

"Get it"

"It's been sitting in the sun...be a little warm."

"Don't care. Get it!"

"Okay." Christian, carrying Wolf, fetched the tainted bottle of wine from the terrace table, feeling only slightly guilty. Another small victory in the personal war being waged among his friends. After all, Paulo had been willing to poison his system with heroin. Paulo grabbed the bottle. Christian no longer felt nauseated watching Paulo drink. "They said you were in a coma."

"Faking. They don't torture unconscious prisoners. The stupid pigs. Some bastard stole my jacket. If I ever get my hands on that whore master."

"You escaped?" asked Christian, steering the conversation.

"Guard looks in, maybe twice a day. If I'm still breathing they go on. I sneak water out of the toilet and piss in the sink, see? No food for days. They would have left me to die like a dog." He takes another drink of wine. "Got my chance when the filthy pig of a guard tried to take advantage. I did him."

"Dead?" Christian felt sick again.

"No, but he won't feel good for a few days."

"Escobar said you were shot."

"Sons of bitches! The passport was a joke. That Escobar…"

"You had drugs."

"Well, yes, but I was talking my way out of that when this other guy was going through my ID. He didn't buy it, so I ran. Also infection in leg from that goddamned dog!" Wolf uttered a low growl. Christian smoothed his hackles. "Are you sure you didn't…you know, kill the guard?"

"No, no, the filthy Spanish bastard! Gagged and covered up with a dirty blanket. Won't miss him…so disorganized. They're all scared of Castro. So much confusion they won't even know I'm gone. What a crazy country…Waiting for Castro or running away from Castro. Such chaos."

"The police'll come here looking for you, eventually."

"Where did you expect me to go?"

"We captured one of the top guys in the Secret Police. Carnero?" Christian asked, to see if the name registered. "Maartyn's got him."

"What!? You captured a cop!?"

"Couldn't help it. He was asking questions. I was doing okay until Maartyn shows up, leaping over the wall like a commando. Then Wolf attacks the cop. By the way, the cop was wearing your jacket."

"Merd! Is it damaged?"

"Afraid so. Let me see your leg."

"That fucking dog!" The skin below the knee cap was puffy, tight and shiny. "Look what you did to me, dog!"

"Infection's pretty bad. Probably gangrene. Have to amputate."

"Jesus Christ! What do I do for a doctor!?"

"Let Wolf chew it off."

"Very funny."

Wolf went on the alert again, nose twitching. Renée peaked cautiously around the door. "Oh, my God!" Wolf squirmed free and ran to greet Renée.

"Hello, little one…and Paulo!"

"Merichault's, back from the dead. About to die again because of that dog!"

Wolf was out of Renée's arms, ready to leap on Paulo. Christian intercepted him. Wolf's enemies were as well defined as his friends. "Easy, boy. Save it."

"Paulo...your poor leg."

"My poor leg. My poor back. My poor jacket. I come to Cuba to find peace and I am attacked, beaten, savaged. Worse than Turkey."

"Christian, you won't believe what we've found!"

"I'd believe anything..." The first shot caused them to freeze. It sounded close but muffled. From the direction of Juanita's Cantina. Wolf was out the door and headed down the hill to investigate.

"God! What now?" asked Christian.

"The police," said Renée as she quickly gathered her belongings and stuffed them into her backpack. "I came to tell you."

Two more shots rang out followed by the crash of broken glass. Then more shots. Singles and pairs. Several bunched together. More broken glass. Wolf returned, flying through the door, followed by a breathless Miguel.

"Señor!...The cops!...shooting up Juanita's," he gasped. Then he noticed Paulo. "Oh, no!...Señor Paulo! This is even worse. Señorita, you must go back to the compound. The cops are looking for Carnero. Juanita told them truthfully that Carnero was in her place, asking questions. There was no other way. Take Señor Paulo to the compound. Señor Christ, you must stay here...Don't be afraid."

Miguel headed for the terrace door. "Pietro! Come with me! Where is the bandito?" Wolf had vanished. Miguel came back into the room. "Pietro! This is no time to play games!" The dog trotted out of the pantry with Carnero's boots in his mouth. "Ah, little one! I recognize those." He took the boots from Wolf and handed them to Renée. "Here, Señorita, Renée. Take these with you." Renée accepted the boots, looking very puzzled. Miguel turned away saying, "Pietro, come! And, Señor Christ, do not forget, the boat's coming tonight." He was gone like a spirit. Wolf, with a longing look at Paulo's throat, followed.

"Whose are these?"

"Carnero's," answered Christian.

"Give them to me!" demanded Paulo. Renée gladly handed over the boots. Paulo sat down, kicking away the guajiro sandals.

"We have to go, now," said Renée.

"Renée...what's going on? What did you find?"

"Caves. The Revolution. You won't believe...no time to explain. Come on Paulo. We better do what Miguel says. Christian, be careful. These Cubans are deadly serious."

"I've noticed."

"Yes, Chris," said Paulo, hobbling after Renée, "these people are also crazy."

"Thanks for the warning."

He watched them go, as he had watched Maartyn and Carnero, working along the garden perimeter. Everybody obeyed the rules but already a trail had been established. And everybody but Christian seemed to know what was going on. A new silence crept over the villa. He felt desperately alone. "It's just a dream. It's just a bad dream. It's just the residue in my blood stream. A pocket of bad stuff released by my illness." That was Escobar's explanation. Where is Escobar? "Who is Escobar?" he wondered aloud. Christian picked up the guitar and went out to the terrace. "Caves. Cops. Revolution. Boat's coming." The familiar vista of the sleepy harbour and anchored islands not as reassuring. He sat down on the wall, cradled the guitar and forced the strings to make notes. Jerky and buzzy at first, but with effort he was able to control the oddities of the old guitar. He found that by pressing the strings closer to the fret bars the sound was better. Also discovered the finger grooves. "So old Jocinto played this thing off the wall." He tuned the strings to open 'A' and strummed a chord. Not bad. "But if my illness released the drugs that caused these hallucinations, then the illness wasn't a dream. It might be a nightmare, but it's no dream and I'm not going to wake up before it gets worse."

So it was no surprise when the front door was kicked open by two serious looking policemen in the uniform of the Servicios Especiales, with pistols drawn, waving them nervously at the shadows. A third man, a thin, overdressed officer, looking theatrical, but with amused dignity, entered behind the Servicios Especiales.

"I'm out here!" said Christian, as calmly as possible. He played a few notes to reassure the policemen. An idle Gringo whiling away the hours in indolence on his terrace.

The first policeman worked his way cautiously through the darkened living room, kicking aside the peasant sandals. Nothing suspicious about cast off sandals. The officer motioned the other cop to ransack the pantry. There wasn't much to ransack but they exclaimed victory when they found the part bottle of wine.

The officer was a white Cuban, short, very trim, turned out as for a parade, complete with medals. He got straight to the point.

"Where's Capitan Carnero?"

"Would that be Captain Yolando Justo of the Secret Police?" asked

Christian, strumming the guitar nonchalantly, as if the Secret Police dropped in regularly.

"You know who I mean. He was here."

"Yes, he was. Señor Carnero came by to ask a few questions. Had a drink. He said he was going to walk, ah, up the road."

"Capitan Carnero never walks."

"Well, he had some wine."

"Where is the French woman?"

"Carnero already asked me that. We had lunch and I went down to the Cantina. When I returned she was gone. Perhaps the Captain has gone to look for her. Why do you want to know about Renée?"

The officer swaggered into the sunshine. His men stayed in the shade of the villa, flipping through the pages of the journal looking for words they understood while sharing the bottle of wine. Christian decided it was a fitting end to the vintage. "We believe the French woman, and a Basque mercenary of many surnames, slipped into Cuba to join Castro. We have the mercenary in jail, as Capitan Carnero may have told you. We just want to question the French woman. She has certain diplomatic privileges, you understand, Señor Christian Joyce?"

The officer was much more tactful than Carnero. Christian assumed that, although he was older, and in uniform, he was an inferior rank to Carnero and could only conclude that it was Carnero's pathological cruelty that got him the higher position over a man of quality. "I can vouch for Renée. She has nothing to do with the Revolution."

"And what of the other mercenary?"

"Other mercenary? Who?"

"The one called Maartyn St. Jacques? He's also just a friend?"

"Ah, that can be explained. You see, I met Maartyn in the Bahamas..."

"You're part of a cadre dedicated to overthrowing El Presidente."

"No!..." Christian didn't want to debate intentions and mistaken identities. He had to change the conversation. "And how do you feel about the Revolution?"

"Why do you ask?"

"Just wondering. Cubans are divided about Castro and Batista."

"Did Capitan Carnero discuss this?"

"Actually, he did. We had a pleasant discussion."

"I doubt that. Carnero isn't given to polite conversation."

"We did talk, about things."

"What did the Capitan say?"

Christian began to sweat. He wished he hadn't tried that gamut.

Maybe it would be easier to throw himself at the officer's feet and plead for mercy. Wasn't good at acting cool under pressure so he retreated to the safety of the music and played a few notes. When in doubt tell the truth. "Carnero said he hates Batista."

The officer smiled. "He told you that?"

"Yes. He told me how he came to the Secret Police and that his mission in life was to, you know..."

The officer turned to his men lingering at the door and dismissed them with a wave of the hand. Christian was relieved to see them go. "May I sit down?"

"Of course. I'm sorry, I have nothing to offer you, only water."

"That's of no consequence. I don't drink on duty. But I will have a cigar, with your permission." He reached into the inside pocket of his uniform and produced two cigars. "Would you join me?"

Christian was surprised by the civility of the request. To refuse might be an insult, but to accept could be worse. He had no doubt the cigars were excellent. Possibly a bribe from a merchant. The bright yellow and black band was simple compared to the Monte Christos. He had seen the billboards in Havana. "Thank you, no...I don't."

"Never smoked a cigar? My boy, these are Cohibas! The most famous cigar in the whole world. Rich men travel to buy a box of these wonderful cigars. Or if they're too busy they may just send a plane. Cohibas have caused wars. Men have died. They're traded like gold. One never knows when a good cigar might be needed." The officer placed one of the cigar's in Christian's hand.

Christian inhaled the complex fragrance, a combination of Viñales' dust, mouldy drying houses, decaying wood, fermented tea leaves with a hint of licorice. Like describing wine, he thought. He stroked the veins of the dark gold leaves, wondering why the officer was being so friendly. "Thank you."

"You're welcome, Christian Joyce."

"What's your name," Christian asked, encouraged by the officer's demeanor, "if you don't mind me asking?"

"No. I don't mind." The officer adjusted the band, turning it over in his manicured fingers. He passed the length of the cigar under his nose, inhaling deeply. Christian waited for him to bite off the end as he had seen old men do. Instead he produced a slim, silver device that looked like a small straight razor. He pulled the slender blade up and inserted the end of the cigar into a hole, then, with a flick of his thumb, nipped the tobacco. Like a guillotine, thought Christian. "My name? Alphonso...Alfonzo José Defencio Marti."

"Marti?"

"You recognize the name?"

"The José Marti? The poet rebel?"

Marti reached into his pocket and produced a small matchbox with a bright red and yellow label of banners and flags, called Liberdad Excelsior. "The very same José Marti, hero of Cuban Freedom Fighters. My grandfather. Poet. Lawyer. Champion of the oppressed."

"I don't understand. You work for Batista."

Marti opened the box and took out a wooden match with the head the same colour as the box, turning the box to reveal a coarse striker. He pressed the match against the striker. A small spark, hissing, with many little rockets flying about trailing smoke before the match flared to life with great violence. Marti waited until the yellow flame turned to a clear blue with orange tip. First he heated the end of the cigar, careful to avoid the flame touching the tobacco, then he put the cigar in his mouth, not clenching it with his teeth, but held firmly by his thin lips and feminine fingers. He measured the flame a little below the end, working his cheeks like a bellows, drawing the flame to the cigar, puffing lightly, blowing out the smoke, looking at the end of the cigar with satisfaction. He smiled. Christian was fascinated by the blue smoke rising around Marti's head, like a wreath framing images of saints and gangsters. He could never understand the mystique of cigar smoking. "That's because you don't understand Cuba."

"Pardon me?"

"I don't work for Batista. Within the Servicios I can keep watch over the dogs of war. Unlike Capitan Carnero, I have no grudges, only my love for Cuba." Christian watched the end of the cigar change to grey ash. "It takes special skills to make a cigar that burns slowly." Marti studied the cigar and pointed it at Christian. "When you know Cuba you will know life."

"Why are you telling me this?"

"A story then..." Alfonzo Marti removed his hat revealing wavy black hair, with streaks of grey at the temples, thinning on either side. Without the hat he looked like a priest. "Many years ago I watched soldiers in the service of the dictator, Machado, beat a young man to a bloody pulp. They dragged him out of the cane field to question him about anti-government activity. He swore he was innocent. They tied him to the wheels of a cane wagon and punched and kicked him until he could no longer talk. They took his refusal to talk as proof of his guilt, because only a fanatic would continue to deny his criminal activity."

"That doesn't make sense."

"You see, my boy, an innocent man might admit to anything. The true revolutionary would defy his tormentors to the death. They left him hanging there on the wheel, like Jesus Christ on the Cross." Marti made the sign of the cross. "The scene made a deep impression on me." Marti paused to study the cigar. "The young man was my brother."

"That's an incredible story."

"It's too common in our country. Witnessing such brutality I grew up wanting justice to be the right of every Cuban." Marti returned the cigar to his mouth and puffed gently. "You understand, my brother was guilty. The beating was because of his name, Marti."

"What happened to him, after the beating?"

"My brother was in the prime of intellectual life. He could no longer take part in anti-government activity so the soldiers accomplished one thing, besides misery. He became a burden on his family who looked after him until the day he died."

"I'm sorry, such a waste."

"José Marti himself said, 'A true man does not seek the path where advantage lies, but rather the path where duty lies, and this is the only practical man'. My brother walked his path, and suffered. Everyone has their reasons to object. Some turn their objections to duty. My brother's duty was to object strongly. My duty is to object wisely, but pragmatically. To work from within until the time's right."

"I suppose there's a moral for me."

"Yes, of course. You may or may not be a threat to Cuba. Only a severe beating will tell. If you protest we'll know the truth."

The all too familiar warning chill coursed through Christian's body. He regretted letting his guard down and felt less fear facing Carnero's lunatic aggression. This smooth, polite officer was capable of intellectual cruelty. "But I'm not guilty of anything."

"There, you see, you're protesting already," said Marti with delight.

"All right, I'm guilty," said Christian, sarcastically. 'I'm a Castro terrorist, that's why I'm hiding out in Los Espiritos, slowly starving to death."

"Be careful. If my stupid officers were still here I would have to let them beat you to complete their day. You see, they've had nothing to do recently except shoot that pest ridden animal in the Cantina. If it were not that the proprietor pays them so well they would shoot her instead. Juanita and her crowd are up to something besides smuggling. Do you know what?"

"I don't, I swear! No one tells me anything."

"I'm to believe your friends are mercenaries, deep into the conspiracy with Castro and you know nothing? I'm to believe that your patron and your house boy are old Castro hands and you are an innocent baby?"

"No. Yes. Does it matter what I say?"

"Not to me." Marti softened. "Be careful, Christian." He drew smoke and let it trail out of his nose slowly. "I know you're innocent of these things."

"If you know, why are you doing this?"

"You chose to come here at an unfortunate time. Another time your stay in Cuba would be nothing but pleasure and you would go away thinking we are such wonderful, generous people. Maybe when this is all over you'll return and find us to be so. In the meantime there's a revolution and what comes out of the struggle must be greater than the parts."

"I don't understand your game."

"Revolutions work from many levels, my boy. You know that."

"Well, yes. I mean, in school we studied revolutions, like in France and Russia."

"Then you know that most revolutions begin with the intellectual class, even the American Revolution. The intelligencia! Those idle and privileged enough to indulge in dangerous thoughts. The intellectuals create the climate for rebellion and teach the rank and file, the victimized, the disorganized peasants. Peasants are the necessary fodder. They seldom grasp the real reasons for the revolution, but they understand their own suffering." Marti paused to puff and savor his cigar. Christian stole a glance toward the compound. If Marti noticed he said nothing. "The leaders give them a few slogans to shout as they march, loot and burn. The intellectuals are often swept away in the hot winds of passion and the revolution is carried along by the masses. The Cuban rebellion started many years ago, before Fidel Castro. Fidel's just a disciple of men like José Marti and Eduardo. No one but Castro himself knows what his real agenda is. If Castro's smart enough to inflame the workers, the guajiros, even the rich farmers, the fisherman, the cane cutters, petty bureaucrats and the military, he can make a rebellion. If he is really smart he will use them to create something good and lasting. A true Revolution."

"You're only confusing me. I mean, I understand the theories but I still don't get where you fit in."

"Don't be stupid, young man. I said I use the Servicios to watch both sides. Batista's the symbol of evil in Cuba, but don't assume that Castro is Saint Fidel of the Sierra Maestra. My concern is that the evil of Batista be erased from our country but I'm afraid that the alternative may be as bad, or worse. At least we know what to expect from Batista and his kind. Carnero's one of them. He says he hates Batista but what he really wants is to raise an army, like Castro, and seize power himself. Greed for power drives untalented men to great heights of destruction and cruelty. You have seen an example of their worst. But have you seen what fanatics can do in the name of revolution?"

"Well, not first hand. But people get hurt."

"Yes, and they can die for a good cause, but only if the results are better than the evil they overthrow. The Leninist Bolsheviks and Marxist Communists promised great things in Russia and China. We know the opposite is true and the people suffer under a greater tyranny. They no longer just suffer and starve, they have no freedom to do anything. They say that now in Russia no one is hungry or without work. But they are forbidden to go to church or speak freely. I don't want that to happen in Cuba. I want to go to church and pray and receive communion and baptize my grandchildren. Everyone has that right in Cuba and the right to die in the bosom of Mother Church, even if it is by government neglect and starvation."

Christian decided to risk the same question he asked Carnero. "So, do you support Castro?"

"No! I don't. I watch and wait."

"Then let's say, you favour any style of government, if it works for the people."

"You begin to understand. Castro wants to change things. My grandfather knew the dangers of sudden change. The people will be dancing in the streets one day and the next day they'll be herded into prison camps by the revolutionaries to protect the Revolution. Then who is the revolution for? If it's not for the good of the people then it can only be for the benefit of the State and the leaders. Do you know of Joseph Stalin's crimes in Russia?"

"Yes, everyone knows about Stalin."

"Not everyone. Many are ignorant of the evils this one peasant man caused because he was a suspicious, evil person who used any means to get power and keep it. Lying to the people, saying that he killed their neighbours for their own good. The purges killed millions. Stalin died the same year Castro began his drive for revolution. But what is Castro capable of doing to get power? What will Castro have to do to keep power?"

"I don't know. The same thing?"

"Very possibly. He seems passionate and hot for revolution but he has always been a cold, calculating manipulator, not above using violence to get his way. I could tell you stories. However, I don't think Castro's interested in power. If I thought that I would work to defeat Castro myself."

"So you, you aren't against Castro?"

"No. I am biding my time. Watching over my Cuba." Marti took a long, contemplative puff of the cigar, almost disappearing in the fog of smoke.

"What will you do if Batista is defeated?"

"Not if, when. I will lay aside my uniform and vanish into the crowds, rejoicing on the Malecon."

"I don't understand about the uniform either. If you are with the Secret Police why do you wear a uniform? Doesn't that give you away?"

"Not the Secret Police. There's no secret police in Cuba. Servicios Especiales. The special police of Batista. Unlike the sneaky Carnero I wear a uniform because it also serves a purpose. If I am known as Servicios Especiales the people understand exactly who I am and what power is behind me. If that power fails I can throw off this uniform and be seen to make the grand conversion."

"Does that work? I mean, aren't you known by the company you keep?"

"Again you misunderstand Cuba. We are a people of passion, yes, but we are also pragmatic. How do you think we have survived four hundred years? To survive one must be like the sugar cane. Bend in the wind. If Fidel Castro is as he claims and the people are free, then I'll put on whatever uniform is required. If Castro shows his true fascist credentials, as I believe he will, but fails to deliver us from evil, I will dedicate myself to bringing him down. I have no hatred, only love for my country."

"Love? I don't know. Seems I've heard a lot about it recently, but not much evidence."

"Love can be a very dangerous thing, just as ideologies can be dangerous in the hands of a complex, cynical political animal. I'm the watcher in the tower, on guard to sound the alarm if the animal gets too close. Now do you understand?"

"Not very much. But, you wouldn't tell me this unless you plan to, you know," Christian made a gesture like a knife across his throat, "the way you trim your cigars?"

"To silence you? No, Christian. You're not a threat to Cuba. You and your friends are only petty bourgeois misfits, even gangsters." He made a gesture of dismissal with the cigar. "Of no consequence. Even Juanita's band of conspirators are not as dangerous to Batista as his own ego and his self deceit. His greed for power will be his undoing. He'll reap the whirlwind. Unfortunately, there's nothing I or my fellow officers can do to stop the tidal wave the hurricane has set in motion. The cane can bend and endure but if you hold it under water it will drown. If you all perish you'll be no more than bits of foreign wreckage washed up on our shores." Marti puffed up a cloud, like a wizard.

"Is that the good news?"

The fog slowly cleared, swirled away on eddies of a gentle breeze curling around the corner of the villa. "There are one or two who must be watched." Alfonzo Marti stood up and held out his hand to Christian. "Escobar's not who he seems to be. Only a warning." Christian shook his hand, feeling a quiet strength. "And there's another person, one that could break your heart. Be careful. We'll be leaving Los Espiritos soon, with or without Capitan Carnero. Personally, I can think of no fate for the bastard that I would regret. But others will come. The military will arrive to do a sweep of this coast looking for Castro's agents. Don't expect them to sit at your table and discuss politics. They'll kick down doors and shoot first." Marti walked briskly across the terrace and through the house to the front door puffing grandly, leaving a trail of smoke like a steam locomotive.

Christian stood for a long time looking at the closed door. How strange, he thought, of all the people who have come through that door, Alfonzo Marti, a police strong man in a theatrical uniform, is the one he would most like to know. The pleasant aroma of the unlit cigar in his hand lingered in the heated air. He wondered if he would ever achieve a time in his life when he could smoke a cigar with such class. "See you around, Alfonzo."

Christian tucked the cigar away in the guitar case, picked up the guitar and lost himself in the chords.

Time slipped away as he concentrated on finding a way to make music, desperately seeking the formula. Just being loud wasn't enough. The notes had to be genuine. No, even that wasn't enough. He wanted to do his best.

A few minutes after Alfonzo Marti left the villa, Christian heard the Ford sedan of the Servicios Especiales grind up the hill on the main road out of Los Espiritos. He could see the trail of red dust hovering over the trees, drifting slowly across the tobacco fields. He should have felt a sense of relief to see the police leave, but instead he felt as though Marti was the first person to really try to explain the Revolution honestly. Everyone else was hiding behind a façade. Marti admitted his rôle in the drama and assumed a costume but didn't try to pretend it was for some other reason. An honest person, thought Christian. A rare commodity.

Christian was daydreaming, unaware that the old guitar was beginning to sound almost normal, and didn't hear the deep, soft purr of the Lincoln convertible creeping effortless up the hill.

"Christian?..."

"Out here."

"Ah, just so." Escobar walked into the sunshine like an actor stepping into a spotlight. Dressed in a light tan tropical suit, looking pale, drawn and worried. "Ah, that's good, practicing for the show."

"Trying."

"But this is not your instrument."

"Technical problems."

"I see. Can I do something?"

"Can you fix a broken saxophone?"

"Uhm...Miguel tells me you've had a visit from Capitan Carnero."

"Among others."

"And, unfortunately you have him in protective custody."

"News travels fast."

"Not fast enough. This is very serious, Christian. I also had a visitor. Major Marti himself."

"Major!? I thought he was just a cop."

"No, a visit from Major Marti is an event."

"I'm double blessed."

"A word from Marti can make you or break you. He plays cards with Batista. Knows everything. The Major and I go way back. Intelligent man. Thoughtful, and compassionate. If there were more like Marti, Cuba wouldn't be in her present difficulty."

Christian remembered Major Marti's oblique warning about Escobar. "Why would Major Marti visit me?"

"What did you talk about?"

"Ah, more warnings. Told me a sad story about his brother, and passed on some fatherly advice. He said we were just a bunch of bourgeois intellectuals. He says you and Juanita and Miguel may be involved with, whatever's happening."

"You do not keep an operation like this from Major Marti."

"Oh, man! This just gets weirder. If he knows about, you know...whatever is going on here...?"

"I told you, Marti and I go way back. I assume he told you his feelings about Batista?"

"He said he likes to see both sides...the dogs of war he called them. But he's also watching Castro."

"Exactly. Unfortunately, he can't interfere."

Christian strummed a cord then put the guitar aside. "What good's knowledge if you can't use it?"

Escobar hesitated, surveying the garden and the compound thicket, as if debating about Christian's right to know the whole story. "There's a great man in Europe who knew many things during the last war. The last World War that is. He had an agency called the London Controlling Section. Their rôle was to know what the Germans were planning and to find ways to deceive them. Winston The Great Illusionist they call him."

"Winston Churchill? Prime Minister of England."

"Briton's symbol of defiance. The glowing fire around which the frightened masses crept during Europe's darkest hours. Some say it was Churchill's power that allowed Spain to remain neutral. Many passed Churchill off as just an orator. He was seen in endless Pathé newsreels strolling arrogantly about the free world, with that scowling bulldog face, a big bowler hat and this incredible cigar the size of a club...perhaps he just waved it around to scare Hitler. He delighted in tricks. His deceptions so confused the Germans that the Hun went running from a force of stick men or cardboard airplanes and inflatable tanks. Sandbag parachutists rained from the skies behind German lines and the Germans were shooting each other in terror."

"If Churchill was that visible wasn't he a target?"

"Disguises were one of his specialties. He once boarded a British navy ship in your own country, disguised as a common sailor, drunk after a night on the town. Admiral Donitz thought his double was on a fast troop ship and sent his submarines after a prize they could not hope to catch, while Winston sailed serenely away in the other direction."

"I read the book."

"Alright, you've studied, but you don't know Churchill's greatest accomplishment. There have always been rumours that England had the means to break the German codes. It's still top secret.

"But you know about it, right?"

"I have sources. The British, with help from the French and the Poles, invented a machine to translate codes. The Germans were so confident in their Enigma machine that they broadcast military tactics openly. They even sold the machine to the Japanese. The British counter intelligence broke the Enigma ciphers. They knew every move Herr Hitler planned. Admiral Donitz deluged his submarines with messages. Herr Goring broadcast numbers of aircraft and destinations openly. Fleet manoeuvres. You know the story of the sinking of The Bismarck?"

"The British navy hunted her down."

"But you didn't know that it was breaking the codes that found her. The British also knew about bombing raids. Submarine locations. Troop deployments. Secret codes of the highest echelons. Everything that was broadcast on the airways. They used the information to prepare for the Battle of Britain and that prevented Hitler from invading England. Someday you'll hear about this espionage game. It's called Ultra. The tragedy was the Allies couldn't use the information to save British cities from the biggest air raids."

"But, that's what I mean, what good's information if they couldn't save lives?"

"Yes, it caused Churchill much consternation. The War Room battles were intense they say. He had to accept losses. But in the long run, the Allies could plan ahead, be prepared to take counter measures. So instead of stopping a raid on a large city like Coventry, they countered with the destruction of Dresden. Imagine, Christian, the heavy responsibility of those men who had to stand by and see their country destroyed piece by piece, lives sacrificed, and say to yourself, there's a greater plan. Accept that some will perish so others may survive. Could you sleep at night with that weight on your mind? Breakfast with your family, knowing that during the night thousands died and you had the secret? How those men must have suffered. In war things are done that no man of compassion should have to decide."

"Only tyrants should get the job?"

"It's too often the case."

"There's another moral or something, right?"

"If you can find one that suits you. Did Major Marti tell you that the soldiers are coming to sweep the village?"

"Yeah, he said that."

"He'll give us some warning. Major Marti's no friend of Batista's. Do you understand what his decisions must be? A man of principle. It pains him greatly to accept that rebellion is necessary. He, like Señor

Churchill, like José Marti himself, must posture, assume disguises. If we perish in this revolution it's of little consequence, but if Castro fails to do the right thing we fail utterly."

Again the mention of disguises, Christian said to himself. "He said that too."

"I thought he might. Pray Fidel does the right thing, Christian."

"I don't pray but I might start, soon."

"Good. Now for your rôle. Pray the boat arrives on time. We cannot contact Santoz and warn him off. Even coded messages are not safe, as the Germans eventually found out, too late. But the Germans paid for Guernicia, didn't they?"

"It took time, but yes..."

"The most important cargo is on board that fishing boat. The last piece of the puzzle."

"Can you tell me yet?"

"Only that the future of Cuba could hang in the balance if we fail."

"But all I have to do is play at Juanita's, right?"

"Your job's almost finished."

"Almost?"

"I don't have time to explain." Escobar glided into the shadows of the villa, like Major Marti, and the others, as if the terrace were a stage and the whole show just for his entertainment.

"Figures." Christian followed. "Story of my life."

"I can't promise you anything, Christian. Your means of survival is over there," he nodded toward the compound, "with your friends."

"Ah, that reminds me...what do we do with Carnero?"

Escobar shrugged. "Kill him, if necessary."

"That's it? Just kill him?"

"Men like Carnero are dross. Chafe in the wind. Insignificant unless he gets the power to reap the whirlwind."

Where had he heard that before? "I get the point."

"Miguel's nearby. Don't leave the villa until he comes for you."

"Leave? Where would I go?"

"Relax, Christian. The Revolution's going well."

"But we're still in danger."

"The real battles will be in the cities. We in Los Espiritos are ready to do our part to assure the success of the Revolution, even if Fidel himself should fall. I don't want to burden you with more information."

"There are times I wish...I don't know what I wish. I'm not sure if I care whether the Revolution succeeds."

"Why should you care, Christian? It's not your revolution."

"I'm just supposed to play my part. And if I blow it, the whole Revolution might fail, is that it?"

"A bit dramatic. By the way...intuition tells me that the shooting will start tonight."

Escobar faded into the night. The big car gliding away with whispers of warnings and dread events. Perhaps the last sounds of a normal world he would hear. Detroit machinery in a Cuban village. The Motor City was far away in a young boy's dreams of loud music and shinny Corvettes. As the Lincoln's sound faded a new silence filled the villa.

Christian was left suspended between dream and reality amid the comings and goings of characters in a dark tragi-comedy. The climax now imminent, said Escobar. But it wasn't time to bring down the curtain and Christian was expected to play his part, wondering how much Renée and the others knew. The compound became a storehouse of possibilities. Renée mentioned caves and Revolutionaries. Perhaps he could simply wander over and have a quick look. Perhaps he could escape on the boat. Perhaps many things, even the last night of his short life and escape from paradise seemed more important than exile.

His passport was gone but the journal was on the table. Major Marti's officers left it open at the last entry. The empty wine bottle standing guard. Christian would never be able to look at a bottle of red wine without remembering Carnero, Maartyn, Paulo and Marti's cops.

The last journal entry was December 22, 1958. It was December 24. No one had mentioned Christmas. Another casualty of conflict and that reminded him of home and childhood. There were few happy memories of idyllic family gatherings around a tree on the Blessed Eve.

Christian practiced the guitar until his fingers rebelled. He slept sitting up on the American couch, guitar across his lap. Miguel and Wolf slipped into the villa from the terrace after dark. Wolf was somewhere in the deep shadows, sniffing the accumulated scents of the day, sorting out friend and foe. Miguel padded softly to Christian's side.

"Señor Christ?"

Christian started. "Wha?..."

"It's me, Miguel."

"Oh, Miguel. I was dreaming. It's dark. Light a candle or something."

"No. The Servicios Especiales are about. Pietro can smell them. Juanita's Cantina? Have you forgotten your mission?"

"At least it's no longer called a date."

"Almost time to go."

"God I'm tired."

"I've brought you something to eat."

"I'm not hungry."

"You must eat, Señor Christ. My mother worked all day to prepare a special dish for the occasion. Just smell the wonderful meat." Miguel lifted the lid of a heavy iron pot. It did smell wonderful, but his stomach said, perhaps not.

"What is it?"

"Ropa vieja. Very special, to make you strong for the gig."

"Means old clothes. Beggar's garments."

"That's close enough."

"And you want me to eat it?"

"It's special, Señor Christ! My mother says..."

"What did she do, cook Old Jocinto's shirt to give me inspiration?"

"No, no! Beef simmered in sauce," Miguel enthused.

"Meat? I'd forgotten there was such a thing. Renée's chicken broth seemed a year ago."

"The beef was very expensive, even if it's a little tough and stringy, but mother cooked it for hours and shredded the beef, worked it until it's as tender as young calf. Smell the spices." Miguel held the pot under Christian's nose.

"Okay, it's interesting."

"She grows the coriander. The peppers, onions, garlic and tomatoes, simmered slowly to make the sauce. And the very special colour, which unfortunately you cannot see, is annatto seeds. I had to borrow the seeds and the bay leaf from Juanita's store. Without the annatto seeds the dish would not have this wonderful reddish yellow colour, which you cannot see, but you can taste. The meat and the sauce are on a bed of fine white rice, resting comfortably, waiting for you to begin...to wake up the feast."

"You sound like some demented food critic."

"What's a food critic? Is it like the dietician?"

"A person who describes food, like a wine critic describes wine."

"Why does one describe wine? Wine is for drinking. Do people describe beer, or rum?"

"No, you're right. Just drink."

"Yes, drink. It's better that way."

233

"I could use a drink."

"The good wine you saved. I'll get a bottle."

"Unfortunately the wine's gone. To a good cause."

"Then you should eat."

"Not sure I can."

"Just try it, Señor Christ, please. Here, I have a spoon. It's near your hand. I could feed you."

"Miguel! I'm not an invalid."

"You might be if you aren't strong enough to play tonight. The unhappy customers will break your knees, or worse."

"Thanks for the encouragement." Christian strummed a chord, flinching from the pain in the left hand. The fingers could be a problem "Jesus! I can't play in this condition."

"Why do you have the guitar and not your beautiful saxophone?"

"Saxophone sacrificed for the Revolution. I'll expect a personal letter of gratitude from Fidel."

"Please eat."

"Ropa vieja won't help my fingers." Christian plucked each string, listening. Tuning, strumming. Not concert clear but recognizable. Fine tuning, leaning down close to the body of the old guitar to feel the resonance. "Miguel...the wine bottle. It's on the table."

"Yes, it's here...but it's empty."

"I know. Take it out to the terrace and break it. Keep the neck and grind the sharp edges on the stones."

"Break it? Why?"

"Just do it!"

"Sure, Señor Christ. I will, if you eat."

"Okay, deal. I'm eating, look."

Christian plunged the spoon into the invisible stew, hoping there were no surprises. "*Uhmm*...good."

"I'll go and break the bottle, as you say. You eat."

"I'm eating. *Uhmm*...You're like my mother sometimes."

Mom and home were distant memories of simple things taken for granted, like baking, bread or cookies on cold winter days. He wished he had understood then what the brief vignettes meant. Protection? Comfort? He heard Miguel break the wine bottle, remembering the sound of falling glass, the night his father broke the bathroom mirror in a rage. The sounds of glass shards in the porcelain sink were like random musical notes. Smashed the mirror instead of his family. Remembered his father sneering at some new art project that failed to produce bragging rights at the corner bar. It was easy to fall into the trap Howie laid for them. They were hurting, as kids hurt when adults turn their backs and authority fails to notice the anger. The rebellion went badly wrong. Rebellions always go wrong. He wondered how badly wrong the Cuban rebellion could go. He felt a snuffling wet nose on his hand. He put the pot on the floor, rubbing the stiff fur on Wolf's neck. He returned the empty pot to the table just as Miguel came in from the terrace. Wolf preened on the American couch.

Miguel picked up the clean pot. "Did you eat?"

"Yes. See?"

"Why does Pietro sound so satisfied?"

"Have you got the bottle neck?"

"Here, Señor Christ."

"Good. Don't ask questions."

"Mother will be very upset."

Christian slipped his left middle finger into the bottle neck and touched the green glass to the metal strings, strummed and slid the bottle neck along the strings. The effect was mournful and gut-wrenching. A train whistle, then a violin. He slapped the guitar to produce a thumping base then drove more chords.

"Señor Christ, I do not wish to criticize, but what is that?"

"Delta Blues. Maartyn The Rhythm King will be amused. It's a poem...get it?"

"Blues? Poem? But you're a jazzman. Juanita wants jazz music."

"She wants loud music. Besides, it's all I can make with this beat up guitar and bleeding fingers."

"Will it be loud enough to distract the Servicios Especiales?"

"Wait 'til you hear me sing."

The Moose Head Cantina was crowded like the previous occasion, but the smoke and the heat twice as thick and fetid. Several of the patrons, including the women, were now dressed in fatigues, side arms in plain view. And the mood was tense, without the hint of a festival. Christian interpreted the tension as hostility for the death of Old Jocinto. He put the guitar case out of sight. Juanita barely acknowledged his presence, preoccupied with serving drinks, although no money crossed the zinc counter. And Juanita had aged ten years overnight.

Miguel took a tray of sweating bottles and worked the crowd, glancing often at the open door. Christian noticed that he didn't collect money for the beer either. Juanita put a dripping bottle of Budweiser in front of him without the usual comments. Christian drank the pleasantly cold beer and looked around at the brown faces shimmering with sweat and the dark eyes that seemed more hostile. He shifted his gaze to the moose head. The glass eyes were missing and the moth-eaten fur around the nose, and ears and forehead showed gaping bullet holes. Kapok stuffing oozed out like the seed fluff on a marsh cattail. Juanita spoke to him in English over the din. "The police have dese-crated my moose, no? The price I pay for silence."

"It could have been worse," Christian answered in English

"Oho, no, I pay too well. But I think it's the last payment."

"I had visitors too. Major Marti."

"Don't mention names!"

"Sorry."

"Drink your beer. Where is Señor Maartyn?"

"Previous engagement."

"You'll have to play alone. The two worthless hombres I hired to work with you have run into the hills."

"They know something?"

"Why do you have only a guitar?"

"Long story."

"Never mind now. Play loud and don't stop for any reason. Do you know Spanish songs?"

"Not many."

"No matter. They aren't listening."

The scene was bizarre. More fatigue-clad locals slipped in until bodies were packed into the cantina like vertical sardines. The talk was loud, almost angry. And there was no singing but the cigars were bigger. The shrine to the Blessed Virgin of the Fields and the smoke-stained crucifix were gone. As were the Santería figures and beads. Casualties of the Secret Police perhaps, or removed for safe keeping. Also miss-ing were the empty pistol holsters dangling from the moose's antlers. Escobar suddenly appeared at the end of the bar. Juanita placed a small glass of the clear liqueur in front of him and Escobar tossed off the drink. "Play!" Juanita said.

The low stage was occupied by tough looking patrons squatting on their haunches, heads bent over beer bottles, in serious discussion. Christian opened the guitar case and slung the unfamiliar instrument. He took the bottle neck out of his pocket and slipped it on his finger. With barely elbow room at the bar he attempted a few chords to warm up. The screeching notes unable to climb above the disparate shouts and curses. He felt helpless and alone.

"Ah, Juanita!...I don't think they want music tonight."

"Play. Play! It's all you have to do, but play loud!"

"I'm playing loud!"

"Play louder. Don't worry, they only have to hear you from the beach!"

"Then I should be on the beach," Christian mumbled.

Using a plastic pick he hammered chords without a tune. He bellowed out some words of hurtin' blues. Broken hearts. Drunken nights on bayous or ungrateful horses adrift in a sea of sagebrush. He tried Spanish songs. Cowboys and coyotes and back to New Orleans riverfront bars and honky-tonk women jilting down-trodden drifters. Whores and drug addicts and car thieves. Problems of the soulful kind. He didn't attempt to make stories, just shouted phrases he remembered. The effect made him lightheaded and giddy. But it was loud. Evil smelling hombres next to him talked louder, and shoved back when Christian tried to make more elbow room.

Escobar nodded and disappeared into the backroom, followed by four men; Santoz and the two sailors from the boat and another man dressed in fatigues, black hair curling out from under a forage cap. Scraggly black beard. A big man. Taller than the average Cuban in Los Espiritos. Familiar face. The photographs in the papers? "Couldn't be," Christian said to the man beside him. The man grunted and grinned. He continued to hammer chords, making the guitar wail like a berserk banshee on a moon-soaked moor. There was no moon over Los Espiritos. A loaded skiff moved back and forth between the beach and the old fishing boat anchored off shore. More men in fatigues entered the cantina and made their way to the back room. Christian played in desperation until Maartyn was at his side yelling in his ear, "What the hell is that, ol' buddy!?"

"Blues!"

"Not any I know!"

"Where've you been!?"

"Man, you wouldn't believe! Can't explain now."

"Course not!" Christian played harder.

"I'm supposed to play to that?"

"Just get on board and make noise."

Juanita thumped a bottle of beer on the counter and grinned at Maartyn. Maartyn downed half the beer and fetched the drum. He and Juanita traded conspiratorial winks. Maartyn pounded the drum and Christian smashed chords, wailing out words that made Maartyn laugh. The atmosphere suddenly changed and the crowd near the bar applauded and whooped. In ones and twos, dark men in fatigues dis-

red into the back room.

"How many of those guys can that back room hold!?" Christian shouted at Maartyn. At least two dozen had vanished into the dark space.

"What about the back room!?"

"Those men! What's going on!?"

"You won't believe it, man!"

"Try me."

Captain Santoz reappeared and motioned for Maartyn. "Chris, just keep playin'. I gotta go! Later, man!"

Maartyn followed Santoz and the mate through the crowd to the cantina door. Was Maartyn leaving Los Espiritos with Santoz? He played. Men, some just boys, dressed in fatigues entered the cantina and slipped into the back room. Four dozen he estimated. Minutes dragged by. Five armed men in fatigues entered the cantina and made straight for the back room. Two or three he thought he recognized. Christian was horse from singing and shouting. Strum and slide. Drink and sing.

Escobar made another appearance, briefly looked at Christian, said 'thank you', and went out the door into the night. He hoped he was relieved of his duty but the tension had lifted and the party seemed to be in full roar. Juanita showed no signs of letting up. Drinks flowed. Something strange was happening. Christian hammered on, loosing all sense of time, but counted no further émigrés to the beaded inner sanctum. Even Miguel had been gone for hours, or so it seemed...

It was after one o'clock when Miguel flew into the cantina, forcing his small body through the crowd to find Juanita. He said something to her and then grabbed the guitar case. "Come on, Señor Christ!"

"What?..."

"They're coming!" shouted Juanita, signaling with her arms for everybody to leave. "Go, go!" Christian was in a trance. Miguel grabbed his hand to make him stop strumming. "Señor Christ! We have to go!"

"Where?..."

"Go now, quickly!" shouted Juanita. The crowd vacated the cantina like jumpy sheep escaping a band of coyotes. In the silence following the swift exodus Christian heard distant gun shots.

"The army," Miguel said. "They're burning the houses. Señor Christ! Can you hear me!?"

"Yes. I hear. The army...just like Major Marti said."

"That's the hombres, Señor Christ. Come on!"

Juanita dumped bottles of beer and rum into a canvas bag and fled to the back room. Christian tried to follow her. "Go with Miguel!"

Wolf was waiting at the door. Christian thought the orange light colouring the dog's fur was the sunrise. Dawn, already? The glow was from the right direction. He carried the guitar clutched protectively to his chest. Miguel carried the empty case.

Wolf led the way to the path and up the hill. The fires began at the far end of the village and spread rapidly through the wooden shacks, aided by a light sea breeze and the dead scrub and drooping fronds of the royal palms. The houses burned quickly and the royal palms flared like torches, as if a troop of destructive trolls stumbled through a village of the Teenie Weenies. The smoke reached Christian before they were half way up the hill. He stopped, gasping for breath, amazed by the sight of the flames and the sound of shooting.

"Come on, Señor Christ!"

The shooting was nearer. Miguel grabbed his hand and dragged him up the hill.

Christian stood in the living room, dazed by fatigue and flight, the growing fires lighting up the interior like a gigantic fireplace. He thought the room looked very cozy in the dancing orange light. "Renée and Esameralda should be here."

"What do you want to take?"

"Take? Where?..."

"To the caves."

"Journal, I guess. Knapsack."

Miguel searched for the journal. Found it on the floor and went into the bedroom for Christian's knapsack, flinging anything loose into the bag. Christian put the guitar in the case, and with the cigar in hand, was looking out the window. The flames were already searing the walls of the cantina, slanting crazily in all directions from the growing fire storm. Armed men were running in the street, trading gunfire with soldiers advancing along the harbour road behind a half tracked truck with a machine gun mounted on a swivel turret. The scene, clearly visible in the firelight, framed by the window resembled a Goya painting. A newsreel rebellion in Mexico or South America. Then smoke and flames blotted out the scene. The fire racing up the slope toward the overgrown garden, leaping over the scrub, exploding dry palms. In moments the garden tangle was a roaring brush fire. Wolf was running from door to door.

"It's too late. The compound's cut off."

"What then?"

"The cold locker!" Miguel dragged Christian toward the pantry and moved the preparation table. He took hold of the ring and heaved the heavy lid aside. He pulled out the empty wine box, took a shirt from Christian's bag and dropped the knapsack into the black hole. "Get in! You'll be safe in here."

Christian had a fear of small dark places, but in the circumstances his phobias seemed minor. "What'll you do?"

"Pietro and I will distract them. We're only a terrified boy and his small yapping dog escaping from madness. Besides, Pietro and I can move much faster. Get in!"

Christian did as he was told. There was just enough room for him to curl up on his side with his head on the knapsack, bare legs and arms on the stones. The stones were damp and cold. Least of his worries. Miguel dipped the shirt into the bucket of water and wrung it out, handed it to Christian and kicked the plank cover back into place.

"Hey! What's this for?"

Miguel lifted the lid a few inches. "Hold it over your face if the smoke gets too bad."

"Take the guitar. It's all I have left."

"Okay, Señor. I'll look after the guitar, now put your head down!"

The *thunk* of the heavy hatch sounded too final. The table skidded on the stones. "Don't worry, Señor Christ, the villa won't burn." Miguel dumped the bucket of wash water over the cover just in case. The cold water poured through the cracks, adding to Christian's discomfort.

Miguel's bare footsteps, sounding hollow through the stones of the floor, were lost in the *clack* and *pop* of gunfire. Christian felt regret at Miguel's going. Maartyn and Renée had left him. Also Esameralda. The shooting was closer but everyone he knew and loved, even some he didn't like, kept running away, leaving him in a dark, damp hole. Only fear of violence kept him from bolting. He tried to explain the violence, curled up like a body in a burial box. West Coast Indians did that to bodies.

Heavy footsteps echoed through the villa. Orders were shouted too quickly for Christian to understand but the girl's voice he recognized. Furniture was overturned and shutters flung open. The rebels were taking refuge in his villa and the battle was going on above his head.

The smell of gun powder and burning brush filtered into his hiding place. Miguel said the villa would not burn but what if the army stormed the place? He didn't want to die in a cold cellar.

The battle for his villa seemed to go on for a long time, until the gunfire became sporadic. Then there was one long burst of machine gun fire from the half track and bullets ricocheted around the interior of the villa. A rifle clattered to the floor, startling Christian. A cry of pain and curses. And much scuffling of feet. A volley of return fire. The rebels were on the terrace, firing over the wall, so the brush fire must have burned it's way beyond the garden. More gunfire from the windows. Taunts and even laughter. What could they be laughing about?

The battle noise became surreal, like a bad radio play with not enough dialogue and too many sound effects. The smoke wasn't so bad with his nose in the wet T-shirt, but the musty, ammonia smell reminded him that he should do his laundry. Concentrate on mundane things. Christian's exhaustion overwhelmed his adrenalin rush. He tuned out the battle that had nothing to do with him. Just a small battle on the fringe of a rebellion. A fire fight. Skirmish...what a strange word for a battle. Kids fighting in a schoolyard with no evil intent, a few wild punches thrown and name calling, or the inevitable prelude to revolutions. It didn't matter. He had done his part...was just very tired.

December 25 1958: *I woke up in the cold cellar where Miguel had left me, but the cover was off and the sunshine coming across the floor from the terrace door was shinning on my face. I guess that's what woke me up, that and the smell of coffee. It was the oddest thing to wake up to the smell of fresh coffee and gun powder...*

Christian dreamed he was in bed and everything was normal. But to be normal it would have to be November or early December, before Maartyn arrived, or Renée and a revolution, and he would be stretched out on the Mediterranean bed. Instead he was cold and stiff. Still in the hole where Miguel had stashed him the night before. His villa had been the centre of a furious gun battle. His fingers hurt. Everything hurt and he couldn't straighten his legs. He smelled the coffee and heard the comforting sounds of his houseboy making breakfast.

"Miguel!?"

"Coming, Señor Christ."

"Get me out of here!"

"At once." Miguel's cheery brown face peered down at him. "I was getting you some breakfast. There isn't much. Just bread and coffee. I borrowed the coffee from Juanita's store. There wasn't much left in the store anyway, just a few things to make the army think we still lived here. Some canned meat..."

"Could you tell me the story later!?"

Miguel, who was wearing baggy fatigues instead of his tattered shorts and T-shirt, took Christian's arm. "You were sleeping so well that at first I thought you had suffocated from the fire but I heard you talking about Señorita Renée and my sisters."

"There was shooting in my house. Rosa was here..."

"Oh, Señor Christ! It was a glorious battle. The army burned the village but we fought them well and have many casualties. Rosameralda's all right. There's plenty of work for Esameralda at Señor Escobar's villa. Señorita Renée's helping with the wounded."

"Wounded? How many dead?"

"Not many. Mostly soldiers before they ran away." The gas jet hissed comfortably. Wolf was asleep on the American couch. The scene was almost normal. Except for the cigar butts, spent cartridges, the smell of gun powder, the shattered shutters that let in crazy patterns of light and the bullet holes around the stone walls, the ambience was domestic.

"You were very brave at Juanita's, and even ran away bravely. You will be remembered as a great revolutionary in our prayers!"

"Great. Now I'm a rebel too?"

"You have always been, as far as Batista's concerned, but that is not our fault."

"You're sure Renée's safe?"

"For the moment. We have named Escobar's villa the Ché Guevara Field Hospital. Maybe Ché himself will visit."

"You make it sound like a community event."

"We've waited a long time."

Christian limped to the window. "Jesus!...look at that mess!"

Los Espiritos was a smoking desolation of charred wood and crumbling stone walls. The naked royal palms, that once supported Juanita's Cantina, thrusting into the blue sky like impotent flag poles. Of Juanita's Moose Head Cantina there was only a suggestion. Christian could see the zinc bar and, incongruously, the moose's blackened antlers, poking out from between deformed panels of the collapsed tin roof. The only building left standing at the beach level was the Catholic church and it had lost it's roof. Everything else that could burn had been consumed. A few villagers sifted through the rubble or stoc talking quietly. The fishing boats were gone, except for Christian's old skiff pulled up on the beach, looking lost and dejected. The Gulf Shrimper was also gone. "What happened to Maartyn?"

"He went with Capitan Santoz. They've had trouble with the engine again and it seems only Señor Maartyn can fix it. They must make one more voyage if the Revolution goes badly in the final move against Habana. Right now they are hiding out in the islands where the navy gunboats can't find them."

"So, Mississippi Maartyn's finally into battle."

"Señor Maartyn's a hero. He promised to come back. I think he likes Rosameralda."

"Who could blame him?"

"There will be problems. Her fiancé?"

"Love finds a way."

"Love does many strange things, Señor Christ, but I do not think it stops machine gun bullets."

Christian had to laugh. "Maartyn can take care of himself. And what of Paulo and our cop friend, Carnero?"

"Señor Paulo has forgiven Carnero but refuses to give back the boots. I think they are, how do you say, kindred spirits?"

"Birds of a feather?"

Miguel laughed in turn. "They were playing cards for cigarettes and rum the last time I saw them."

"And where was that?"

"In the caves."

"Right." Christian scanned above the charred village to Escobar's villa. "I want to see Renée."

"And Esameralda?"

"And Esameralda, yes. Why do you know so much?"

"It's my job to know so I can tell Señor Escobar."

"Does he care about my love life?"

"Of course, your affairs are our affairs."

"Really?" he asked sarcastically.

"Have some coffee, Señor Christ."

Christian took the mug and moved to the east window to get the morning sun on his cold body. He sipped the surprisingly good black coffee with only a few grounds rising lazily in the hot currents. He was looking across the burned-over garden at the stone building, starkly visible among the blackened trees and gray ashes, wondering how they would keep it secret now, when three men dressed in fatigues, ran from the compound gate and dropped down the hill. "Miguel! There's something going on..." The stone building suddenly rocked and jumped and debris flew outward. The soft *carrumph* of the explosion followed immediately. The tin roof lifted majestically and came down almost intact, panels flapping like a giant bird settling on its nest. Smoke and dust boiled outward from under the roof. The shock wave rolled over the villa. Stone chips and wood splinters rained down like ice pellets in November. In Montreal.

"What the...!?" Wolf, a veteran of explosions, just raised his snout, sniffed the air, and went back to sleep. "Miguel...!"

"Sorry, forgot to warn you, Señor Christ."

"Oh...makes sense. I mean, who should know?"

"We had to blow up the tunnel."

"Under the no-longer-secret warehouse, right?"

"One of the entrances to the caves."

"Trap door. Is anybody going to tell me? Wait, let me guess. Last night, all those rebels..."

"Another is behind Juanita's. That Juanita. You'd think she'd be inconsolable about her cantina."

"People...soldiers, kept going into Juanita's back room. Some guy went in who looked awfully familiar."

"The comrades entered the caves through Juanita's. That's all you need to know, for now."

"No you don't, Miguel. Not this time. Explain."

"The army will come again."

"Again? You said I was in no danger."

"There was no danger. Now you know too much, but not everything. Until I take you to the caves and you become our prisoner."

"Prisoner!? Now wait a minute!"

"It's war."

"Maartyn's a hero. Renée's a nurse, how come I get to be a prisoner?"

"Just kidding, Señor Christ. For you it will be more like baby sitting."

"Thanks. Why didn't Renée come back this morning?"

"I told her you were sleeping and I'd bring you after breakfast. Besides, the girls are busy. There were people killed down the coast."

"I can't believe you're taking this so calmly. The army ransacks the place. The village burns. People get shot. Buildings blow up."

"We should finish and go. First to Escobar's...Ché's Field Hospital."

They didn't take the skiff to Escobar's villa. There was no need for deception. Miguel and Wolf led him across the ashes of the garden by a narrow path to the dirt road that skirted the top of the first plateau. The earth was still warm and eddies of grey ash swirled in Wolf's wake as he raced ahead. The vegetation was burned away so they had an unobstructed view of the battle zone. It was like an aerial surveillance of a disaster. Los Espiritos was a total loss. Soot-blinded elders were searching the wreckage for their small lives. The rest had vanished.

"Where is everybody?"

"In the hills. Señor Escobar made us prepare months ago. Food and guns. Little hideaways that no one could find. You see, Señor Christ, every child knows the hills like they know their mother's breasts. We defended the village only to make the army think we're desperate. That's why the army loves to destroy things. They think they're hurting the people, to make us weak so we'll stop being rebels and love El Presidente because we have no choice, except to die. But we moved to the hills and so the people have lost very little. Those old people you see down there are just Churchills."

"Churchill's? Churchill's what?"

"Decoys to make the army spies think we search in desperation for our lost village."

"I see. Escobar's obsession."

"Yes, he likes this Churchill. He tells many stories to inspire us."

"One day you won't talk, next day you explain too much. When you explain too much I think it's because you're hiding something."

"There's no need to deceive you now. As you can see. Only Juanita lost almost everything because she couldn't move the cantina without suspicion. A great sacrifice for the Revolution."

The journey to Escobar's villa was a brisk walk in brilliant sunshine under a high azure sky with puffy white clouds floating above the islands. The burning blue of the Gulf to their right. The blackened hillsides to their left. The light sea breeze, although tainted by the acrid smell of smoke, was still pleasantly cool. It should have been just an idyllic outing for a tourist in a subtropical paradise. Wolf ranged ahead checking everything. They passed the cemetery. The blackened markers and charred wooden crosses stood out like sign posts on a desert highway. Fresh graves glowed red in the sun. He thought of Old Jocinto, the lost guitar and the Cuban girls. Esameralda a clear image now. Renée hovering, almost in shadow.

The villa looked undamaged. He expected to see bullet holes in the white plaster and broken shutters. Nothing seemed touched by the fierce battle except that the tall, narrow, pornographic windows were missing.

"Those windows look like gun slits," he said to Miguel's back.

"It's no coincidence, Señor Christ."

"Why wasn't Escobar's place attacked last night?"

"The Señor has immunity, but I think that's all done now. Major Marti can no longer protect him, and Batista would slit his own mother's throat if he suspected she sympathized with Fidel. Señor Escobar is ready to come out, as they say."

"I see." Christian wondered if Miguel appreciated the double meaning. It was just a silly notion, probably a reaction to the tension.

They mounted the wide steps and entered the shaded portico. Christian was reluctant to leave the warming sun for the chill of Escobar's gaze. Miguel walked straight to the big wooden doors which opened inward as if by magic. Wolf darted in first.

A pair of young rebels, like twins, dressed in new fatigues, with their dark eyes and dark hair and broad handsome features, stood aside for Miguel. "Miguelito, and Pietro...you can go in, he's expecting you." One moved to block Christian.

"It's alright, Mateo; he's a friend of El Comandanté. Señor Christ, this is my cousin Mateo and his friend Enriqué. Enriqué's a Spanish student from Madrid who stayed to fight for Fidel."

They regarded Christian and his guitar case with suspicion. Perhaps they'd seen gangster movies from America in which the comic gangsters always look as though they're on their way to music lessons or Symphony Hall. Across the marble foyer, in the sunlit courtyard, groups of young men and women dressed in clean fatigues, stood about the trimmed flower beds and classic statuary, smoking and talking. They could have been students on a lunch break, except for the guns slung over their narrow shoulders. There was nervous laughter, masking the tension their body language could not hide. They lacked the *savoir faire* of their combat-hardened comrades in the east, five year veterans of deadly ambushes, running fire fights and bloodshed. Rosameralda was in the centre, obviously in control, looking cool and poised.

"Rosameralda's here too?"

"Oh yes," said Miguel proudly. "Rosameralda's the boss of the cuartel. El Capitan next to Comandanté Escobar."

"Comandanté Escobar? Why am I not surprised."

"Christian!..." Renée ran towards him, heavy combat boots clicking on the marble floor. It was a scene in a railway station from an old war movie, except it was the beautiful woman in uniform rushing into the arms of her civilian lover. Christian put down the guitar case and the knapsack in time to catch her. Wolf stood guard as they embraced. They didn't disappear in a cloud of steam from the locomotive, nor did an orchestra play in the background. Esameralda entered the frame to throw her arms around both of them and plant a big wet kiss on Christian's mouth. He and Esameralda kissed again. Then he kissed Renée, comparing the effect. They both kissed him back.

"Christian, so much has happened," Esameralda said.

"We were worried about you, Cheri," Renée whispered. "Miguel told us about the cantina and the battle, and how brave you were."

"I was hiding in the cellar," he protested.

"The casualties are here, look..." Esameralda drew him closer.

The hospital beds were turned perpendicular to the walls and each bed was occupied by a casualty covered with crisp white sheets. One child, a burn victim, whimpered through her pain.

"This is what Batista has done to us!" Esameralda swept the ward.

"Jesus..." Christian breathed. His stomach churned. The stark reality of the Revolution was like a dash of cold water. No longer rumours about innocent Cubans beaten up by Batista's army, nor the reality of Maartyn bloodied by the police, nor endless stories about atrocities in a distant province. The scene was more shocking than being face to face with the dead engineer. "I have to get back to my little one," said Esameralda, reluctantly freeing herself from their embrace. "I don't know what I'm going to do for her, my poor darling."

Esameralda returned to tending the small body swathed in bandages. "That's Ezy's little sister. She's burned very badly. Poor Ezy's so upset."

"Jesus!..." he breathed again.

"Come and see what we're doing," said Renée, taking Christian's hand. The galleries had changed. He was relieved to see that the stained glass priests and fornicating bishops were gone. A young rebel lounged at each narrow slit with a rifle pointing out. The fake paintings were gone also. Miguel wandered out to the courtyard to mingle with the young rebels and to tease Rosameralda.

Wolf found a new scent and *zig-zagged* around the foyer looking for the source. No one paid any attention.

"We've been here all night," Renée said, sounding fatigued. "The wounded just keep coming. And now there's farmers and their families from far away. The army killed many before they got to the village. Brutal. These poor people had no warning."

"I knew they were coming," said Christian.

"You, Cheri? How?"

"A Major Marti."

"Why you?"

"Another warning. Marti's the head of the Pinar del Rio Police but seems to be on Fidel's side, for now. Escobar warned me too. Now it's too late."

"Try not to think about it. Be busy."

"Renée, this is just crazy!"

"I know. It's dangerous too. I was worried about you. The last few days in the caves were too incredible, and you won't believe what else...What's Wolf doing?"

Christian turned to see Wolf intently checking each bed. "He's looking for somebody."

"The caves are full of people, Christian. Soldiers and just tons of supplies and the wildest thing of all..."

Renée was interrupted again by Escobar. "Christian...It's good to see you in one piece!" Ernesto Escobar, dressed in a white surgeon's coat splattered with blood, was working on a wounded rebel whose stomach was torn open by machine gun bullet. The young face contorted in pain as Escobar injected morphine. "So, you got through last night. Miguel told me about your escape."

"Does it matter...compared to this?"

"It's good you survived. We have need of your skills. Señorita Jalobert will explain."

"Skills? I play in bars."

"Interpreters," Renée said quickly.

Christian noticed that Escobar was wearing an officer's uniform under his open white coat. "You're the Comandanté."

"By default. I was with the Republicans, against Franco. My views were well known and my family, staunch Nationalists all, disowned me. Castro knew this of course so I was recruited, so to speak, by Fidel to organize the locals. Fidel's Western Front. I've no stomach for combat, so I choose a more creative approach, as you'll see. But, Christian, you must excuse us..." Wolf suddenly howled, racing through the ward. "Pietro! Come back!" Escobar said sharply. Wolf continued searching for something along the gallery. At the seventh bed Wolf attacked a wounded man. The fury of the attack was startling in the context.

"Pietro!...No!" Miguel reached the bed first.

The man scrambled from under the sheets, kicking wildly, trying to shake off Wolf who dangled from his bandaged arm. The man flashed a stiletto but Wolf found flesh first, the sharp teeth opening a vein. The knife missed the dog and sliced through the bandage. Miguel grabbed Wolf and the man ran, dodging and pushing startled nurses aside. Wolf twisted out of Miguel's grasp and leapt on the escapee's back, sinking his teeth into his neck. The terrified man went down hard, sliding on the marble floor. Wolf hung on like a surfboard rider until his prey stopped skidding at Escobar's feet.

"Pietro!" Miguel tried to pull the dog away. The man was choking, eyes bulging with fear. "Pietro, let go..."

"*Ahhhg*!...Get the Devil off!"

"Make him stop, Miguel," Escobar said in a low, even tone.

"I can't, Señor. Pietro has a prize."

A crowd was gathering. A strange standoff. An innocent man, attacked by a vicious dog, and no one knew what to do. "There must be a reason," offered Rosameralda.

"I know what it is," said Miguel, looking more closely at the man's face turned to him for help. "Carnero's man. The one's who beat up Señor Maartyn. Pietro hates them with all his heart."

"Is this true?" Escobar bent down to address the victim. The man pleaded with his eyes, realized it was hopeless, then turned away, pressing his face into the cold tiles. "Is this true, impostor!? Tell me or I'll let the dog chew your head off."

"Yes..." he choked. "Yes!...get this Devil off!"

Escobar made a sign. The rebel named Mateo threw the bolt of his rifle and pointed it at the man. The smooth metallic slide action reverberating in the shocked stillness.

"Pietro..." Miguel stroked the stiff, erect hairs on Wolf's neck. The small dog's muscles were taught. "Easy, Pietro. Let go now. It's all right to let go. Pietro..."

Wolf slowly eased his grip, ready to renew the attack if the man moved. An instinct awakened from a distant time. He relaxed his hold because Miguel asked softly and stroked gently. The impostor wisely remained rigid. Blood flowed from the wounds across the marble floor. Blood mingled with the black hair slick with Brylcream. Perhaps it was the barbershop smell that Wolf objected to. Carnero's smell.

"Get up!" Escobar ordered.

The man slowly stood up, holding his thrice wounded arm.

"Come away, Pietro," Miguel said gently. Wolf backed away and sat down.

"Who are you?" Escobar asked.

"I have nothing to say."

"Chivato! A Batista spy. Strip off his bandages."

Esameralda came forward with scissors. She reached for the man's left arm. He pulled away and Esameralda jumped back. The man glared at her. Wolf growled, ready to leap again. "Hold still!" said Escobar. "Esameralda, you may cut the bandages," he said firmly. She held the man's arm by the wrist and quickly cut the muslin wrappings, the bandage peeling away in strips like wood shavings. There was brown skin and Wolf's deep teeth marks and the fresh knife wound. And above the elbow there was a crusted, shallow slash, made by the same knife, just deep enough to draw blood.

"Self inflicted," said Escobar.

"Your mother's a whore." The spy spit on Escobar's blood stained slippers.

"Brave talk. Very well..." He signed to Rosameralda. "Capitan Diez, take this spy to the courtyard and shoot him."

Rosameralda nodded to Mateo. The young rebel prodded the condemned man with the end of his rifle. Mateo was no more than sixteen years old, thought Christian, but there were years of hatred in the action.

Renée put her arms around Christian and buried her face in his chest. "Christian, they can't." He held her close, numbed himself by the life and death tableau. He knew Escobar could order death but the look of triumph on Rosameralda's face was even more chilling. And in the aftermath of revolution many would die. It has always been a legacy of rebellion, Christian knew. Now they would witness events that seemed so remote from their lives while growing up in the fragile security of a country at peace. The condemned man, head bowed in resignation, was pushed ahead of the mob. The young voices of the rebels buzzed with excitement.

It happened quickly. Rosameralda gave the orders and the chosen rebels shuffled self consciously into position. Her commands rang out clearly in the morning air. Renée and Christian were still holding each other when the ragged volley crashed around the villa; the man thrown against the wall like a rag doll. Cheers erupted from the young Turks tasting blood for the first time. And when the cheers subsided they could hear the frightened whimpers of Esameralda's little sister. There were no words to explain to a small child, why such things could ha, pen on Christmas Day.

The mood in the shocked villa hospital was somber. Death in the heat of battle was acceptable, even necessary. The violent end of a life in the bright sunshine of a peaceful courtyard was harder to understand.

"Well, Christian, you are truly part of the Revolution now," said Escobar. He and Escobar were seated at a cluttered desk in Escobar's bed chamber; the office of El Comandanté of Pinar del Rio.

"I don't know which part."

"In time."

Juanita entered with a tray. "Coffee, gentlemen." She looked clinically efficient in a long white coat that covered her like a sofa dust throw, hair controlled by a bright orange bandana. Nurse Juanita, no longer the Haitian Zombie of the smoky cantina. Big gold earrings gave her an Afro-Cuban flamboyance at odds with the atmosphere. Christian saw a different Juanita. Still colourful but with an aura of power and freedom.

"So, my young Gringo tastes real life in Cuba," she said as she placed the silver tray on the carved desk.

"Hello, Juanita."

"Enjoying your holiday?"

"Things change. And you?"

"I help out where I can. Amputations. Clean up. Meals. Service is what I do best. What can I do for you, pretty boy?" The intended humour was unmistakable.

"Amazing. You people actually enjoy this."

"And why not?" she asked, the open smile belonging to someone that Christian had not seen in the cantina. "If I could run and carry a rifle I would be at the gates of Camp Columbia right now demanding the head of General Batista. But, since I am only a fat bar maid, I serve those who'll shake that little pig until he squeals."

"I'm glad you're okay."

"I am wonderful!"

"Sorry about your cantina."

"*Phew*...think nothing of it. I would have done the same eventually. The army just moved me out sooner than I expected."

"You knew the army was coming last night?"

"Oho, yes. It was a very close thing. And, Christian, you are officially a hero of the Revolution. Capitan Santoz could hear you bellowing like Batista will all the way from the beach."

"Bellowing? Is that what he said?"

"Well, his words were a little stronger."

"Thanks. Is there anything to eat?"

"So, you witness your first execution and already have a stomach. That's good! Could you have said that the first day you arrived in Los Espiritos?"

"Kidding!?"

"I'll see what I can find for our hero." Juanita flowed out of the room like the Queen of Africa.

"Christian, you're in luck," beamed Escobar. "Capitan Santoz remembered my special food packages."

"More Joe Louis?"

"Only a few left I'm afraid. What the *cargo* didn't consume on the voyage from Tampa."

"Cargo? The men dressed like soldiers? Mercenaries or something, right?"

"Not mercenaries."

"Churchills? A deception."

"Have you guessed the deception?"

"I'm not sure. I assume they're soldiers, guerrillas. Renée said the caves were full of soldiers and supplies."

"You're almost there."

"I can only guess...a local cadre. The Western Front?"

"Close, but no cigar."

"Major Marti gave me one for being a good tourist. Can I ask more questions?"

"Of course. You're one of us now."

"What does Miguel have to do with the smuggling? And why the mysterious trips to Havana? You put him in a lot of danger."

"He's our best agent. A ragged urchin on the Malecon. Watching and reporting everything, and he knows everything. Even I don't know how he does it. That boy and his disreputable dog should be honoured with a bronze statue, if we succeed."

"Can you tell me what Miguel's fish selling has to do with anything?"

"You're perceptive. You may have a career in espionage."

"No thanks. I'm just concerned about my house boy."

"You know of course he's there to keep an eye on you?"

"I guessed that."

"The fishing boat's what it appears. Santoz catches shrimp along the Gulf Coast."

"Maartyn told me that much."

"They also collect money donated by friends of Cuba. The Yankee dollars come ashore and Miguel takes the packages of money, sews them into the bellies of the fish he catches, then delivers the fish to the passenger boats. The captain is paid for the guns he smuggles into Habana under the nose of Batista's police. As I told you, the real battles are being fought in the streets. Fidel's playing guerrilla in relative safety while the city fighters take great chances. Batista would be livid to know how simple it is to supply his enemies. I would love to have the opportunity to tell him face to face."

"That explains a lot."

"The payments are only part of it. By the way, you can stop worrying about Miguel. We won't be making any more trips into Habana. Not after the action of last night. Once Batista hears of our little game he'll order an attack at all costs, if only to punish me."

Escobar rubbed his eyes and sighed deeply, the parchment skin pushed into thin, lingering folds. Christian sipped his coffee, watching the enigma, the veteran of the Spanish Civil War, and wondered how human beings, who seem weak physically, can be so strong in conviction. There were the stories, folk tales already becoming legend, about Comandanté Ché Guevara, the young doctor from Argentina. Ché suffers from asthma attacks almost daily but marches over mountains and through humid jungles, carrying the Revolution. Ché joined the small band of Cuban rebels because of his convictions; help for the poor and oppressed. Christian wondered if his own life would ever be the same. "The same as what?" he asked himself aloud.

"Pardon, Christian? I'm sorry. It's been a long night. Who knows what this day will bring. Freedom? Death?"

"Señor Escobar...was it right to kill that man?"

"The Chivato!? Properly executed. Military firing squad. No, my boy, but it was necessary."

"Too extreme, I'd say." Christian felt foolish saying the obvious. The word felt strange on his tongue.

Escobar thought for a moment, searching for a simple explanation, like a parent educating his child. "It was extreme, for a reason. You see, Christian, the Revolution's like a young animal that must be nourished. A jungle cat kills to show her cubs how, and to know the smell of death. Death also means life. Our young fighters are full of rhetoric, yes, and passion, but most of them had never been under fire. They need to hold life in the sights of a rifle. But no, the man did not need to die except as a lesson. His death is only a small element of Cuba's history."

"Shouldn't he at least have had a trial?"

"Trials are for liberals, after rebellions, when the victors have time to look back on their deeds. Victor and vanquished. Maybe we won't be the victors. Maybe nothing will come of all this except the destruction of idealism and the execution of thousands."

"You at least have a cause."

"Cause. Such a trite word, don't you agree? Causes, even righteous causes, can be corrupted. The Crusades were merely waves of self-indulgent fanatics who used Christianity to bolster their chances for a heaven. A grand excuse to expand their empires at the expense of the Muslims. Even then it was a battle of ideologies. Cause? An idea fostered by a succession of popes and kings to tempt even women and children to sacrifice themselves in the name of Christianity. They died horribly, far from home, for what? For more worldly gains for the Pope! And the clergy filled the papal coffers by selling indulgences. Christendom was no better than your Modern Imperialists. Andalusia did very well by the Moors, however. We learned much science and medicine. We used their knowledge to become a stronger nation instead of wasting our energies trying to kill them. We were more interested in killing the British." Escobar chuckled and sipped his coffee.

"That's not the way I learned history."

"Of course not. Northern European history. What did you know about Cuba before you arrived?"

"Ah, Cuba got a bad deal, starting with Columbus."

"Yes, my own people were the problem."

"You're Spanish."

"Yes, Christian. Cubans don't need a foreign cause. Now we fight amongst ourselves. I must give Fulgencio his due. He tried to do right, in the beginning. But somewhere on the road to democracy he stumbled, perhaps tripped up by his greedy friends who saw the chance to become wealthy. I'm sorry for Fulgencio. I cannot hate the man. I can despise the cruel, suspicious dictator he became. I loath the dogs that lick his boots for the scraps. Fulgencio's a sad, desperate man. Now he cowers alone, at Camp Columbia, shaking in fear that the peasants are coming to seek revenge." Escobar became silent, eyes fixed in space, reviewing Cuba's turbulent history, or so Christian thought.

"Ah, Señor Escobar?..."

"Fidel Castro and his Comandantés preach democracy and socialism. We'll see what happens when Fidel's forced to deal with the appetites of his own fighters, the new bureaucrats and policemen, once the fighting's over and the blood lust is satisfied. We'll see what his cold, calculated strategy creates."

"You sound like Major Marti. Is everyone suspicious of Fidel?"

"Fidel's dangerous because he's the most ruthless of all political animals; the man of vision. Only a handful of men in history have had that power. We'll see if the Revolution is for Fidel or Cuba. He'll have powerful men around him, even enemies who will use him, with never a thought for the Revolution. Let's hope Fidel's smart enough to know that he's the Rebellion but not the Revolution. A man with a mission. You can call it a cause, if you will. Fidel's spoken cause is to carry the Revolution to Habana. He says he does not want to be Presidente, El Líder Maximo. Claims to rejects the trappings of power. We'll see what he is forced to choose."

"If he wins he has free choice...doesn't he?" Christian asked, curious about Escobar's ambivalent feelings about Castro.

"No one has a clear choice, Christian. We do what we have to do because of circumstances. Did you have a choice about Cuba?"

"Well, I decided to come."

"Bad choice, but certain things made you stay. You don't have a choice now. I'm sorry, Christian, when I am very tired I talk too much. Now then, people out there need me."

Escobar stood up slowly, as if age had suddenly caught up. He looked small and frail. Christian had the feeling that Ernesto Escobar would not live to see what Fidel Castro would do.

"Juanita has instructions. If the Lords of the Apocalypse decree, we may yet become friends, if not, I hope you'll remember me. Goodbye, Christian." The handshake was brief but firm. Escobar opened the door and entered the ward. New casualties were arriving. He could hear Renée and Esameralda giving orders.

Christian gazed around the large room filled with expensive statuary and artifacts from the antiquities to the modern era. The fake paintings were stacked facing the walls, as if Escobar had rejected a former way of life. 'Intellectuals cause revolutions and are swept away by them', Escobar had lectured. Why did Escobar stop being a doctor? What had happened during those twenty years since the Spanish Civil War? He could hear the distant mutter of the diesel generator. The dead engineer was in the deep freeze, and now the executed police spy. He thought of Maartyn's father, Simon, deposited in a freezer in Mississippi. Refrigeration is important in the warm countries. In Canada bodies could be dug into the permafrost, covered with muskeg and left forever...

Juanita entered by the service door from the kitchen area holding a canvas bag. The aroma of chicken broth and roasting pig wafted in with her. The diesel sound was loud and intrusive. The new Ché Guevara Hospital hummed with activity. The smell of the broth reminded Christian of Renée and chicken soup and his memory was racing back to childhood. He rejected the visions. He wanted the chicken soup of the present. Juanita held up the canvas bag. "Ernesto says you like these," she said grandly.

"José Louis' and Twinkies...right?"

"José who? Are you sick?"

"Yes, thank you. I'll save them for Maartyn."

"It's okay with me, Gringo." Christian accepted the bag, almost laughing at the absurdity. "Comandanté Ernesto orders you to go. Miguel says the army's returning. They hold the road from Pinar. Señorita Renée will show you the way to the caves."

"What about you and Esameralda?"

"Comandanté Ernesto sent Miguel to meet the army. The villa's now a hospital and only wounded civilians are here. We'll be fine. And Christian, God will be with you, but be careful just in case He's distracted." Juanita folded Christian to her bosom and hugged him like a mother sending a child off to camp.

"Thanks, Juanita. Be careful yourself."

They hurried through the crowded ward to find Esameralda. She was changing bandages on a wounded farmer who had been left beside the road to die. The rotting wound and the antiseptics competing in the warm air. Christian felt sick. The goodbye was brief. She took off her purple and orange bandana and knotted it around Renée's neck. "You might need this."

"Come with us," said Renée.

"I am with you, and so are Jesus and Mary..." She embraced Renée and then Christian. They kissed. Christian was torn. Run for safety? Stay to help Esameralda? What could he do? What did he know about medical things? Or freedom fighting?

Climbing through the underbrush, then into the tree line they could see the column of troops on the winding road below. Christian stopped to watch, fascinated by the nearness of war.

"Christian, come on!...It's not far, Cheri."

It was a torturous route through the trees. Christian stumbled on the loose rocks. A fire fight erupted on the road to the hospital. Gunfire crackled in the heavy air, sounding like firecrackers at a Chinese festival. A rapid, prolonged exchange, then a pause as each side assessed the enemy. "I hope they're okay," said Christian, trying to see through the brush. More shots defiled the clear air.

The army had been stopped by the blockade and the outnumbered rebels were putting up fierce resistance. A new sound rose over the sporadic gun fire. Roaring engines and squealing tank treads sent shivers through the spectators. A WWII Sherman tank, followed by the half track, *clanked* to a position at a bend in the road east of Escobar's villa. The tank's turret swiveled, the cannon elevated and fired. The shell whistled over the hospital. A moment later Christian's villa erupted in a cloud of smoke and broken stone, like the top blowing off a volcano. "Jesus!" shouted Christian. The shock wave hit him like a body blow to the abdomen as they watched the darkening cloud rise from his beloved villa and drift slowly inland. "You bastards!"

"Come on, Christian. It's just a house."

"We could've been in there! You rotten bastards!!"

"We weren't."

"It's my home!"

"That's right, but now we have to think of ourselves."

Renée tugged on Christian's arm until he picked up the knapsack, guitar case and canvas bag following her through the trees toward the white hills and the blue pines. He was having trouble keeping up.

"Give me the guitar," she said impatiently.

The rebels pulled back when Miguel informed Rosameralda that Christian and Renée were safely into the hills. Then Miguel and Wolf vanished back into the bush. Rosameralda and her rebels made for their own enclaves. Los Espiritos, what was left of it, was open to the army.

The Ché Guevara Hospital was occupied by the medicos and the casualties, even the rebel guards had been sent away. Escobar insisted that he and his small staff face the army alone. The only way to defeat Batista, he said, was to offer no excuse for retaliation. The plan might have worked if someone had not informed the advancing army commander about the execution of the police spy in the hospital courtyard, under Escobar's orders.

They stopped to rest and lay down in the dappled shade of a stand of Viñales pines. René toyed with the damp curls matted across his forehead. "Did you miss me?" she asked.

"Yes, of course."

"Really?"

"I don't know," he admitted. "It was pretty intense."

"I missed you." She put her fingers on his tanned arm and followed the fading needle marks to the bend of the elbow. She started across his bare chest. What direction would she go? he wondered. "It seems like years since we made love," she whispered, moving closer.

"Long time. But only days, I guess."

"Has something happened to your feelings for me?"

"No, not really..." he lied, with difficulty.

"Esameralda?"

"I...I'm a little confused."

"I'm not jealous, you know. I love her too."

"I don't know what to call it."

"Love's good enough."

"Okay..."

"She loves me too."

Christian digested the news. "Have you?...you know?"

"Not that way, yet," she said sadly.

"But you would?"

"I don't know, perhaps, but then I think of you and Esameralda. I wouldn't want to spoil it."

"Renée...you always make things so complicated by trying to make things simple and perfect. If you want Esa I'm a big boy, I think I can handle it!"

"Can you, Christian? You've matured but I don't think enough to handle competition from your girlfriend." Renée giggled and rolled onto her back. The baggy fatigue jacket lay open and her small, firm breasts heaved with her laughter. Golden hair spilled around her face and shoulders, and the dappled sunlight did interesting things to the skin between her breasts which glistened with sweat. He could almost taste the salty nipples. But Christian was still weak from his illness and the tension. He wanted to make love to her but the signals were confusing, there was a war going on around them and Renée wasn't helping. "If I told you that Ezy wants you, would that help?" she asked innocently.

"No."

"Does it excite you to think of Ezy and me, and making love with her and me at the same time, and thinking of me making love with her while you watch?"

"Renée!..." He didn't answer because he would have to be honest.

The idea was new. Christian considered the previous morning. exciting and dangerous. And exotic. He desired Esameralda b of the special chemistry that draws people together. But even if things were normal, that is, if they were on a beach on Andros Island and rum and tequila were the stimulants instead of war, it would be difficult for Christian to handle the confusion of his emotions. He was not used to the libertine ideologies of the Bohemian crowd who experimented freely and confused love with lust. He was shy as well as confused. That understanding was for the future, when relationship parameters and sexual stereotypes became blurred.

"Christian? My question is too direct?"

"No comment."

"It excites me to be so close to death, and be alive." She unbuttoned and rolled to his side, and put his hand into her baggy fatigues, closing her eyes.

Christian ran his tongue across his dry lips in preparation for the kiss...A volley of shots rang out like an alarm bell, from the direction of the Ché Guevara Hospital. Christian jumped to his feet. He could see the red tile roof against the green brush that escaped the fire. The picture was too beautiful for a killing. The tank and the half track had moved to a position along the road between his ruined villa and Escobar's hospital. Troops were standing in groups near the tank, as if proximity to the steel machine was protection against rebel snipers. He couldn't see into the courtyard of the hospital but he could make out a thin cloud of smoke wandering up, dispersing in ragged wisps like shy spirits in sunlight. They waited in fear for another volley. The silence told them nothing. Soldiers shambled out of the front entrance of the villa, formed up behind their officer and marched along the road above the village, the officer glancing nervously toward the hills.

Christian was thinking he might never see Esameralda again. The slight figure of a boy and a small dog moved cautiously through the protective brush and palmettos towards the villa. It was like watching a movie. "It's Miguel...He's going down to the hospital."

"Tell me it wasn't a firing squad."

Christian sat down heavily, as if the knapsack was full of lead, but it was a different kind of weight. Bodies of the dead were heaped on his back. Another life ended, perhaps two. Another violent act as the Revolution crept nearer. He had nothing to do with the Cuban Revolution, he told himself again. An innocent tourist in the wrong place and time. Or had Escobar been right? Had he been drawn to Cuba by some cruel force and into the fire storm of rebellion for a reason?

"We should go," said Renée. "Miguel will tell us."

He could barely move. To get up was agony. Every step was a step closer to the centre of the storm. He wanted to live, but so had those who had already died. Why should he be special?

"Christian, please..."

A soft footstep in the brush above made them tingle with fright. Christian put his hand on Renée's arm and drew her down into the shade of a palmetto, the spear points of the fronds hardly a comforting refuge. "*Shhhh...*" he whispered. "I don't think it's the army...and I know it isn't Miguel."

Something was moving toward them. Too many rustlings to be an animal. The sounds seemed to come from all directions. Then the clink of metal and they were surrounded. "It's only rebels," said Renée, buttoning her fatigue jacket in a rare show of modesty.

"Okay, but what will they think we are?"

"Hands in the air," a young voice said in a horse whisper. Christian turned slowly. He was staring into the end of a long rifle. Could smell the oil. He was tired of having guns pointed at him and seeing deadly black holes inches from his face. "Who are you?" the nervous young voice asked in the rural Cuban dialect.

"Friends...we're friends...of Señor Escobar's," stammered Christian.

"It's just the Gringos," the young voice whispered to someone behind him. Five small rebels in odd sized fatigues and military gear appeared through the undergrowth, keeping low so they could not be seen by the soldiers on the road. "What are you doing here?" the leader asked.

"Nothing...on our way to the caves."

"You're the lost Gringos. Our captain has been looking for you. My name's Oscar Remirez Ortiz. What's yours?"

"Christian James Joyce. This is Renée. Señorita Jalobert," he said, thinking that Oscar was an odd name for a teenager with a rifle. But teenagers with odd names grow up to be adults who suit their names.

"That's right. Exactly as our captain said."

Oscar Ortiz said something to a boy, hardly older than Miguel. The boy nodded and scuttled away. The others sat down on the tough grass. In their fatigues they looked like Cuban Boy Scouts, except for the new rifles and heavy ammunition belts slung across their thin chests. Sweat darkened their fatigues and they were bare foot and dusty, but they looked healthy and happy. Bright smiles softened the tension. One boy took out a crumpled package of Lucky Strike cigarettes and offered them around. Oscar shook his head but took the package and offered them to Christian.

"No, thank you, Oscar. I don't. But do you think it's a good idea for them to light up? The soldiers?" he pointed down the hill.

"Exactly right," Oscar said. He turned on his companions. "Don't light up you fools!"

"Are you Gringos really lost?" asked a darker skinned boy named Hepté, the unlit cigarette dangling from his full lips. It gave him a comic expression as if impersonating a famous movie detective.

"No," answered Renée. "We're going to the caves."

"Then you are definitely lost," said Oscar. "Not very lost, but if you keep going in this direction you will run into the soldiers. There are twenty of them at least. They're Batista's commandoes. Trained to fight in the mountains, but they were too late to do any good in Oriente so have been sent here to punish us. The stupid army down there are just for show. To make us think all we have to do is stay in the hills to be safe."

"How do you know all this?" asked Christian.

"Miguelito saw them coming. Señor Comandanté Escobar said that Batista would try something like that. Major Marti warned him."

"Does everybody know about Major Marti?"

"Sure. He wants to join us soon."

"When will the soldiers be here?" asked Renée.

"They're moving slow, so as not to be noticed," said Oscar, too cheerfully. "But they'll be here soon. That's why Rosa, I mean, Captain Diez sent us to find you."

"I think someone was killed at the hospital."

"Yes, we heard the shots. Capitan Diez sent Miguel down to see."

"How old are you?" asked Renée.

"Nearly sixteen years old," said Oscar importantly. "I am a lieutenant already. Someday I want to be a Comandanté just like Camilo."

"I want to be a Comandanté and a doctor just like Ché," said the boy named Muñoz.

Boys and their heroes, thought Christian. Just like kids back home who want to be hockey stars like Rocket Richard or Jean Beliveau. Cuban boys should be talking about baseball heroes like Joe DiMaggio and Mickey Mantle or the local Cuban hero who might make it to the major leagues. Instead they're peach-fuzz rebels hunkering in the dirt and heat, sucking on unlit cigarettes, waiting their chance to draw blood for the Revolution. Talking casually about guerrillas and battles and casualties. They discussed Fidel's chances against the Moncada barracks, his old nemesis. Christian day-dreamed about his own youth, growing up poor, but not desperate. Certainly not in any real danger. He couldn't remember anything to protest. Life was a passing show, a carousel of possibilities. One need only to select a pretty horse to ride into the future, released from the angst-ridden boredom of adolescence. He expected the Cuban boys to bring out trading cards and begin swapping favourite rebel leaders. Christian no longer loved Cuba. He wanted to shut his eyes and escape to Montreal. In the fall. The magic season of colours and crisp air, relief from the moist heat of the Cuban coast. Montreal is also an island...a refuge once rejected.

"There you are, my lost children." The sweet voice was like a sparkling fountain, playing over the small clearing. "Thought we'd lost you."

"Rosa!" Renée had to suppress her joy. The two girls held each other like sisters at a funeral. "Rosa...someone's been shot."

"Come on...we can't stay here. Let's get to the caves and wait for Miguel."

Rosameralda ignored Christian, put her arm around Renée and they walked together away from the dangerous path into the bush. The young rebels formed a line and followed; Christian stumbled along behind Oscar Ortiz.

The column moved obliquely across the slope. There was no path that Christian could see but Rosameralda walked around stands of trees with a sureness that made him more at ease. The slope was gentle at first but when they reached the prominent white rocks and the taller pines the walk became a climb in the loose talus. Christian was sweating and breathing hard, the knapsack and the canvas bag growing heavier. His pace slowed. He slipped on loose rocks and went down. Oscar turned to help him. "I'm okay."

"Give me your knapsack. Muñoz, take Señor Joyce's arm."

"I'm okay, really."

"I'm sorry, Señor Joyce...It's not okay," said Oscar, shouldering the knapsack. "You are slowing us down. If the soldiers come before we reach the cave we'll have no chance unless they lay down their rifles and join the Revolution."

"But isn't that happening everywhere?" asked Christian, naively or hopefully. "We've heard the reports. Maybe you could talk to them?"

"These are Special Forces, trained by the Americans. They need desperately to kill Fidel's guerrillas. We need to kill some to stay even."

"You're just boys!"

"We're not boys, Señor Joyce."

"Right..." Christian wished Oscar would stop addressing him as Señor Joyce. It made him feel old and feeble. As Miguel did. Where is Miguel? "You're right. I feel..." He bent over, hands on knees. "Just a dizzy spell."

"Are you sick?" asked Rosameralda, who had doubled back.

Renée took his arm and the bag of cakes. She handed the bag to one of the boys. "Cheri, it can't be far now."

"No, we're close," said Rosameralda. "Just over that ridge. But we must be very careful."

"Oh, God...Just stash me in the bushes."

"Don't be ridiculous, Christian. We can't leave you," chided Renée.

"Don't you want to be a hero?" prodded Rosameralda.

"I just want to rest."

"Let's get moving. Muñoz, climb that big rock and signal if it's clear to the caves." Her tone had changed. Muñoz lopped off through the brush. Rosameralda gestured for the rest to follow her.

They walked in silence for several minutes; only the sound of their feet dislodging loose rocks disturbed the mid-day somnolence. Christian was wearing sandals and had to stop frequently. The cool breeze of morning had given way to thick air, heavy with the weight of an approaching storm. The sun's heat was stifling in the clearings. Renée was sweating freely, making dark stains on her fatigue jacket down her back and between her breasts. Christian was dehydrated and perspired only a little. With every stop to clear his sandals it was harder to start again. Tiny insects seemed to like the conditions and feasted well.

The Sherman tank started up and moved off, creaking like a knight in rusty armour. "I wonder if they ever oil that thing?" said Christian, trying to make light of the situation. No one commented.

They stopped to rest in a level clearing where they could see Muñoz climbing an outcropping near the crown of the hill. He reached the top and peered cautiously over the edge, inland, toward the east. The rock was the highest point in the first ridge and had a view of the plateau with its tobacco fields and farmer's shacks, drying sheds and skinny cattle. There must have been some movement. He ducked down, pointing over the rock, making a five finger sign that could have meant five miles or five minutes. He turned to look over the edge again, scanning intently. The shot that knocked Muñoz off the rock was muffled by the ledge but they clearly saw him thrown back violently and fall straight down. He made no sound landing.

"Mother of God!" Rosameralda cursed, rocking slowly from side to side. "Muñoz, Muñoz...I sent him to his death."

"Rosa...don't." Renée knelt beside Rosameralda, holding her close. "Don't blame yourself."

"He's my mother's sister's only son." She didn't cry. She knelt with her head on Renée's shoulder. She looks small and pathetic, thought Christian. Tragic beauty. Of course, beauty is not immune to grief. The other boys were in shock at the loss of their comrade. Yesterday they were boys. Today they are still boys, expected to act like hardened fighters. It takes longer than one battle and one or two dead. "Just over the hill. That's what Muñoz was trying to tell us. Now they know we're here. It's too late to run for the caves."

"I'm a fast runner," said Oscar. "I could go that way," he pointed to the northwest, back across the slope, "and distract them."

"Some. The rest would search. No."

"As you say." The disappointment obvious.

"Get into thick brush, and hope they pass, but if they don't we'll fight!"

"What if we all make a run for it?" asked Renée.

"Run?...Where? Back to the villa? Into the hills and be chased down like animals? Down the hill and face the tank? Run to the caves and destroy Señor Escobar's plan? Is your man able to run fast enough and far enough to avoid a commando knife? Do we run together or go it alone?"

"You're right, Rosa," sighed Renée, "but I don't want to die under a bush."

"There are worse places."

"Maybe, but not many."

"No time to talk." Rosa pointed to a patch of scrub.

Christian looked alarmed. The thicket was too small. The cover too thin. The palmettos too spiked. "There's a better place, over there. More trees."

"Yes, and the first place the soldiers will look, or maybe just throw in a hand grenade."

They could hear the soldier's approaching; equipment *jinking*, military boots crunching on rocks as they slipped over the crest of the hill. The officer directed his men to check for the body.

"In there!" Rosameralda ordered in a harsh whisper.

Hepté took the guitar from Renée. She hesitated but Rosameralda gave her a look. She worked between the palmettos and branches of scrub pine. Christian took the guitar from Hepté and pushed it ahead of him, having difficulty forcing the rigid case through the tangle. "Hurry!" whispered Renée. A sense of panic gripped Christian. The guitar meant many things and they all came flooding into his consciousness. He pushed the case, sending the suffering guitar flying into Renée who had returned to help. "Ohh! Christian, you moron!" "Sorry…"

"Will you two stop. You next." She pointed to the youngest rebels. They went on all fours, dragging their rifles by the barrels. Ammunition belts getting caught in branches. "Quiet…Oscar, get in."

Oscar had to drag his rifle and Christian's knapsack, as well as negotiate his machete, canteen, holster and ammunition belts, through the maze. The sound of twigs snapping were like gunshots. Rosameralda, using a leafy branch, dusted the area. When Oscar was finally into the thicket she followed, backing in, using her fatigue jacket to mask their tracks. "Put dirt and leaves on yourselves. Then be quiet."

Rosameralda got down, head close to the dirt, seeing what the officer might see from ground level. She heard a noise outside the thicket and silenced her charges.

Muñoz crawled through the small clearing, dragging his precious rifle. One leg was obviously broken and blood streamed from a head wound. The soldiers, moving carefully from cover to cover, were close behind Muñoz who passed only a few feet away from his compadres, effectively erasing more traces but leaving tracks as well as a trail of blood in the soft soil. Muñoz didn't see Rosameralda and it was too late to call to him. She rejoiced that Muñoz was not dead but her heart ached to know that the soldiers might catch up and cut his throat. She clutched her pistol, ready.

The soldiers had the trail. Running footsteps approached the small clearing like bloodhounds on a scent. There were two dozen of them in commando gear. The officer, a young lieutenant, followed the tracker, scanning left and right, directing his men to search thickets, waving his pistol at the ones he wanted checked. He sent two men crashing through the large thicket that Christian had wanted to hide in. As he passed the small thicket where the fugitives buried their faces and held their breath, the officer stopped, examining the oddly disturbed ground. Rosameralda could see the dusty black boots.

Christian imagined he could smell the polish. The boot kicked at the dirt, mingling the lighter dusts from the hills with red dust from the clearing, Christian noticed with fascination. Rosameralda had more pressing things to digest. If discovered she would spring up firing and hope to let the others escape. The officer bent down to examine the ground more closely, about to direct soldiers to sweep the thicket. The tracker called, "Lieutenant! I've found something, over here."

The officer moved away, signaling his men to follow. More boots hurried past and the dust drifted through the thicket in veils, like lace curtains. The military sounds drew away. Then they found Muñoz' ammunition belt. "There's blood...one person."

"There are more," the officer surmised.

"The wounded one went that way," the tracker insisted.

"All right. He'll lead us to them."

The soldiers moved off, following the fresh trail. Rosameralda made a sign to remain quiet. "Muñoz is alive," she whispered to Oscar.

"Muñoz lives," Oscar whispered to the next boy who told the next.

"Poor Muñoz," she said sadly.

"We could ambush the pigs from behind before they get to Muñoz," offered Oscar.

"You're a brave boy...Renée, you and Christian wait for the fight to begin, then go that way until you come to the big pines."

"Muñoz might still get away," Renée said, knowing Rosa's mind was set.

"They'll run him down like an animal."

Rosameralda fought her way out of the thicket. Oscar and the other boys crashed out after her, holding rifles above their heads as if wading through deep water.

Waiting. The silence was nerve wracking. Christian and Renée held on to each other, unable to speak. Renée cried softly on Christian's chest, her tears mingling with their sweat and dust. Life was disintegrating around them and he wished he could explain why Rosameralda was rushing to die and Esameralda was in danger and Escobar had probably been left to die in a pool of blood in the courtyard of his beautiful villa. And what about Miguel and Maartyn?

The fire fight was announced by shrill battle-cries; the boys' contraltos and Rosameralda's clear soprano, followed by a pistol report and more shouting. Then a ragged exchange of gunfire between rifles and automatic weapons, the automatics drowning out the slower rifles. Renée buried her head deeper into Christian's chest.

"Let's go," he said, during a brief lull.

"But Rosa!"

"Renée!...we can't do anything for her. Come on!" Christian dragged Renée out of the thicket. "Which way? Renée!...which way to the caves?"

"That way."

"Wait. I forgot the bag."

The fire fight intensified, moving further down the slope toward the village. Then gun fire from the road joined the chorus. The regular army troops moving above the village came under stray fire from the rebels shooting at the Special Forces between them. The army soldiers, thinking they were being ambushed, fired blindly up the hill without waiting to see who was shooting at them. There were curses and orders flying about. Above the chaos rose the clanking and screeching of the tank, accented by the sweeping staccato *chunking* of the machine gun. Bullets whined through the dry trees, spraying the slope with lead slugs, *thuncking* into the soft earth like the first big drops of summer rain.

Batista's elite mountain force was pinned down on an exposed slope where the scrub thinned out at the verge of a tobacco field. The field, on a narrow plateau, and then another scrub slope, separated them from the regular army but they couldn't cross the field and there was too much noise to communicate. The lieutenant tried waving a white hanky but it was invisible from the regular army's position.

The lieutenant assessed his situation. An unknown number of obviously savage rebels held the higher ground. The regular army force, about fifty men, was coming up the slope behind the tank and the half track. His exposed position was untenable at best, but he was much closer to the rebel force. The tank broke through the brush at the edge of the tobacco field and sprayed the thin cover, wounding two more of his men. The officer made his decision. "Fire at the tank!!" His men opened fire. The tank stopped advancing, firing wildly. The officer scrambled up the slope towards Rosameralda's position, calling, "Don't shoot!!" Waving his hankie, holding his pistol above his head. "Talk! Want to talk!"

Rosameralda was suspicious. It could be a trap, but the army was engaged and the Special Forces location was being raked by gun fire. Cries of the wounded cut through the noise. "Hold your fire!" Her own boys stopped firing. "All right, Imperialist! Tell your men to come up the hill, backwards, and keep shooting at the tanks!"

"What? Back up? Are you crazy!?"

"You heard me! If one turns we'll shoot!"

"I can't surrender backwards!" he croaked.

A random hail of machine gun bullets sent them both sprawling on the ground. Rosameralda felt a hot sensation in her left arm. "Damn! Don't surrender then. Go back and fight the tank!"

"All right...all right!"

Rosameralda heard one of her boys moaning. She signaled for Oscar. Oscar crept to his fallen comrade. A bullet had torn through his thigh. There was an exit wound and lots of blood. Oscar tore up his sweaty undershirt and made a crude bandage.

The officer fled back down the slope and relayed the order from one bewildered soldier to another. Each man turned, a look of incredulity on his face. But at a signal from the officer the men grabbed arms and legs of their wounded and backed up the hill, dragging their burdens. Those not encumbered with the wounded continued firing down the slope toward the army's position. The ploy worked. The indifferent regular army troops lay low as bullets ricocheted off the tank and careened through the trees.

The shooting gradually subsided. The Special Forces troops concentrated on negotiating their wounded comrades over the rocks. When the shooting stopped the wounded were carried to Rosameralda's position. It was too late for the Special Forces officer to change his mind.

Rosameralda stepped out from her hiding place, pointing her pistol at the officer. "Tell your men to place their guns on the ground."

"A woman!? I can't surrender to a woman."

"Your choice."

A sudden spray of machine gun slugs whined through the brush. "Do as the woman says," the officer ordered. It was well known that Fidel Castro's Comandantés treated Batista's soldiers well if they surrendered. Besides, this guerrilla leader was a beautiful woman. How tough could she be?

The American trained mountain troops unslung their automatic rifles, letting them slip to the ground. Their expressions were more embarrassed chagrin than defeatist angst. They didn't look like hardened commando specialists. Nor had they been in the hills of Pinar del Rio long enough to grow beards or even stubble, but most had moustaches. They were all white Cubans of a consistent height and age, selected for youth and looks. Batista's personal guard sent to avenge his wounded pride. And except for some blood and dust, their camouflage uniforms were fresh and relatively clean. Escobar would be amused, thought Rosameralda.

"Pistol belts and knives!" ordered Rosameralda.
The soldiers unbuckled and dropped them in the dirt.
"Ammunition."
Ammunition pouches dropped beside the rifles.
"Hand grenades. Carefully. No heroics."
Hand grenades were unclipped and tossed onto the piles.
"Look after your wounded," she said, turning her back on her prisoners. "Oscar, collect the weapons. The rest of you!..." she called out, as if addressing a large number of rebels, "the rest of you keep two guns sighted on each man."
The lieutenant swaggered towards Rosameralda, hands out in pathetic supplication. Without weapons he was forced to use what he considered his Latin charm on this beautiful guerrilla.
"Don't come a step closer or I'll shoot your tiny cojones off."
"Señorita...please," he whispered. "This is embarrassing."
"Send a message for the army to take your wounded. The rest of you are coming with us."
The second battle of Los Espiritos was over.

The steep, brush-covered hills were crawling with heavily armed rebels, the regular army commander concluded and withdrew. The tank backed away, spun in its length and lumbered down the hill. The half track defiantly wheeled around, tearing up a half moon strip of the tobacco field, and followed the tank. The hills where no place for armour and the troops weren't going anywhere without them. The regular army gladly retreated back to the road to await orders.
Rosameralda ignored the lieutenant and watched as Oscar shuttled armloads of weapons to the thin rebel firing line, wondering what she and her four children were going to do with her dangerous prisoners. The weapons they could bury but the prisoners could not be abandoned. And what had happened to Muñoz? She'd send Mateo to look for him as soon as she secured the prisoners. It was only then that she turned her attention to her own wound.

Renée and Christian, convinced that Rosameralda had perished in a hail of bullets, climbed through the rocks toward the stand of pines. Their own safety was no substitute for their sense of loss. It seemed that everyone they knew was being violently swept away by the tide of war.
The stand of pines surrounded a natural bowl in the rocks and the well hidden entrance to the cave. They approached the entrance over a

thick mat of pine needles, through a jumble of upturned rocks and bush; a labyrinth cul de sacs. The entrance itself was behind an over-lapping cleft in the rocks.

Christian followed Renée in and out of dappled sunshine, gazing around at the beauty and peace of the hills. The fresh breeze from the north sighed in the tops of the pines. He had always loved pine trees. Of all the trees in Canada, pines are the most dependable. He was a city boy but his limited exposure to pine trees had been pleasant. A park on the fringes of Westmount. An oasis of sandy soil where tall pines and oak trees defied the city below. The fallen needles dry and hospitable. The pines spoke softly in the wind and remained on duty during the winter months when the leaves of seasonal trees fled the scene, leaving behind only skeletal remains and cold, bony fingers that reminded him of the dead.

"Through here, Cheri."

"Wait."

"What is it? You hear something?...Christian?"

"No. I just don't want to go in, yet."

"We must. The soldiers?"

"Let's just sit awhile." Christian sat down, back to a rock, facing the afternoon sun, tilting his head to the healing rays. He held his eyes shut tight and watched the amoeba shapes and krill images dance across his personal viewing screen. His mother told him that if he faced the sun the rays would burn right through his eyelids and his eyeballs would shrivel and fall out and his brain would fry like bacon. There was a time when he believed her, but was fascinated by the odd shapes. "My brain's fried, Renée. Can't you smell it?"

"Christian, please. This is no time for one of your moods."

"My moods? Do I have moods?" he asked sarcastically. "I didn't know that. I thought I had problems and that my problems gave me an excuse. So, it's only a mood. Moods can come and moods can go. Let's just wait 'til this one goes."

Renée sighed and sat down beside him. "What are you talking about?"

"Let's play a game of wish-away. You know, most people wish for things. Let's un-wish things."

"It won't help. Whatever has happened..."

"Not true! Nothing has happened if we don't let it. Let's go back to that time on Andros. We were sitting under the palm trees close to the edge of the lagoon. Remember, we watched Joseph repairing his fish-ing boat? His kids climbed over the gear and he never got angry with them and they never seemed to get in his way. There was Joseph's dog, what was her name?..."

"Lady Moogie."

"Lady Moogie...acted like she owned the place. Moogie slept under the boat with her puppies and got splattered with red paint and then Joseph had to drag her and the puppies out from under when he wanted to launch. Then the kids and the puppies climbed over everything and Joseph just worked around them. His wife made us food but you said we shouldn't eat her food because you were embarrassed that you had so much money.

"My family."

"Same thing. But she wouldn't take the money and it was a problem because to refuse the food would hurt her feelings. So we accepted the food. Then we hired Joseph to go sailing and he dove for conch and fed us like royalty, then wouldn't take your money."

"It was a very difficult time for us."

"Very difficult trying to do the right thing. So did we do the right thing by not giving them money?"

"Yes, because...I don't know."

"And remember what Maartyn said?"

"Maartyn. He said they were just stupid niggers."

"Were they stupid not to take the money?"

"No, their reward was friendship."

"So, we were all in the right, except for Maartyn."

"Maartyn was just being Maartyn," said Renée impatiently. "Can we go in now?"

"Miguel says Maartyn has it bad for Rosameralda."

"I know. Rosa's confused."

"He would have to change his attitude, wouldn't he?"

"I hope Maartyn and Rosameralda are alive," she said irritably.

"Hope? You have to wish it."

"What about Esameralda and Miguel?"

"I am un-wishing that they died. Maybe they're dead, but I'm un-wishing. Come on, help me."

"Christian, don't do this." Renée began to cry again, softly, inside, like a big girl, then slowly she crumbled. She cried from the very bottom. He held her close and let her cry and felt closer to her than in their wildest, deepest love making. He realized for the first time that love has many levels and that passionate love is only one level. Nothing compared to the feeling of truly being inside a lover's skin.

"Joseph and Trina were true lovers," he said. "Remember, we could hear them at night. She screamed so loud with pleasure we pretended it was a jungle cat and that we were camped in Africa. But now that I think about it, it was during the heat of the day that they really loved each other. She was so calm. Even with all those beautiful kids everywhere around them. Like little brown monkeys. And the puppies."

"She's a wonderful mother." Renée sniffed and wiped her eyes and nose, but remained buried in Christian's chest. She needed to be held. "Trina's been pregnant constantly since she was fifteen," she said.

"She would come down to the beach with a cup of tea for Joseph. Trina asked us to come to her neat little home. They couldn't have been happier in a mansion."

"Like my home in Paris?"

"Is it a happy home?"

"Not very. Well, there were times, when affairs didn't get in the way. I had happy days as a child, before things changed and my father started going to the whores. My mother lives in a dream. Now he's dying. How happy could it be?"

"Mine did the same. It was never discussed, but the hints were there and I think it's what caused the break. How did your mother take it?"

"Like a saint, naturally. Like a proper French wife. The way French women are supposed to accept that husbands cheat. They retaliate by taking lovers. It's normal to adjust one's thinking."

"So, if Maartyn wants to have Rosameralda, he has to accept her ancestors."

Renée rallied to the argument. "It's not the same thing, Christian. Rosameralda doesn't have a choice about her ancestors. My father had a choice about his behavior. My mother had a choice to accept or make trouble."

"They chose to pretend. They un-wished the truth," he said in triumph. "Why didn't she go back to Asia?"

"Too proud," she said, the ache of that reality a condition she wanted avoid. "I don't feel like doing this."

"And I don't feel like being in that cave."

"Fine, we'll just sit here until the soldiers find us and kill everybody. The Revolution will fail and Cuba will be in a worse mess."

"I can't take responsibility for Cuba."

"Come into the cave. I'll show you what you're responsible for."

"I don't like dark places."

"It's a big cave with high ceilings."

"You're just saying that."

The birds suddenly stopped chirping. Renée gripped Christian's arm. Golden finches and Cuban parakeets feeding in the pines flew away in a splash of colour. "Something's coming!"

"I don't hear anything."

"That way."

Wolf bounded into the clearing.

Christian jumped to his feet. "Wolf!"

The little dog leapt at Christian, almost knocking him over.

"Señor Christ!" Miguel entered the clearing on the run. "Señorita!"

"Thank God!" cried Renée. "At least somebody's alive."

"Miguel! What happened at the villa?"

"Many things. Some not good," he shrugged.

"Who?"

"First, I must tell you...about Rosa."

"Is she dead?" cried Renée.

"No, no! She's wounded, but she's okay. She told me to tell you..." Miguel stopped for air.

"What?" demanded Christian. "Miguel, get it out."

"Just that...she's okay. I found Muñoz crawling down the hill. He's wounded, and has a broken leg. I took him to the Ché Geuvara Hospital. We had to sneak past soldiers patrolling the road. Then, as I was coming back up the hill, I met Rosa with her prisoners."

"Prisoners?"

"Yes, she and Oscar and Hepté Santamaria, my cousin, and Domonic Garcia, captured the soldiers sent by Batista. Hepté and Domonic are wounded too, but not badly. The army's still on the road."

"What about the hospital? Miguel, tell me," demanded Christian.

"Señor Escobar...in his courtyard. We put him in the freezer with the engineer and the police spy. Now he lies beside that one but they still aren't speaking."

"Escobar. Is that all?"

"Yes. The others were warned. Soldiers attacked Esameralda but Juanita bravely drove them off with a knife and gave them a good scolding."

"Esameralda's okay? You're sure?" asked Christian.

"Yes, Señor Christ. She's the only one left, except for Juanita and some old women in the kitchen."

Christian felt weak and had to sit down. "Is that it?"

"No, there's more. Rosameralda's the Comandanté of Pinar del Rio. She sent me to find the fighters camped in the hills, to tell them to march toward Habana to draw off the army."

"I should go back and help Ezy."

"No, Señorita. It's too dangerous. Juanita can't hold off the whole army."

Christian put his head back and shut his eyes. Wolf sat down beside him.

"Are there no doctors?" Renée asked.

"Major Marti will send doctors from Pinar, soon. Santa Clara's ready to fall and Camilo Cienfuegos's coming to Pinar del Rio to open the Western Front."

"He's asleep," she said, irritably.

"Señor Christ can't sleep! The army's waited long enough. Rosa said it was funny to see Batista's soldiers shooting at each other."

"I don't think it's funny. Christian?" Wolf walked to the edge of the clearing, sniffing the air. "Christian?... Oh dear. Help me." Renée and Miguel steered him toward the cave entrance, one of many entrances to the complex of natural tunnels under the hills, called Los Casas. The main entrance was a half mile away, guarded by a force of guerrillas preparing to move against Havana.

Two young rebels guarded the outer entrance. Miguel signaled in his way, like a cicada in the heat. They took Christian in hand, helping him negotiate the low entrance. Christian stumbled over the rocks but made only a token protest. The sloping tunnel gradually enlarged as they approached the first cavern. Once inside the cavern they eased him down. Miguel went back to the clearing for the guitar and canvas bag. The young guards looked closely at Christian in the diffused light. "Is he wounded, Señorita?"

"No. He's pretending to be asleep."

"He looks to be sleeping very well," said one of the guards, his white teeth flashing. "Should we carry him to the cavern?" asked the other.

"The army's coming. About fifty."

"That's nothing. We could hold off twice that many."

The boastful young rebels were well protected in their tunnel. Their idea of warfare was heroic hand to hand combat, seen only in American movies and comic books, ignoring the reality of hand grenades and flame throwers. Miguel was back with their gear. He shared some cakes with the guards. "I have to report back to Rosameralda."

"Alright, Miguel, go now. I'll look after him," Renée said, tugging Christian to his feet. Miguel and Pietro faded away like ghosts.

"Okey dokey, Señorita. We'll be back," his voice rebounding from all directions.

Christian stumbled reaching for the wall of the cavern. "Why's it so dark?"

"Can you walk?"

"It's cold in here...smells."

"It's better below. Hold on to me. The first part's rocky."

They started down the uneven slope. There was residual light from many directions but it was too dark to see more than black shadows.

"Are there monsters that grab your ankles, and pull you down and eat you?"

"No. It's just a cave."

"No maidens in distress...dragons?"

"No. Be quiet and stay close."

"Are we having an adventure?"

"No!"

"I haven't been this close to you for days. Seems weeks."

"Only days...watch this hole. Step over."

A larger cavern opened and light slanted through a fissure in the roof revealing a small grotto and a stone alter with carved wooden heads, clay figures hung with glass beads and colourful wood and straw masks. Stubs of candles with wax flowing around the base were positioned in front of a painted icon. The face in the painting was black and sensuous, but distorted, almost abstract. A primitive portrait done with a heavy hand. The face reminded him of Juanita.

"A church? Down here?"

"Santería. African myths," said Renée impatiently.

"Yeah, there's stuff like this at Juanita's."

"This is her mountain shrine. The faithful come here during Carnival in July."

"Never thought of Cuba and caves."

"Viñales is limestone, rivers running underground. The rocks collapsed to make valleys, careful here...ready? Step."

"This could fall on us?" Christian scanned the ceiling of the cavern.

"I think it'll hold up for few more days."

"Days?"

"Joke. Batista will collapse before this cave does." At the top of the cavern mid-day sunlight poured through the long fissure, slanting down in a wide blue shaft of dust and humidity. Flying insects darted in and out of the rays, flashing like tiny Christmas tree lights. Renée pointed. "A vent. Sink hole. Like a drain?"

"How do you know all this stuff?"

"Father wanted me to go into politics so I studied geology. Totally useless for a Parisienne. I was left out of discussions about politics."

"You're a true rebel."

"I hadn't planned on this."

They passed through a big cavern, still descending. The going was easier as Renée promised and the tunnels much bigger. But the deeper into the ground they penetrated the more Christian felt his claustrophobia. And it was cold and damp. He began to shiver. It wasn't just the temperature; body forces ebbing, sucking away his fragile strength. She felt him trembling.

"Almost there, Cheri. Hold on."

"I'm holding."

"I mean, your spirit."

They left the light behind again but the grade was gradual and they descended in almost total darkness, trusting to Renée's memory. The floor of the tunnel leveled out after they had passed a junction. "That's the way to Juanita's and the compound. There are many tunnels. One could get lost."

"I don't want to be lost."

"We're not lost."

"I smell something."

"Kerosene. Escobar's generator must have stopped again."

"The freezers," Christian said, thinking of the bodies. The freezer room would be dark and cold, just like a cave...He heard laughter ringing along the tunnel, squeezed from the large cavern, bouncing off the rock walls. The laughter should have been reassuring. "Who's there?" he asked.

"You'll see. It's a surprise."

"I don't like surprises."

"Christian, you're being very grumpy. You should be happy we're alive."

He didn't feel happy. He was disoriented by the darkness, the distant echoes. It all came crashing down. Felt sick to his stomach. He considered the possibility of epilepsy. Father's side...but the dizziness confused him. He didn't like the dizziness and the distorted sounds. "What is it this time, Cheri?" He wanted to tell her...

He woke on a metal army cot, under a coarse wool blanket. Renée was close by, but the face peering down at him was not Renée's. It was a strong Mediterranean face, with a dark, curly beard and nervous, inquiring eyes, topped by a green forage cap. The man smelled of cigar smoke. He remembered the face from the newspapers. Fidel Castro!

Another face. A long bushy beard, and a cowboy hat. Comandanté Camilo Cienfuegos. And another, short, dark patchy beard. Thin intense face with dark probing eyes. The young doctor, Ché Guevara. Maybe he was in the Ché Guevara Hospital, or Havana and the Revolution was over, but he could still smell the stench of the kerosene lamps and the bat guano in the damp, stale air. His senses seemed sharper. He heard Renée speak in English. "His name's Christian. The musician at the Cantina?"

"Ahh, yes, of course. The Gringo with the golden hair," said Fidel Castro with a fairly good Cuban accent and a touch of Brooklyn. "He played and sang so badly the captain of our stinking boat knew everything was okay. How are you, young man? That was quite a performance. Couldn't have done better myself." There was the laughter again. Then the faces withdrew.

"Renée?...What's going on?"

"He meant that as a compliment."

"What's happening?"

"You need to eat something."

"Not Joe Louis'."

"Joe Louis? You mean the things in the bag?"

"Yeah, I couldn't."

"No. Chicken soup."

Matches flared. Cigars were being lit. Coughing and cursing punctuated Spanish nonsense talk. Unconnected words and phrases, like musicians warming up. The smell of cigar smoke masked the smell of the kerosene fumes and the guano dust. Not a great substitute, but better. The smokers went back to their card game. Another face was hovering near. Paulo. And then another. Yolando Carnero. Christian drifted off, hoping it was just another bad dream. But Renée was near, making soup on a gas burner, so it wasn't a dream.

Renée worked in the kitchen area, watched closely by Fidel Castro.

"He's still delirious?" asked Fidel.

"Poor Christian," Renée said sadly. "Takes days to recover."

"Days!? What if I need him tomorrow?" asked Fidel, this time in plain New York English.

"I'm sorry. He can't travel."

"Travel again? Castro's at the other end of the goddamned island! I thought I was going to die on that ill gotten boat from Florida. A short sea cruise, they said. Jesus! If I'd known.."

"I'm sorry...what's your name?"

"Ramon."

"Ramon? That's too much," she giggled.

"Ramon's my professional name. Alvin...Alvin Mario Francisco Augustine, son of a brick layer. My mother's Puerto Rican, that's the Francisco part. My agent said, 'get a proper stage name'. Can you imagine going through life as Alvin? The producers would think I'm one of the goddamned chipmunks!"

"Look, Alvin...Ramon...You see how he is."

"This Escobar guy assured me everything was taken care of. The interpreter, the speeches, wardrobe? He promised a plane. I get a rotting old fish boat and some loony Latinos who seem to know nothing about engines. A near death experience. He promised the Palace. Then, instead of even a hotel, you stick me in a cave with bats and thugs. And outside there's a goddamned war going on! All this for a lousy thousand bucks and expenses. I don't see the expenses, just the chance to get shot in your stupid revolution!"

"Ramon, this isn't my revolution," Renée said testily.

"And my interpreter sleeps!" Ramon gestured, playing to the balconies. "Sweet, sweet repose...arise, you fallen knave..."

"It's not Christian's fault. I doubt he knows your purpose."

"My purpose? I'm here to act, not die of arthritis inside a filthy Cuban cave. And these damned cigars!...man! How am I ever going to smoke these dog turds!?"

Camilo Cienfuegos said, "Just wave it around when you make your big speech in Havana."

"Maybe you need a bigger cigar," said Ché Guevara, "...to defend yourself when the mob finds out you're not their beloved Fidel."

Ramon sat down at the table feigning disgust. "Me? I'm not getting that close. Escobar said that if Castro's killed I only have to look good from a distance and make a speech or two."

"Open your mouth, they'll tear you apart. Let's play."

"Are you saying I can't get this part down?"

"I'm saying nothing, let's play."

"I'm sick of cards!" Ramon swept the cards from the table, knocking over a bottle of rum. It smashed into shards. The three characters and Paulo and Carnero watched the rum draining into the cracks. Ramon suddenly jumped up and roared, "Oh, see how the piquant liquor flees from my anger, like the tide flees from my mighty armies. Like the rain retreats to the very clouds when I cast but one black look to heaven..."

"Enough!" shouted Camilo. "You sound like fucking Moses on the

Mount."
"No, he thinks he's the Great Khan, crossing the Alps."
"That was Hannibal, you great ape."
"Guerrilla. Me mountain man, barbudo."
"Peasants! Amateurs," said Paulo, picking up the sopping cards.
"Stop this!" commanded Renée. "Christian needs rest."
Ramon turned to Renée, dramatically wounded. "Mea culpa, my beauty. You're too skinny, my Puerto Rican momma would say, but you have lovely hair, and a nice derriere." He stroked a golden tress flowing over her shoulder. Renée ignored Ramon and stirred the soup. "So fragile. So pale. So...domestique. A French woman's touch gives a common cave such ambience. Some flowers here. A comfy chair there. Look, a sleeping cat." He cut the dramatics and asked softly, "So, this guy's your boyfriend, huh?"
"We've been lovers."
"Doesn't look like he could satisfy a passionate woman like you."
"You on the other hand could, I suppose?"
Ramon was taken aback by Renée's directness. He tried another approach, changing characters. Bogart. "When this is over, doll, we'll see the country. The beaches. Passion food. Daiquiris in the shade of a palm tree..."
"Then you would fuck me so well I would never look at another man's dick?"
"Whoa!..." Ramon backed off. Girls don't talk that way, even the tough girls in his old New York neighbourhood. "I, ah, didn't mean..." The others laughed and made rude gestures. Ramon pulled a pistol from his holster and wheeled around, waving the semi automatic in their faces. Cagney. "All right, youse dirty rats! I've been waiting for a chance to plug you suckers. Prepare to die, dogs. Take that! *Blam! Blam!* And that! *Pow! Pow!*" He shot Camilo, Paulo, Carnero and Ché in turn, then blew into the end of the pistol.
Paulo and Carnero were not amused. Camilo and Ché laughed. "Sit down, you idiot," said Camilo. "If this fucking revolution depends on that performance you might as well turn in your union card."
"You'll never make Broadway with that Cagney shtick," giggled Ché, a slightly built actor from California, named Benny Lerner. Benny chewed his unlit cigar. He seemed nervous, as if the Cuban army was about to rush out of the darkness.
The six young rebels guarding the cave lounged and smoked on the periphery, bored with the crazy Gringos, restless to be with the real fighters moving on Havana. Daily Rebel Radio listed towns and cuar-

tels falling to the advancing brigades as Camilo Cienfuegos, Ché Guevara, Húbet Matos and Raúl Castro moved westward through the provinces. Castro himself was attacking Santiago de Cuba, the ultimate insult to Batista. Less than three thousand dedicated guerrillas routing Batista's demoralized army. The boys could sense victory and resented being left to guard American actors.

Renée turned off the burner. Christian was asleep again. She went to sit beside Paulo who was stretched out on his bunk examining the festering wound on his leg. She spoke to him in French. "That must be treated. I wish you had gone down to the hospital when there was a chance."

"There's medical supplies here. Can you do it?"

"I don't know medicine."

"Just put something on it that smells worse than this infection."

"Paulo..." she hesitated, "Escobar's been...executed."

"Too bad," he said without emotion.

"I thought you'd want to know."

"Why? So I can weep? He's nothing to me. Look what he did? He got me shot and thrown into prison."

"It wasn't his fault. You ran."

"I didn't want to go back to prison."

"How will this end, I wonder?"

"How should I know? Maybe we'll rot in this cave until doomsday."

"Did you get the radio reports?"

"Yeah. The crazy announcers were going on about, 'Zero. Three. Cee'. They kept repeating it over and over and singing this really stupid song, most of which I couldn't understand. I got 'zero cinema' and 'zero cabaret'. Then they sang, 'If all of Cuba is at war, don't go to the cabaret'. Must be code."

"Probably. Anything else of interest?"

"The hairy mountain guerrillas are closing in on Havana. Same as yesterday."

"There, you see. It'll be over soon. What will you do then?"

"Poke my eyes out and sell pencils."

"You're not being good company either."

"Pardon me, Princess, if my humour has escaped from this hole in the ground leaving a cynical shell behind."

The first warning of more trouble was the snarling rush of Wolf who flew into the cavern on the trail of his old enemies, Paulo and Carnero. Renée moved quickly to intercept the dog. It had become a ritual. Perhaps Wolf thought it was a game. He faked to the right. Renée fell for it, as usual. Wolf went left, out flanking her and, using the table and the Americans as blockers, put himself between Paulo and Carnero. The Americans scattered. Paulo rolled onto the floor and squirmed under his cot. Carnero fled behind Renée. The rebel guards laughed and cheered.

"Wolf!...Pietro! Stop!" Renée shouted in Spanish. "Stop this, right now!"

Wolf sat down, tail wagging, tongue lolling, satisfied that he had instilled sufficient chaos over the glum atmosphere. Miguel entered on the run.

"Pietro, you bad dog! Sorry, Señorita Renée. I can do nothing with him sometimes."

"It's all right, Miguel. A little excitement can't hurt. Paulo, you can come out now."

"I'll kill that dog, first chance," whined Paulo.

"It's not a good time for games, Señorita," said Miguel. He looked closely at Christian, touching his damp hair gently. "The army has reinforcements and tanks. Soldiers are coming up the hill. Tanks and trucks full of soldiers are going east to circle the mountain. Jésus is with them, the little traitor! Rosameralda's coming behind me but she has her prisoners. The soldiers will find the entrance for certain this time. The trail now looks like the road from Los Espiritos to Habana."

"What should we do?" asked Renée.

"Rosa's going to blow up the western entrance."

"Then there's only one way out."

"Even the stupid army knows about the main entrance now."

"Did Rosa give you instructions?"

"Just to wait."

"I see," said Renée. "What else can we do?"

"Obviously my captivity is about to end," said Carnero with a smirk.

"Not so fast, Señor Copper," said Miguel coldly. "I told the Special Forces lieutenant that we had an important Servicios Especiales who had turned traitor."

"That's a lie!"

"Not a lie, Señor. You want us to help you flee Cuba. And even if they didn't believe me they'll be suspicious. You had better do what Señorita Renée says, and be a good boy."

Ramon became agitated with the chatter. "Hey, tell me what's going on!"

"The army's in the hills," answered Renée calmly. "Get your things together, ready to move."

"Terrific! Just terrific! Escobar assured me this gig's a piece of cake. I want to talk to Escobar!"

"I'm afraid Escobar is no more."

"Dead?"

"Firing squad."

"You're kidding! They only do things like that in Russia...don't they?" Ramon sat down heavily on a cot, head in his hands. "I need my therapist."

"You need a good kick," said Renée.

"There's more news. Señor Maartyn's with Rosa. The boat was attacked but Señor Maartyn escaped. He was lucky to get past the patrols. I found him on the beach but couldn't leave him at the hospital."

"Is he all right?"

"Pretty much all right. Well, not so good. He has many little wounds. But he was more lucky than Captain Santoz."

"Miguel, go to the east entrance. We need to know how much time."

The explosion was a muffled *whump*. The mountain shook and pieces of rock fell from the roof, clattering to the floor and rattling down the walls like falling ice. The shock wave blasted into the cavern like the bulge of air ahead of a subway train. It tasted of dust, cordite and guano. Bats shrieked in protest. Christian started in his sleep, waking from a troubled dream.

"Rosa has blown the entrance," Miguel said as he moved toward the main entrance. Miguel stopped at Christian's cot. His fingers brushed loose strands of hair that had blown over his face. The touch lingered. He looked up at Renée and smiled. "He's damp but cool."

"He's cool, indeed," agreed Renée.

"Come on, Pietro." Miguel grabbed a handful of Hershey bars from a stack of grey ration boxes marked US Navy and vanished into the shadows.

"I don't want to die in Cuba," moaned Ramon, rocking, holding himself in a tight embrace. "I have too much to live for. My work. My art..."

"He's acting," said Camilo Cienfuegos. "Let him go on. He needs the practice."

"Oh Wayne! You're so insensitive!" whined Ramon.

"You're so weird," replied Wayne Rozniki. "How they ever picked you to play Fidel Castro is beyond me."

"You know central casting," said Benny 'Ché' Lerner. "If a Pollack can be a Cuban, an Italian can be anything."

"I'm Ukrainian!" protested Camilo. "There is a difference you know."

"What? The difference between horse meat sausage and pork meat sausage?

"And I suppose a Jew could be Pope?"

"Before a Pollack."

"Look at him, he's pathetic!"

"I can get up for it!" said Ramon. "I need is inspiration."

Rosameralda lead her prisoners into the cavern as if she and a group of children had been out for a romp in the park. But the pistol in her hand wasn't a toy. The lieutenant swaggered as if he was an associate of the beautiful rebel. Rosameralda motioned for him to keep his hands up. His troopers followed, escorted by a dozen armed boys, stumbling out of the tunnel, all brothers of the same father, Batista. They lined up beside their officer, gazing in wonder at Fidel, Ché and Camilo.

"It's him!" whispered one.

"Esta Fidel!"

"Líder Maximo!"

"Esta Ché et Camilo!"

"Fidel! Yoy!..."

Ramon realized the soldiers were talking to him. El Maximo. He rose majestically from the cot. Pulling himself up to full height, towering above the Cubans. "Companeros!..." he began grandly, but calling them farmers. "No Batistianos...Morir por la Patria es Vivir! Eh, Fidelistas?" He scanned their faces, pausing for effect, unable to discern the special troops from the rebels. Then his eyes fell on Rosameralda. "Oh, my God, she's back!" he breathed. "Ah, ah...Atención, atención, ya viene el general!" The Cubans looked around the cave to see which general Fidel meant. He searched his brain for recent clips. "Iré a Santiag, eh? Iré en coche de aguas negras!," he shouted, which is a broken line from a Garcia Lorca poem sent to him by Escobar. Translated it means, *I am off to Santiago in a coach decked with mourning waters.* The soldiers took it as a battle cry and repeated, "Iré Santiago! Iré Santiago!"

Ramon, pleased with the results, shouted, "Morir a los americanos! La granjita!!"

To the soldiers he was saying...*Death to the Americans. At the ranch.* They cheered again. It did make more sense to kill Yankees than each other.

"Iré a Santiago! Iré a Santiago!" a soldier shouted again. The others took up the cry again.

Rebel Radio was reporting that Fidel's column Number One was moving on Santiago de Cuba. It didn't matter that Santiago was seven hundred miles to the east, Fidel was in their cave above Los Espiritos. Maybe he *was* a magician. A Spiritualista! They had already decided that, to a man, if their mission went badly they would change sides. Who better to surrender to than El Maximo himself, and it was much better than submitting to a girl, even Rosameralda. Real Cuban men knew the proper order of things. The soldiers urged their lieutenant to consummate the union.

"Ah, Señor Comandanté Castro...my men and I are at your service."

Carnero just shook his head in disbelief, but said nothing. These confused soldiers could be useful. Christian struggled to understand what all the shouting was about. Paulo lounged on his cot, bemused, studying the attributes of the soldiers, making eye contact with one. Indifferent as to which one, since they were a matched set.

Ramon turned to Renée and whispered, "What did he say? Servicios what?...""

"They want to surrender to you. Just say 'excelente'."

"Excelente! Excelente!" He turned to Renée again. "Now what?"

"Go and stand in the corner and pretend to be busy. Smoke a cigar or plan an attack. I'll speak to Rosa."

Ramon smiled benevolently on his growing army and strutted imperiously away, looking for a corner, ordering Camilo and Ché to his side.

Rosameralda and Renée embraced. She held Rosa at arm's length to assess her wound, afraid to fall into those eyes. "Rosa, help me out of this. Talk to them."

"This is not my doing," she teased. "You started it."

"Please. You must. We can't keep up this ruse."

"That lieutenant, Carlos the Octopus, can't keep his hands off me. If I talk to him it will only encourage the little roach and I'll be forced to shoot him."

"But if your prisoners discover the truth about our *Castros Americanus* there could be a riot."

"All right. How's Christian?"

"He's improving. How's Maartyn?"

"He's so strong, won't admit to his injuries. Such a man, that one."

"Good," said Renée. "Now please say something to those men before they catch on. Wait! Where *is* Maartyn!?

"He was behind us in the tunnel." Rosameralda rushed past the surprised prisoners and disappeared into the darkness.

Renée was left at the epicentre of the group of rebels and converts waiting for a pronouncement. Leadership. She composed herself, wondering what her father would do faced with a tense diplomatic situation. She experienced an unexpected longing to be with her family. She looked around the stinking cave, with its dampness and danger and the grotesque shadows thrown onto the walls. Shadow plays. Trolls, she recalled from childhood stories. This was no fairy tale adventure. She realized the absurdity of her situation and longed for her clean mansion in Paris, even in winter. Paris in winter has compensations. The lights, the boulevards, the steaming sidewalk cafés, her maids, her bedroom with its ornate walk-in fireplace...I am not a revolutionary! she screamed inwardly.

They had blown up another escape route. The army was outside La Casa with tanks and flame throwers. They all faced a gruesome death and the person in de facto command was a delicate French girl with long, sunshine coloured hair. For some reason the prisoners believed she had a rank higher than Rosameralda's, whatever that was. She had poise and strength for a foreign woman in sweaty fatigues. Fidel had confided in her. Well Renée, she said to herself, it's now or never.

"Compadres. Cubans. El Comandanté Maximo welcomes you to the Revolution. You are brave soldiers. If you swear allegiance to Fidel he will grant you immunity when the Revolution is over...and, if you take up arms at his side he will bestow upon you all the rights of the members of the July 26th Movement."

"Si! Si!!" The special force lieutenant shouted his acceptance of conditions. His men took up the chant, "Iré a Santiago! Iré a Santiago!" The sound was deafening in the confines of the cavern. The bats took flight again and wheeled about their heads. Ramon turned from his mime of strategy planning with Ché and Camilo to make gestures as if he were the Holy Father bestowing a papal blessing. He glowed with power. The new recruits shouted, "Iré a Santiago! Iré a Santiago!" Renée waved for silence.

"Compadres. El Comandanté Líder Maximo has given you, the sign. You are officially sworn as..." all she could think of was The French Foreign Legion, "...Legionnaires. Legionnaires of the Revolution!"

The soldiers received the new honour with more cheers and handshakes all around. The lieutenant rushed over to Fidel and embraced him. Ché and Camilo pried the lieutenant away and made him understand that they were very busy with strategy for the attack on Santiago.

"Ah, Señorita Comandanté," said the lieutenant, mincing over to Renée, "My men and I are most happy to join the cause of the Revolution. I, personally, have never supported Fulgencio Batista, and assure you that, even though I was a trusted member of the Palace Guard, I only acted as a soldier in the service of my country."

"I'm sure, lieutenant...what's your name?"

"Carlos. Carlos Octavio Garcia Manuel Sancto Fuentes, at your service. My father is Senator Octavio Sancto Fuentes. I was El Presidente's personal cigar carrier. I also helped to count the money from the parking meters. And on Sundays..."

"Well, Carlos Octavio Garcia, I'm sure your skills will be useful..."

"Help me!" Rosameralda shouted from the tunnel. Four of her boys rushed into the darkness. The three Americans suspended their pantomime. Lieutenant Octopus stared at Fidel, Ché and Camilo, twitching his nose, flickers of doubt lifting first one side of his mouth and then the other. His soldiers, now sworn rebels but with no guns and no orders, shifted and shuffled uneasily.

Renée was out of ideas. The remaining rebel guards were uncertain if they were to keep their guns trained on the prisoners or to mingle. Ramon was rehearsing a speech. He had a short list of Spanish words and phrases but Fidel was known to talk passionately for hours. They decided to light more cigars.

Rosameralda returned with Maartyn before the cigar ritual gave the Americans away.

Maartyn looked like a hand grenade victim. "Put him down here," Renée said, indicating the cot next to Christian. Maartyn struggled to stay on his feet. They had to force him down. Rosameralda knelt next to the cot and soothed him with her hands. His upper chest and one arm, the one he used to shield his face, were peppered with bullet fragments and splinters of wood. Renée brought clean towels and the first aid kit.

"It's worse than I thought," said Rosameralda.

"Maartyn's very tough," said Renée. They began cleaning away blood, assessing the many entry wounds. But clearing the weak clots caused the blood to flow. "He's lost too much blood." She took Maartyn's pulse at the carotid artery. "His pulse is erratic. Is there any blood for transfusion?"

"There's Red Cross boxes," answered Rosameralda. "We've been bringing in supplies for months. But I don't know how to give transfusions. Do you?"

"No." She stood up and approached Lieutenant Fuentes. "Do any of you have medical training?"

"My apologies, Señorita Comandanté, we had a medical person. Unfortunately our doctor was injured during training, in Miami. Actually it was a fight, in a bar."

Renée confronted the actors who where trying to hide in a cloud of cigar smoke. "Do any of you have medical training?"

Ramon shook his head. The Camilo character likewise. Benny Lerner lowered his eyes. He looked as if he was about to be sick.

"Well?" Renée prodded.

"I, ah, was at medical school. California. Berkeley. Before I went into acting."

"Good, you know how to give blood."

"Not really."

"You've at least read a book?"

"Well, yeah, and...I, ah, attended a seminar once, battlefield trauma. This was just after the Korean War. Battle wounds. Very graphic. I got sick"

"I don't care how sick you get. If there's blood give it to Maartyn."

"Blood requires refrigeration. Your supplies will be plasma."

"Whatever it is, do it."

"I, ah, quit medical school, actually, before, ah...."

"See that woman? Rosameralda. If you don't give Maartyn a transfusion she'll probably shoot you."

Benny's eyes went wide. He dropped his cigar and followed Renée to the large stack of medical supplies. They searched the Red Cross cases until they found one marked plasma. Inside was an aluminum container, like a briefcase. Rows of tightly packed plastic bags, standing on end, looked encouraging. There were also packages of apparatus.

"We'd need to know his blood type. Medical problems?"

"His medical problem is that he'll die without blood!"

"I know, but, giving the wrong plasma…"

"What's the right plasma?"

"There should be Type AB positive...safe to give Type AB to anyone."

"Well, I don't see Type AB."

"Then he needs his own type."

"What do you need to know?"

"Me?...in general? His blood type, and Rh factors."

"There's a test, right?"

"Yeah, lab tests."

"What do they do on a battlefield?"

"Read the dog tags."

"Dog tags!?"

"Yeah. Rank, serial number, blood types, all that."

"Benny, you're a genius!" She kissed Benny on the prominent nose. "Maartyn wears dog tags!"

"What?" said Rosameralda. "Dogs?"

"Look!" Renée pulled on the chain around Maartyn's neck. The tags jangled free of his blood-splattered T shirt. "Dog tags!" She examined the stamped printing.

Benny was reading over her shoulder. "That's it. Look. Blood type...O-Rh-positive."

"You have to match the type. That's all, isn't it?"

"Fortunately he has a wide choice." But Benny looked grave. "You have to hook the apparatus...the tubes, to the bag and hang the bag."

"Yes? What?" demanded Renée.

"Then you have to shove this needle into his arm."

"Okay. Do it!"

"Couldn't do it...be sick."

"You have to!"

"I threw up. I feinted."

"I'll do it," said Paulo.

Three faces turned to Paulo. "Paulo...of course," said Renée. "Benny can tell you what Maartyn needs."

"What are you talking about?" asked Rosameralda.

"Paulo can give Maartyn the transfusion," she said and couldn't help adding, "the needle. It's the one thing in life he's good at."

Benny and Renée carried the equipment to Maartyn's cot while Rosameralda tried to clean the wounds. Maartyn wasn't clotting. "He's bleeding badly. Hurry," she implored as they set up the unfamiliar apparatus.

"Ah, I'd suggest to the lady, to Rosa, that she stop dabbing. He's a bleeder by the looks," said Benny.

"What's that mean?"

"Probably low in fibrinogen. Clotting agent? His blood clots slowly and if she keeps cleaning him he'll just keep bleeding."

"Rosa, Benny says to stop rubbing his wounds. Maybe just hold his hand."

The inhabitants of the cave edged closer forming a tight circle. No one thought about allegiances. Christian opened his eyes, trying to focus on the scene, but it all came in a jumble of blurred bodies and whispers.

"Hurry, please hurry." He recognized Rosameralda's voice, or was it Esameralda?

Benny finally found the right combination of tubes and needles. There was a metal stand to hold the bags which clipped to the frame of the army cot. Benny attached the bag to the tube and then the tube to the needle. He handed the needle to Paulo then stood back. "Wait!" he said. "I have to clean the spot." He opened the bottle of surgical disinfectant, tore open a cotton swab packet and began dabbing the liquid over Maartyn's dirty arm above the wrist. Paulo traced the blue veins standing out co-operatively on Maartyn's muscled arm. The needle in Paulo's hand was poised a few inches from the skin.

"Don't!" cried Christian, hurling himself off the cot, lunging at Paulo. His shoulder caught Paulo on the right side, on the infected wound. Paulo cried out, going down hard, dropping the needle which swung free like a pendulum. Benny captured the needle on the second pass before it could touch anything. Christian and Paulo sprawled on the dirt floor, Christian on top. He pulled back his fist to throw a punch. Renée recovered from her shock and grabbed Christian's arm. "No, no, no! It's all right. Paulo's giving him blood."

Christian looked closely at Maartyn. "Jesus! What…?" Maartyn was slipping into shock.

"I'll explain," said Renée. "Get off Paulo."

Christian stood up and offered his hand to Paulo. Paulo slapped it away. "Fucking idiot! Between you and that dog I'll be a cripple for life. Someone help me up."

Rosameralda and Ramon pulled Paulo to his feet. Christian sat down on his bunk, looking at Maartyn. "What happened to him?"

"The boat was attacked," said Renée, whispering in his ear. "Maartyn was the only survivor. Bullet fragments and splinters. Paulo and Benny are giving him a transfusion."

"I'm sorry. I just saw Paulo, and the needle."

"It's okay, Cheri."

Christian scanned the faces. "Hey, that's not Fidel Castro…"

"I'll explain that later also."

Paulo took the needle from Benny. Benny began swabbing the spot again. "Not there," said Paulo. "There." He pointed to an area mid way between the inside of the elbow and the wrist. Benny dabbed where he was told. "Open," said Paulo. Benny opened the clip valve below the bag. Amber liquid and bubbles flowed down the tube in a chain, like little railway cars, and dribbled out the end of the needle until it was a steady stream. "Stop." Benny released the clip. Paulo took hold of Maartyn's arm below the spot and effortlessly slid the needle into the prominent vein. "Open." Benny opened the clip valve. Blood flowed in and out and the amber liquid flowed again, although there was no indication of movement. Clear plasma with no air bubbles. "How many bags should he have?" Paulo asked Benny.

Benny shrugged and bit his lip. "How much blood has he lost?"

"A lot," offered Renée.

"Need to be more precise," said Benny. "Give him two bags and see how it goes."

"Why not just say, take two bags and I'll send you the bill if you don't die," said Ramon.

"That's helpful," snapped Benny. "Too much plasma and blood pressure goes off the dial. Cardiac time. Two bags, and then we monitor."

"Good call, Doc," said Camilo.

"Hey, I've only read about this stuff."

"How long will it take?" asked Renée.

"Two hours a bag. Depends."

They waited in silence, mesmerized, watching the plasma level in the bag, and watching Maartyn as if they expected him to swell up or change colour. He didn't swell up but he did change colour, imperceptibly, from ghost white, to feint pink. Two hours crept by. The cave was silent. Many slept. Benny reached up and shut off the flow before the bag was empty. He disconnected the tubes and hung a full bag in place. "Should we pull the needle?"

"I don't know," answered Paulo. "How much of a problem is one small bubble?"

"Enough to stop the blood to the brain? They didn't tell us much about that part."

"Maybe that's the part where you puked."

"Shut up!"

"Okay, boys, enough. I say pull the needle," said Renée.

Paulo pulled the needle. They repeated the procedure for clearing the tubes of air, watching a tiny bubble curve down the tube, and vanish. It was like watching a single car following a curving highway.

Christian revisited winter nights on Mount Royal, in a narcotic induced tunnel, mind bent but vision clear, watching headlights on Montreal streets through the skeletal fingers of winter-dead trees. Zombies swathed in wrappings lurched through the streets exhaling frosty breath volcanoes. The sound of footsteps like snow explosions. The endless wails of stereo sirens as the great city pulsed below, wondering whose lives were forever altered. It seemed to Christian that the bubble took a long time to travel four feet of plastic tubing.

"Clean."

Benny swabbed a new spot and Paulo faltered as he jabbed the needle into Maartyn's arm. His hands were shaking. Maartyn flinched, eyes fluttering, and almost immediately a large brown patch appeared around the needle.

"Bruising," Benny said. "You missed the vein. Change arms."

They went through the ritual again, on the right arm, but Paulo was shaking too much to insert the needle. "My side...I'm sorry."

Rosameralda squeezed Renée's arm. "Señor Lerner, now."

"Benny, Rosameralda says you insert the needle."

"I can't."

"Do it, Señor." Rosameralda said, before Renée could speak. Benny blanched, appealing to Rosameralda with his eyes. Miguel and Wolf reentered the cavern on the run, but stopped outside the circle. Wolf sensed something was happening and sniffed at the new arrivals. Only Carnero noticed the vicious dog patrolling the perimeter. The old antagonists glared at each other. Miguel balanced impatiently on one foot. He had news for Rosameralda. "Do it, now!" she said, in a low voice. Miguel had been observing Christian.

"Miguel...What did you see?" Rosameralda asked finally.

Miguel looked at his sister, struggling to refocus on the coming battle. "Tanks. Trucks. Many soldiers. They left the road and are coming across the fields. I used Cesare's binoculars."

Benny took the needle. He swabbed the spot where Paulo pointed. Paulo staggered to his cot. Benny drew a deep breath, fighting down the nausea, and touched Maartyn's skin with the tip of the needle. He broke into a sweat, hands trembled slightly, as Paulo's had, but he concentrated and pushed. The needle slid in cleanly and blood backed into the liquid. "Open," he said calmly. Renée opened the valve. Those who had been holding their breath, exhaled. Benny put a piece of tape over the needle and reached for Maartyn's wrist. "Good, good. He's steady. Slow but steady. And there's some strength."

"Well done, Doc," said Camilo. "That calls for a drink." He held a bottle out to Benny.

"No, thanks. I want to keep an eye on his vitals. I'm still concerned about the clotting."

"The bleeding's slowing down," observed Renée, lifting a bandage gently. "The clotting's better."

"Picking up agents from the plasma."

"Benny, you'd better look at this guy," said Ramon, indicating Paulo. "He passed out just now."

"Should have done it before." Benny went to Paulo's bunk and knelt beside him. The few onlookers drifted away, rebels and soldiers mingling, sharing cigarettes and news.

Rosameralda took Miguel aside. "You've done well. Rest for now."

"That little traitor Jésus Gonzáles is riding on the lead tank. I'm going to kill him with my own hands!"

"No! Miguel, don't talk that way," scolded Rosameralda. "He's only a child."

"He's a traitor for a chocolate bar and a ride on a tank!"

"How long?"

"Half hour. Less. They go quickly through the tobacco but they'll take time coming up the hill. Rosa?"

"Yes, they know. Did you tell Cesare?"

"He's waiting for orders."

"Santa Maria!" Rosameralda sounded weary of it all. "Renée? I need you." Renée left Paulo's side. She had cut away Paulo's shirt and pant leg. Benny probed the infections, swabbing, ordering Ramon and Camilo to find certain medical supplies. He asked routinely for sulfur, morphine and syringes. "Renée, the army's near. Tanks, flame throwers, heavy artillery. They may try to seal the cave or use flame throwers...you understand?"

"I understand."

"You also understand it's too late to run."

"Yes. We couldn't leave anyway."

"I know." Rosameralda looked at Maartyn. "I don't trust Fuentes."

"Then it's up to you."

"There's no way out, Renée. Our men are in the hills but I can't order them into the cave. We have only fifty, if Fuentes's with us. We could hold out for a time." Rosa was silent for a long moment looking about the cave at the faces waiting for her orders. "There's another problem."

"I'd be surprised if there wasn't."

"The hole in the top of the cavern?"

"The vent near Juanita's grotto?"

"Yes. As children we could squeeze through, until we developed in certain ways." The girls shared a tense smile. "The vent lets in air so they can't suffocate us. The big problem is that Miguel saw one of the children leading the tanks. He also knows about the vent. The army could use gasoline."

"To burn us out?"

Her expression said much.

"I see." Renée shivered. She had seen her government's classified films of Algeria, Korea and French Indochina, in the comfort of her movie room. Napalm in the jungles, flame throwers and hand grenades in cave fighting in Asia. Imagined the stench of burning flesh. "What should we do?"

"Cesare will put up a strong fight and hope the others can keep the army from the vent."

"Rosa," interrupted Miguel. "Jésus must be stopped. I'll do it."

"Miguelito...no." She gathered Miguel to her and hugged him tightly, the tears flowing freely. "Our little sister. It's too much."

Miguel gave her a quick kiss, putting her off guard. She relaxed her grip. Miguel kissed her again then tore himself out of her embrace and ran for the east tunnel. "Keep Pietro with you!" he shouted over his shoulder. "Don't worry!" He was swallowed up by the darkness. Wolf came bounding through legs. This time Renée was ready. Wolf deeked right. Renée shifted, but immediately changed direction as Wolf went left. She scooped him up. "Got you!" Wolf went limp but Renée wasn't taking any chances. She carried the dog to Christian.

"Hold this little Houdini," she said. "How are you?"

"I'm okay. What's happening?"

"We aren't sure. Miguel's gone to see."

"What's really happening?"

"I have to check on Maartyn." She turned to Maartyn and stared at the plasma bag. Christian was left to contemplate their future with little information, or return to the dubious safety of sleep and distorted dreams. Either way he had been summarily set aside while Renée contemplated her own options. There wasn't much time for self absorption.

Maartyn was breathing easier, his pulse almost normal, the bandages no longer soaked with fresh blood. She couldn't see Paulo for spectators watching Benny work. They were obviously starved for entertainment and an impending battle wasn't enough. Watching someone else's pain, the ultimate voyeurism, the new television technology's appeal, would make hospital emergency room's popular.

Renée retreated to the kitchen area and lit the gas burner. She stared at the blue flames of the gas jet, imagining what it would be like to burn.

"Renée," said Rosameralda, "I'm taking Fuentes. My boys will protect you. El Comandanté of the cave."

"Why me?"

"Who else?" She unbuckled the pistol holster and drew it around Renée's slender waist, settling in on her hips. "Use it."

"Imagine what my poor mother would say."

The two friends embraced briefly. Nothing was said. It wasn't necessary. Rosa turned away, signaling Lieutenant Fuentes. "Arm your men and come with me."

Fuentes and his soldiers looked startled. Shouldn't El Líder Maximo be giving the orders? Castro and his Comandantés were hovering on the periphery watching Benny, like spectators at an industrial accident. It was known that Ché Guevara was a medical student in Argentina. He was called The Doctor, his mountain clinics already legend, but still. Why is this woman ordering us around? wondered Fuentes. And why is Fidel, who is known to have the largest ego in all of Cuba, even larger than El Presidente's, not in command? Rosameralda could see the doubt in their expression and body language. It was time to end the charade.

"Yes, Lieutenant, our Fidel Castro's an impostor. An important part of the Revolution. Camilo...Ché. The reasons are obvious. The Revolution must succeed with or without Fidel Castro Ruz. You have chosen to fight against Batista. Now's the time. Issue yourselves rifles, ammunition and hand grenades. Make certain you each have a knife and a bayonet. My boys will return your handguns."

The soldiers immediately set upon the arsenal. "Viva Castro! Viva la Revolucíon!" shouted Fuentes, attempting to reassert his authority. He enjoyed command, the posturing at least, and would have done well in a touring troupe with the Americans.

Rosameralda sat with Maartyn while Fuentes pretended to be in charge. She had many things to consider, not the least of which was Fuentes' new loyalty. Was he to be trusted? Could she use him?

"Maartyn..." she said softly. Maartyn's eyes fluttered open. He tried on a brave smile. "Maartyn, I know you cannot understand me, but, I have to go. Renée will look after you. Rest." She leaned down carefully and kissed his dry lips with a lingering softness. It was a kiss to make a person want to live, if only to experience the promise. Just to make sure he got the message she took his hand and placed it inside her fatigue jacket. Her breasts were firm and warm, the erect nipples cool and hard, like bullets.

Maartyn got the message.

Renée had been watching the moment, unashamed. She turned off the soup and stood gazing at Rosameralda and Maartyn, feeling used up, at twenty a veteran of the game.

"Fuentes, you are now Captain," Rosameralda said abruptly. "Señorita Jalobert is the Comandanté. Those staying behind will take orders from her. Carnero, care to join us in a real fight?"

"Many thanks, Señorita, but I have no boots, you understand."

"Very well. You don't wish to redeem yourself. You boys stay with Señorita Jalobert. Protect her and our doctor. And watch Carnero carefully, especially when the battle starts. Do not come to the entrance unless I send for you."

Rosameralda reviewed her troops. She searched the eyes of each man for a sign of weakness. With the commando makeup rubbed away they looked much younger, no longer boys, but still innocent, untried young men only recently bloodied. Only Fuentes, who would not meet her eyes, was a question. Perhaps he was still chagrined about being compromised by a woman. Or dubious about the reasons for an impostor Fidel Castro. Perhaps it was simply hormonal conflict.

Rosameralda strode quickly into the dark tunnel. Fuentes motioned for his troops to follow. As the last man entered the tunnel Wolf made his escape, bolting from Christian and dodging past Renée. He raced through the tunnel, beating Rosameralda to the encampment at the eastern entrance. He wouldn't stop running until he found Miguel.

Renée was left behind, leaning against the rough plank dining table, contemplating her situation, surrounded by ration boxes, cooking pots and gas bottles. The designated leader of an odd collection of misfits, casualties and children, holed up in a Cuban cave, waiting for the third battle of Los Espiritos to begin. She had no idea what to do, other than make soup. The rebel boys smoked and talked glumly in small groups. Christian and Maartyn slept. Ramon and Wayne, relieved of their ridiculous charade, watched Benny working on Paulo.

From exploratory conversations Benny already knew the circumstances of Paulo's wounds. "I apologize for not attending to these sooner. I didn't take the oath."

"What oath?"

"Hippocratic. I'm not a doctor." He probed the ugly looking flesh around the gun shot wound.

"Ahhh, damnit!...That's bad!"

"Sorry. My technique's only theoretical."

"Fucking pain!...killing me."

"Pray or something." He shook out a thermometer and stuck it into Paulo's mouth to keep him quiet. "I can give you morphine but we need antibiotics."

"Uh huh...goo...ge...sum."

"Unfortunately, I can't find the antibiotics."

Renée overheard the conversation. "Antibiotics are at the hospital."

"How do we get them?" asked Benny.

"The cave's sealed."

"Immune system's very low. This wound should have healed days ago." Benny probed and swabbed, pulling away stinking flesh. He suddenly got up and rushed to a dim area of the cave used for the chemical latrines. He came back, wiping his hands with disinfectant. After a swig of rum which he spit out, he continued probing. He placed a large gauze pad on the gunshot wound, checked Paulo's temperature and began to work on the torn up leg. Unfortunately Wolf wasn't there to savour his handy work. "This's very bad."

Renée decided they needed a diversion. It was, after all, Christmas. "Does anyone know a Cuban Christmas dinner recipe?"

Ramon was the first to respond. "As a matter of fact I do," he said, using the opening to get close to her. "While studying up for this gig, I came upon a recipe for a Cuban dinner, guajiro style. It's called Moors and Christians. It ain't nothing like the real thing back home, but here it is..." Ramon gestured and postured. Renée waited. "Black beans and rice."

Renée frowned. "That's it? Black beans? Rice?"

"Well, the recipe also calls for spiced roast pork and cassava bread, with a Spanish almond dessert, but I don't see a pig roasting on an open fire, do you?"

"Doesn't sound much like Christmas," said Renée.

"Can you come up with something more appropriate?"

"No, it's just that, at Christmas we entertained properly. I miss the ritual."

"Oh, excuse me, Princess. We peasants would love to hear what you consider an adequate Christmas feast."

She rejected the idea, at first, then realized any chatter was a diversion. "Even at Christmas it was about presentation," she began, as if giving a lecture. "An intimate dinner party for sixty dignitaries required seven varieties of wild country game, roasted on spits on the terrace. The centre piece would be a suckling pig on a bed of fresh mangos flown in from the colonies, as well as fresh flowers. No point wasting government planes. Of course there were the usual plum, orange and apple eau claire sauces. There was always a baron of beef hung from the ceiling, for the barbarians from Russia and Romania. The poor cow was tied in the orchard and fed Brittany apples for three months, and milked to make cream, before she was slaughtered and marinated to become mock steer. But very tender. The Russians would never suspect. Her babies provided the veal and sweetbreads with brandied raisin and walnut sauce on the side. Smoked Atlantic salmon sliced so thin they were transparent. Icelandic herring fillets wrapped around sea turtle eggs and dipped in mourning dove mayonnaise. The vinaigrette was made from turned Chardonney or a Bourdeau, Grand Cru at least. Did I mention dried and sautéed truffles over saffron risotto? That was to impress the Italian diplomats. Portobello mushrooms stuffed with escargot, and Normandy oysters smeared with Lake Baku caviar for appetizers, and about twelve different liqueurs, imported, as recognition that other countries do make spirits. But with France being the vineyard to the world, there were vintages, signed by the maitres, from every region, each with its own cheeses. Heaps of Mediterranean vegetables and exotic fruits. Patés of rare bird livers on Jewish flat bread in honour of Captain Dreyfus. I won't even try to explain desserts. But there is at least one rich confection from each colony France likes at the time, including, a flaming maple syrup and Cognac on butter pastry from Quebec. We even condescend to allow desserts from countries we don't like, if they are special, like Baklava. As a finale, Turkish cigarettes or Cuban cigars with thick Moroccan coffee topped with fresh clotted cream, and more Cognac of course. Then there's the midnight buffet...the leftovers."

"Oh, my God! Leftovers? Imagine. And what did you do for breakfast?"

"That was special too. Our family time. After mass, at Notre Dame, if it was cold, Daddy made us walk to this incredible little Moroccan restaurant across the river from Notre Dame, for the most divine paper thin crépes d'oeuf with tangerine advocat sauce. We'd sit bundled up on the terrace and drink steaming cups of sweet coffee made with clotted yak cream and topped with shaved Belgian truffles, spiced with an exotic North African liqueur made with dates and oranges. It was sinful!"

"You miss Paris and all that?"

"I didn't realize how much," answered Renée. "Not for the excess. I left home to get away from *all that* overdone *joie de vivre*. But I wouldn't mind just a tiny bit of luxury."

"Like a bath," said Benny.

Ramon saw his opening. "When we go to France I'll take you to this little Italian spot I know in Montparnasse. Never mind Moors and Christians, the risotto con aragosta will knock your socks off, darling. Cheese? How about real water buffalo Mozzarella? They have their own Chianti wines and olive oil brought in from the family vineyard in Tuscany. You'll meet movie stars and writers. I could go on."

"What's the name of this famous restaurant?"

"Maison de Domaine Montepulciano."

"Sounds awfully pretentious for Montparnasse."

"It's just a hole in the wall, actually, known to the locals. In New York it would be considered a dive but they have the best kitchen in France. It's never been discovered by Michelin. I know the owner, Luigi. His wife's second cousin married my old man's older brother. They live down the street. Practically family. Luigi would give us the special table at the back with a view of the garbage cans. Candles in Chianti bottles. Table cloth, red and white of course. Clean napkins. Fork...spoon. Wilted flowers. Very romantic. So, marry me?"

"Never give up, right Fidel?"

"Seldom."

"Well," sighed Renée, still lingering in Paris, "since this is Christmas in a Cuban cave, we have black beans and rice. Without roasted pork. I'd settle for Spam. At least that's pork."

Benny overheard the conversation. "Nothing with pork," said Benny.

"What do you care about Christmas dinner, Hebe?"

"I celebrate everything, just in case one of us is right."

"I'd better get on with dinner," said Renée.

Ramon lost interest in the local cuisine and went back to rum and playing cards with Wayne Rozniki and Yolando Carnero. Renée explored the boxes and sacks of supplies, already inventing variations of black beans and rice. Her Parisienne blood demanded something more than Bohemian ascetics. She wanted life and excitement. And what else? On the edges, creeping into her awareness, was a new feeling. She couldn't help being attracted to the pushy American. He was the opposite of Christian. Tall and powerful, if somewhat quirky, and seemed to have two personalities; explosive artistry or given to fey whining. He was dark and exciting and, he knew Paris. She found her-

298

self staring over the boxes of rations at Ramon, hunched over cards, hazy in cigar smoke, as if they were in the green room waiting for their cue. How could they play cards knowing they could all die for the Revolution? Christian, Maartyn and Paulo were in danger, damaged by the rebellion in a country they knew little about. Her mind rejected the nearness of revolution and the coarse excesses of her current Bohemian experience.

Renée found a big sack of Italian rice and another of black beans stamped USA. Black beans, she remembered, had to be soaked for hours before cooking. "We don't have hours!" She wanted to cry. Instead she searched for a substitute. Canned kidney beans or pork'n'beans. Benny would object. All she had to do was open the cans and heat. Make the rice. "What's the point?" She decided not to soak the black beans. Christmas dinner would be delayed, or postponed or, it wouldn't matter. Then she spotted a wooden case in the middle of the grey boxes. It wasn't grey, it was rough, natural wood with stylish stenciling. She moved boxes until she freed the case. Château Bouscaut, Bordeaux. "Château Bouscaut! Here, in Cuba? I don't believe it." Behind that case was another with the name, Marqués de Riscal, Elciego Espagne. Escobar had good taste. "Heaven exists! There is a God!"

While Renée pondered the irony of excellent wines and instant death by flame thrower the boys were getting acquainted. "You should go back to medical school," said Paulo.

"My technique's worse than my theoretical knowledge, I know."

"I didn't mean that," he said, looking into Benny's eyes. "You have a nice touch. You'd be a good doctor."

"I don't have the stomach. This was hard enough. Just probing the surface. My father wanted me to be a heart surgeon, like himself. Surgeon at least. Nothing less. Can you see me? Throwing up in your patient's chest cavity is not good ethics."

"Then be a massage specialist. With those hands?" The meaning was subtle. Benny just nodded.

Renée was concentrating on food and Christmas in Paris. "Even a scrawny chicken would be good," she said to break the silence. She was looking for the salt and pepper when the battle began. A tank shell exploded near the entrance and was answered immediately by small arms fire. More explosions. Each burst sent a tremor through La Casa. Renée put a lid on the pot to stop debris from falling into the rice. She found the box of canned Spam and a box of canned black beans, just heat and serve. The Spam was cut into cubes for frying. There was even olive oil. The mountain trembled and shook. Dust and rock fragments fell. She realized that the cave dwellers were staring at her. She was El Comandanté. "Rosa said to wait!" She wondered how long the rebels could hold off the tanks.

They all waited in silent fear. And waited through the explosions and tremors. The tanks were having trouble manoeuvring in loose talus. Firing from a low angle, too far away to use the flame throwers. And the entrance was protected by a rock outcropping so the shells exploded in spectacular bursts, with smoke and flying shrapnel, dangerous only if the rebels ventured out. They stayed well inside the cave and darted out to return fire. The Major in command of the army was reluctant to launch a full attack. He had sketchy information about the size of the rebel force and it's armament but it was known that a unit of elite commandos had disappeared, presumably defeated, or they defected, and their automatic weapons captured.

A line of soldiers armed with jerry cans, crept along the valley and up the hill through the dense brush. The tank commander seemed content to lob shells at the cave and wait. And the ground troops camouflaged in the brush had been, at first, amused, then annoyed by the actions of a strange little dog that harassed them until they had to move from their positions. Shooting at the dog didn't work. Each occurrence brought a withering hail of gunfire from other rebel units dug in above the cave opening.

Their main tactic, that of burning out the rebels, was delayed when the young guide, Jésus, mysteriously disappeared. The patrol sent to search for the vent were harassed by the pockets of rebels in the hills but it was only a matter of time. In the meantime the Major was taking casualties and the morale of his troops was falling. It was supposed to have been a swift punishment detail. Batista badly needed a victory.

In desperation the army major ordered his soldiers to use the flame throwers to set fire to the brush below the cave entrance. He would smoke the rebels out and destroy the ground cover.

The smoke of the burning vegetation did find its way into the cave, and most wafted out the hole in the cavern. And that's how the army found the vent.

Renée ordered her people to lay low. "And put out the cigars!" She attended to Maartyn with wet towels, holding them lightly over his face. Christian, left to muse about his isolation, was determined to make amends. But how? Renée was more distant and war didn't help.

Rosameralda sent a runner with a commentary on the battle but there was no word about Miguel. Cesare had been killed by a tank shell. His body blown over the edge and down the talus slope. Wolf had been seen harassing the troops. When the brush fire burned itself out and the smoke cleared Renée resumed her Christmas feast preparation. It was that kind of Christmas. The tank shells landed. Small arms fire crackled sporadically. Kerosene lamps flickered. The bats circled and complained every time a tank shell exploded. The waiting continued. It was neither day nor night in the cave and the hours dragged. Finally the bats left the cave. "It must be dark outside," she said to Ramon who was watching the final preparations for Christmas dinner.

"You'd make a good wife under fire. You can work in the dark, and look great in fatigues. You'd do okay in Queens."

"What's Queens?"

"New York. East side?"

"Is that another marriage proposal?"

"Yeah, but you don't have to answer right now. I want to taste dinner first."

"I have a big surprise..." She was interrupted by the arrival of Wolf.

"There's the dog!" Ramon said. Wolf was unsteady, tired and grey. The tan hair burned away on his left side. Ugly red patches showed through the ashes.

"Oh, Wolf...not you too? Come here, little one." Wolf advanced toward Renée slowly, in obvious pain. His whiskers and eyelashes gone. Ears singed. He looked like an orphaned seal pup too long out of water. She picked the dog up carefully and stood him on the table, then set about cleaning away the ash and burned hair. Wolf submitted without complaint. "What should I do for him, Benny?"

"Petroleum jelly or sterile oil to stop the loss of fluids, light gauze bandages and antibiotics."

"We have olive oil."

"Paulo and your friend Maartyn need antibiotics," added Benny.

"Should I use the olive oil?"

"Try the olive oil."

"Poor Wolf. You're a tough little dog." Renée made him lay down while she swabbed the oil carefully on the burns. Wolf didn't look tough. He looked miserable. Defeated. "Where's Miguel?" Wolf's trusting eyes looking up at her. "Don't know, do you. Or you do know. This stupid war!"

Wayne wandered over to have a look. "Amazing dog. Sure knows who his friends are."

Carnero followed, not understanding the conversation but aware of the feelings the others had for his arch enemy. "That dog will get very sick, like your friends," he said in Spanish. "He needs antibiotics too."

"Yes, we know," said Renée. "But we can't get to the hospital."

"Send the dog," he said.

"What?"

"Send the dog before he gets too sick."

"He's in bad shape!"

"He got here. He could get to the villa," stated Carnero. "Look, this cursed dog's very smart. I trained him to deliver messages and carry things. Send a message to the villa."

"Do you think it would work?"

"How should I know? I'm just his trainer. Was, until the little thief turned traitor and joined Castro."

"Benny," said Renée, "how much antibiotics do we need?"

"Half a dozen vials at least, I think. Make it a dozen."

"Talk to Wolf. Make him understand," she said to Carnero.

Carnero approached Wolf and leaned down as close as he dared. Wolf bared his teeth. "Listen, Marlon Brando, you ungrateful, ugly little dog. You and me go way back. I was good to you...better than you deserved. Now you have a job to do, just like the old days. Remember?" He turned to Renée. "He's listening. Write a note and tie it up in something to put around Marlon's neck."

"Esameralda's scarf." She untied the purple and orange bandana and held it in front of Wolf's nose. "Esameralda. Take this to Esameralda," she said and spread it out on the table. "Benny, write down what you need."

Benny turned to Wayne. "Gimme your cigs." Wayne reluctantly handed over his last pack of Camel cigarettes. Benny ripped open the soft package and dumped out the cigarettes. "As your doctor I advise you to quit smoking. I don't have anything to write with."

Carnero understood and offered a gold plated fountain pen.

"That's a very fine pen," said Benny, turning the Mont Blanc pen over, admiring it's elegance, much the way Major Marti had appraised his Cuban cigar. He pulled the cap, revealing a long, engraved, hand split nib. "This could be a dangerous weapon," Benny said with some irony. Renée caught the double meaning. He wrote down the type and quantity of antibiotics and handed the pen to Renée. She translated and wrote a brief note to Esameralda and gave the pen back to Benny, saying, "A good doctor should always have a good pen." Benny smiled and handed the expensive pen back to Carnero.

"Keep it," he said simply. "I won't be needing such a fine pen."

Renée folded the paper and rolled it into the bandana. She tied the roll around Wolf's neck. "Wolf, take this to Ezy...I don't know if he can make it."

"He can make it," responded Carnero. "I've seen this dog do things a dog should not do, believe me."

"We can't send him out the entrance," Renée said.

"It's dark. Maybe they won't see him."

"Too risky," she said, then remembered Rosa's warning. "The vent!"

"The vent?" asked Carnero. "What's a vent?"

"A hole in the roof. Rosa says it's just large enough for a dog."

"Where's this vent?"

"The small cavern. Carry Wolf. Follow me."

"Okay, dog, I have to pick you up," Carnero said softly. "Marlon, try to think of me as a friend, at least for now. Your pals, Paulo and Maartyn, need the medicine. Okay?" Carnero extended his hand slowly toward Wolf's nose. The dog's lips twitched. Carnero's hand trembled. Wolf's eyes flitted from the hand to Carnero's throat. Carnero touched the scarf. "You must take this to Esameralda at Escobar's villa. Esameralda. Escobar's." Wolf tried to get up but Renée held him.

"I think he understands," she said.

"Marlon understands. The dog hates me but he understands. It's the way we did things. He understands names and places. If I said, El Presidente and Palace, he would run all the way to Habana and hide under Fulgencio's bed. If I said Palace and bomb, Marlon would run all the way to the Palace, ignore El Presidente and search for a bomb, or deliver one. I could send a message to my inside man at Meyer Lansky's and a sum of money would be deposited in a special bank account for El Presidente. We would get a small fee. Who would suspect a miserable looking Sicilian rat dog?"

"We should be going," interrupted Renée.

"Of course, Señorita." Carnero put his hand on Wolf's head. "Okay, Marlon, I'm going to pick you up." He gently gathered Wolf into his arms. Wolf's muzzle passing close to Carnero's neck.

Renée turned off the gas burner.

"Should I go with you?" asked Ramon.

"Not necessary," replied Renée. She took a kerosene lantern

Renée held the lantern low, glancing back to see how Carnero and

Wolf were doing. Wolf was playing limp dog again. "He's accepted you."

"Marlon Brando's just biding his time. I know this dog."

"The shelling has stopped. What does that mean?"

"They won't attack tonight," said Carnero with certainty. "Batista's army does not fight in the dark. More afraid of the spirits than Castro's guerrillas. It only takes one superstitious man to infect a whole regiment. There are plenty of Santerias. With such an army we cannot resist Castro."

"Are you still against the Revolution?"

"I don't know, Señorita. Cuba's worth fighting for but I don't know about this Castro. He might be better than Batista but my life's worth nothing if his Comandantés are running things. I can tell you that Batista plans to leave Cuba but there won't be a place on the plane or money in a Yankee bank for me."

"What happens to his loyal followers?"

"The servants, the go boys, the peasants who do his dirty work while the Batistianos get richer? Castro won't be merciful."

"If there's a way out, will you go?"

"Where would I go?" Wolf began to squirm. "I'm putting Marlon down. He'll be fine." Wolf limped on ahead. "And that woman, Rosameralda Diez. Don't trust her. She's in too deep with Escobar. I know some things. But her boys, they have something to fight for. I've done nothing except kill and steal. That gold pen? I took that from a judge…"

"Careful here."

"…A good man. An old man, defenseless except for his honesty. I beat him. Why? Because he stood up to Batista. I was paid well. Blood money, and I made certain there was plenty of blood."

Renée walked ahead of Carnero, puzzling over his confession and the comment about Rosameralda, tingling with the knowledge that danger was only a pace behind. Carnero was a cold, cynical assassin; the same hands that beat an old man bloody, could close on her throat. Wondering what the philosophers would do with such a situation. A crushing reality of the human condition and she felt helpless to change anything, but was strangely unafraid. Carnero had no reason to harm her, for the cause or for his own selfish existence. From that moment she rejected the Existentialists. The Bohemians. The poets. The intellectuals. She thought about the milling, faceless masses, with no future other than anonymity and submission. She was too much of her father to continue to deny the advantages of power. She had to find a way back to grace.

They arrived at the cavern and began working up the rocks, passing Wolf from hand to hand until they reached the top, just under the roof. The fresh night air coming over the hills from the sea was like warm silk wafting across her sweating face. It was hard to imagine Cuban soldiers pouring gasoline through the opening. "Hand Wolf up."

"Listen, Marlon Brando, it's time to go to work. Esameralda. Escobar's villa. Got that?" Carnero passed Wolf to Renée.

Renée steadied Wolf on a ledge. "Time to go little one. Go on." Wolf looked back once and made a short leap to the next level. He hesitated, as if testing the air. "Go to Esameralda. Go on," Renée prodded. "Go on, little one."

Wolf scrambled to the opening, sending a small avalanche of rocks down over Renée. The dog wiggled through the crack and disappeared gradually into the blackness, like diving into an inverted pool of ink. Renée remained looking up at the stars, breathing the good air. "I don't want to go back." She opened her fatigue jacket, breasts fully exposed to the air and Carnero's gaze. She wasn't thinking. Carnero was.

"Very nice, Frenchie. Very nice." He played with the lantern, making the shadows shift and move, toying with her. "I could take you now, Señorita."

Renée buttoned the jacket, waiting for the fear to surface or Carnero to make his move. Neither happened. She looked at the man for a moment. "Yes, you could, but raping me wouldn't get you any closer to heaven."

Carnero laughed. "Heaven?...I should weep."

When Christian woke Renée was gone. Perhaps it was the absence of comforting kitchen sounds or his spiritual need to have her near. "Where's Renée?" he asked no one in particular. "Renée?..." He sat up seeing first Maartyn attached to the plasma bag, then Benny and Paulo and finally Ramon, sitting at the table with Wayne 'Camilo' Rezniki, who was looking back at him grinning. "Who are you?" Christian asked in Spanish, then in English.

"Me? I'm Comandanté Camilo Ceinfuegos. The trusted lieutenant of this moron who thinks he's Fidel Castro," Wayne answered.

"Then who are you?" Christian asked Ramon.

Ramon got up, slowly unfolding his long body, and sauntered over to Christian, peering down condescendingly. "Ramon. The name's Ramon Augustine. I'm going to marry your girlfriend."

Christian could smell the rum breath. "Oh, really? How long have I been asleep?"

Ramon snickered, thinking that Christian was making a joke. "This time? An hour or so."

"You work fast."

"Thank you. You should try staying awake."

"Where's Renée?"

"She's gone, with that Carnero person."

"Jesus Christ!"

"I've been Him too. Philadelphia. Easter pageant. They had me hanging on this goddamned cross for six hours."

Christian tried to stand up. "Bathroom."

"Latrines." Ramon held Christian's arm to steady him. "You're in the army now. Over that a way."

"Thanks. What day is it?"

"Christmas Day."

"Christmas!? I'm...Jesus!" He felt light headed.

"You too? Happy birthday."

Maartyn moaned and lashed out at some demon in his dream. "Is he all right?" Christian asked.

"Give a little, get a little. He's coming along. Benny pumped him up. How about you?"

"I don't know. Woozy. Right now I need to go."

"You don't mind if I don't hold your hand? I signed on to be President of Cuba. For nursing services see Benny."

"Who's Benny?"

"The Hebe with his finger in your buddy's knee."

"Oh, God," Christian sighed. "I'll figure this out later." Christian negotiated his way toward the place Ramon indicated. Ramon returned to the table and poured a glass of rum.

Renée entered the cavern followed by Carnero. Ramon jumped to his feet. "'Teenchun! Hey, everybody up. It's the Comandanté."

"Cut it out, Ramon." She noticed the empty cot. "Where's Christian?"

"AWOL, mam. Away without leave. Over the top. I sent out a search and recover patrol with orders to shoot him on sight."

"Ramon, stop it!"

"Aye, sir...Mam."

"Christian? There you are. Are you all right?"

Christian reentered the circle of lantern light. "Who are all these people?"

"Sit down, Cheri." She helped Christian back to his bunk. He sat down, studying Ramon myopically. "Ramon Augustine, from New York. He's playing Fidel Castro," she explained, like a patient parent.

Ramon waved. "We've met, darling."

"That's Wayne Rose...something."

"Rozniki?"

"Wayne Rozniki. He's Camilo Cienfuegos. And that's Benny Lerner from California. He's Ché Guevara."

"I can see that, but why?"

"Escobar plans to continue the revolution even if one or all the leaders are killed."

"So, that's why the big lecture about Churchills. But, what are they doing here?"

"We were supposed to send them on to Havana, unfortunately the army's surrounded the mountain. You might as well know, Christian. We're trapped. Rosameralda's fighters are holding off tanks and things. In simple terms, Cheri, we could all die."

"Great." Christian looked at the walls of the cavern. "It's worse than I thought. What are we supposed to do?"

"Have Christmas dinner."

"Christmas dinner in a cave. Wonderful," he said sarcastically.

"Good. You're getting your sense of humour back. And, I have a surprise." Renée held up a bottle of wine, the Château Bouscaut. "A good Bordeaux, with a distinguished pedigree."

"At a time like this?"

"If we have to die we might as well go with a bottle of the best French wine. My father's brother owns the Château. It's the most beautiful château in Bordeaux."

"Of course it is."

"Don't be rude. I can't help it." Renée handed the bottle to Christian. She lit the gas flame and set the cubed Spam to fry, then opened cans of black beans. "Would you open the wine please? The Bouscaut's only a '52. It'll want to breathe. The Riscal also. Let's see. There's twenty of us for dinner. Better open six of each. Oh dear, we don't have glasses. We'll just drink from the bottle. Mommy would feint."

"Horrors." Christian used the blade of his utility knife to cut the foil.

Ramon and Wayne carried the rest of the wine to Christian's bunk. "Want I should do that, little fella?" asked Ramon, holding a bottle of Bouscaut up to the lantern.

"No, thanks."

"A Fifty-two Bouscaut. Throws a nice sediment. Worth about sixty-five bucks a bottle, American, in a good restaurant," said Ramon.

"Expensive dinner." Christian inserted the auger and handed it to Ramon.

Ramon pulled the cork effortlessly and offered the purple-stained cork to Christian. "Sir?"

"You don't do that. It's vulgar and silly," said Christian, taking the bottle and glaring at Carnero as he inhaled the strong essence. "It's not ready." He passed it to Ramon. Ramon tasted the wine and passed the bottle to Wayne. "He's right. Needs time. What do you think?" Wayne took a big mouthful and had trouble swallowing. "Not quite ready, is it?" Wayne shook his head, eyes watering. "Better open all the bottles and let them breath," said Ramon, gesturing limply. "But it does have interesting hints of black cherry and cat urine. Voluminous without being pretentious." He handed the bottle back to Christian.

"Subtle nose, with a touch of petrol, or barnyard and licorice," Christian said, rising to the challenge. He ventured a sip. "Ahhh, dry, full bodied, bit harsh, but with much promise. Should still drink well in about ten years." Another sip, he held the bottle against his lips. Carnero was watching. "I detect overtones of oak and an edge of tannin, and yes, a definite burden of barnyard. It may smooth out to butterscotch given air. But it lacks a certain Cuban touch." He offered the bottle to Carnero.

"Ah, why did you do that?" asked Ramon.

Carnero had not followed the English but there was no mistaking the intent. He accepted the bottle without taking his eyes from Christian's. Christian suddenly grabbed the pistol from Renée's holster and pointed it at Carnero. It took everyone by surprise.

Renée reacted first. "Christian!?"

"Just a game, Renée. A little game that Señor Carnero and I like to play when we get together for a drink. Eh, Yolando? My turn."

Carnero grinned. Christian hadn't pulled the slide to arm the pistol.

"What are they doing?" asked Ramon.

"I don't know," answered Renée. She looked at Christian. "What are you doing?"

"Did I spit in the bottle, Carnero?"

Carnero addressed the bottle, grinning. Defiant. Christian pulled the slide the way he had seen Rosameralda chamber a bullet. The bullet slid smoothly into the chamber. Carnero's grin faded. Tiny beads of sweat began to build on his forehead. Christian stood up, unsteady, but that only made him more dangerous. He shuffled toward Carnero until the gun was a few inches from his face. "How do you like that, eh, Yolando!? A gun looks different from that end, eh?" Christian was shaking badly and had to hold the heavy gun with both hands.

Carnero faked a grin. "All right, my friend. I'll drink. Please, be easy. Very easy. Look, I'm taking a drink."

"Christian?"

"I know what I'm doing. This guy put me through some bad moments, yesterday. And this might be Christmas Day so I'm sharing a drink with my good friend, Yolando."

"This isn't like you."

"No, you're right, Renée. This isn't me. None of this is me. I'm not even here. I never came to Cuba. I'm still in a hospital in Chicago and you're all just wicked dreams. So what have I got to lose in this nightmare? You know?...dreaming...when you pull the trigger the gun just melts, or the bullets roll out on the floor, or they fly out and snap back, or the gun goes limp like a failed erection. They say it all has to do with libido and not being able to get it right. So why don't I just pull the trigger and see if I wake up?"

"Hey, Chris!..." Maartyn was sitting up. "Chris, ol' buddy, give me the gun. I'll shoot'im for ya."

"No, Christian. I definitely think you should shoot him yourself," said Paulo. "Good experience."

"What do you think, Ramon?" asked Christian.

"Would you stop this!" demanded Renée.

"I think you're all nuts," answered Ramon. "What do you think, Wayne?"

"Definitely nuts. Too long in Cuba, I'd say. The damp air. The cigars. Too much rum. What do you think, Benny?"

"Tough question. I'm new to this compassion for my fellow man gig. But, I'd have to say that Christian probably should *not* shoot Mr. Carnero, unless there is just cause."

"Is there just cause?" asked Ramon.

"Oh yes. There definitely is just cause. Justo causo, eh Carnero? This hombre goobed in my last bottle of wine then stuck a gun in my face and tried to make me drink it."

"Oh, that's so sick!" said Wayne, with exaggerated disgust.

"Was it good wine?" asked Ramon, trying to keep it light.

"You *are* all crazy," said Renée.

"Yes, it was good wine. Not a great wine like a Laffite or a Bouscaut. Just a good Spanish red. Not in the same class as a superb

Bordeaux, but it had character. And it *was* the last bottle."

"Then y'all should definitely shoot the fucker!" said Maartyn with delight.

"Yeah, shoot his balls off first!" giggled Wayne.

"Please shoot to kill!" pleaded Benny. "I don't want any more wounded."

The young rebels gathered around, mystified by the antics of the Gringos. They had no sympathy for Carnero so they began to shout too. The scene grew ugly. Taunts. Gestures. Then Christian started to laugh. "Okay, I'm going to shoot him now. Take another drink, Amigo!" The gun wavered badly.

"Wait! Let's all drink to the execution." Ramon began opening bottles. Carnero was still in a fog about the conversation but there was no doubt about the tone. The mob pressed closer. Christian continued to laugh, stumbling around, waving the pistol. Wayne and Benny held him up. Renée gave up trying to reason with them and retreated behind the supplies. Ramon opened bottles as fast as he could and passed them around. The Cuban boys shook their heads. Wine wasn't part of their upbringing. Fidel forbid it and they didn't want to go crazy like the Gringos.

"Here's to whatever it is that pissed Chris off!" said Ramon. Bottles shot into the air. "Salut! Skol! Cheers!" They drank.

"To pissin' Chris off!" shouted Maartyn. They drank again.

"To the Cuban Revolution!" said Wayne. They drank.

"To Fidel Castro, Maximo Lider," shouted Ramon. "My mentor and my future. If he's a good boy I'll let him play me sometime!" They drank.

"Hey, Carnero!" Christian said, steadying the gun on Carnero's face. "It's Christmas, man. Feliz Navidad."

"Feliz Navidad, Señor," he replied, meekly.

"Hey, that's right!" said Ramon. "Buone Feste Natalizie. I drink to the bambino."

"I know that one. Ah, Greek, isn't it?"

"Italian, you moron!"

"To morons!" They drank.

"I know one," said Maartyn. "Boas Festas," he said in his Louisiana dialect.

"What language is that?" asked Benny.

"Portuguese. My ol' man used to go aroun' huggin' an' kissin' everyone. Even the niggers got Boas Festased!"

"Boas Festas? Oh, that's good, but listen to this!" said Paulo. "Noeliniz Ve Yeni Y iliniz Kutlu Olsun. Try that one."

"What the fuck was that, man!?" roared Maartyn.

"Turkish. Probably means, *Seasons Greetings you stupid Americans.* I spent a Christmas in a Turkish jail. It was like this cave only the food was better."

They all laughed, even Carnero. Anything to delay his own execution.

Christian said seriously, "Did you know that St. Nicolas, better known as Santa Claus, was a Turk?"

"What!?" exclaimed Ramon. "Get out! St. Nicolas's Italian."

"No, he was Turkish. The Turks call him Noel Baba. He gave money to the poor. There's a church in Myra dedicated Noel Baba. And Ramon, you might be interested to know that Italians stole the remains of Noel Baba and built a church called San Nicola di Bari. That's your Italian connection. Thieves and grave robbers. The Mafia had a religious beginning." Wayne and Benny laughed at Ramon who made a face. "And, if Paulo had spent time learning something about his hosts he'd know the customs and legends about St. Nicholas. Here's to a Turkish Santa Claus!"

They didn't believe him but toasted the Turkish version anyway. Christian traced the spread of St. Nicholas throughout Byzantium, Europe and Russia to the New World, toasting each progression. Bottles passed. And when a bottle was empty another took its place. The Spanish Riscal was broached.

Renée rescued the last bottle of Château Bouscaut and sat behind the supplies on a hand grenade crate. Drinking alone, resigned to let the boys do moronic male things. She hoped that Carnero would not be shot, but didn't really care one way or another. Listened to the silly chatter and the uproar, biding her time.

"Wait! Wait..." said Christian. "We can't forget Ernesto Escobar who died for our sins on Nochebuena."

"What was that Easter? Good Friday?..."

"Okay. I wasn't there. But here's to Escobar...sorry Paulo...the man to whom we owe our deepest gratitude for allowing us to be a part of this great big show, this three ring circus called the Cuban Revolution!"

"To Ernesto's circus!" shouted Ramon.

"To the Revolving Revolting Revolution!" said Benny.

"Hey, Benny! How do you say Merry Christmas in Hebrew?"

"Merry Money, you ass!" screamed Ramon.

Benny tossed a bloody bandage at Ramon. "You're all first class dick-heads and Santa Claus should bring you painfully swollen hemorrhoids so I could treat them with chili peppers!"

The laughter was explosive, manic, heard at the entrance to the caves and down the mountain. The major of the army force surrounding the mountain passed the word to his troops to be alert. The Santeria rebels were obviously invoking the spirits, working up to a murderous rage. A suicide attack possibly. Rosameralda sent two fighters back to the cavern to see what the uproar was about.

Christian waved his bottle. "Wait, wait. I've got another one. You'll never get this. Nodlaig mhait chugnat." Christian waited for a response.

"That doesn't even sound like a language," said Ramon.

"You made that up!"

"No, no. I swear. It means Merry Christmas."

"Is it Yiddish?"

"No! What am I?"

"A flamin' Canuck from Mooseland!" said Maartyn, taking a large mouthful of Spanish red, which dribbled from the corners of his mouth and mingled with the bloody bandages.

Christian pretended to be annoyed. "No, you idiots. Nodlaig mhait chugnat. It's Irish. Gaelic."

"I thought Irish were little green people with funny shoes."

The two rebel fighters sent by Rosameralda were red-eyed and fatigued from the shelling. "Señorita, Comandanté?" one addressed Renée politely.

"Yes? Who are you?"

"Manuel and Carlos," said Manuel. "Comandanté Diez sent us to ask what the commotion is about. Are you having a problem?"

Renée looked very tired and unhappy, nursing a bottle of wine like the bag lady in a dusty alley. "No. The children are just celebrating Christmas." The sarcasm was overdone and went over their heads.

"Christmas!?" exclaimed Carlos. "Santa Maria. We'd forgotten."

"What's happening outside?" she asked, offering the young man a drink.

"Thank you, Señorita, no. Outside is quiet. The army's lying low."

"Did you see the boy, Miguel?"

"Miguelito? We saw him just before dark. He ran down the hill toward the tanks. Then we didn't see him any more. Then we saw his little dog chasing two soldiers around a tree. It was very funny. But I think the dog is burned to death."

"No, Wolf's all right. We're okay here. Tell Rosa, Comandanté Diez, not to worry. See those two big pots. Christmas dinner. Take them with you. And there's chocolate bars in that box."

"Many thanks, Señorita. Feliz Navidad."

"Joyeux Noël," she replied, without enthusiasm. The young men stuffed their pockets with chocolate bars, took the heavy pots and returned to the entrance. Renée leaned back against the boxes, sipping wine, caring less and less about the battle, the revolution...

"Merry Christmas," Ramon said, sitting down beside her.

"Vesele Vanoce," she replied.

"Vesele Vanoce? Never heard that one."

"Bohemian salutation. The real Bohemians. Bohemia? The area in Europe, not the condition of one's mind or wardrobe."

"You're in a mood, Princess."

"If I ever get out of here I'm going straight to New York and the nearest Hilton, order room service and shower for a whole day. Then sleep for twelve hours. A Turkish steam bath the next day. And a full body massage. On the fourth day I'm going to eat my way down Fifth Avenue. Then I'm going to shop my way back up until the French national debt's in crisis. On the sixth day I'm going home."

"What? Without giving me a phone call?"

"I might call, then I'm going to get on a diplomatic flight out of La Guardia, drink Champagne and eat caviar in first class, and when we land in Paris I'm going beg my family to forgive me."

"Forgive you for what? Being headstrong? An error in judgment only. Haven't you heard? The young are allowed a couple. I'm up to half a dozen and my family are always glad to see me. My current error in judgment is leaving Harvard Law School to be an actor, after my father practically mortgaged the business to pay my tuition...not only that, I asked him for the money for acting school. His restraint was monumental. He should get an Oscar, or at least a sainthood."

"Are you a good actor?"

"Not very."

"Then why are you doing it?"

"Someone told me I couldn't."

"Yes, I understand that method of making decisions."

"You said, we, before."

"Pardon? What about, we?"

"You said, when *we* land in Paris. Am I going with you?"

Renée looked sideways at Ramon. Their eyes focused through the pleasant distortion caused by the good wine.

The cave dwellers were somnolent, content to lounge quietly, smoking, waiting for dawn. Renée slept sitting on the hand grenade crate with her head on Ramon's shoulder, cradling the bottle of Bouscaut, whose memories were stronger than just a good Bordeaux. She spent glorious autumn days as a child skipping through vineyards in the way of the pickers, wandering the great rooms of the Château and playing hide and seek between the oak barrels in the dark, damp chai, with the wine master's children. Those were happier memories of dark places, when the stories were of ancient ghosts and things that rattled only in the imagination of a child. She was longing for a return to a happier childhood that she knew only in brief sojourns in other people's castles, planning her return to Paris and the society she had rejected for the lure of Bohemia. Freedom, like everything, has it's price and she found the price too high. She was dreaming about the crumbling elegance of Château Bouscaut and the tower, going around and around the winding staircase, descending dizzily to the chai. The chai, the cellar, bodega. Rebellion in Bogotá. Chai, like Ché, Comandanté Guevara, the rebel doctor marching to Los Espiritos to save Christian...She felt the wet nose on her cheek. She thought it was Ramon.

December 26. Dawn. *I don't remember much about that morning but Renée and Miguel filled me in the next day...It was almost unbelievable, but here goes...*

"Ramon?...Wolf!"

The dog had a small package in a nylon stocking tied around his neck. Barely able to stand. Spots of blood on the dirt floor from his shredded pads.

"Poor Wolf," she said, hugging the little wreck. She removed the stocking roll and put down a bowl of water. Wolf lapped a few drops, too tired to bother. He lay down and put his head between his paws, gave a deep sigh and went to sleep. Renée covered him with a blanket and tucked it under, trying to avoid the burns. Wolf was too far gone to care. He had fought the battle in his own way, to the limit.

Renée untied the stocking. Inside, wrapped in cotton bandages, were the twelve vials of antibiotics, and a piece of paper. A barely legible note of sorts from Esameralda. *'Ren...Dog come. Good. God look after. Love, eternity, Esa.'* Renée's throat tightened. Esameralda was almost illiterate. Of course, what chance did she have to go to school? A prostitute by age twelve. Below Esameralda's childish scrawl was a

314

short note from Juanita. *'Esa ask me to write. We are fine. Army threaten to kill us if we help you. Said they killed most of you, so not until Pietro arrive did we think you are alive. It be nightmare here but this day doctor arrive from Pinar with more med. We fine now and hope you too. Don't let them kill you and when dog is better send word. Love...Juanita.'*

"Benny..." Renée shook Benny by the shoulder. The good doctor had passed out on Paulo's cot with Paulo's arms around him. Paulo opened his eyes. "He's very tired. He needs to sleep."

"Wolf's back with the antibiotics."

Benny pulled himself together and administered the antibiotics to Paulo, Maartyn and Wolf, hands no longer trembling. No nausea when the needles penetrated flesh, remembering things he had learned in medical school. Feeling the rush, the epiphany, the blinding light of discovery and the clear picture of what lay ahead.

Paulo slept. Maartyn rallied and got up to go to the bathroom, stopping to cover Renée who was asleep on Ramon's cot. Ramon had gone for a walk to the cave entrance, to watch the dawn and get the news broadcast from Rebel Radio. Christian sat on the edge of his cot, reading over the note from Esameralda, watching Renée sleeping, sensing that he was losing her. The feeling was a sickening ache, deep in his body, creeping slowly up toward his heart. Too late.

The drone of a large airplane could be heard in the distance but Wayne, Carnero and the young rebel boys slept on, until the bomb crashed into the entrance of the cave. Lieutenant Fuentes was blown apart where he stood. Five of his men were killed. Two of Rosameralda's lookouts died instantly and several were wounded. The Cuban Air Force B-26 that delivered the deadly bomb came out of the rising sun over the tobacco fields, engines idling. A flame thrower on the ground below the cave, acting as a pathfinder. It may have been a lucky drop but the bomb's accuracy was devastating. The machine guns in the nose of the plane strafing the hillside, cutting down more mountain rebels where they slept. The death plane peeled away and was gone before the rebels could return fire. It was Batista's last victory.

Ramon was in shock when he reappeared in the cavern with a wounded boy in his arms. The carried the dead and wounded, shuttling back and forth while Renée and Benny administered emergency aid. The young rebel guards were sent to the entrance to replace the casualties, rejoicing at the chance to take their places on the front line for Cuba.

The army poured everything they had at the cave entrance, wounding more rebels trying to rescue their comrades. There was a continual shuttle of torn bodies to the cavern field hospital.

Conversation in the cave was limited. Stop bleeding. Stitch up the worst wounds. Ease pain. They were out of Type O Negative and only the Special Force troops and army personnel wore dog tags. Benny assessed and guessed. When the cots were filled the new wounded were put on tables, or crates, then the dirt floor. The dead were shunted to the latrine area. Medical supplies were used up. Morphine rationed. Only the most severe traumas were treated with other than the basics. By noon Benny had completed two years of internship at street level medical school and was qualified to man the emergency ward of any inner city hospital.

At mid day there was a lull in the fighting. Both sides exhausted in the stinking, smoking heat, but there was little rest. The walking wounded were patched up and sent back to the front. The army dug in below and waited for orders.

The army launched another heavy barrage in mid afternoon. This time using mortars, as well as the tanks. Shells arched with deadly accuracy into the entrance driving the rebels further back into the cave where they couldn't return fire. The army major, sensing the advantage, ordered a ground assault. It was a foolish manoeuvre, born of need for a victory or his own ego. The opportunity was for himself in the eyes of General Batista. The barrage was suspended while the soldiers scrambled up the loose talus slope. In the lull Rosameralda ordered her rebels back to the entrance of the cave to prepare for the attack.

The first platoon, tired from a night of tension and breathless from the climb, were ordered to charge the cave without a rest. Young, scared and uncommitted, worse, untrained for close combat, they were perfectly silhouetted against the glowing Cuban sky. The rebels were only dim shadows behind boulders and in dark places. The first wave was slaughtered on the apron of the cave. The second wave made it into the opening and were cut down by point blank volleys and hand to hand combat with knives and bayonets. The survivors of Fuentes' Special Force and the determined young guerrillas fought like demons. There was no third wave. A few soldiers fled back down the slope leaving weapons and helmets behind. The younger rebels, only teenage boys themselves, called after them, "Casquito! Casquito! Little helmet. Go on back to mamma, darlings!..."

316

More bleeding bodies were carried into the cavern. Rebels and army. It didn't matter. They were Cubans. The war was over for them. It remained for Benny and Renée to save as many as possible.

Rosameralda was sure the army would not attack again that day. She regrouped the strongest of her dwindling force safely inside the entrance and tried to sleep sitting against a rock.

Renée organized the walking wounded to serve meals. Rice, chocolate bars and cold canned beans. Hot coffee was consumed by the gallon. Christian, Ramon, Wayne and Carnero drank their coffee and ate canned beans on the run, their heads still pounding, regretting the Christmas bash. Maartyn and Paulo dished rice and poured coffee while Renée divided her time between kitchen and clinic. The cavern was almost full and resembled a London subway or a Berlin train station during the War. It was only a very small Cuban war, but the faces were the same.

"We'll run out of water soon," Renée reported to Rosameralda.

The activity level in the crowded cavern was chaotic, so when Miguel and his prisoner, Jésus, entered from the inside of the mountain no one noticed, except Wolf. But Wolf was too exhausted to do more than just wag his tail. Renée noticed the familiar greeting as she passed Christian's bunk where Wolf convalesced. "Miguel!..."

Miguel was dirty and tired but beaming. "Señorita, Renée, you don't know how glad I am to see you. And there's Pietro! You little bandit, what have they done to you?"

"Wolf's had a very difficult day. And so have you." Renée checked Miguel for injuries and then hugged him again. "Miguel, you had us worried."

"I'm very fast on my feet, even though this traitor has slowed me down."

"Who's this?"

A small boy Miguel's age, face distorted and puffy, was standing meekly in Miguel's shadow."

"Jésus González, the traitor, who I have taught a lesson. He's only lucky I didn't kill him. The fighting was bad?"

"We have twelve dead. Your friend Cesare, and more than twenty wounded. Seven army soldiers wounded. Just boys. They also have many dead.

"Cesare's, my cousin. He's been like a brother." Miguel scuffed the dirt floor. "There's also more dead and wounded up on the hills," said Miguel, "but we can do nothing for them. And Rosa?"

"Rosa's okay. She's with the fighters at the entrance."

Christian was on his way to the latrines with a pot. "Miguel! Thank God. We heard you attacked the tanks all by yourself."

"Just one. I got this little traitor for my efforts." He pushed Jésus forward. In the light the damage to the terrified boy was more obvious. Miguel had given Jésus a good beating.

"Miguel," said Renée, shaking her head with fatigue, "where did you come from just now?"

"Juanita's tunnel."

"Juanita's!?"

"Yes. The part that collapsed is mostly dirt. The fire burned the supports. We've been digging for hours. This little traitor has atoned for his sins. I told him, either he works or dies. He dug like a dog. But we must get everyone out of here soon. Jésus says they're going to pour in gasoline."

"We know," said Renée, abstractly, not willing to accept the vision.

"Can we get out through Juanita's tunnel?" asked Christian.

"It will be a tight thing, but we can do it."

"Then what do we do with the wounded?" asked Renée.

"We can take them to the Hospital along the beach. No one's watching the village."

"Shouldn't we wait for dark?"

"No, Señorita. The army could find the hole any time."

"Go to Rosa. Tell her we need as many boys as she can spare." "Okay. But be fast. If the army pours the gas...Juanita's tunnel is also down the hill."

"I know. Go."

Miguel raced for the entrance. Jésus, forgotten, looked for a place to hide. Renée and Christian had no time to comfort him. "Christian, tell everybody we have a way out. I'll talk to Benny."

Benny was exhausted, almost out on his feet. "Leaving? Now?" asked Benny. "Some of these boys'll die if they're moved."

"Benny, they'll die if we stay."

"What if we just surrender?"

The simple logic stopped Renée cold. "Surrender? The thought never occurred to any of us. Rosa told me a story about Moncada. The attack went wrong from the start and most surrendered. They killed almost all the rebels in their cells. Do you think the army would hesitate to kill these rebels, including you and I?"

Ramon overheard the conversation. "She's right Benny. But it was the police who did the deed. Carnero's buddies. We should have let Christian shoot him." He looked at Carnero who'd been listening to the conversation. Carnero just shrugged and turned away.

"Oh, God. This is awful. We'll lose some, I know it," lamented Benny.

"We'll lose them all, if we don't go now."

"Okay. Least wounded must help the worst cases."

Preparations to evacuate were slowed by great confusion and language problems. Rumours of the gasoline plot spread quickly. The cavern was a tense mass of frightened people, moving about in the semi darkness. There was talk of surrender. There were denunciations and accusations. Jésus González crept into a dark place and remained out of sight. Rosameralda returned to the cavern with Miguel and called Christian, Renée and Maartyn aside. She addressed Christian coldly. "Ask Maartyn what condition the boat's in."

"The boat?" He gestured with his arms, large boat. She nodded gravely. Christian turned to Maartyn. "Rosa wants to know about Santoz' boat."

Maartyn looked at Rosameralda. He knew what she was thinking. "The boat's okay, if the Cubans haven't got to'er. She's pretty well shot up but the important things were workin'.."

Christian translated for Rosameralda.

"Good," she said. "You'll leave for Habana tonight."

"Havana?" asked Christian, surprised. "We could go to Florida and get clear of all this. What if Fidel loses? Batista's going to be some pissed about this mess."

"The Revolution's not over! It's our duty to deliver the actors to Habana. Ernesto was specific. The army has the roads blocked and it would take too long to cross the mountains. Get them to Habana by the 28th!"

Maartyn understood what Rosameralda was saying by the passion of her speech. "Sounds good to me. I'll do whatever it takes to kick ol' Batista's butt!"

"Maartyn," said Christian dryly, "I recall, like it was only yesterday, you had a different opinion about who should kick whose butt."

"Yeah, well, y'all weren't givin' me the straight story here."

"You mean you hadn't met Rosa."

Maartyn looked at Rosameralda who was preoccupied by the scene of death, dying and escape. Renée became impatient. "Rosa, we can take the wounded on the boat."

She turned on Renée as if she was a lowly recruit. "No boat. Miguel assures me that you can get them to the hospital. We're wasting time talking. I'll send some boys to help."

"Aren't you coming?"

"We'll occupy the army."

"Please be careful."

Rosa was a distant stranger. "Make every person carry a rifle and ammunition. No exceptions. Ernesto, and Fidel, are very clear. A rebel fighter is of no use without his weapon."

"Rosa..." Renée would have embraced her friend but Rosameralda turned away. Renée had no time to contemplate the rejection. They were all under stress. The grim business of preparing to transport the injured had taxed everyone's strength and the extra weight of rifles, ammunition and hand grenades would make the task even more difficult.

Rosameralda picked up an ammunition belt and said to Miguel, "Miguelito, get them to Juanita's!" And she was gone.

Miguel would lead the way to Juanita's tunnel with a lantern in one hand and a chocolate bar in the other. A rifle and ammunition belt slung over his narrow shoulders.

The first group, the mobile wounded unable to carry cots, followed Miguel, after a fashion, stumbling up the slope. Monstrous shadows of the lurching, halting procession were cast on the cave walls by flickering lanterns. And as the lantern lights withdrew the morale of those waiting to go ebbed with their strength. Fear was another burden. The army meant to burn them alive. They would be helpless and vulnerable shuffling through the darkness toward the small cavern. How would the spark happen that touched off the conflagration? The slow exodus became a test of courage as well as endurance. The temptation to run was intense.

The fire fight began again at the east entrance and the pace of evacuation quickened. Renée emptied her knapsack and stuffed in medical supplies. "Has anyone seen the boy, Jésus?..." she asked in English and Spanish. No one answered. Benny picked up a case of plasma. "Okay, nurse," he said to Renée, "let's go."

"Benny, you have to carry a rifle at least, orders."

"No way. Medical stuff, that's me."

"Come on, Renée," urged Ramon. Ramon and Wayne carried a cot with a boy who was badly torn up by the first bomb. Paulo, rifle and ammunition weighing him down, held a bag of plasma and limped along beside the cot. Beside the small boy lay Wolf, unconcerned about the commotion. Content to be carried. They fell in at the end of the line.

Renée slung a rifle over her shoulder and gathered up her knapsack. She was leaving everything behind, except for her precious French passport with the United Nations diplomatic stamp, a hair brush and a tube of lipstick. It was as if she was abandoning a lifetime in a tomb for the archeologists. Artifacts of a Bohemian life-form recently extinct. She also carried a lantern and a case of morphine. She took a last look around the chaos of the cavern; the open crates, weapons, food, bloody bandages, the empty bottles, the discards, the dead. Then she noticed Christian talking to Carnero. Carnero was sitting on a supply case, cradling a wine bottle, shaking his head.

"Christian! Time to go," she called.

"He won't leave."

"We must go, now, Cheri. Let that man decide his own fate." Renée followed Ramon to the tunnel.

Christian watched the dim form of Renée fading into the shadows. He felt the deep ache rising. He was a ship adrift again on a black ocean. The last lantern that was sitting on the stack of supplies, a dim lighthouse on a dangerous coast.

"Carnero...Come on, man! We've got to go."

"You want to drink with me, Amigo? I didn't spit in it this time."

"No, thanks...look...you know what's going to happen."

"Yes. The war will end and then the real bloodshed will begin."

"You can get away on the boat. Just like you wanted."

"To Habana? No friends there," he said sadly. "I'll stay here and get drunk. You can shoot me if you want. I have no life. I have no boots. But, I wish I had one good cigar."

"Wait..." Christian opened the guitar case. "Here."

"Ahh, Cohiba!...very good! Thank you. I wonder if Batista will smoke a good cigar when they come for him?" Carnero found matches in his pocket. The same brand of Liberdads that Marti used.

"The Cohiba," said Christian, "is a gift from Major Marti, but I wouldn't light it now. The gasoline?"

Carnero shrugged. "Marti!? You know him too?"

"We met. A good man, the Major."

"Yes. A good man." Carnero studied the cigar, regretting his own life of brutality. "Go, Christian Joyce. Good luck. By the way...I'm sorry about the...you know? The horn."

"It's okay. Listen, I have running shoes."

"No, no. Thank you. Go...I have my bootless future to look forward to."

Christian shouldered his heavy knapsack and a rifle. He too had crammed his pack with ammunition, like a good revolutionary. He picked up the heavy canvas bag. The Joe Louis' discarded for hand grenades. Behind him he heard the match flare. The bright light competed with the lantern momentarily. Carnero puffed on the cigar. Christian could smell the fine aroma but didn't look back. "What a strange man," he said. He picked up the guitar and followed Renée's lantern light. Renée, the lady of the lamp, he thought, hurrying to catch up, leaving Carnero to face his own version of eternity.

The sounds of the gun battle diminished as he made his way up the slope, along the black tunnel, eyes focused on the light ahead. He didn't notice Jésus still cowering in the dark place near the tunnel entrance. On the mountain side Cuban soldiers struggled to pass jerry cans of gasoline. A human chain, like stranded motorists, intent on filling a bottomless tank. Christian could smell the gas fumes as he reached the junction that led down to Juanita's Cantina. It would take many gallons to create a proper inferno. Rosameralda and her rebels had to escape the same way, he realized with a rush of fear, not for himself.

It was late afternoon when Miguel reached the end of the small tunnel behind the ruins of Juanita's Cantina, but too long to wait for dark. Too necessary to get the wounded to the hospital and proper care. It was also obvious that the cots would not fit through the long, narrow tunnel. The stench of gasoline fumes was filling the cavern system. "Leave the cots," ordered Miguel.

The wounded were dragged to freedom, blinking into the sun sliding towards the Gulf of Mexico. Christian caught up to Renée at the junction and they were together when the last of the wounded reached safety. Miguel worked his way back through the ruins of the Cantina to crouch beside Christian and Renée under a twisted section of tin roof. The refugees were strung out along the bottom of the slope, hidden by the charred remains of Juanita's many enterprises. Benny went from group to group checking bandages and plasma bags, giving instructions to the helpers, mostly through sign language, but Benny was very good at mime.

"Are you the last out?" asked Miguel.

"No, there's Rosameralda and her group."

"Santa Maria!"

322

"She can't come that way!" said Renée.

"...And Carnero," added Christian.

"Where's Jésus?" asked Miguel.

"I thought he came out with you?"

"No, Señorita. Jésus'...too scared I think. He's bad, that one, but he's my friend."

"I'll go," said Christian. "You're needed here. Jésus might run away if he sees you." It wasn't what Christian meant to say. The whole episode of the battle for Los Espiritos had passed over his head. He had a gut wrenching fear of the gasoline inferno but the fear wasn't as strong as other feelings. "I was the last person out. I should have searched for stragglers." He crawled back into the tunnel before Renée could object.

The first part of the return journey was accomplished in semi-darkness, feeling his way along the metal cots, some sticky with blood, and then the damp walls. Since the tunnel was the main artery for movement between Juanita's and the cavern, the floor was smooth with few surprises. But when he reached the junction, the smell of gasoline had increased and it made his stomach turn and his breathing shallow. He could hear the gasoline trickling over the rocks.

The wider, main tunnel to the cavern was more dangerous because it was necessary to keep to the side. What he feared most was putting his hand on a bat or a snake. There was diffused light from the cavern where the vent opened to the sky but not enough to define loose rocks or outcroppings. Then he could hear shrill voices at the vent. An argument; the rapid Cuban dialect almost incomprehensible to Christian. Ahead he could just make out the weak yellow light in the cavern. The periodic shooting and return fire from the entrance was a distant noise but everything was connected. Then he heard a single shot. Much closer.

As Christian made his way slowly toward the cavern the Cuban army crept through the low brush toward the main cave entrance. Rosameralda and the remainder of Fuentes' force maintained the fire line, advancing to the edge of the cliff, taking shots, then scurrying back before the machine guns could answer. The army established positions to wait for the results of the fire brigade on the mountain, ready to gun down the survivors.

Another group of soldiers, led by a young officer named Gabriel Salvador, who would die alongside Ché Guevara, fighting for Socialist ideals in Bolivia, crept closer to the entrance from above. Between exchanges of fire, Gabriel made a daring run and leapt down to the cave apron, rolling into the cave to sprawl at Rosameralda's feet. The extraordinary feat took the rebels by surprise. No one moved. Gabriel just looked up at Rosameralda and smiled. "Señorita...we have heard of your courage. My men are just up there, behind the bushes. Not much cover if the soldiers see them."

"What do you want?"

A mortar shell arched toward the cave. Experienced soldiers have a sixth sense about trajectories. Can hear the bomb coming and know if it has their number. Rosameralda grabbed Gabriel by the shirt collar and dragged him further into the cave. The explosion threw dust and debris over the rebels. "Thank you," Gabriel said, brushing dirt from his uniform. "My platoon is supposed to be pouring gasoline into the cave. We did pour some and now it's very dangerous. We were ordered to use hand grenades to start the fire. But we couldn't do it, Señorita. We're Cubans. We do not fight that way, against fellow Cubans. We aren't like those Fascists in Germany."

"Won't your officer just send more soldiers?"

"Undoubtedly. The Major badly wants a victory and is willing to kill us all to get it. I left some of my men to guard the hole. But it's only a matter of time."

"You're taking a big risk."

"We can't fight Batista's war."

"How many of you feel this way?"

"Most in my platoon. Maybe half the army here in Pinar del Rio. The rest are loyal to Batista and would die rather than join Castro."

"That means we're still cut off from Habana. We'd have to fight our way there...Is this just a trick?"

"No, Señorita...Are you the Comandanté?"

"Escobar's dead."

"My men are in danger up there."

"You think it's safer in here? You could just walk down the mountain and join your officer."

"Ideologically I cannot. The power of Batista oversteps the bounds of moral authority."

"We can't stand here arguing ideology." Rosameralda sighed. "Okay, tell your men to come in. We'll give them cover."

Rosameralda motioned to her rebels to lay down covering fire. They sent a hail of bullets flying into the army lines. Gabriel signaled for his men. Seven soldiers, minus their weapons, scampered through the brush and dropped into the cave. The rebels retreated to wait for the return fire.

"You didn't bring your weapons," scolded Rosameralda.

"Sorry, we thought we were surrendering."

There was only silence from the army below. Silence more menacing.

Christian felt his way into the cavern. "Jésus González! Are you here?...Jésus!?"

"I'm here," a small, frightened voice said from behind the mound of broken supply cases. Christian took the lantern, working around the scattered crates to find him. Jésus was standing near the body of Yolando Carnero. Carnero was still clutching the wine bottle, and the smouldering cigar, red wine mingling with the blood trickling from a dark hole in the middle of his forehead. Jésus held the pistol in his small, trembling hands. Rosameralda's pistol. The pistol Maartyn coveted. The one she gave to Renée. The one Christian used to threaten Carnero. Carnero must have palmed the gun. "He told me to, Señor."

"You shot him?" Christian took the gun away from the boy. "What do you mean, he told you to!?"

"First he begged me. Then he ordered me. Then he said he would fuck my mother if I didn't do it. That made me angry."

"You sad, disillusioned little bugger." Christian stuck the warm gun into the band of his jeans. "Let's get out of here."

The first part of the return trip was accomplished in silence and without mishap. They were at the junction when Christian again heard the sound of voices at the vent, shouted orders, and the no familiar gurgling sound. The stench of gasoline fumes were almost unbearable. Christian felt the cold gasoline wash over his sandals. "The lantern! I didn't put out the lantern!"

"We're at Juanita's tunnel, Señor."

"Rosameralda. Damnit! I left the lantern for them."

"Go to Juanita's, Señor." Jésus was off on a dead run down the slope to the big cavern. Christian could hear his bare feet splashing in the gasoline. Fear clutched his guts. It was no use going back to the cavern, he reasoned. Carnero was already dead. Rosameralda might be dead. Jésus would redeem himself or die trying. They could all die. He felt his way to Juanita's tunnel, passing the junction to the compound, remembering Renée's curiosity about the trap door in the stone warehouse. "Exciting? Could never have imagined this."

Christian was gasping for breath by the time he crawled out of the tunnel. "You didn't find Jésus?" Renée asked as soon as Christian calmed down.

"He went back...for the lantern."

"The lanterns. Oh, my God! Christian! We were carrying lanterns through the petrol!"

"The fumes...weren't bad enough yet. Probably the dampness, you know? But now."

Miguel slid down the burned over slope sending a cloud of dust and ash over them. "Jésus? You found him?..."

"Yes, but he went back...I left the lantern for Rosa."

Miguel looked disappointed. "I have to go after him. He's my responsibility."

"No! He's not," said Renée.

The boy tried to dodge past Christian. Miguel wasn't as fast as Wolf and Christian pinned him to his own body. Miguel went limp, the old trick, but Christian wasn't buying it. "I was stupid. He's my responsibility," said Christian.

"You're exhausted, Cheri," said Renée. "You'd never make it."

He thrust Miguel at Renée. "Hold on to him!" Christian peeled off his shirt. Maartyn, still holding his plasma bag, heard the commotion.

"Hey, Chris, you dumb fuck! Don't do it!"

"Christian, you can't. Don't...!" Renée pleaded.

"Get to the villa." He scrambled back into the tunnel.

"What's he doin'!?" Maartyn asked.

"Jésus went back to put out a lantern."

"Man, that Chris needs a good shake." Maartyn ripped out the plasma needle and scrambled into the tunnel after Christian.

"Maartyn! No!...Oh, you fools!"

Another dispute broke out among the Cuban soldiers at the vent. Both factions took cover and fired at each other from close range. The sound of bullets ricocheting and whining around the mountainside could be heard by the runners in the tunnel and the medical refugees huddling in the debris of the burned Cantina. They knew it might determine their immediate future.

Christian was used to the cave by now and made good time. Maartyn groped blindly through the fumes, no hope of stopping Christian. He had no plan other than to find his friend.

Rosameralda's fighters, the remnants of Fuentes' platoon, and eight new converts of Gabriel's force, were just entering the cavern when Jésus doused the lantern. The conversation in the dark was confusing and protracted until Jésus finally convinced Gabriel not to light a match. Gasoline was again pouring into the cave and if they were going they had better decide.

"We can't surrender," said Gabriel Salvador. "And if what this boy says is true, my men have been defeated. I'm a dead man in the Cuban army."

"You might die anyway," said Rosameralda.

"Then I'll die fighting," said Gabriel.

"Against your comrades?"

"To die with a gun in my hand is one thing. To burn Cubans alive is another."

"Guns and ammunition boxes. Find them!" ordered Rosameralda.

Someone had a flashlight. Rosameralda and Gabriel stood together as his men crawled about the supplies searching for the long crates with the rifles and the square crates of ammunition or grenades.

"I've found grenades!" said a voice.

"Here's bullets!" rejoiced another.

"What do you suggest?" asked Gabriel.

"Fight our way out when it gets dark."

"We're only a few against a hundred."

"But we're more desperate," Rosameralda said.

"You're right, Comandanté. Fear gives wings to the feint of heart. Terror makes men do the impossible."

"Only men?" she asked.

"Sorry, Señorita. Your boys don't look like guerrillas."

"These men were trained by the Americans." She indicated Fuentes' troops.

"Ah, the famous Special Force that vanished in the mountains."

"They're good fighters. Ernesto says that it's better to be few and be furious."

Christian could hear voices. "Hello? Rosa?...you there?"

"Christian?"

"Yeah. Is Jésus with you?"

"Yes, he's here."

Maartyn also heard the voices. He plunged ahead toward the sounds, cursing obstacles. Then Christian heard Maartyn coming behind him.

"Who's there?" Christian called out. "Give me the flashlight."

"It's me, you moron," Maartyn called. "Who'd y'all think'd be dumb enough?"

"Maartyn, ahh, man...why?"

"Couldn't let y'all do this shit by yerself."

Once more Rosameralda led her fighters to the front. They carried boxes of ammunition and hand grenades. She set her men in firing positions and at her signal they unleashed a steady barrage of small arms fire. Maartyn showed Christian how to load and fire the single shot rifles. Christian inserted bullets and threw the bolt, closed his eyes and fired. He had no idea where the bullets were going. Maartyn slammed in bullets and whooped every time he pulled the trigger. In his glory, finally shooting at something. Jésus flung hand grenades as fast as he could pull the pins.

The tanks moved ahead to answer the barrage. Maartyn signaled for Jésus to toss him a grenade. Maartyn pulled the pin and flipped the safety hammer free. The hand grenade was armed. He had only seconds to get rid of it. Christian stopped firing, watching in awe. The lead tank was three hundred feet away but Maartyn had the advantage of height. He judged the distance and hurled the grenade. Pretending it was a blue crab and the tank a fat pelican on a dock post. The grenade sailed high in a lazy arch, exploding above the tank's turret as planned. The explosion did little more than blister the drab green paint but the downward concussion and the rain of shrapnel stunned the tank crew. Three men abandoned the tank and fled into the brush. Maartyn lofted another grenade and flushed a machine gun crew. They were cut down by rifle fire. Soldiers began to pull back or broke from hiding in ragged groups. The Major, in a rage, stood his ground and threatened to shoot deserters until he was also cut down by a bullet, fired by one of his own boys. Retribution for the bloody attack he had ordered that killed so many of their young comrades.

Maartyn lofted more grenades at the remaining tanks until they backed away to safety. The mortar crews were next. A well timed grenade exploded directly above a position, wounding both men and terrifying the rest of the crews. They abandoned their weapons and fled back down the hill. The tanks, one by one, spun about and ground down the slope. Foot soldiers slipped away to safety. And still the rebels kept up the furious fire. The return fire from the army diminished to sporadic volleys as officers exhorted their soldiers to stop running away. When the isolated groups of rebels in the hills saw their chance they made their way down to the cave and joined Rosameralda's fighters.

Rosameralda did not relent. The barrage continued until their fingers bled from slamming in bullets and pulling triggers. Jésus could barley lift his arm to fling grenades. Christian watched Maartyn in his element, in awe of the noise and violence. They couldn't move without slipping on brass shell casings. She kept up the constant fire until an hour before sunset.

"Stop firing!" Rosameralda motioned for Gabriel.

Gabriel slipped to Rosameralda's side. "Comandanté, that was wonderful. Poetic. Did you sense a certain rhythm to the music of our guns?"

"No. I saw Cubans die and it breaks my heart. Why don't they just go away?"

"Some do what they're told."

"Do you think the army will return?" she asked, weary rather than worried.

"I saw the Major fall. His next in command, Capitan Duarez, is the Major's man, only twice as cruel. I'm sure he'll ask for reinforcements. The Air Force will return with napalm. That is, unless all the planes are needed to fly Batista and his pals out of Camp Columbia."

"He's leaving soon, do you think?"

"There's talk. Castro and his barbudos should have been crushed before they left the Sierra."

"Escobar would never fight their war. How can the army defeat us if we won't fight in the open?"

"Well, Señorita Comandanté, here we are, slugging it out with them, running out of ammunition. If we stay here..."

"You're right. I'm taking my boys down to the village to regroup, then we're fighting our way to Habana. You're free to join us, or make peace with the army."

"I'm going with you."

Rosameralda was not surprised. She looked at Maartyn who was absorbed filling his pockets with rifle shells. It was dark. Time to go.

The medical refugees struggling along the margin of the beach could hear the constant barrage from the other side of the mountain. They mistook the grenade explosions as the work of the army obliterating the rebels. Their friends and relatives. This time Renée was sure her friends had been killed. She sobbed openly as she helped Benny prepare the worst cases to move again. Benny sent the walking wounded ahead with Miguel, those who could walk but could not carry more than their rifles and ammunition. He cursed the need to transport weapons but dared not counter Rosameralda's order.

Renée tried not to think of the fighting, the wounded or the reasons. She wished she could just walk away from the chaos, back to her life in Paris. She wondered how the world functioned in a never ending cycle of war, death and destruction, but began to understand how her father could make a career directing the suffering of others. He had often said that it was the duty of the enlightened to teach, if possible, that war is not an answer, to have compassion for those who suffer because they cannot avoid war, and to smash those who insist on using war to their advantage. He had also said that the world did not understand the French. To the French, democracy was a hard earned privilege. They had wrenched control out of the grip of the monarchy, created a democracy, suffered destructive invasions, resisted the Germans and then the Communists in their own ranks. No country on earth had a better claim to democratic principles, shed more blood in the struggle, or held the prize higher. Some day Renée would understand, he said, even if the world did not. At some point in her life she would see that nothing is perfect but there are levels of perfection and perception. She had only to choose. Would he accept her own imperfections?

Rosameralda motioned for her small ragged army to be silent. They had reached the high point of the hills, the spot where Muñoz had seen the Special Force. She was kneeling on the place where Muñoz landed, his fall broken by young pine trees. It seemed so long ago. She signaled for Gabriel. He knelt beside her and inhaled her scent. She thought she smelled like a workhorse, or worse. He breathed the rebel musk with great pleasure. She whispered, "From here we have to cross the slope to reach the village. We know that half of the army was on this side of the hill yesterday. We don't know if they're still here. We must get the boat driver, that Gringo," she signaled to Maartyn crouched beside Christian at the back of the column, "is the boat driver. If we run into a patrol someone has to protect him. The boat driver must get to the beach. See to it."

"What about you?"

"Right now it doesn't matter."

"It does to me."

"Gabriel Salvador, we could both die."

"Then I would be happy to die beside you."

"Oh, my. You are a persistent boy. My other boyfriends could be very jealous. One has a machine gun."

"I'm not afraid, if you're the prize."

"Look at me! I'm filthy. Do I smell like a prize?"

"The best Cuban cigar could not compete."

"That's not a compliment."

They both began to giggle. It may have been nerves.

Christian and Maartyn worked their way to the front of the column and Christian overheard the conversation between Rosameralda and Gabriel. She ignored Maartyn. He felt badly for Maartyn. It was unfair, but what was one heart more or less in their situation?

Rosameralda signaled for the column to move. They worked their way cautiously across the slope.

It was Gabriel who spotted the patrol. He motioned everyone down and pointed to a clearing ahead. A squad or a platoon, it was hard to tell, but both groups were on a collision course and in moments the fire fight would start.

"Christian..." Rosameralda whispered. "We can't avoid them. You and Maartyn make a run for the beach. Go straight down that way. Get the boat and wait for us below Ernesto's. If I don't make it you must get the Americans to Habana. Here's a contact." She took a pencil and a small note pad out of the pocket of her fatigues and wrote a name. "Here, don't lose it. This man's our agent. Deliver the Americans to Habana at all costs. Get ready to go as soon as we attack. Don't stop running for anything."

Rosameralda used hand signals to position her troops, the cold professional, without a look or a word for Maartyn. It was as if they had never touched, or allowed her dark sensuality to change a lifetime of attitudes. She turned her back. They were dismissed.

"What was that all about, man? Is she mad at me or somethin'?"

"No, she's...too busy, to, you know...say anything. There's going to be a battle. We run."

"No way! We stay with Rosa!"

"We go. Rosa's orders. We follow orders...Maartyn, okay?"

The attack was swift and deadly. Rosa's rebels had the element of surprise and position. But the army had numbers. Jésus was off on the first crack of a rifle. They never saw him again. Christian dropped his rifle and ran through the brush, Maartyn close behind. They didn't stop until they crossed the plateau on the level of Christian's villa. There they waited in the bushes to catch their breath. The beach was below, and the darkening harbour, so placid and tantalizingly peaceful. The fishing boat was a half mile out where Maartyn had left her at anchor. They decided to wait until full darkness, but it was agony sitting in the brush, listening to the fire fight in the hills above them. Christian played the wish-away game, trying to pretend the sound had nothing to do with him or anyone he knew, puzzling over Rosameralda's behaviour.

When it was dark enough Christian and Maartyn made it to the beach. The fishing boat's tender was gone, a spoil of war, confiscated by a poor fisherman perhaps, but there was Christian's old, water-soaked skiff. They launched the heavy boat and rowed away from the beach. The fishing boat was an ominous black silhouette against the after glow of the western sky.

"She's ridin' pretty low," whispered Maartyn.

"You mean it's sinking?"

"She'll be half full by now's my guess. I just hope it ain't up to the engine. Diesels take a lotta shit but they don't' like salt water in big doses."

They rowed the rest of the way in silence, feathering their oars, as if the splash from the narrow blades could be heard above the constant booming and chatter of the fire fight still raging in the hills.

It was pitch dark when the skiff bumped the bullet riddled hull of the foul smelling shrimp boat. They could have found the thing in a dense fog. They held on to the gunnels for a long moment, listening to the sounds from shore. A tank creaked and clanked along the road toward the hospital, followed by the half track and trucks loaded with soldiers. The remnants of Batista's army was on the move.

"The battle's over, I guess," said Maartyn. The pain was obvious.

"Don't worry, Maartyn. Rosa can look after herself, you know, they might have just called it off."

"Thanks ol' buddy. You lie like a rug."

Maartyn climbed over the rail and tied the painter to a cleat, crunching over broken glass on the deck. The wooden fishing boat was a shambles. Bullet holes. Broken equipment and shredded nets. Wood splinters mingled with the broken glass. Most of the wheelhouse windows were shot out. "Jesus. What a mess," Christian said in awe.

"I want y'all to take these guys ashore."

"Who?"

"Captain Santoz an' his mate."

Christian climbed reluctantly over the rail and stood only a few inches from the two bodies. Flies buzzed and crawled. "Jesus Christ!

They're dead."

"Yeah, an' they stink. But I want them buried proper. I'm not goin' to dump'em for the sharks. They're good guys, dig? Treat'em nice."

"Oh, man...you're going to help me?"

"Can't. Got to pump this sucker an' make'er run. When the tides high I'm goin' to run on over to Escobar's to pick up the others. You take these dudes ashore now an' get them in the freezer, an' tell Renée an' the others to wait near the beach at midnight. I'll come in as far as I can. It'll be high tide an' we won't have much time. Don't want to hang this ol' bitch up on a sand bar. Give a lift."

Christian gingerly raised Santoz up by the feet. Maartyn dragged a line under his body and tied a bowline and made it fast to a lifting hook. Using the net gantry and hand winch they lowered the two bodies into the skiff. The mate nuzzled his captain on the bottom boards in dirty bilge water. Christian was untying the line when they heard the soft *carrumph* of a big explosion. Orange flames shot out of the hillside in many places. From under the collapsed compound warehouse, out the sealed off west entrance, and from Juanita's tunnel. The explosions at the east entrance and the vent itself were only an orange glow in the sky, like a sunrise through mist. The contents of La Casa were being incinerated. Maartyn and Christian stood close together at the rail watching as the fires flared and died. Then Los Espiritos and the harbour were in darkness again.

"Some friggin' Christmas, man!"

"Maartyn...she might have made it...even if they had to surrender."

"Get goin', asshole! I've got work to do."

The hospital was as chaotic with casualties as the cave.

"Renée!!..." Esameralda came running through the crowded ward. "I'm so happy to see you! Pietro came last night."

"That poor little dog. He made with the vials, and your note. You don't know how relieved I was."

"Oh, Renée...Renée. What's the news of Rosa?"

Renée sighed and sagged into Esameralda's arms, the fatigue that she'd been fighting for days taking over. All she wanted to do was lay in Esameralda's arms, shut her eyes and sleep. "We don't know, Ezy. There was fighting at the east entrance. Christian and Maartyn are with her, I think."

"The big explosion?"

"The army blew up the caverns. That's all I know."

Esameralda stood for a long time staring at the dark mountains. The hills and caves under the blue pines where they had played as children. Where she had learned her trade. The refuge for her village, also the killing fields for many villagers and soldiers, and possibly the final resting place of her sister and her friends. She willed the tears not to come, yet. "Oh, I wanted to tell Rosa about our little sister. They took her to Pinar. Army trucks are coming for the wounded. We made a truce with the captain of the Pinar cuartel. I think he's looking for mercy if Batista goes. He'll let us bring in our wounded if we swear not to help the rebels."

"We're considered rebels, aren't we?"

"I'm afraid so."

"We have wounded. Can you take them?"

"I'll find room, but you can't stay here. For your safety as well as ours."

"We'll leave for Havana tonight, if the boat comes. Otherwise, I guess we're on our own. It could be worse."

"I'm sorry, Renée. We have to think of the wounded. What will you do in Habana?"

"I'm taking the first flight to New York."

"You can do that? It's that easy?"

"It's embarrassing. My father was very specific. I could throw away my career but I'm to carry my diplomatic papers. A kind of traveller's insurance for the over privileged."

"Will you ever come back?"

"Of course. Wherever you are."

"I'll be in a convent in Pinar del Rio, I hope."

"I pray. We've got almost thirty. Some critical. Is it safe to bring them up?"

"Miguelito's gone to check. The army went past a few minutes ago."

Christian angled the big skiff across the bay in the general direction of Escobar's villa. It was a long, lonely row in the dark with two stinking stiffs for company. Couldn't help thinking that in Canada, in late December, the dead wouldn't stink. He turned often to check his line, but avoided looking at the dim figures dressed in dirty white pants and shirts. Only the white material was visible in the residual light from the stars but that made the bodies appear to float. He wondered what happened to Santoz' wide brimmed hat that made him look like a cowboy. The night was warm. Another front, he thought...a warm front, probably means a blow. Tonight? Tomorrow? A late December storm from the northwest. A Northerly like the Christmas Eve blow. All the way from Canada. Home. Where it was Christmas and cold. He was homesick for Montreal but not ready to leave Cuba. He hoped Maartyn was a good sailor, not that he would be on board when the boat left. He already knew that. He also knew that Renée would be aboard, going to Havana with Ramon. What would he do? Row a skiff full of the dead forever. He thought of the River Styx. Crossing the black river to the Underworld with a load of condemned souls. "Why me? What did I do?" Better question...what could he have done differently? "Just about everything." He swore an oath to Styx; if he survived the night he would begin a new life course, as soon as he figured out the previous journey. The oath was irrevocable.

The skiff grounded on the last of the rising tide below the villa recently known as the Ché Guevara Hospital and Morgue. An invisible group of people huddled in the darkness at the fringe of the beach. Renée recognized the way the boatman moved. She ventured out of hiding and approached Christian engaged in trying to pull the heavy boat up on the rocky shore. The gently lapping waves masked her careful footsteps. She whispered, "Christian…"

He jumped. "Oh, Jesus!...Renée."

"Thank God! We heard the battle, and then the explosion. I thought...Are you alone?"

"Not exactly. I brought along a couple of Maartyn's friends. He wants me to look after them. Are the others here?"

"Yes, all except Benny. He's staying at to help Ezy until the boat comes."

"He's taking a chance."

"I told him so, but he insists."

"What about Miguel?"

"Right now he's sleeping. He's not going on the boat without Rosa."

"Rosa was in a big fight. That's all I know. How many are you?

"There's Ramon. Wayne. Paulo. Some of the boys who want to join Fidel. It's over here, but Castro's winning. It's just a matter of days now, so the Pinar doctor says."

"Yeah, it's over here," said Christian, a hint of sadness in his voice.

"It would be something to see. History...Castro in Havana."

He felt awkward. "Yeah, it should be something. The Revolution..." Christian was quiet for a few moments, sensing the distance growing between them. The tension of wars and relationships pushing them further apart. "You're going of course," he said with an edge of bitterness.

"Yes, Christian. I'm going. But you're not?"

"No, I guess not."

"I understand," she said.

"Stay with me, Renée."

"Cheri, look around you. Your villa...the town. All gone. There's nothing left."

"I have to stay, awhile. Can't explain."

"Miguel will look after you," she said quickly, as if she had foreseen the moment.

"Yeah, Miguel, funny. Too bad we never got a chance to enjoy this."

"Next time."

"Where?" he asked.

"I don't know. Spain. Morocco?"

"I might go to Montreal, then Ireland. I have family in Dublin."

"Come to Paris."

"I will."

"Kiss Esa for me."

Then they held each other long enough to replay the events of their revolution...They had shared much, and there was a fragile, unspoken bond.

Christian pulled back. "Renée...I do love you."

"I know. But it's not enough, right now."

"When?"

"When you're ready. When I'm grown up. Right now I have to go home to my real life. Start over."

"Enjoy Paris for me."

The things said. The distance bridged. They embraced and kissed like brother and sister.

Ramon and Wayne stashed the bodies of Santoz and his mate in the freezer with Escobar, the police spy and the engineer. The crew of the fishing boat were back together.

Christian and Renée remained on the sand, side by side, holding hands.

"Do you think Rosa will make it?" she asked, letting go of his hand.

"I don't know. It was a wild battle."

"It's so crazy. How can this be happening?"

"Who knows? Maartyn's taking it hard."

"But we don't know that she's dead."

"If he has to leave without her it's the same thing. But it's better, I mean, she's not what he thinks..." He didn't want to explain.

"I know. But I'll miss her."

They heard gun fire from the distant hillside. A brief fire fight as Rosameralda's survivors engaged in a running battle with the army patrol, trying to draw them away from the hospital. Renée walked past Christian to the water's edge, looking out across the harbour to the blackness of the Gulf. Out on the bay they heard the rumble of a diesel chugging to life. "Is that the fishing boat?" she asked.

"Yeah, he'll be along soon. Regular bus service...like Dorchester Street."

"Christian, I want you to know that the girl who came here a few days ago died in this stupid little war, but her feelings for you have survived."

"Well, that's the good news. Here, take this thing." He handed her Rosameralda's pistol.

"Shouldn't you keep it?"

"No way. Never again."

She put the heavy weapon in its holster. They stood together listening, watching for the old shrimp boat to materialize out of the darkness. The others came down to wait, keeping a respectful distance.

Maartyn brought the boat in gently, the big engine idling but still loud, broadcasting their location. The forefoot of the hull kissed the sand a few yards offshore.

Christian shuttled the actors and the small band of heavily armed rebels and their gear out to the shrimp boat. He and Maartyn shook hands but Maartyn was distracted, looking toward the sound of sporadic firing; scanning the dark beach for any sign.

"I guess she ain't gonna make it," Maartyn said sadly.

"She'll make it, somewhere," Christian lied again.

"Can't wait ol' buddy. The tide's turnin'. If she shows up, tell'er...well, tell'er whatever y'all want. I ain't much good at it."

"Sure. Hey, Maartyn...Thanks for coming."

"Yeah, man, it was a blast. See, y'all round. Let me know next time you find a quiet little place in the sun."

"You'd be bored silly," he said. It was true.

"Screw you, man!" Maartyn laughed and stepped into the shattered wheelhouse. The transmission gear engaged. A swish of white water and sand boiled up from under the stern, pushing the skiff away.

Christian watched for her at the rail. Renée's fair complexion only a dim mask. Ramon was standing beside her, arm around her waist. He couldn't tell if she waved. The shrimper backed into the darkness, leaving only the stench of diesel and a throbbing noise that carried over the ink-black water. Christian let the skiff drift. Suspended in nothing, caressed by a soft breeze from somewhere.

December 27 1958 The Villa. Afternoon: *I slept in the skiff last night. Somehow my pack survived. They unloaded the bullets and hand grenades and most of my stuff. My journal survived. My black tam, sunglasses and my old running shoes. The pack was here at the villa when I returned. The old guitar's here too. Miguel must have known that I'd come back. The kid's spooky. I'm just going to sit here on the terrace and wait to see what happens. What else can I do? And after yesterday, what else could possibly go wrong?...*

When he woke the sun was in his eyes. But the sun was headed for a dark bank of clouds and the wind puffed up with a sharp edge of cold. The skiff bumped the rocky shore below Escobar's villa in annoying little motions as the ruffled water pushed and shoved at the old hull. He was lying on the hard bottom boards, feeling abused, alone...

"Señor, Christ?" The voice sounded far away.

"What?..."

"I thought you were never going to wake up."

"Morning, Miguel."

"It's afternoon. You've been asleep hours. I've been watching to make sure the boat didn't drift away."

"Thanks," Christian said too sarcastically. Miguel sat down on the sand to resume his vigil. Christian dozed again, unable to move, too depressed to care that he was wet and cold.

Later they beached the skiff and walked up to the villa hospital. The gallery wards were almost empty except for a few rebel boys who had been with Rosameralda and arrived too late for the trucks to Pinar del Rio. Wolf occupied a bed near the sun drenched courtyard.

"Hello, old dog," said Christian. Wolf wagged his tail and tried to sit up, but flopped down and let Christian explore the burned and battered little body. "You sure took some beating fella. Maybe Fidel will give you a medal too."

Rosameralda was sitting on a bench in the courtyard, her back to him, near the spot where Escobar had been killed by the firing squad.

338

She appeared to be in mourning. The remains of her rebel army bivouacked in the shade of the logia. Gabriel Salvador hovered near, like a guardian angel. All the events of the last few days began rushing back. He should go to Rosa, but he wanted to retreat from the rush of memories. Then Esameralda was at his side.

"Christian?..."

He took Esameralda in his arms and held her close, crushing her warm body to his for many reasons. She was life and nourishment. He would hold on to this one. But there was just one question. "Esa...are you staying?"

"Christian...I can't breath."

Juanita was watching from the doorway to the kitchen. She smiled her incredibly big, but sad smile and turned away. Miguel shook his head and wandered into the courtyard to sit with Rosameralda.

"Sorry." He relaxed his bear hug. She took his hands, looking deep into his eyes. Esameralda's were a deeper darkness that he couldn't fathom.

"Christian...I have to tell you something."

"I'm going to stay here, with you," he said quickly, before he could change his mind.

"I'm going to Pinar del Rio to join the American doctor."

"When?... Why?"

"As soon as we're finished here. There's a hospital."

"I'll go with you."

"It's a hospital run by the Sisters of Mercy."

"That's okay. We could all use some."

"You wouldn't want to leave the coast. Pinar's hot and dirty. There's nothing for you to do there."

"I'll find something. Anything."

"Then you would have to become a nun."

"What!?..."

"Christian...It's my dream. Since I was a little girl."

"Oh, well, then..." Off balance, Christian stood a long moment staring beyond the woman he was about to give himself to, feeling the chill of the void he would never understand. Wanting and not wanting, what exactly? Being and not being, like the guy said? Renée would know. He kissed her tenderly on the lips. "That's from Renée."

The Cuban army was gone. The third and final battle of Los Espiritos was over. In spite of the cool breeze a heavy tranquility had settled over his altered paradise. He left the skiff below the villa and walked the beach past the destroyed village. People were rummaging through the ruins, hauling out anything usable, dragging away the charred timbers, salvaging their small lives. Swirls of grey ashes blew inland.

He passed the church. A mound of charred rubble was piled outside the doors. Pieces of the cross. Penitential benches. Sacrificial alter. Confessional of sins, mortal and venal. The ruined remains of the ornate tapestry that hung behind the alter. Blessed roof tiles. A sacred waste dump. Inside, women dressed in black garments knelt on the blackened tiles before a makeshift alter lighting small candles; chanting, swaying, the colourful Santeria beads moving and rustling with their motions. The fat priest wept, hands uplifted to the roofless sky, imploring a celestial contractor to come down and repair the damage. What a strange country, he thought.

Passing the remains of Juanita's Cantina he spotted the moose's blackened antlers sticking up through the twisted tin roof panels. He remembered something about the colour he had seen in one of the bullet holes. He picked his way carefully through the debris. The moose head had been burned again by the blast of the gasoline fire belching out of the tunnel like a blow torch. The antlers were brittle and broke away when Christian touched them. He tripped, clutching at the head for support. The hairless parchment crackled and pulled away and thick wads of burned paper tumbled out. Money. Fives and tens. A few twenties. Canadian money with a picture of King George VI. He looked around to see if anyone had witnessed the discovery. He picked up a wad, thumbing the edges. Most of the bills disintegrated. The heat had baked the mouldy paper, turning it to crispy brown flakes, running through his fingers like dry snow. But some on the inside of the wad survived and he estimated hundreds of dollars. He took off his shirt and stuffed in the undamaged bills, tying the sleeves to make a small bag.

The feeling of guilt weighed heavy as he walked up the hill to his villa. The money was his ticket out of Cuba. Enough to buy a passport on the black market, but manna from heaven came with a heavy moral dilemma. It was Juanita's money.

The villa was not as badly damaged as he had imagined. The tank shell hit the thick stone wall of the house on the terrace side. The terrace was littered with chunks of stone and red roof tiles. The wall of the pantry was fractured. A gaping hole in the roof creating another terrace in the living room. The bedroom, and the big bed, though full of debris and rock dust, was mostly intact.

The guitar and the knapsack leaned against the wall where Miguel had placed them. He tilted the bench to dump pieces of stone and mortar and sat down, back to the remains of the wall, facing the sun, with the bundle of money between his feet. He put on his black beret and his sunglasses. He dozed and tried not to think. He slept and dreamed...

"Señor Christ?...."

"Miguel?...."

Miguel, dressed in his over-sized fatigues, with a forage cap at a jaunty angle, was standing in front of him, rifle over his shoulder and a pistol stuck in his webbed belt. "You've been sleeping again."

"And you've been watching again."

"I see many things."

Christian felt a rush of prickly guilt on the back of his neck. He glanced down to see if the bundle was still there. "Did you see me at Juanita's?"

"Not if you don't want me to."

Christian exhaled. "It's Juanita's money. I'm going to give it to her."

"Juanita knew the money was there."

"She did?"

"Sure. I was only eight years old when the big crate arrived. There was a note from her lost husband. It said that he was sorry he couldn't come back but he was doing very well in Canada and that her life insurance was in the big head. She put her hand into the mouth of that thing and pulled out that funny looking money. I played with it for a few days then she put it right back in, saying that she wasn't interested in funny money and that he had probably gotten it illegally in the first place. It's been there ever since. Now you've found it."

"What should I do with it?"

"How should I know? What does anybody do with money from some Canada. You can't spend it."

"You can in Canada."

"Well, Señor, that seems to be the problem of not being there and being here, where you don't need money. I brought you some food from the Ché Guevara Hospital."

"Not more Joe Louis'!"

Miguel laughed and held up a pot. "No, Señor Christ. Juanita sent you some roasted chicken with black beans and rice. When they took away the wounded in the trucks they left Juanita with all this food to feed the village. A gift from Major Marti."

Miguel found two spoons in the rubble of the pantry. They ate the warm chicken, beans and rice from the pot and talked about the Revolution, their revolution, until Miguel announced that he had to go. "Rosa has a new boyfriend, Gabriel Salvador."

"I know."

"Rosa and her new man are going to steal a truck and fight their way to Habana. I'm going with her. I promise to return as soon as I meet Fidel."

"I'll starve while you're gone."

"No you won't. Go to the Ché Guevara Hospital and visit Pietro and Esameralda. Juanita has plenty of food."

"Good. You take care of yourself."

"Sure, I'll be okay...Señor Christ, you're the one I worry about."

Juanita arrived that evening after feeding the villagers. Pietro was with her, stiff and sore, panting from the effort. The climb up the hill left her breathless and glistening. Christian made a wider clean place for her on the bench and got Pietro a drink of water from the pantry. Pietro curled up beside his knapsack, sighed as if he was home, and went to sleep. Christian sat against the terrace wall facing the sunset as always. Juanita settled herself and smiled, looking satisfied. They sat for a while in contemplative silence while Juanita caught her breath. She surveyed the ruins of her villa. "I've got a gift for you, my Gringo, rebel hero. I saved a bottle before the pigs of army brats burned down my cantina." She held up a bottle of Cuban Dark, the brand that melts away all worries and cares and depressions. She twisted off the wooden top and handed the bottle to Christian. He took a cautious drink. He knew what Cuban Dark could do. Wondered if Juanita just wanted to get him drunk.

"Juanita...I found something of yours, in the moose head."

"I know. Miguel told me."

"Of course he did."

"You keep it. I don't need Canada money. I have plenty of real money in the bank in Habana, as long as Castro's people don't help themselves and Batista doesn't take too much with him when he goes."

"So, you think he'll go soon?"

"He'll go soon. Ernesto said it was planned long ago. These evil dictators are crooks but not stupid, so they steal enough money to keep them in their old age, some place like Miami or Santo Domingo. He'll go by New Years."

"Then it's over. Finally." Christian began to relax. "What a story."

"Story!?" Juanita took the bottle and downed a good mouthful. "Gringo, you don't know half the story."

"What do you mean? I just survived the Cuban Revolution. The intrigue. Secret caves. Weapons. Actors. Three battles, well, most of them. But I've seen all the people and watched the play, and counted the dead and the wounded, lost my girlfriend, both girlfriends, and now it's over...isn't it?"

"Here, have a good, long drink while I tell you the real story."

Christian did as he was told. The rum burned all the way down and the alcohol charged through his body. He put his head back against the wall so that the sunset was full against his face, and waited for Juanita to tell him the real story of a revolution in Los Espiritos.

"First of all, my beautiful but naive Canada Gringo, Ernesto Escobar was not who you think."

"Am I surprised?"

"Ernesto burned to be King or El Presidente. He could go either way. He and Señor Frank the Butcher Bartuchi had this plan, you see. They knew there was going to be a revolution. Bartuchi was to provide American money to finance the coup in return for control of Cuba's corruption, but Bartuchi got too greedy. He tried to make his own smuggling business while they waited."

So Escobar's story about Bartuchi and the drug operation was at least true, thought Christian. But the tale of greed and deception wove a strange and sticky web that enveloped not only Los Espiritos and Pinar del Rio Province, but spread to Havana and beyond to Las Villas, Camaguey, and even to the Sierra Maestra in Oriente Province.

"You see, Christian, the reasons for the three American actors smuggled into Cuba was only partly true. Escobar's plan was to eliminate Castro himself before he reached Habana."

"Eliminate!? You mean...?" The implications of the plot to kill Fidel Castro and his Comandantés, substitute the impostors in the confusion of battle and seize control of Cuba, left Christian limp. The powerful rum helped, but it sounded too fantastic. Pure fiction, and yet, he had seen the evidence. The caves. The preparations. The impostors. Escobar himself. Frank Bartuchi was only a drawn character, but he was living in the man's house.

"So, now you understand. If it hadn't been for Escobar's execution?"

"Who told the army about Escobar's firing squad?"

"The execution of the spy? I did of course."

"You!? Why?"

"I knew what Escobar would do once in power and Cuba does not need another dictator. The unfortunate spy was sent to watch Escobar because Major Marti knew Escobar was up to something. Carnero was just a diversion. Marti came to visit you to find out what you knew and to see if you were in with Escobar in some way. He asked me many questions about you in private while his stupid men shot up my moose to keep suspicion from me. If he had suspected you he might have had you killed on the spot. You see, Christian, my innocent lover, Escobar tried once before to be the man of power."

Juanita paused for a good dollop of her rum. "He told you he was a doctor and an officer in the Republican army during the Spanish War. What he didn't tell you was that he plotted to seize control of Spain as soon as the Republicans had defeated Franco. But it didn't happen. Franco won the war with the help of that Nazi, Adolf Hitler and the Fascists. Escobar was denounced as a traitor. It was a great blow to his family, all good Loyalists, true Spanish aristocrats. But Escobar himself is the bastard son of a German count, it's a long story of power and intrigue. Some day I'll tell you that one. He was an embarrassment to his family even before the incident with the plot to take over Spain. They gave him money and an allowance if he promised to leave Andalusia and never return. He fled to England and then to Cuba and lived like a Latin playboy, exiling himself to Los Espiritos because of his unfortunate attraction to young men. Here he smouldered for the chance to rule. The Revolution and Castro were his chance. He wanted to be either King or El Presidente. I couldn't let it happen."

"But the impostors are on their way to Havana. Maartyn has the name of an agent."

"Yes, Escobar's agent. The organization goes very deep, even into Fidel's July 26th Movement."

"Then, you mean, the plan could still work?"

"Yes. The plan could still work, even without Escobar. Fidel has many enemies among the other movements who would like to take power. Now, listen to this…"

The full story of Fidel Castro the Rebel Prince, Escobar the Pretender and The Butcher Bartuchi, took a long time to tell. It was dark when Juanita and Christian shared the last of the warm rum.

"Escobar. King of Cuba? That's incredible!" said Christian.

"There's one or two things more."

"Do I want to know?"

"You do. For your own good. Rosameralda was to be queen, at least his consort."

"Rosameralda!?...No way!"

"Our Rosa. The most beautiful, most dedicated revolutionary in Cuba."

"Who's about four hundred years younger than that Old Fag?"

"One has to think of the future."

"Jesus Christ! Do I know anything?"

"Now you know almost everything. One small detail and then I'm finished. I was to be the Director of Casinos for Escobar. My reward for being a good conspirator."

"Wow!...So, what happens now? Escobar's dead. The conspiracy's finished?"

"Rosa's on her way to Habana. If she gets there anything could happen."

"You mean, she?...no, that's too ridiculous."

"Is it? The thirst for power is a powerful drug. You understand that power don't you, Christian?"

"Afraid I do."

"The afflicted one will do anything, use anyone, to get power or to keep it. But don't concern yourself with Cuba's problems. Young Gabriel Salvador is one of Major Marti's best men. His allegiance is only to Cuba."

"Jesus!...Rosa. They'll kill her?" The pain was like a knife going very deep into vitals. Nobody, it seemed...not Rosameralda, Escobar, Juanita, Esameralda or Wolf, not even Renée or Maartyn, was who Christian thought they were...except Miguel, sort of. And Paulo. "I liked the other story better. The simple one about a clean, honest revolution where people only get killed for right and obvious reasons."

"Sorry, Christian, my pet. We tried not to tell you anything in the beginning, if you will remember? Now you know everything."

"Never should have asked."

"We must bury Ernesto and the others. They have thawed out and begin to smell badly. Would you like to be at the service?"

"Thanks. I'll pass." He was drifting again.

"And, by the way, Christian, Esameralda asked me to give you a message." He wasn't there. "...Christian?"

"Uh huh..."

"Esameralda says to tell you that she's not going to be a nun, for a while."

"Amen..."
Christian digested the news and decided that maybe he would just sit on his terrace for a week or so, the rent was paid, catch up on his writing, play his guitar and wait for his warrior house boy to return. He had one more question to ask Miguel.

January 16 1959: *The Revolution's over, or has it just begun? Batista's gone. Renée's gone too. Is it only four weeks since Maartyn and Renée arrived? Miguel's back from the war. He had some bad news. Rosameralda was killed in a battle with the army on the road to Havana. He wouldn't tell me how she died. Miguel buried her near San Antonio de los Banos. It was the last battle of the war. Renée flew to New York after turning Ramon, Benny and Wayne over to Escobar's agents. Maartyn and Paulo left Havana with the shrimp boat, headed for Louisiana. Fidel Castro's in Havana, at least we think it's Castro. There's much confusion in Havana but the July 26th Movement has control of the cities and most of the island. And so it begins, what Carnero feared. The reprisals. The aftermath and the executions. The trials started in Santiago de Cuba. I woke up this morning in bed with Esameralda. We both need consoling. Should I miss Renée? I can't decide. I didn't ask Miguel the question; too complicated. It's been like that lately. It was a strange and confusing year, '58...*

The End of Book One

Surviving Well is the Best Revenge Cuba: 1958 is Book One of the Christian Joyce series following the exploits of Christian James Joyce as he travels the world, outpacing his demons, searching for that elusive paradise: an island of tranquility.

If you enjoyed this book you can write a review and post it on Amazon.com. Send me an email or go to my web site.

Book Two, *Surviving Well is the Best Revenge Montreal: 1960* will be released in September 2014. Available at your local Indie Book Store or on Amazon.com, on ebook or contact us at Sarawak Studios Press.

Surviving Well Montreal: 1960. Christian reluctantly leaves his Cuban friends behind and makes his way home to Montreal. His family has gone. He's broke again, alone, on the streets. Befriended by an intense young French Canadian radical, he's introduced to a new gang of misfits and another rebellion. The fledgling FLQ are about to explode onto the political scene. Maartyn St. Jacques is determined to find his friend and Renée arrives in time to rescue him from the consequences of his latest error in judgment. But Christian has met Breeze O'Sullivan, a beautiful and talented young student from Newfoundland. The affairs are intense, the politics volatile, and there's a baby to protect. How will Renée react to this turn of events? And how will Christian and Breeze escape from Isle Royale before the Québec Surité descend on the old warehouse; headquarters of the FLQ over-looking the mighty St. Lawrence River? For a hint; *Surviving Well is the Best Revenge Newfoundland: 1962* will be available in early 2015.

To follow Christian, pursued by his friends, on his journey to troubled islands, the reader will travel next to Ireland, Ile de la Cité in Paris, then Malta and back to Cuba to continue the unfinished Cuban Revolution, this time as a celebrated journalist to interview the real Fidel Castro.

Made in the USA
Charleston, SC
16 March 2014